DOING BUSINESS
BEYOND
AMERICA'S
BORDERS

The Do's, Don'ts
and Other Details of
Conducting Business
in 40 Countries

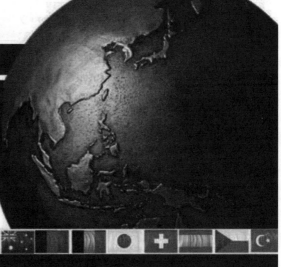

LAWRENCE W. TULLER

Jere L. Calmes, Publisher

Cover Design: Desktop Miracles

Composition and Production: Lesley Rock for SquareOne Publishing Partners

This publication is designed to provide accurate and authoritative information
in regard to the subject matter covered. It is sold with the understanding that the
publisher is not engaged in rendering legal, accounting or other professional services.
If legal advice or other expert assistance is required, the services of a
competent professional person should be sought.

Library of Congress Cataloging-in-Publication Data

Tuller, Lawrence W.

Doing business beyond America's borders / by Lawrence W. Tuller.

   p. cm.

  ISBN-13: 978-1-59918-257-5 (alk. paper)

  ISBN-10: 1-59918-257-2 (alk. paper)

1. International business enterprises—Management. 2. Small business—

Management. 3. International trade—Handbooks, manuals, etc. 4. Globalization

—Economic aspects. I. Title.

  HD62.4.T85 2008

  658'.049—dc22

                     2008023175

Printed in Canada

11 10 09 08   10 9 8 7 6 5 4 3 2 1

contents

acknowledgments

MY HEARTFELT THANKS TO TED WONG FOR INSIGHTS INTO CHINA, GENE MAKAR for India, Kathryn Dankowski for Eastern Europe (especially the Czech Republic), and René Duvekot for Brazil. Teo Babun for valuable suggestions related to the Latin culture. Susan Tuller for clear and concise opinions about the opportunities in several Pacific Rim and Latin American countries and especially an analysis of the behavioral characteristics of ordinary people. All of the speakers and attendees at the Latin America/Caribbean Productions conferences that I hosted. The courteous and hard working men and women in U.S. embassies and consulates around the world who are truly ambassadors of goodwill for America and our first line of defense. And last, but certainly not least, my clients and hundreds of friends from around the world. Without contributions from all of you, this book would not have been.

preface

URING MORE THAN 40 YEARS OF DOING BUSINESS THROUGHOUT THE WORLD, mainly with or for American smaller and mid-market companies, I have lost count of the number of times entrepreneurs have asked me for advice about getting started in exporting or foreign sourcing. Everyone, it seems, has the same questions. These valiant crusaders want to expand to new foreign markets but don't know which ones offer the greatest demand for their products. They need to know how to assess the market-entry risk of a specific country. They need to know how to market and distribute their products in foreign lands, how to transport those products to overseas markets, and how to ensure that they will get paid. They need to know where to source low-cost production materials and labor. And they need to know the best ways of dealing with unique cultural differences and unfamiliar languages.

Today, more than 200,000 U.S. companies export goods and services, accounting for about 12 percent of America's GDP. Predictions from the SBA, the International Trade Administration, and the U.S. Chamber of Commerce indicate that exports will double or possibly triple during the next decade, drawing in even more smaller and mid-market companies. Canada gets the lions share of these exports and will continue to be America's largest trading partner. However, the major emerging markets of China, India, Russia, Brazil, and Mexico will demand ever greater shares of America's products and services. Certainly, a weak dollar increases U.S. exports. So do continuing advances in high-tech products. And with a soft dollar, America's attraction to foreign travelers will continue to increase. But the biggest demand now and in the foreseeable future originates in rapidly growing emerging or less developed nations.

This book looks at markets in 40 countries that comprise four emerging regional markets—Latin America, Eastern Europe, South and Southeast Asia, and the Middle East. Of these four regions, Latin America, led by Brazil, takes far and away the largest share of U.S. exports, increasing about 12 to 15 percent per year. Close on the heels of Latin America, Asian countries, led by China, absorb the next largest share. Competition from European Union countries limits U.S. involvement in Eastern Europe, including Russia, but the opportunities there are so great that to ignore this region would be unconscionable. Although Middle East countries have very small consumer markets, many have practically unlimited cash and desperately need to import every type of product and most business services.

Without doubt, the future for smaller and mid-market companies willing to jump on the international trade bandwagon looks as bright as glistening ice. Not only will they benefit from exporting to these emerging markets, they will also increase profits from foreign sourcing. Many will eventually set up offshore warehouses, manufacturing plants, retail stores, and service establishments. *Doing Business Beyond America's Borders* is the premier international trade resource for these entrepreneurs. It is the first authoritative book to answer the questions all new global trade entrepreneurs ask—How to I find the best markets for my products? How do I sell my products? How do I finance these transactions? And where can I get help?

But prospering in international trade is not a sure bet. Many obstacles await the unwary. Foreign markets challenge even the most progressive, innovative entrepreneur. Widespread corruption, violence, extreme poverty, and religious and racial intolerance permeate all emerging world markets, much as they do rich nations. Radical changes continue to alter the business landscape. Unstable political regimes and convoluted financial markets tend to blur the horizon of market opportunities.

Despite these challenges, markets in emerging nations offer much greater profits and long-term growth than rich countries—including the United States. Although we will delve into opportunities and hurdles in all 40 countries, we will emphasize profitable possibilities in those markets that are projected to be the largest and fastest growing over the next 10 years—Brazil, Russia, India, and China.

International trade has its own set of rules, semantics, and peculiar ways of conducting business. To introduce these standard, fairly universal topics,

Part I: A Global Trade Primer deals with the basics of global trade, the global financial system, protectionism, and free trade pacts and provides street and website addresses for a variety of sources of information and assistance. Part II: Analysis of Key Countries and Regions examines market opportunities in each of 40 countries, along with the major barriers to market entry. A brief description of American habits that confuse or irritate foreigners, followed by anecdotes that crystalize the more important cultural traits and business protocols of Russia, Brazil, India, China, and Middle East countries, highlight Intercultural Relationships in Part III. This section also looks at the obstacles and opportunities for women in global trade and suggests ways to mitigate language barriers and win negotiations. Part IV: Managing Global Trade brings to life the nuts and bolts of getting started in international trade, including such topics as market research, country risk assessment, strategic alliances, marketing channels, e-commerce, advertising, trade finance, countertrade, and the essentials of importing. The Appendix lists the street and website addresses of additional contacts that should be helpful for entrepreneurs looking for assistance.

Two underlying themes anchor this book: (1) that foreign markets are more profitable than U.S. markets and (2) that every business owner or manager who genuinely wants to expand his or her business can, with very little risk, be successful in international trade. Yes, serious barriers exist. Yes, transnationals provide intense competition, especially in rich nation markets. And yes, assistance from Washington varies all over the board. On the other hand, the time is ripe to take advantage of a weak dollar and the robust thirst for American products among emerging nations. Unique financing options beckon the global trader. Risks pale when compared with those in many U.S. markets. And the potential for future expansion in foreign markets tops that present in the United States.

Now is the time to break out of the box and reap the benefits of global trade. Many smaller and mid-market companies have done so and you can too.

—L.W. Tuller

PART I
A GLOBAL TRADE PRIMER

chapter one
The Basics of Global Trade

I T'S TIME TO CHANGE. MARKETS ARE SHRINKING. SOME ARE SATURATED. YOU CAN'T
compete with backroom jobs outsourced to India. Competitors always seem to be one
step ahead with low-cost, partially assembled goods
from Central America. You can't locate or retain skilled
managers or workers. Your bank won't stretch your
line of credit. Chinese imports steal your customers.
Taxes sap too much of your income. Government
regulations stifle initiative. Profits evaporate. It's time
to change. But to what?

A whole new world of eager customers, ready financing, and high margins awaits the innovative entrepreneur. Where? Beyond America's borders in Latin America, Eastern Europe, Asia, and the Middle East. Like lava flowing from an exploding volcano, globalization barrels forward snuffing out protectionism and blanketing the earth with free market economies. At last count, the SBA reported more than 200,000 U.S. companies regularly engaged in international trade—more than 90 percent of them small businesses. And this number mushrooms exponentially each year.

Thousands of small business owners recognize that globalization is the answer to their prayers.

Thousands of small business owners recognize that globalization is the answer to their prayers. They understand that attacking new markets in foreign lands will ease the burden of stifling government regulations, competition from imports, and bankers' reticence. Twenty years ago, America's entrepreneurs were hesitant to even think about selling in overseas markets. Now the onslaught of globalization clearly marks the path to future growth and profitability, outshining many U.S. markets.

All global traders agree that theirs is a complex world, challenging even the most progressive, innovative entrepreneur. According to Forrester Research Inc., 85 percent of small businesses that sell their products over the internet cite the complications of shipping overseas as the number one reason they do not fulfill international orders. Widespread corruption, violence, extreme poverty, and religious and racial intolerance permeate all emerging world markets, much as they do rich nations. Radical changes continue to reshape the business landscape in Latin America, Russia, Eastern Europe, the Middle East, China, India, and Southeast Asia. Unstable regimes and convoluted financial markets cast a darkening glow over many otherwise fascinating opportunities.

Despite these challenges, overseas markets offer much greater profits and long-term growth than U.S. markets. Developing countries are especially ripe for new products and services. Low labor costs and easily accessible production materials provide foreign-based manufacturing, research and development, and even certain service industries viable alternatives to high cost Stateside operations. While thousands of owners of smaller companies are beginning to realize the magnitude of these benefits, they are also learning that getting started can be frustrating. If you are one of these entre-

preneurs—and if you aren't, I can't imagine why you're reading this book—
you must have a raft of questions that need to be answered.

➡ Which markets sport the heftiest demands for your products?
➡ What are the best ways to sell your products?
➡ Which means of transport are the most cost effective?
➡ How can you be sure if you'll get paid?
➡ Where do you find the lowest cost production materials and labor?
➡ How do you deal with the unique cultural anomalies and unfamiliar foreign languages?

By the time you finish this book, you'll have your answers. You'll uncover opportunities in Brazil, Russia, India, China, Israel, and 35 other countries. You'll find a methodology for calculating the risk of entering these markets. You'll get tips for coping with unfamiliar languages and recommendations for selecting strategic partners to smooth out the tangles of foreign customs and regulations. You'll be shown a program for tapping the benefits of export trading companies. You'll learn about which countries are ready for e-commerce. You'll read about winning negotiating tactics and creative financing options for imports, exports, and investment in overseas facilities. Baffling cultural traits and business practices from around the globe will be highlighted. And American habits that drive foreign customers and bureaucrats up the wall will be pointed out.

Choosing the best country in which to do business is by far the most difficult decision you'll have to make—and also the riskiest. Selling products (and by products I mean goods, services, technologies, franchises, and know-how) in a foreign country is virtually impossible without a thorough grasp of its laws, customs, economics, market demand, customer demographics, and business protocol. Since these vary country to country, what works in Russia won't work in India, and doing business in China isn't the same as doing business in Brazil. Attracting customers, checking credit, setting sell prices, negotiating contracts, helping customers arrange financing, delivering goods, and collecting receivables must be consistent with the business practices of the host country.

Choosing the best country in which to do business is by far the most difficult decision you'll have to make—and also the riskiest.

Not only do you need to choose a country where the mode of doing business jibes with your own practices and objectives, you also need to choose a country whose customers, infrastructure, and political stability meet your specific needs. Having swallowed media hype about its high-growth future, hundreds of U.S. companies of all sizes seized on China as a target for exporting, sourcing, and even foreign direct investment. Clearly, some continue to reap enormous benefits. But others have failed. While China's enormous population, gigantic landmass, and pockets of free-wheeling capitalism offer some companies the potential for hefty profits, others find only massive roadblocks. For instance, rising wages and suffo-cating air pollution are causing more and more foreign companies to abandon this fast-growing country in favor of other Southeast Asia markets (according to AmCham Shanghai, 17 percent have already made the shift). However, despite these setbacks and many other disastrous experiences in China (and previously in Russia and Mexico) U.S. companies continue to export to these giant markets. In fact, the dollar amount of exports from U.S. companies to a specific country indicates how easy or difficult it is to do business in that country and serves as a good starting point for our analyses.

A GLOBAL PERSPECTIVE

While Washington is preoccupied with guaranteeing healthcare and flushing out terrorists, American businesses have taken a different tack. They are excited about offshore opportunities in the emerging markets of the world. Global trade is big business. In fact, worldwide exports topped $13 trillion in 2006, of which $1 trillion or 8 percent came from U.S. companies.

Excluding Canada, the greatest benefactors of U.S. exports continue to be Mexico and the rest of Latin America. Exports to this region have grown 12 percent over the last five years. And Latin trade shows no sign of abetting. In fact, as Figure 1-1 shows, more than one-fifth of total U.S. exports go to Latin America.

Over 200 countries dot the global landscape. However, examining the pros and cons of doing business in each is well beyond the scope of this book. Therefore, I have chosen to look at those 10 emerging nations in each of the four regions of the world (Latin America, Asia, the Middle East, and Eastern Europe) that have attracted the most U.S. exports. I have chosen

	U.S. Exports ** (million $)	Percent	U.S. Imports** (million $)	Percent
FIGURE 1-1 U.S. Exports and Imports				
EMERGING NATIONS				
Latin America	214,195	20.7	326,437	17.6
Asia	165,456	16.0	470,029	25.4
Middle East	44,433	4.3	94,569	5.1
Eastern Europe	18,472	1.8	39,383	2.1
Subtotal	442,556	42.8	930,418	50.2
RICH NATIONS				
Canada	230,656	22.3	302,437	16.3
European Union (original 15)*	181,718	17.5	298,878	16.1
Japan	59,612	5.8	148,180	8.0
Other	122,092	11.6	174,025	9.4
Subtotal	594,078	57.2	923,520	49.8
Total U.S. Exports and Imports	1,036,634	100.0	1,853,938	100.0

* Original 15 countries: Austria, Belgium, Denmark, Finland, France, Germany, Greece, Ireland, Italy, Luxembourg, Netherlands, Portugal, Spain, Sweden, and United Kingdom
** Excludes expenditures by international visitors to the United States and U.S. citizens traveling abroad
Source: International Trade Administration

emerging nations rather than rich countries because they offer U.S. businesses beginning global trade the fastest-growing markets and the least amount of competition from transnational companies. Figure 1-2 shows the key statistics for each of these 40 countries, ranked in descending order by the amount of U.S. exports to that country.

When looking at these markets, bear in mind the criteria that you believe are the most important to the success of your specific products. Although Russia may be the perfect choice for a company manufacturing oil well pumps or cables, it could be a disaster for one producing curbside mailboxes. Just because the U.S. Commercial Service highlights healthcare products as a viable market in Brazil doesn't mean that dietary supplements will sell there as well. Even within a broad category of products such as edu-

	FIGURE 1-2 Key Statistics						
Country	2006 U.S. Exports to (million $)	Population (million)	Annual per Capita GDP (PPP)	GDP Growth (percent)	Un-employment (percent)	Inflation (percent)	2006 U.S. Imports from (million $)
Mexico	133,978	107.5	10,600	4.5	3.2	3.4	198,253
China	55,185	1,314.0	7,600	10.5	4.2	1.5	287,774
Singapore	24,683	4.5	30,900	7.4	3.1	1.0	17,768
Taiwan	23,046	23.0	29,000	4.4	3.9	1.0	38,211
Brazil	19,231	188.1	8,600	3.1	9.6	4.2	26,366
Hong Kong	17,775	6.9	36,500	5.9	4.9	2.2	7,946
Malaysia	12,544	24.4	12,700	5.5	3.5	3.8	36,533
U.A.E.	11,648	2.6	49,700	10.2	2.4	10.0	1,385
Israel	10,864	6.4	26,000	4.8	8.5	1.9	19,166
India	10,056	1,095.4	3,700	8.5	7.8	5.3	21,830
Thailand	8,146	64.6	9,100	4.4	2.1	5.1	22,466
Saudi Arabia	7,639	27.0	13,800	5.9	13.0	1.9	31,689
Philippines	7,617	89.5	5,000	5.4	8.4	6.6	9,694
Chile	6,786	16.1	12,600	4.8	8.3	2.1	9,565
Columbia	6,708	43.6	8,400	5.4	11.1	4.3	9,265
Turkey	5,723	70.4	8,900	5.2	10.2	9.8	5,359
Dominican Republic	5,350	9.2	8,000	7.2	16.0	8.2	4,532
Argentina	4,775	39.9	15,000	8.5	10.2	10.0	3,979
Russia	4,701	142.9	12,100	6.6	6.6	9.8	19,828
Egypt	4,132	78.9	4,200	5.7	10.3	6.5	3,844
Costa Rica	4,132	4.1	12,000	4.7	6.6	12.1	3,844
Guatemala	3,511	12.8	5,400	5.6	3.2	6.6	3,102
Indonesia	3,078	245.4	3,800	5.4	12.5	13.2	13,424
Peru	2,926	28.3	6,400	6.5	7.2	2.1	5,880
El Salvador	2,152	6.9	5,200	3.4	6.2	4.3	1,856
Kuwait	2,087	2.4	21,600	8.0	2.2	3.0	3,981

	FIGURE 1-2 continued						
Country	2006 U.S. Exports to (million $)	Population (million)	Annual per Capita GDP (PPP)	GDP Growth (percent)	Un-employment (percent)	Inflation (percent)	2006 U.S. Imports from (million $)
Pakistan	1,989	165.8	2,600	6.5	6.5	7.9	3,672
Poland	1,961	38.5	14,100	5.3	14.9	1.3	2,253
Trinidad and Tobago	1,615	1.1	19,700	12.6	7.0	8.0	8,362
Qatar	1,278	0.9	29,400	7.2	3.2	7.2	261
Hungary	1,187	10.0	17,300	3.8	7.4	4.7	2,584
Czech Republic	1,122	10.2	21,600	6.2	8.4	2.7	2,346
Algeria	1,101	32.9	7,700	4.6	15.7	15.0	15,455
Morocco	878	33.2	4,400	6.7	7.7	2.8	521
Oman	829	3.1	14,100	6.5	15.0	2.0	909
Lithuania	566	3.6	15,100	7.2	4.5	3.6	570
Romania	554	22.3	8,800	6.4	6.1	6.8	1,119
Slovakia	510	5.4	17,700	6.4	10.2	4.4	1,405
Bulgaria	293	7.4	10,400	5.5	9.6	7.2	458
Latvia	245	2.3	17,700	10.3	5.9	6.3	299
Sri Lanka	227	20.9	4,100	6.0	6.3	15.6	2,065
Estonia	221	1.3	21,800	7.9	4.7	4.4	526

Source: CIA Factbook 2007; International Trade Administration; U.S. Department of Commerce; U.S. Commercial Service

Note: PPP stands for purchasing power parity. According to the Organization for Economic Cooperation and Development (OECD) purchasing power parity is the "currency conversion rate that converts to a common currency and equalizes the purchasing power of different currencies. In other words, it eliminates the differences in price levels between countries in the process of conversion." Economists believe this presents a truer picture of economies than traditional GDP per capita calculations. Perhaps PPP is a little easier to understand when one thinks of it as a mechanism to state that exchange rates between two countries are in equilibrium when the purchasing power for a given basket of goods is the same in the two countries. The Economist magazine issues it's McDonald's Big Mac Index once a year. This hamburger index, otherwise known as the Big Mac PPP, is the exchange rate that would leave a hamburger in any country costing the same as in the United States. For many people, PPP is a difficult concept to grasp. Rather than spend any more time on it here, check out The Economist website www.economist.com for a full description of the Big Mac Index.

cational supplies, imported school desks may be in great demand in Shanghai while Chinese producers corner the market on blackboards, chalk, and erasers.

The moral, of course, is to ignore markets that are hyped by the U.S. government or the American media and cautiously investigate only those countries whose consumer and business needs, infrastructure capabilities, and sociopolitical strata support your specific products and goals. This sounds more difficult than it really is. Plenty of data is available from a plethora of sources—both public and private—that describe in a fair amount of detail the types of products most needed in each country (see Chapter 4). If it yields a market that fits your capabilities, you're home free. If it doesn't, move on to another country. And remember that one man's garbage is another man's treasure. Violent pockets in Latin America keep most foreign traders at bay but could be the best possible markets for your handcuffs, uniforms, and bulletproof vests.

On the first pass, you may find that none of the data precisely meets your needs. Does that mean you should abandon your plans to enter global trade? Absolutely not. It only means that you will need to dig deeper and be more creative in ferreting out opportunities. This is where experts in global trade can be an immense help. Hiring an international consultant may seem like an extraneous expense; however, the benefits of sound advice from one who knows your product and has extensive experience in international trade will more than offset the cost. Such advice will also save you an immeasurable amount of time sorting through reams of data on your own. Before you ask, no, I can't take on any new clients. But you'll find plenty of choices on the internet.

Even with expert assistance, however, certain matters must be addressed immediately. The following are the most common questions asked by entrepreneurs planning to begin trading in global markets:

➡ How can I identify the best overseas markets for my products?
➡ How do I sell to customers who speak a different language?
➡ How can I prevent foreign governments from expropriating my property or products?
➡ How do I deal with wide fluctuations in currency exchange rates?
➡ How can I sell in foreign markets that are government controlled?

➡ How can I determine the creditworthiness of foreign customers?

➡ How can I ensure payment of my invoices?

➡ What recourse do I have if a foreign customer doesn't pay?

➡ Where do I find out about shipping containers and shipping documentation?

➡ Don't high customs fees distort selling prices?

➡ How can I compete with host country companies when I have to add overseas shipping and customs costs to my prices?

➡ What if the ship sinks or pirates steal its cargo?

➡ Since we're not a wealthy company, how can we afford to finance export customers?

➡ What if customers pay in currencies that cannot be converted to dollars?

➡ How do I move money between countries?

➡ How can I communicate with my overseas locations?

➡ With international travel so costly, how do I cost effectively supervise my people stationed in a foreign country?

➡ Am I subject to double taxation, once in a foreign country and again by the IRS?

➡ If I deposit collections in a foreign bank, how do I get my money back to the United States?

➡ Where do I find a lawyer that understands foreign laws?

➡ What should I know about doing business in a specific country?

➡ How do I learn local business protocols and customs?

➡ Where do I find foreign personnel to sell my products or manage my facility?

➡ How do I train foreign personnel?

➡ What fringe benefits are legally required for foreign employees?

➡ How do I get an audit done overseas?

➡ Where do I get passports, visas, and work permits for my employees?

➡ If I want to sell in Saudi Arabia, for instance, how do I locate other American companies doing business there?

➡ What U.S. government agencies can I go to for assistance?

➡ Are there any private sources of expert assistance, so I don't have to get involved with government bureaucrats?

➡ How do I become familiar with a specific country's laws, tax statutes, labor codes, and other rules of doing business?

To answer these questions, we need to look at the various market-entry options. But first, a lesson learned from AllTemp Aluminum.

INSIGHT...

AllTemp Aluminum Extrusions Inc. (ATAE) supplied the East Coast restaurant industry with large pots, pans, and other cooking utensils. ATAE also sold aluminum parts used in automated restaurant dishwashers. Although this company had the capability to manufacture several of its products, the owner, Mr. Borus, chose to purchase most of them through a network of distributors. I was engaged to help them devise a long-term strategic plan that would expand markets beyond the East Coast and ensure steady growth. Such predictability was important because within seven years Mr. Borus planned to turn the reins of his company over to his son.

Mr. Borus was not risk averse. Although he was conservative in many ways, he knew that steady long-term growth required at least of modicum of risk. Also, competitors were beginning to import low-cost cooking utensils from China, undercutting his prices and stealing an increasing number of his long-term customers.

After completing my analysis of ATAE's operations and interviewing the company's managers and key customers, I came to the conclusion that the least expensive, fastest, and most profitable long-term solution was to begin a program to export cooking utensils to a handful of markets in Columbia and Ecuador. Mr. Borus was delighted. After I explained how he could market his products through an export management company without leaving home and could finance the program with one of the off-balance sheet transaction finance companies, he couldn't wait to begin.

Before we implemented the plan, however, I cautioned my client that while exporting seemed to be the best alternative for the present, before his tenure was up, he probably would want to seriously consider stocking his own warehouse in Columbia or even establishing a manufacturing subsidiary there. A decade later, under the leadership of Mr. Borus' son, ATAE acquired a small aluminum manufacturing company in Bogotá, as exports to Ecuador expanded.

Global trade is a four-legged beast comprised of exporting, sourcing (importing), foreign direct investment in local markets, and foreign direct investment to produce goods for shipment back to the United States (e.g., maquilas, also known as twin plants or assembly plants) or other countries. Of the four legs, exporting from the United States has generated the greatest dollar profits for smaller U.S. companies. And that's where we will begin our journey.

EXPORTING

Manufacturing companies *export* goods to customers in Germany, Argentina, or India and *import* products from Malaysia, Italy, or Mexico. That's straightforward. Absolutely, no confusion. But when it comes to exporting and importing services, definitions get a bit sticky. For instance, U.S. contractors export services when they construct buildings, roads, or utilities in a foreign country. Consultants export when they perform services for foreign clients. U.S. investment banks export when they arrange financing from global sources or assist customers in structuring foreign business acquisitions. On the other hand, the opening of a Sheraton, Hilton, or Marriott hotel overseas is not considered exporting.

One of the quirks of the government's definition of service exports and imports involves foreign visitors to the United States and Americans traveling abroad. Every dollar foreigners spend on food, lodging, recreation, gifts, or airfare are considered U.S. exports. And that's a fair chunk of the total. In 2006, international visitors dropped $107.4 billion. Of course, the reverse—American travelers spending U.S. dollars abroad—is considered importing. That seems like a stretch, but that's Washington's way.

The sale or purchase of technology or management know-how is also convoluted. For instance, a U.S. company that licenses a French company to use its technology for the manufacturing of products in France is considered an exporter. A U.S. company that purchases the right to use German designed engine components is an importer. When McDonald's franchises restaurants in Russia it is an exporter. But when Coca Cola opens a plant in Burma it is not an exporter. Publishers that sell book rights to English publishing houses export copyrights. But a television network with overseas reception does not export broadcasted news.

Confusing definitions notwithstanding, exporting is certainly the most popular form of global trade. Companies that don't have sales personnel with international experience can easily contract an export trading company or export management company to handle overseas marketing. These specialized agents can also manage all the shipping documentation. Collections can be assured through the use of letters of credit, customer bank guarantees, or credit insurance. In fact, exporting is usually more profitable and carries less risk than selling in U.S. markets.

Once your export program is up and running growth strategies that involve foreign sourcing or foreign direct investment will be a natural progression in the building of a competitive market position. Imported materials, parts, and components are, in many cases, less costly than similar items purchased or manufactured in the United States. Assembling labor-intensive products with low-cost labor in emerging nations can increase profit margins. The judicious use of foreign trade zones in the United States and in other countries avoids the extra cost of import customs duties and taxes. Direct shipment from an offshore manufacturing plant to foreign customers may reduce shipping costs below those incurred when shipping from the United States. And capital raised in Europe, Latin America, or Asia is, in many cases, less costly and more available than U.S. financing.

One major difference between exporting (either from the United States or from an offshore facility to a third country) and selling in U.S. markets is that in order to close an overseas order, U.S. exporters are expected to help foreign customers finance their purchases. Buyers will expect you to provide trade credit as well as government financial support and bank guarantees. This close interaction of marketing and finance can be confusing and a hard pill to swallow, especially if your company follows the traditionally American custom of a strict demarcation between these two functions.

A second major difference between exporting and selling in U.S. markets is that normally the former carries very little collection risk. Bad debts that may plague your U.S. business can be virtually eliminated with irrevocable letters of credit confirmed by a U.S. bank, government guarantees from Ex-Im Bank, or credit insurance from a private carrier.

Margins are also generally higher on export sales. American goods continue to be sought after in virtually every offshore market, especially in emerging nations, so you should be able to get higher prices than you can get in competitive U.S. markets. The exception, of course, is generic products manufactured in-country. To the extent that the market cannot distinguish between your imported goods and locally produced goods, the prices of both will be similar and margins will be lower.

In addition to or in lieu of exporting, you may find it profitable to get involved in foreign sourcing. This sounds more difficult than it is.

American goods continue to be sought after in virtually every offshore market, especially in emerging nations, so you should be able to get higher prices than you can get in competitive U.S. markets.

FOREIGN SOURCING

The terms *foreign sourcing* or just *sourcing* can be confusing. Both refer to the purchase of foreign produced parts, components, and raw materials. Sourcing also refers to the use of foreign labor for the making of assemblies or components to be shipped back to the United States for integration into finished products and to the raising of capital through offshore capital markets or from foreign banks. In addition, it also refers to the acquisition of patented processes from foreign suppliers.

Globalization has clearly brought many benefits to consumers, not the least of which is lower prices from foreign sourcing. Labor-intensive products that have been assembled in very low-wage emerging nations flood the shelves of our stores. Virtually every piece of clothing we wear has been produced partially or completely offshore, mostly in Southeast Asia, Central America, and the Caribbean. The vast majority of our electronic appliances, equipment, and components have been produced in China, Malaysia, Thailand, and other low-wage countries. Automobile parts and assemblies, aircraft components, toys, and school supplies originate in Mexico, Canada, China, Japan, and Eastern Europe. On and on it goes.

Globalization has created worldwide manufacturing capabilities, a global storeroom, an all-inclusive choice of products, and an international caldron of financial services. We are no longer restricted to goods produced in the United States or limited to state-of-the-art innovations conceived by American inventors. Foreign sourcing enables American businesses to supply us with anything that's available in any other country.

INSIGHT... Something as simple as buying a book is a good example. The other day I wanted to buy a specific title by one of my favorite authors, Mark Burnell. After combing the shelves of Barnes & Noble and Borders and searching in catalogs of several book distributors, I finally located the book on Amazon.com at The Book Depository, an English company based in London. An e-mail credit card order that including a shipping cost of $3.99 (the same as the cost of shipping a book domestically through the U.S. Postal Service) brought me the book in five days.

Basic materials can be sourced from offshore sites, usually at prices significantly lower than the same materials purchased within the United States. Hardwood lumber from Canada and Brazil, fragrances from India, cement from Mexico, and steel from South Korea are a few examples.

Foreign sourcing does present a few challenges, however. Depending on your supplier, you may have to pay in advance for the goods. You should buy marine insurance to cover the possibility of losses should the boat sink or pirates steal your products on the high seas. Deliveries may be hard to coordinate with your local production schedule. You will definitely have to arrange and pay for overland or air transport of the goods from the port of debarkation to your facility. Still, in most cases, foreign sourcing will be less expensive than purchasing your materials from Stateside suppliers. Be careful of quality rejects, however. Many exporters from Russia, Eastern Europe, China, and some Latin American countries tend to pawn off inferior-quality products on foreign buyers.

What Uncle Sam taketh away, he sometimes giveth back. Despite onerous U.S. Customs procedures requiring reams of paperwork (mostly done by computer now) for each shipment, you may be able to avoid U.S. customs duties completely through the use of foreign trade zones that pepper the landscape. Be sure to check out those nearest your facility. Depending on the particular foreign trade zone, you can store imported products, assemble imported parts, and even reship finished goods, without incurring customs duties.

FOREIGN DIRECT INVESTMENT

By *foreign direct investment* (FDI) we mean setting-up, acquiring, or otherwise investing in a manufacturing plant, distribution center, retail outlet, or sales office on foreign soil. These facilities may be used for producing, holding, or selling products to local markets; exporting to other foreign countries; or producing finished products or parts, assemblies, and components in maquila factories for shipment back to your U.S. company, as in foreign sourcing. For those of you who may not be familiar with it, the term *maquila* refers to a factory on foreign soil that imports materials and equipment duty-free for assembly or manufacturing and then reexports the assembled products back to the originating country duty-free. The term comes from Spanish and means the practice of millers charging a miller's portion (a maquila) for processing other people's grain. Twin plants is another term signifying the same type of arrangement. In Mexico, these factories are called maquiladoras.

Returning to foreign direct investments, an FDI may involve the complete acquisition or a majority or minority interest in an ongoing business or facility. It also can refer to investing in a majority or minority interest of an infrastructure project (a power utility, port authority, or toll road) or an equal or unequal interest in a joint venture or other strategic alliance. Additionally, it can refer to building a facility or starting a business from scratch.

Although exporting opens the door to global markets, over the long haul, you can maximize worldwide profits with an FDI in an offshore facility. Such a local presence enables you to carve out market niches in the same way that Toyota, Subaru, Siemens, Lukoil, and other foreign competitors have done in the United States. It also permits more competitive pricing than exporting because a local presence obviates extra shipping costs and tariffs, reduces the timespan in moving goods to market, allows more efficient after-sales service, and lets pricing policies flow with rapidly changing market conditions. Furthermore, goods can usually be produced with lower labor and material costs than if they were made in the United States. Before investing in a foreign facility, however, you need to become familiar with the intricacies of doing business in that country and the risks that it entails.

TECHNOLOGY LICENSING

For some businesses and in some countries, the nature of the product, restrictive government regulations, or lack of management talent may preclude either exporting or developing an FDI. Yet market demand for your products may be strong. This is especially true in the worldwide branding of many low-tech consumer goods, such as toothpaste, bar soap, breakfast cereal, and so on. Licensing technology to foreign companies enables them to produce these products in-country, which may lead to significantly more trade in the future while you collect royalties. This technique has been used extensively by transnationals in the developing markets of Asia and Latin America.

The major advantage of licensing over either exporting or FDI is that it provides an entree to global markets without financial commitments. The biggest disadvantages are:

1. Difficulty in collecting royalty payments.
2. Complying with local tax laws that might delay or reduce royalty payments.
3. Losing control over the technology as well as the production processes and marketing strategies of proprietary products.

However, loss of control may pose less of a problem as time goes on and you develop newer technologies or products to replace those licensed overseas. U.S. software producers learned that this was an effective way to beat the piracy of computer programs. Overall, the ease of entry into local markets and the low cost of technology licensing frequently outweigh the risks.

FRANCHISING

Franchising also offers an opportunity to enter the global arena without significant cost or financing commitments. However, most companies that have franchised overseas for years, such as McDonald's, Kentucky Fried Chicken, and Radio Shack, assist in the financing of startup franchises either through leasing arrangements or short-term working capital loans. Foreign franchisees will probably expect you to do the same.

Companies that have successfully started franchises offshore have always had a working franchise base in the United States. They learned early on that without franchise experience in the United States overseas franchising can easily backfire, costing more than a business startup. The case of Weltight Sash and Door Company demonstrates how the lack of franchising experience can lead to horrendous decisions and ultimate failure.

INSIGHT . . . Weltight, a manufacturer of aluminum doors and windows, distributed these products throughout the Midwest from a series of home remodeling centers. The company's owner heard about terrific opportunities in several large residential developments underway in and around Mumbai. Wishing to tap this apparently enormous new market, he traveled to India to survey conditions for himself. While there he noticed several franchises sporting American names. Unfortunately, he didn't take the time to investigate how they were set up or if they were profitable.

Returning home, the Weltight owner announced that his company would immediately begin franchising Indian distributorships. Franchise agreements were negotiated with three Indian companies in metropolitan Mumbai and Madras. Weltight transferred $300,000 to each distributor for startup working capital and agreed to guarantee loans from local Indian banks for the purchase of installation tools and vehicles.

The franchising experiment lasted about two years, during which time all three distributorships folded. Weltight lost its initial investment of $900,000, and as a guarantor, they were liable for another $1,315,000 to settle bank debts. That was the last time franchising or global trade were mentioned at Weltight.

If you are already franchising in the United States, however, you should have little difficulty doing the same overseas, assuming your product lines, distribution policies, franchise procedures, and contracts are all adapted to the specific market being served. Now let's shift gears and take a look at how the American public, and hence Washington, view global trade.

A PUBLIC VIEW OF GLOBAL TRADE

Historically, the U.S. government and the American people have viewed global trade more as a necessary evil than as a major benefactor to the U.S. economy, contributing more than 12 percent of GDP. Driven mostly by trade unions and now environmentalists, elected officials have succumbed to arguments about how global trade steals American jobs and denigrates the world's environment. Vice President Al Gore and other environmentalists condemn industrialized nations and, by inference, global trade for being major contributors to global warming. Trade unions rant against free trade pacts and foreign sourcing as the major causes of jobs shifting from the United States to emerging nations. As is so often the case, he who makes the most noise gets heard. Trade unionists and environmentalists, both very small minorities, have shouted loudly for some time and Washington has listened. While not overtly against global trade, enough legislators are skeptical of its benefits to fight fiercely against enacting new trade pacts. Some senators have even made noises about withdrawing from NAFTA. A good example of the power of these voices is that trade agreements already negotiated with Colombia, South Korea, Malaysia, and Panama languish in congressional committees awaiting ratification.

> Whatever the reason, the relationship between the American public and Washington, on the one hand, and international traders, on the other hand, has been at best rocky and at worst downright antagonistic.

Whatever the reason, the relationship between the American public and Washington, on the one hand, and international traders, on the other hand, has been at best rocky and at worst downright antagonistic. Still, since 1989 various administrations have made modest attempts at changing this negativism into a more positive approach to international trade. For example, the proposed Free Trade Area of the Americas conceived of during the later stages of the elder Bush's administration was an attempt to bring all Western Hemisphere nations under a unified trade umbrella by 2005. Unfortunately, a consensus among those nations was not forthcoming and the effort died a natural death. Furthermore, NAFTA continues to bring the economies of the United States, Mexico, and Canada closer to a single standard. And the many bilateral trade and multilateral trade agreements that have been implemented, agreed on, or are being negotiated will certainly benefit U.S. businesses both large and small. Thanks to these agreements, U.S. companies of all sizes can hold their own on price as well as prompt delivery with fiercely competitive European and Asian transnational corporations.

Although billions of dollars continue to pour into Israel and Egypt to further our interests there and additional billions stream into Colombia and Central America in an effort to stem the flow of illicit drugs across our borders, international affairs are given short shrift by the U.S. media. Yes, trade issues occasionally make the nightly news, but by and large, they are overshadowed by the wars in Iraq and Afghanistan. Daily catastrophes in the Balkans and the Middle East, African lawlessness, massacres by teenagers with guns, the exploding economic growth of China, terrorist threats, outsourcing to India, the revival of Japan, these are the featured stories behind today's headlines. With a few exceptions, global trade and direct investment by the American business community hardly make a byline. It certainly seems that the American public does not have an overriding interest in worldwide trade. And this indifference is the driving force behind Washington's staccato approach to global trade policies.

Fortunately, the American business community sees things differently. It recognizes that the future lies in globalization and that global trade is the anchor. The Summit of the Americas, originating in 1994, is a good example of the political clout a unified American business community can bring to bear.

OPPORTUNITIES ABOUND

It is now clear that every emerging nation has benefited from market reforms implemented over the last 10 years, some more than others. While governments are becoming more closely aligned with what passes for democratic institutions (with a few noted exceptions, especially in the Persian Gulf states), capital continues to flow from the IMF, the United States, Canada, Europe, and Japan as well as the private sector. Business has been legitimatized by new laws governing consumer protection, foreign investment, intellectual property rights, capital markets, agent/distributor relationships, and a host of other matters necessary to sustain free market economies. And most importantly, consumers in record numbers want to buy American products and services. These booming commercial and industrial markets that hunger for American technology and management know-how are just too inviting to pass up. Free trade pacts that give U.S. companies a competitive edge over European and Asian rivals are too strategically beneficial to dismiss out of hand. With the fires of global competition burning cross-border barriers, smaller U.S. companies that have waited for the right time to enter global markets must move forward now.

> With the fires of global competition burning cross-border barriers, smaller U.S. companies that have waited for the right time to enter global markets must move forward now.

This is not to say that entrepreneurial businesses are strangers to global trade. On the contrary, U.S. technology, management know-how, goods, and services from smaller companies in a wide range of industries have contributed significantly to the growth of foreign economies, especially emerging markets. Moreover, many foreign governments actively solicit foreign trade and investment from American companies of all sizes. American made consumer and industrial products fill the shelves of emerging nation stores and the aisles of their factories. In fact, doors that have previously only been ajar are now swinging open for smaller companies in all industries.

Several emerging economies are rapidly maturing, no longer satisfied with being treated as backwater frontiers. These countries have thrown off the yoke of less developed status and are ready to join the more economically developed regions of the world. Still, many barriers remain.

DEFICIENCIES THAT STILL REMAIN

Although progress has been made and many risks of doing business in emerging nations are less intrusive today than they were 10 years ago, it's impossible to escape the conclusion that serious problems still lurk in the shadows. Many educational and healthcare facilities lack modern technologies, supplies, and trained staff. Landline telephone service is a scarce commodity. Electricity has yet to reach many rural populations. Water supplies and waste disposal plants fail to meet the needs of 21st century citizens. Although vastly improved in commercial and industrial centers, rural roadways, bridges, and ports remain in dismal shape. And environmental degradation has not abated.

The social issues have also not been properly addressed. Poverty and its evil sister, unemployment, remain huge deterrents to future growth. Unleashed corruption runs wild through bureaucracies, law enforcement, and businesses. Crime turns urban streets into battlefields. Drug trafficking through defenseless smaller countries poisons a whole generation of young people. Openly hostile military regimes and failed legal systems have caused street crime, kidnappings, and homicide to double and even triple in several capitals of the world. Organized crime—the Mafia, Triads, and the Yakusa—has taken over legitimate businesses. These very serious problems must be dealt with quickly and decisively to ease the apprehensions of global traders and travelers.

No one should be misled into thinking that doing business in the global economy is easy. Whether exporting, sourcing with maquila operations, or manufacturing or distributing for local consumption, doing business offshore is far more complex than it is in the United States. Competition is intense. Shipping costs are high. Language and protocol barriers are very pronounced. And the business climate is unique in each country. The entire mode of conducting business can be tricky for foreigners, especially America's entrepreneurs.

INTRA-REGIONAL CULTURAL AND BUSINESS VARIATIONS

Although many similarities exist among the emerging nations of the world, several differences stand out and should be recognized by anyone entering global trade. Every nationality has unique cultural traits. Every country has seemingly strange business practices. When you start looking at specific countries as potential markets, keep a sharp eye on the possibility of encountering the following.

➡ Informal underground markets. Many countries have thriving and openly available underground markets in goods imported from the United

States as well as knockoffs of these products. This tends to destroy the efficiency of distribution systems and disrupts financial systems.

➥ Weakened judicial systems. Although the judicial systems of most emerging nations have improved markedly since the early 1990s (except in the Arab states), some are still fraught with corruption.

➥ Environmental degradation. Brazil stands alone as having probably the worst history of environmental debasement in the world, caused mainly by logging companies, farmers, and ranchers in the Amazon Rainforest. Chinese air and soil pollution continue to exacerbate rapidly. Indonesian forests have been stripped. Indian water supplies are contaminated. Russian mining, oil well drilling, and waste disposal have despoiled thousands of acres, making them no longer suitable for agriculture.

➥ Crime. Some countries, notably drug trafficking drop-off countries, have virtually uncontrolled street crime. And organized crime is becoming more pronounced in several countries.

➥ Passive vs. aggressive cultures. Ordinary people as well as government officials in some countries seem to be much more aggressive in their behavior than those in other countries. Russia and some Eastern European countries come to mind as prime examples. The contrast between them and mild mannered Indians is remarkable.

➥ Impact of foreign cultures. Immigrants, American retirees, and American expats have had a major impact on the economies and cultures of several countries, especially in Latin America and the Middle East. Such an impact is visible in the adoption of the English language, American dress codes, and American business protocol.

In some countries, these conditions are not pronounced. But in others, they are very evident. Recognizing and integrating variations in cultures and market risks is a crucial part of your long-term strategic marketing program. We will see in succeeding chapters, just how crucial such an integration is.

chapter two
Global Financial System

I REALIZE THAT YOU PROBABLY HAVE VERY LITTLE OR NO INTEREST IN THE GLOBAL financial system. Most people don't. All you really want to do is get an export program underway. Still, it's very difficult—if not impossible—to become involved in any aspect of global trade without at least a modicum of knowledge about how money flows throughout the world, the instruments needed to make it flow, the organizations who control and govern the flow, and a smattering of the vernacular used by finance professionals. Therefore, I strongly suggest you at least give this chapter a cursory look.

Like a skier descending Mt. Everest, the evolution of the world financial system continues to gather speed. After centuries of central bank control, the combination of advances in global communications and transportation, and international dependence on Middle East controlled oil has opened global doors to the flow of money. Individuals, companies, banks, and nations instantaneously move money to investments that bring the highest return and offer the greatest security. Although an overworked cliché, the fact that money knows no national boundaries definitely describes the modern day global financial system. Globalization has taken over.

Although an overworked cliché, the fact that money knows no national boundaries definitely describes the modern day global financial system.

The entire financial system, and especially the global banking system, is experiencing a massive reshuffling of priorities. The various parts of the system have become so intertwined that a hiccup in one part causes pneumonia in another. This interdependence of the world's stock exchanges, government debt obligations, currency exchange rates, and private and public financing foretells an even greater upheaval in the future.

The complexity of capital makes it impossible for any nation or group of nations to control its flow. In the future, there will inevitably be an even greater need for an international body with granted authority to maintain order throughout the financial world. Some combination of the Bank for International Settlements, the World Bank, and the International Monetary Fund might be the answer.

The global financial system has received many shocks during the past 60 years. One of the most significant was the introduction of the European Union's euro currency. At its inception, the euro was merely an accounting nicety. By 2002, however, euro coins and bills were issued, making the euro the official currency of the European Union's Eurozone, which consists of 13 countries (Austria, Belgium, Finland, France, Germany, Greece, Ireland, Italy, Luxembourg, the Netherlands, Portugal, Slovenia, Spain, and in 2008, Cyprus and Malta).

GLOBAL BANKING

In addition to other aspects of the international financial system, globalization has brought enormous changes to the banking industry. The ability to move money anywhere around the world simply by clicking a computer mouse has forced central banks, whose main concern is doing nothing to disrupt the flow of money, and mammoth international banks, whose businesses extend far beyond deposits and loans, into an entirely new global banking business model. And these changes have not ended, yet.

Dramatic innovations continue to revolutionize the industry. Macroeconomic reforms, domestic deregulation, high-tech communication, and new types of securities have made capital markets more efficient than ever before and have boosted cross-border lending beyond the dreams of even the most flamboyant optimist. This, in turn, intensifies competition on a global scale.

In response, banks have diversified into nontraditional financial services. Nonbank institutions entered the trade finance market. Creative financial instruments and near-money currency, such as American Depositary Receipts (ADRs) and euros, drain productive demand from banking channels. Moreover, excess capacity in the world banking community has further encouraged cross-border rivalries. The Bank for International Settlements' (BIS) (we will look at the BIS in more detail later) recommended guidelines for increasing capital ratios was the final straw, forcing banks in country after country to restructure their balance sheets and national regulators to reexamine outmoded bank legislation.

The impact of a restructured banking system on global traders is both devastating—and exhilarating. The worldwide credit crunch of 2007–2008 forced banks to be more interested in cleaning up their balance sheets and cutting costs than seeking out new lending opportunities. Part of this effort was reflected in a tidal wave of worldwide bank mergers. It can also be seen as an attempt by banks to further specialize their portfolios while shedding the yoke of one-stop shopping.

As national regulatory agencies begin to grasp the significance of these changes, more creative approaches will become available to finance global trade as well as foreign direct investment. Cross-border financing will further permit exporters and investors to utilize financing sources in host countries. Multilateral and bilateral donor aid is already finding its way directly to the private sector, bypassing bank quotas and government siphoning. Development banks are becoming more aggressive in raising local capital for private sector direct investment. Unique strategic alliances channel cross-border funds from a variety of sources for single projects. Competition from nonbank alternative transactional financing continues to force commercial banks to lower demands for inordinate amounts of external collateral. So many changes, in such a short amount of time, boggles the mind.

Before we get too far along, it might prove helpful to set the stage by reviewing the major developments in the world financial system that have led to the current upheaval in global banking.

EXCHANGE RATES

In 1944, Bretton Woods, New Hampshire was the site of a series of meetings between the Allied Powers of World War II that shaped the world's financial system as no other set of decisions has done—before or since. For the first time, a united opinion established a system of pegged but adjustable exchange rates among the currencies of the major world powers. For 26 subsequent years, exchange rates endured prolonged periods of only minor oscillations and a few large but closely controlled swings.

By 1970, sustained payment imbalances together with substantial shifts in international reserve holdings forced the United States to abandon the gold standard (a fundamental underpinning of Bretton Woods). The 1944 agreement collapsed and floating rates took over. To this day, however, two-thirds of the members of the International Monetary Fund continue to limit their exchange rate movements, pegging their currency's value to the U.S. dollar, the euro, the Japanese yen, the IMF's Special Drawing Rights (SDR), or some other global standard.

In 1979, the European Community began experimenting with the European Monetary System to establish a regional standard. Member states agreed to keep their exchange rates within a certain range of values relative to one another. Theoretically, movement beyond this range would urge the monetary authorities of the two countries involved to intervene in the market to stabilize both currencies.

After the collapse of Bretton Woods and the abandonment of the gold standard, the world's major currencies—the U.S. dollar, the British pound, the Japanese yen, and the German mark—floated against one another in a relatively free market without major fluctuations. During the 1980s, conditions changed. Exchange rates became extremely unstable. During the early 1980s, the U.S. dollar experienced skyrocketing ascents despite a mushrooming trade deficit. Then, between 1985 and 1988, it lost nearly 40 percent in a tumbling free fall.

Such wild fluctuations created an extremely unstable atmosphere in which to set national budgetary policies. The fluctuations distorted national monetary and fiscal policy. They prohibited intelligent evaluations of international investment strategies and product pricing. In fact, unstable exchange rates upset the entire global marketplace. This caused a fiery debate among economists, government policy makers, and the financial community about whether or not the world monetary system required reform and, if so, what type of reform needed to be implemented.

These protagonists argued from three perspectives: (1) floating rates are good, encourage speculation on future trends, which is the way a free market system should work, and should be left alone, (2) a fixed rate system should be reinstated based on either a gold standard or some other universally acceptable medium, and (3) a compromise should be reached between a floating rate and a fixed rate system, allowing rates to fluctuate within a narrow band. The later was the direction taken by the European Monetary System, leading to the introduction of the euro in 1999.

The management of exchange rate risk is crucial for any company involved in international trade.

The management of exchange rate risk is crucial for any company involved in international trade. To minimize adverse exchange rate fluctuations and maximize gains, exchange rate management must underlie the choice of financing methods for virtually any long-term project or transaction. This anomaly of international finance is an important criteria for your choice of one funding source over another.

The fact remains, however, that exchange rate fluctuations are less a function of specific tactics than a fallout of a whole conglomeration of economic forces experienced on a worldwide level, such as inflation rates, interest rates, political unrest, financial market aberrations, and commodity prices. Furthermore, currency exchange rates respond wildly to major economic shocks, such as wars, OPEC maneuvers, natural disasters, and anticipated political and economic actions of the world powers. Nevertheless and regardless of the difficulty, effective tactics for raising global capital must recognize the strategic importance of exchange rate fluctuations and deal with the issue as expeditiously as possible.

UNITED NATIONS FINANCIAL INSTITUTIONS

A second major event emanating from Bretton Woods was the formation of two international monetary organizations still very much in evidence today—the World Bank and the International Monetary Fund.

Member countries make contributions to the World Bank, which subsequently issues bonds and notes to raise its lending reserves. The original purpose of the World Bank was to mobilize capital for postwar European reconstruction. Over the years, the bank's focus has shifted, eventually becoming a source of funds for emerging nations to finance investment projects when private capital could not be raised. Today, it makes medium- and long-term loans mainly to governments. A modest amount of financial assistance has been directed to the private sector, which the host country government always guarantees with collateral.

The mission of the International Finance Corporation (IFC), one of the four arms of the World Bank, is to promote local capital markets and private industry in developing countries. It accomplishes this by providing large transnational corporations with debt and equity capital, technical assistance, and financing for preinvestment studies.

The original purpose of the International Monetary Fund (IMF) was to stabilize exchange rates through the coordination and regulation of member country currency movement. It no longer coordinates and regulates, although it does promote stability through surveillance and consultation with member countries. The IMF also provides minimum short-term loans to member countries for the purpose of resolving payment difficulties.

The IMF's role in the international financial system has increased significantly over the years. Today, it is one of the most powerful and important financial institutions in the world. Its major activity in recent years has been to support the building of infrastructure projects in emerging nations. Such support translates mainly into serving as a super numerary policeman. It does this by exercising approval authority over specific projects and developers prior to the awarding of financial assistance by development banks.

To obtain IMF approval, countries must keep inflation and budget deficits under control, curtail money supplies, and achieve at least a modicum of political stability. Critics cite the high unemployment and social unrest that such stringent policies bring, but so far, the IMF has held its ground.

THE BANK FOR INTERNATIONAL SETTLEMENTS

The Bank for International Settlements was founded to coordinate the collection and rescheduling of German reparations after World War I. It has survived to this day as sort of a central bank for the central banks of its 10 member countries. The BIS serves a useful purpose in that it functions objectively as an international financial ombudsman. With consensus approval from its member central banks, the BIS acts as a standard setting body for the global banking system.

Although the beginnings of the global integration of financial markets can be traced to the 1960s when Eurocurrency and Eurobond markets developed from excess deposits of Marshall Plan U.S. dollars in European banks and Citibank originated certificates of deposit, only since the 1980s has this integration of domestic and international markets been extended.

> The BIS serves a useful purpose in that it functions objectively as an international financial ombudsman.

The global credit crunch of 2007–2008 hit bank balance sheets hard. The free flow of money during the last decade and unrestrained credit—primarily in the United States—resulted in a major capital inadequacy problem for banks around the world. The BIS recognized that overextended loan portfolios resulted in a deterioration of capital ratios, not only of U.S. banks but also of financial institutions throughout the world. In an effort to correct this untenable situation, the BIS encouraged member country banks with significant operations outside their local markets to adhere to its 8 percent capital asset ratio guidelines.

It is certainly possible that the credit crunch of 2007–2008 could promote a global funding crisis for years to come. At a minimum, adherence to the BIS guidelines has rattled the global banking system. This, in turn, has produced a profound effect on the availability and form of trade finance and investment capital for companies of all sizes and from all countries.

NATIONAL CENTRAL BANKS

Stepping down from the multinational level, a central bank is at the apex of national banking industries. In the United States, it is the Federal Reserve Bank (the Fed), in Great Britain it is the Bank of England, in Japan the Bank of Japan, in Germany the Bundesbank, and so on.

The Fed is independent of government fiscal policy. The Treasury Department determines the division of government finance between taxation and government debt issues, and the Fed determines how much the private sector will hold in government issued interest-bearing paper that cannot be used to purchase goods or services and how much will be held in noninterest bearing coins and bills. The Fed also has the authority to alter the amount of government securities held in the private sector by engaging in open market trading.

In emerging nations as well as most rich countries the central bank and the federal treasury are one and the same. Regardless of how they are structured, however, investors and depositors view central banks as risk free with no possibility of defaulting on obligations. This proved to be a faulty assumption as recent defaults on government debt by Argentina, Brazil, and several African countries clearly shows.

Central banks originate and control their respective national monetary policies. They influence the growth of money and credit and the level of interest rates on short-term securities. Central banks attempt to influence long-term economic growth through the control of the aggregate demand for money. Their principal method for achieving this is to convince the private sector that the central bank views price stability as a prominent, long-range objective and that bank policies reflect this objective. The Bundesbank has been eminently successful in convincing German industry. Central banks in Argentina and Brazil failed miserably during the 1980s. The Fed's scorecard was only average until Chairman Alan Greenspan took over, when it improved markedly. The jury is still out on Chairman Ben Bernanke.

With the globalization of financial markets, central banks have had an increasingly difficult time exerting major influence over national monetary swings. They can no longer control the availability of credit merely by increasing or decreasing discount rates or by buying and selling federal securities. The market determined price of credit, based on the global financial markets, is now the prime determinant of how much credit is allocated to industrial economies as well as its price. This move to a financial world where the market determines interest and exchange rates has cast a new light on the role central banks can or should play in influencing economic stability. And this continues to be a difficult lesson for central bankers to accept.

Although the long-term goal of central banks remains essentially unchanged, new global financial instruments, markets, and institutions direct the effectiveness of national credit. A whole new language has insinuated its way into global banking circles. Nonbank lenders, off-balance sheet credit, securitization, and so on have shattered the traditional definition of a bank and even of money.

In the face of revolutionary global banking innovations, federal regulators and the accounting fraternity (represented in the United States by the Securities and Exchange Commission and the American Institute of Certified Public Accountants, respectively) continue to grapple with how, when, and where to ensure accuracy and meaningfulness in financial statements.

COMMERCIAL BANKS

Commercial banks represent the next tier down in the global banking hierarchy. Aside from semantic differences, commercial banks in one country differ markedly from commercial banks in another country. The structure of national banking systems is the most visible difference.

For example, approximately 10,000 banks operate in the United States, ranging from giant money center banks, such as Citibank and Bank of America, to tiny rural banks. On the other end of the spectrum, in Great Britain, Switzerland, and Canada four or five banks hold nearly 90 percent of all bank deposits. Between these two extremes, the 10 largest banks in Japan account for approximately 50 percent of deposits.

Although the long-term goal of central banks remains essentially unchanged, new global financial instruments, markets, and institutions direct the effectiveness of national credit.

Government regulations that control the type of activities a bank can engage in and the maximum value of loans it can make vary significantly between countries, as do constraints on new entrants into the banking system. The levels of reserves that banks must keep on deposit at the central bank also differ markedly between countries. In effect, these controls make banking a controlled monopoly within a nation's borders. In a global sense, the banking industry closely resembles a commodity business, with little or no product differentiation. At the same time, paradoxically, the largest global banks are well known. Even though bank products are the same, customers choose one brand name over another based on reputation, advertising, and other forms of brand recognition.

To further confuse the competitive nature of international banking, banks from various countries are interrelated. They borrow from and lend to each other. They participate in syndications and joint ventures. They maintain interbank near-money deposits. They share cross ownership. Money flows freely throughout global banking as if the industry consisted of only one group of banks in one country.

Global banks also engage in nontraditional banking activities. Through holding company structures, banks freely compete in leasing, securities brokerage, shipping, insurance, real estate management and development, healthcare, investment advisory services, and a variety of other industries (except in the United States where bank regulations are more restrictive).

Cross-border ownership creates an even greater diversion from traditional banking activities by providing access to services and products prohibited by national regulations. Within national boundaries, banks may enjoy monopolistic advantages, but on the global scene, immediate access to vast hoards of money, services, and products makes the industry both intensely competitive within capital markets and a viable competitor in other commercial industries.

The impact of cross-border bank ownership and the ability of global banks to raise capital worldwide have profoundly changed the global economy. Such cross fertilization promotes the integration of global objectives and adds financial stability to otherwise erratic financial markets. It opens the doors of European, Asian, and Middle East financial markets that were previously closed to all but the largest transnational corporations.

Twenty years ago, the British government's decision to grant foreign firms permission to trade in British securities and the concomitant raising of foreign capital to finance the privatization of many previously state owned English firms during the 1990s signaled the real beginning of the internationalization of capital markets for smaller companies. Now companies of any size can raise capital for global trade or expansion without relying on their home banks, stock exchanges, or government programs. Cross-border debt and equity securities can be issued on exchanges in London, New York, Tokyo, and many other exchanges around the world. British, Japanese, French, German, and American banks participate in short- and long-term loans in each other's backyards. Investment banks, merchant banks, and nonbank institutions have all entered the credit business and together with commercial banks provide a never ending source of funds for companies from virtually any nation.

TRADE FINANCE SERVICES

Commercial banks are an essential partner for any company engaged in global trade whether through exporting, foreign sourcing (importing), foreign direct investment, countertrade, foreign exchange, or government projects. Whenever monetary payment is made or received it funnels through the commercial banking system. Major international banks maintain branch offices around the world, and it behooves you to develop a working relationship with one or more of these behemoths prior to entering global trade.

Collections, Payments, and Transfers

Even if you bypass commercial banks in favor of transactional nonbank financing, you still need a bank to handle collections, payments, and money transfers. Collections from foreign customers or payments of foreign invoices are very seldom done with bank checks. Bank notes, drafts, or bills of exchange are common international payment instruments, although wire transfers are favored for most transactions.

> Major international banks maintain branch offices around the world, and it behooves you to develop a working relationship with one or more of these behemoths prior to entering global trade.

   Banks throughout the world maintain loose associations with other banks called *correspondents* and credit balances from these correspondents are maintained in money center banks in every rich nation. The periodic notification between banks of debits and credits against these balances are referred to as *wire transfers,* although no money actually changes hands. This system works well throughout the world except in those emerging nations without correspondent relationships with major international banks, such as Myanmar, North Korea, and Cuba. In those countries, the transactions must flow through an intermediary bank probably in Britain, France, the Netherlands, Switzerland, Germany, or Japan, which adds to the cost and transfer time.

Wire Transfers

Nearly all cross-border movement of money is done by wire transfer. U.S. money center banks and major international banks act as clearing houses for most wire transfers regardless of the country of origin or destination. Wire transfer services remain highly competitive with significantly different currency exchange rates and fees. Therefore, be sure to get quotes from several banks before transferring currencies from or to an overseas location.

In those countries that sport a wide proliferation of banks, such as the United States and to a lesser extent Japan, the time element on receiving end wire transfers also varies. International banks prioritize daily disbursements of transfers received from their correspondent banks. If a local or regional bank happens to be in an unfavorable position with its correspondent bank it could take three, four, or even five days to get the funds transferred. A favored correspondent bank receives its money—and so do you—in one day.

Wire transfer services remain highly competitive with significantly different currency exchange rates and fees.

Currency Arbitrage

All international banks engage in currency arbitrage. To maximize gains and minimize losses they buy and sell future deposits of foreign currency in anticipation of rate changes. Banks do this for their own accounts and most will also open arbitrage accounts for customers. Currency arbitrage is definitely not for beginners, and it certainly is not a necessary facet of global trade. On the other hand, when the need arises a bank geared to handle this type of transaction can be a big help.

Export Trade Finance

Most trade finance flows through commercial banks as the transfer point, whether funds originate with government or private sources. Export credit or guarantees from government agencies, such as Ex-Im Bank, require commercial banks to be in the middle of the loop. Guarantees as well as money flow from the government agency through a commercial bank to you, the exporter, or your foreign customer.

Trade credit instruments always emanate from commercial banks, and collections from foreign customers flow through commercial banks. Commercial banks are involved in every aspect of trade finance and cash management but each bank is different. The transaction efficiency and fees of each vary considerably. A commercial bank's expertise in handling international transactions is the most important criteria in choosing a bank. The size of the bank isn't as important as its international expertise and the status of its working relationship with correspondents.

Exchange Conversion

Larger commercial banks also offer exchange conversion services. Most global traders prefer not to accept foreign currency as payment for an account. Even with hard currency, the exchange differential and conversion fees cut into profit margins. Sometimes it is necessary, however, especially when doing business in emerging nations. Why? Because some less developed nations prohibit the transfer of local currency out of the country, converting to hard currency within the country is the only way to repatriate profits. Normally, local branch banks of hard currency nations make the conversion at a significantly lower cost than host country banks. In countries without this convenience, the only solution is a countertrade arrangement or a letter of credit.

The size of the bank isn't as important as its international expertise and the status of its working relationship with correspondents.

Letters of Credit

Many international transactions require payment with a letter of credit (L/C). Commercial banks serve as both the source and the recipient of L/Cs. Bankers' acceptances and forfaiting are other common techniques, but L/Cs are still the most popular. A letter of credit grants a commercial bank the authority to charge its customer's account or credit line for the amount of the L/C and associated fees. The receiving bank then notifies the originator bank that it is holding the instrument. Credits and debits move between the banks as described earlier, and the seller draws cash against the L/C. As long as the L/C reads *irrevocable* and is placed in a bank in the seller's country, the seller can ignore exchange rate variations. A *confirmed* L/C guarantees that the seller's bank will make payment.

This procedure easily becomes garbled when the commercial bank representing either the seller or the buyer doesn't understand how letters of credit work in international trade. Valuable time can be wasted in processing the documents and collecting the money. Therefore, the choice of a bank with an experienced international department is just as important as it is in other aspects of global trade.

Guarantees

Payment and performance guarantees are essential elements in global trade. Commercial banks get into the act by issuing *standby* letters of credit. These L/Cs serve as guarantees and can only be drawn on in the event of default of payment or performance. Most companies and government agencies accept standby L/Cs in lieu of surety bonds, providing the L/C comes from an internationally recognized bank.

NONBANK INSTITUTIONS

The high demand for creative trade finance has spawned a flurry of financing institutions outside traditional banking circles. Partially in response to overly conservative American commercial banks and partially as a result of confusing federal assistance programs that are often biased against smaller businesses, these nonbank institutions provide new, creative trade finance. Although several large corporations have formed trade finance companies, mostly focused on parent company needs, the biggest impact is being made by U.S. subsidiaries of foreign companies.

The range of services offered by these nonbank institutions spans the spectrum of trade finance. A few of the more popular services include transactional financing independent of a company's other credit lines or balance sheet debt; documentary credits; coordination with government export/import credit and insurance agencies; forfaiting and factoring; spot, forward, and futures exchange transactions; international leasing; maquila financing; countertrade management; trade alliances; capital and interest swaps; asset-based loans; project loans; guarantees; loan packaging; foreign government subsidized export financing; and conversion of developing country debt instruments. Many of these services involve near-money; that is, transactions with the liquidity of money but not directly transferable as a means of payment.

Best of all, these nonbank transactional trade finance organizations welcome smaller business customers. If you are being shut out by your commercial bank give one of these transactional finance institutions a shot. Transactional trade finance has existed for many years in Europe and elsewhere, but only during the last approximately 20 years has it impacted the American scene. (See Chapter 21 for a further discussion of transaction trade finance.)

HAWALA: A QUESTIONABLE ALTERNATIVE TO THE GLOBAL BANKING SYSTEM

Hawala (also known in Pakistan and India as *hundi*) is an alternative or parallel payment system to global banking. It is an informal value transfer system based on the performance and honor of a huge worldwide network of money brokers. These brokers are mainly located in the Middle East, Africa, and Asia, but several now have small offices in the United States, primarily in New York and Detroit.

The origins of hawala are not entirely clear. However, experts citing mention of hawala in Islamic texts as early as the 8th century believe that it first started in the early medieval period as a way to finance long distance trade. In Pakistan and India, it developed into a full-fledged money market. Not until the first half of the 20th century was hawala replaced in those countries by a formal banking system. Although used for a variety of purposes—many of them illegal—hawala is probably best known as a way for migrant workers' to transfer remittances to their families in their home countries without going through a bank. Hawala is also used to finance export trade when other more traditional financing methods are unavailable.

In hawala's most basic form money is transferred via a network of hawala brokers called *hawaladars*. A customer gives money to a hawaladar in one city with instructions to transfer the funds to a recipient in another city that is usually in a different country. The broker contacts a hawala broker in the recipient's city, tells him what to do with the funds—minus a small commission, of course—and promises to settle the debt at a later date.

The unique features of the system are that: (1) no instruments such as bank drafts or promissory notes are exchanged between the hawala brokers, (2) the transaction takes place entirely on the honor system, and (3) it is outside and independent of any national or global banking system. Since the system does not depend on legally enforceable claims, it can operate even in the absence of a legal and judicial environment. No records of individual transactions are produced. Only a running tally of the amount owed by one broker to another is kept. Settlements of debts between hawaladars can take a variety of forms and need not take the form of direct cash transfers.

In addition to commissions, hawaladars earn profits by bypassing official exchange rates. Generally, the funds enter the system in the source country's currency and leave the system in the recipient country's currency. Settlements often take place without any foreign exchange transactions, so official exchange rates never enter into the deal.

Hawala is a fast, convenient, and cheap way to transfer funds. Its greatest advantages occur when the recipient's country has restrictive exchange rate regulations, as is the case in most Middle East countries. It also works best when the banking system of the recipient's country is very rudimentary, as is the case in less developed economies. Moreover, hawala transfers are informal; they aren't regulated by governments. Therefore, governments cannot control the amount of currency in circulation, collect taxes, or interfere with illegal immigrants making the transfers.

In the United States as well as in many other Western countries the hawala system is definitely illegal. But it is in constant use and gaining favor with both legal and illegal immigrants. The U.S. Treasury has attempted to break the hawala chain to no avail. After 9/11 and in line with terrorist prevention policies, the federal government claimed that hawala was used extensively by terrorist organizations such as al-Queda to finance their operations. Money laundering accusations have also been leveled against the system. Interestingly, however, advertisements from hawaladars still appear in several ethnic magazines and newspapers circulating throughout the United States.

FOREIGN EXCHANGE MARKETS

Unless both the exporter and foreign customer use the same currency, such as the United States and Ecuador who both use the U.S. dollar, foreign exchange will impact all global trade transactions except hawala transfers. Whenever a company in one country exports raw materials, products, or services to a company in another country it must accept payment in the currency of its own country, the currency of the importer's country, or the currency of a third country. Importers face exactly the same decision process, only in reverse.

A similar decision must be made for foreign direct investments. When a company from one country makes a direct investment in a facility or project in a country with a different currency, the denomination of the currency used for payment must be based on tactical projections of foreign exchange rate movements.

When all is said and done, supply and demand probably have more influence on the movement of exchange rates than anything else.

In many respects, foreign exchange rates react to the same forces as on the world's stock exchanges. Just like movements in securities prices, the world is full of experts who believe they have the answer to predicting foreign exchange rate movement. Statistical trend charts, formulas, the relationship between interest and inflation rates, a country's balance of payments, and a variety of other factors lead foreign currency players to a plethora of special techniques and theories for explaining why foreign exchange rates move in one direction or another. The fact is, however, that no one has come up with a surefire method for explaining these movements. No one can accurately predict movements in the stock market, and no one can accurately predict future currency relationships. When all is said and done, supply and demand probably have more influence on the movement of exchange rates than anything else.

The supply of and demand for various currencies are functions of the perceived influence of current conditions on a country's economic fortunes and expectations of future global developments. In financial market parlance, currency supply and demand are derivatives of the *coincident interaction* of fundamental economic factors and technical conditions in the market. The following are the typical supply and demand conditions that influence exchange rate movement:

A. Factors Affecting the Supply of Foreign Currency
   1. Exchange controls. Formal rules and regulations established by a country's central bank that govern the flow of funds in and out of the

country, including the official bank rules for foreign exchange transactions within the country.

2. Quantity of outstanding currency. The amount of a country's currency available for foreign exchange transactions as determined by the country's total currency in the interbank markets.

3. Growth in the domestic money supply. Growth rate of a currency within a country monitored and regulated by that country's central bank.

B. Factors Affecting the Demand for Foreign Currency
   1. Comparative value of exchange rates. Determined by commercial banks and dealers who buy undervalued currency and sell overvalued currency. A country's currency value increases when export sales exceed import purchases of goods and services.
   2. Interest rate differentials. Influenced by foreign currency trading by professional dealers who buy currencies of countries with higher interest rates and sell currencies of countries with lower rates.
   3. Inflation rate differentials. Volatility and uncertainty of a country's economic future as reflected by inflation rates that influence dealers to buy currencies of countries with low inflation rates and to sell those with higher rates.
   4. Real rates of return on government securities. Countries that provide high real rates of return on their government obligations increase the desirability to hold their currencies.
   5. Central bank intervention. Central banks buy and sell their own and other country's currencies in the open market to maintain predetermined rate relationships of their own currency.
   6. Confidence in government. Stable political systems and leaders who are unlikely to enact major changes in monetary or fiscal policies give investors confidence that their investments are secure. This feeling of safety, more than any other demand factor, influences major currency buy and sell decisions.

Wars, famine, internal political actions, central bank manipulations, societal opinions, and a variety of other uncontrollable events exert more influence on supply and demand curves than interest or inflation rates. The ability to predict currency exchange rate relationships is as much a matter of guesswork as forecasting, six months in advance, when the next snow-storm will occur. Nevertheless, to maximize your profits from global trade you should make an attempt. The viability of many global trade transaction depends to a large extent on how well you manage your foreign exchange.

One misconception—that letters of credit or other trade finance instruments insulate a company from foreign exchange rates—needs to be dispelled immediately because nothing is further from the truth. Instant payments on the shipment of goods are affected as much by perceived future foreign exchange variations as straight cash transactions. For example, if Company A from the United States exports goods to Company B in Germany, payment may be made by an L/C drawn on a New York bank denominated in U.S. dollars. Assume the contract is negotiated on June 1 when the exchange differential between the dollar and the euro is 50 cents. Company B forecasts that the differential will increase in favor of the dollar by 10 cents by the time the shipment is made. When negotiating the price of the goods, Company B insists on a low enough price to compensate for the drop in the euro's value, even though the invoice is in U.S. dollars. Conversely, if Company A sees a drop in the dollar vs. the euro by the time of shipment, it will insist on a higher price to com-

The ability to predict currency exchange rate relationships is as much a matter of guesswork as forecasting, six months in advance, when the next snowstorm will occur.

pensate. To the extent that the forecast in either case is correct, both companies come out whole. However, if wrong, either Company B will pay too much for the goods or Company A will receive too little.

Foreign exchange is not as mystical as finance professionals would like us to believe. Certainly, foreign exchange dealers and brokers have a vocabulary all their own, as do brokers who specialize in commodities, stocks, or bonds. When communicating across borders in several different languages, common terminology is essential. Aside from confusing semantics, however, the principles of foreign exchange that you need to understand to manage the financial side of your business are relatively straightforward. To effectively engage in international trade, you must be as cognizant of the role of foreign exchange as you are of other basic economic conditions controlling the market. You must watch your company's exposure currency by currency, period by period and take appropriate actions based on the likelihood of adverse currency rate movements. You must arm yourself with sufficient global economic and political information to form rational judgments consistent with advice received from your banker and consultant. Most importantly, you must develop an internal foreign exchange policy consistent with your long-term trade objectives and staff your finance department with qualified personnel who can manage foreign exchange transactions.

> To effectively engage in international trade, you must be as cognizant of the role of foreign exchange as you are of other basic economic conditions controlling the market.

THE ROLE OF MAJOR WORLD CURRENCIES

When you read the international business section of any daily newspaper, at one time or another, you will certainly find references to the currency reserves of China, Russia, Brazil, or other countries. The best way to explain a country's currency reserve is to liken it to a company's working capital or an individual's checking account. Reserves provide a country with immediate cash or credit with which to purchase goods and services or to meet short-term debt service payments. Reserves may be held in a country's own currency; in gold; in an artificial currency, such as the Special Drawing Rights issued by the International Monetary Fund; or in a rich country's zone currency, such as the U.S. dollar or British pound sterling.

In the same way that a manufacturing company needs a greater amount of working capital than a service company, a country that predominantly has a manufacturing base and converts imported raw materials into exportable finished goods needs more working capital (reserves) than an agricultural economy. Reserves may be stored in a country's own central bank, the central bank of a foreign country, commercial banks (either at home or in a foreign country), or all of the above.

No simple guideline exists to determine how much of a reserve a country should hold. Many years ago, economists felt that an amount equal to one-half the value of total imports was sufficient. However, when commodity prices skyrocketed this proved insufficient. Inadequate currency reserves can lead to liquidity problems, especially for emerging nations.

The global liquidity squeeze in 1969 gave rise to a study from the International Monetary Fund under the auspices of representatives from the

United States, the United Kingdom, West Germany, Italy, France, Japan, the Netherlands, Canada, Sweden, and Belgium. The outgrowth of this study was the formation of a new reserve medium called Special Drawing Rights (SDR). The SDR is an international reserve asset, created by the IMF to supplement the existing official reserves of member countries. The SDR also serves as the unit of account of the IMF and some other international organizations. Its value is based on a combination of the key international currencies of the United States, the United Kingdom, the European Union, and Japan in weighted proportion.

SDRs are allocated to member countries in proportion to their share of world trade as periodically determined by the IMF. They are actual pieces of paper which one country can present to another country as collateral to borrow that country's currency. These are short-term interest bearing loans. No country is obligated to accept more SDRs than allotted by the IMF. The basic idea is to provide each country with an avenue to raise short-term working capital when, and if, it is needed without regard to the level of its own currency reserves. However, SDRs cannot be used for long-term capital investments in a country's infrastructure that will take years to repay.

Although the idea seemed reasonable at the time, in practice only those countries that don't really need help benefit from SDRs, namely those countries who already have a firm industrialized base. Less developed countries benefit very little because they have such a small proportion of total world trade.

Meanwhile, in the pragmatic world of international trade, certain currencies have become major or *zone currencies*. For years the British pound sterling served as a zone currency for the Commonwealth of Nations. The U.S. dollar serves as a zone currency in the Caribbean and for several countries in Central and South America.

A zone currency represents a currency that other national currencies are pegged to and move in tangent with. Zone currencies may also be called *reserve currencies*. This means that, in effect, the currency can be held freely and invested and traded easily throughout the world. It also means that anyone—of any nationality—can hold and use this currency without restriction by the national government.

First level or *lead currencies* go a step beyond reserve currencies. A lead currency must hold its value, offer flexibility in world markets, be accessible, and in sufficient quantity to enable its use for long periods of time. Since 1945, the major lead currency in the world has been the U.S. dollar.

An interesting advantage of being the lead currency is advanced by those who advocate increasing the federal trade deficit as the primary means to promote growth in the United States. They argue that the greater the deficit in the country's balance of trade, the more U.S. dollars are held by foreigners and that these dollars will ultimately find their way back to U.S. banks. Whereas this may work for a while, there is no assurance that the U.S. dollar will remain the lead currency indefinitely, and furthermore, there is certainly no guarantee that foreigners will spend the dollars on U.S. goods and services. Foreigners may very well choose to build their own reserves in dollars.

If you feel uncomfortable with exchange rates, currency transactions, and the entire global financial system you're not alone. Very few entrepreneurs are conversant on these topics. And that's OK. You don't have to be a financial whiz to profit from global trade. Still, you need to know the bare rudiments of how the international system works. Also, be sure to read Chapter 21, which covers the type of trade finance you'll need to help your customers pay for your exports. By referencing this chapter and Chapter 21, no banker, bureaucrat, or customer will be able to pull the wool over your eyes when it comes to global finance.

chapter three
Protectionism and Free Trade

ISN'T IT AMAZING HOW MUCH GLOBAL TRADE IMPACTS OUR EVERYDAY LIVES—THE variety of goods we choose from; the prices we pay for goods; our multiple financing options; the recruiting of gardeners, laborers, maids, and nannies; and the contributions of a seemingly endless supply of highly qualified scientists, engineers, and medical practitioners. This tremendous influence of global trade is caused not only by the economics of free markets but also by the policies and overt actions of governments, multilateral organizations, and the international financial system.

Every government enacts international trade policies that it perceives will benefit its own citizens and economy. Policies of the United States, Britain, the European Union, and Japan are extremely complex—replete with hundreds, if not thousands, of side agreements, formal and informal understandings, and shifting priorities as elected administrations come and go. Each government gives lip service to the benefits of free trade among nations. Yet each also enacts laws to protect its own industrial, commercial, and agricultural bases as well as select groups of its citizens. Such protection acts as a solid barrier to free trade.

Emerging nations also view international trade through two lenses. On the one hand, the governments of these countries fear being swallowed up by one or more of the world's economic giants. On the other hand, by encouraging imports and foreign investment their countries benefit from Western technology and cultures. Some countries, notably the giant emerging nations of Brazil, Russia, India, and China, adhere to extremely restrictive trade policies. Fortunately, these policies are beginning to give way as governments recognize that restricting trade and foreign investment only stifles their own economies. Latin American countries are a perfect example of how the abandonment of protectionist trade policies gave every economy a major boost toward free market growth. The common element of all restrictive trade policies is that they significantly impact the ability of foreign companies to transact profitable business within a host country's borders.

PROTECTIONIST TRADE POLICIES

Protectionist trade restraints (also referred to as *protectionism*) are real or artificial barriers to free trade. They are consciously or unconsciously erected by government policy to protect specified industries, wage earners, or regions of a country from imports made with low-cost labor or materials and, therefore, priced lower than domestically produced goods. Every nation enforces such policies. In the United States, there are payments to farmers for not growing crops, price supports to Florida's Big Sugar industry, special tax breaks for the oil industry, tariffs and quotas to protect the pharmaceutical industry, anti-dumping legislation to safeguard the steel industry, exclusion of foreign carriers to prevent competition in the airline industry, and many, many more trade restraints clog Washington's law books. During the 1950s and 1960s, in an effort to reestablish a manufacturing base after World War II, Japan banned all but a few imports of industrialized products that could not be made at home. Brazil protected its computer industry for many years by insisting that all PCs bear the logo of Brazilian manufacturers.

Protectionism may take the form of high tariffs on imported goods; quotas on specific imported products; anti-dumping laws that prohibit foreign exporters from selling goods in the United States at prices lower than those charged in their own countries; industry subsidies; tax breaks; or even direct government intervention, such as has happened several times in the American banking and securities industries. Every government has a vast arsenal of methods to protect its domestic industries and workers from foreign competition. Clearly, such tactics are the antithesis of globalization and conflict directly with free trade. But everyone does it.

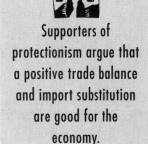

Supporters of protectionism argue that a positive trade balance and import substitution are good for the economy.

Supporters of protectionism argue that a positive trade balance and import substitution are good for the economy. Prior to 1990, failing Latin American countries followed this argument for decades until free market reforms finally began to replace state directed economic policies. In the United States, the traditional excuse for restricting imports was to protect the jobs and income of blue-collar workers and farmers. Recently, however, offshore outsourcing has shifted the rationale to protecting the jobs of engineers, scientists, designers, and other high-income, white-collar employees.

Some people feel that protecting jobs is more important than paying lower prices. However, a consensus has yet to be reached by either the U.S. government or the business community as to whether protectionism provides a tradeoff between more jobs on the one hand and lower prices on the other hand. Protectionists point out that free trade, that is, the lack of an ineffective national protective trade policy, shifts workers from manufacturing jobs to low-wage, service-sector jobs, such as store clerks. Still, according to several surveys, 95 percent of professional economists support free trade, the highest percentage of agreement by these theorists on any subject.

One final note on protective trade barriers. Many rich countries, including the United States and a few emerging nations, have found that high tariffs and anti-dumping laws do little to help their economies. One alternative has been the increased use of a nontariff barrier called the *voluntary export restraint* or VER. A voluntary export restraint is a governmental restriction on the quantity of particular goods that can be exported *out* of a country during a specified period of time. The word voluntary is somewhat misplaced, however, because these restraints are typically implemented after the insistence of importing nations.

In the United States, VERs are used to restrict trade in textiles, clothing, shoes, steel, automobiles, electronic products, agriculture, and machine tools, to mention just a few of the affected products. Since VERs are essentially informal agreements between two specific countries to restrict trade, they act as a convenient loophole to the multilateral trade rules of the now defunct General Agreement on Trade and Tariffs and the more recent World Trade Organization.

THE WORLD TRADE ORGANIZATION

Created in 1995 by the Uruguay round of trade talks that took place between 1986 and 1994, the World Trade Organization (WTO) is an outgrowth of the General Agreement on Tariffs and Trade, an organization formed by the world's trading nations after World War II. Today, the WTO remains the only nonaligned international organization operating in the world's multilateral trading system. Its mission statement affirms that it is the "only international organization dealing with the global rules of trade between nations. Its main function is to ensure that trade flows as smoothly, predictably, and freely as possible."

That sounds wonderful, but translated into business language it means that the WTO monitors compliance with and adjudicates mutually agreed on rules for trading goods and services between countries. These rules have been negotiated and agreed to by the trade ministers of all member nations. When a dispute involving subsidies, trade barriers, or other protectionist trade practices arises, the WTO serves as arbitrator between the parties. On paper this makes sense. In practice it doesn't work very well unless both parties agree to implement the WTO's recommended changes. For instance, the WTO has tried to no avail to get the European Union to stop or at least reduce farm subsidies. It has also tried to get the United States to discard its export tax subsidy, the Foreign Sales Corporation, and its successor, the Extraterritorial Income Act. Still, the WTO does provide a valuable service by acting as a court of last resort where trade disputes can be aired.

 World Trade Organization, Centre William Rappard, Rue de Lausanne 154, CH-1211 Geneva 21, Switzerland; www.wto.org

It seems clear by this time that agreements reached under the WTO cannot be relied on to open borders to global trade and, at the same time, keep the playing field level for all competitors. Rich countries abide by WTO rulings only as long as it suits their national purpose. Emerging nations on the brink of full economic revitalization—Brazil, Russia, India, China, and Mexico—find it impossible to exercise influence over the United States and other rich nations and, therefore, ignore those provisions of WTO rulings that they believe might slow their own growth. Very poor nations like Haiti, Guyana, Myanmar, and Belarus are so far removed from the global trading system that the WTO has little meaning, if any, to them. The fact that serious grievances brought by Japan, the United States, and several emerging nations have languished for years in the WTO's committees with little chance of changing the trading practices of any defendant shows how ineffectual the WTO has become.

The reasons the WTO seems to have little effect on day-to-day trading practices are twofold. First, the efforts of governments to protect their economic and political self-interests will never be abandoned for grandiose global rules. Secondly, influential business groups (cartels in some countries) will not sacrifice their profitability, economic growth, or political power for the sake of a global agreement that does not provide for equal treatment of all members, often citing the protectionist policies of the United States and the European Union and the preferential treatment granted to groups of emerging states.

Although the WTO and trade talks similar to the Doha round (which has now been abandoned) may be the answer over the long term, most international traders would probably agree that multilateral and bilateral agreements are the only practical way to ensure progress in global trade. All governments know that protecting their national interests and those of their business communities is politically more rewarding than relinquishing sovereign control to a world body without teeth. To satisfy such national self-interests and, at the same time, open their economies to global trade and investment, countries throughout the world are placing increased emphasis on bilateral and regional trade pacts. Therefore, you must also be in a position to take advantage of these tariff reducing trade agreements.

TRADE PACT FEVER

Trade pacts such as the North American Free Trade Agreement (NAFTA), South America's Mercado Común del Sur (MERCOSUR), and the European Union (EU) exert a powerful influence on the strategic plans of companies in all industries. Take, for instance, the impact of NAFTA on the entire Western Hemisphere. Clearly, this trilateral agreement has broadened many market opportunities for U.S., Canadian, and Mexican companies. More important than that, however, NAFTA introduced the concept of free trade to our hemisphere. Many people in the U.S. business community who had never thought of becoming involved in international trade are now aware of the advantages to be gained by broadening their horizons overseas.

Although two governments will never see eye to eye on economic policies, exclusion from trade pacts coupled with the apparent ineffectiveness of the WTO, has opened many eyes to the reality of radically changing trading patterns. Recognizing the strength in numbers, countries around the world have pushed forward with their own free trade agreements, their own versions of common markets, economic unions, and free trade areas, not only to increase trade among themselves by lowering tariffs, quotas, and other import barriers but to also present a more unified front for parity treatment by the United States and other rich countries.

The United States has also moved forward with many bilateral and, in some cases, multilateral trade pacts. The following agreements, as of this writing, have been implemented, negotiated, or discussed.

Latin America

1. NAFTA with Canada and Mexico
2. Dominican Republic–Central American Free Trade Agreement (DR-CAFTA) with the Dominican Republic, Costa Rica, El Salvador, Guatemala, Honduras, and Nicaragua
3. United States–Chile Free Trade Agreement

4. United States–Peru Free Trade Agreement
5. United States–Caribbean Basin Trade Partnership Act of 2000
   (replaced the expired Caribbean Basin Initiative)

Asia–Pacific
6. United States–Australia
7. United States–Singapore

Middle East–North Africa
8. United States–Bahrain
9. United States–Israel
10. United States–Jordan
11. United States–Morocco

Proposed Agreements Discussed But Not Yet Finalized
12. Transatlantic Free Trade Area (TAFTA) with the European Union
13. Middle East Free Trade Area (MEFTA) with most Middle East countries

In addition, free trade agreements that have been negotiated with Colombia, Panama, South Korea, Malaysia, and Oman gather dust in Washington, awaiting ratification by the U.S. Congress. A free trade agreement with Ecuador is being considered, and both Egypt and Uruguay have expressed interest in beginning similar discussions. The United States has also been negotiating free trade agreements with several other countries including Ghana, Kenya, Mauritius, and Mozambique in Africa; Thailand and Indonesia in Asia; and Kuwait, the United Arab Emirates, and Qatar in the Middle East. One indication of the importance of trade pacts to the U.S. business community is that in 2006 42 percent of all U.S. exports went to countries that had executed agreements with the United States.

Although each U.S. trade pact is slightly different, they all deal with reducing or eliminating tariffs on goods shipped from a foreign country to the United States and on goods shipped from the United States to that foreign country. Some pacts also cover such diverse subjects as protection of intellectual property, permission for foreign direct investment, liberalization of customs procedures, and strengthened judiciary practices. NAFTA, of course, is a special case. It covers a multitude of matters especially germane to trade among the United States, Canada, and Mexico, including references to environmental protection and labor practices.

Critics argue that the main effect of free trade pacts has been to move U.S. jobs to low-wage countries, thereby depriving American workers of their livelihoods. Certainly, many jobs have moved offshore. But the trade-off is a huge plus for the American consumer. Being able to choose among a wide range of imported and domestically produced goods, consumers enjoy a plethora of products at competitive prices. Without free trade pacts that enable U.S. companies to produce offshore for shipment back to the United States or enable foreign companies to ship duty-free to U.S. markets, our choices would be limited, and we would be paying a lot more for everything we buy. As it is, goods produced by American-owned factories in Central America, the Caribbean, and Asia are competitively priced with products imported from China, other Asian countries, and Eastern Europe. Just look at the clothing we wear. Nearly all of it is now sewn in DR-CAFTA countries. U.S.-owned maquila plants in Latin America and increasingly in Southeast Asia, continue to produce clothing, shoes, and a variety of electronics for shipment back to U.S. markets.

Critics argue that the main effect of free trade pacts has been to move U.S. jobs to lower-wage countries, thereby depriving American workers of their livelihoods.

And look at the range of products that have been introduced through both importing and foreign sourcing. For instance, offshore call centers and backroom financial services in Barbados, Jamaica, and the Dominican Republic—all of which predate those in India—increase the efficiency and reduce the prices in a vast array of industries. Beautiful varieties of Colombian flowers grace our tables at very competitive prices. Chilean wine and grapes, Honduran fruit, Ecuadoran seafood, Guatemalan bananas, and many other crops and products from trade pact members fill the shelves of our stores. Of course, some countries can produce goods at low prices, even with the added cost of U.S. tariffs and ocean shipping, making free trade pacts unnecessary. China is a good example. She is not a member of any U.S. trade pact and yet supplies America with such diverse, competitively priced imports as toys, clothing, electronics, and auto parts. Most countries, however, cannot match China's low wages and free trade pacts fill the void.

It seems abundantly clear that free trade agreements have in the past and continue now to benefit all Americans, even those whose jobs went off-shore, with greater varieties and low-priced products needed in everyday life.

WHY TRADE PACTS?

Why trade pacts? Why struggle with extensive negotiations and then fight for congressional approval? Can't we find a better way to keep prices competitive? Maybe. But each trade agreement brings something different to the table. Some provide for minimal tariffs among member nations. Some agreements, such as MERCOSUR, provide for a common external tariff that discriminates against nonmember countries. Some agreements, such as the European Union, provide for a common currency as well as the free movement of goods, people, and capital among member nations.

Major free trade agreements have one or a combination of four primary goals:

1. To protect domestic industries from foreign competition. For a variety of reasons, every country has industries it wants to protect. The United States protects textiles, steel, milk, and other farm products. Brazil protects automobiles and computers. The European Union protects a variety of farm products, and so on. Member nations may exclude from trade agreements, without WTO recourse, any products or industries they choose to protect, effectively blocking complaints of protectionism from nonmembers. This is a clever way to sidestep tariffs, subsidies, anti-dumping laws, and other trade barriers.
2. To present a unified front. The only way smaller, emerging nations stand a chance of negotiating fair agreements with such powerful trading partners as the United States or the European Union is to ban together as a unified body that matches or comes close to matching the trading strength of rich nations.
3. To placate world opinion on nontrade issues. In this day and age, very few governments want to risk the wrath of world opinion by asserting (or inferring, for that matter) that protecting the environment or promoting workers' rights aren't worthy goals. Yet few nations will enact

policies as stringent as the United States would like. Trade agreements give nations a venue in which to pay lip service to these worthy goals without actually implementing unpopular laws.

4. To increase trade and investment among member nations. NAFTA and the European Union have had enormous success in increasing trade and investment among member countries, but the Association of Southeast Asian Nations (ASEAN) has been less successful.

Impact on Corporate Strategies

Why should I care about these trade pacts? They are government-to-government agreements that only peripherally affect my small business. What impact could free trade agreements possibly have on my market strategies? As we have learned from NAFTA, the impact of well-designed free trade agreements can be much greater than originally anticipated. However, at a minimum, your company will benefit in three ways:

1. The reduction of tariffs between the United States and its trading partners will make the pricing of U.S. exports to those countries more competitive with in-country producers.
2. Common external tariffs will make imports from nonmember countries less competitive than imports from member nations, such as the United States.
3. The reduction of tariffs among member nations will make the pricing of materials and components sourced from those countries more competitive with imports to the United States from nonmembers.

You must have seen an increase in your business attributable either directly or indirectly to NAFTA, especially for the first few years after it was implemented. Trade between the United States and Singapore, Israel, and Australia grew substantially after free trade pacts were enacted with those nations. Similarly, we can expect trade with Central America to increase under DR-CAFTA.

Potential Negatives

Perhaps one day someone will find an alternative to free trade pacts. Perhaps another way will be found to gain global advantage. Perhaps the United States will not remain the economic superpower that it is today. After all, the world is constantly evolving and as one powerful empire descends, other economies ascend. This seems to be the prediction of some economists who believe that Brazil, Russia, India, and China (referred to as the BRIC countries) will overtake the United States as the world's superpowers, at least in the economic sphere. Perhaps the four of them will join forces in the world's largest free trade pact. Or maybe they won't.

Here's a different but equally probable look into the future. Whether we like it or not, and notwithstanding the efforts of the WTO, we could be heading toward a tripolar world—a world comprising three massive trading blocs: the Western Hemisphere, the European bloc (including all of Europe, Russia, and Turkey), and the pan-Pacific bloc (including Australia, New Zealand, Japan, South Korea, Taiwan, India, China, and ASEAN nations), with each bloc enforcing its own common external tariffs.

Events appear to be moving steadily in that direction. Through a series of regulations and standards aimed at protecting national industries, the European Union is getting ever closer to discriminating against nonmember competition. On the other side of the world, China, Japan, South Korea, Taiwan, and several ASEAN countries, along with Australia and New Zealand, are making noises about a pan-Pacific trading bloc aimed at doing the same. It is even possible that India would join such a bloc.

Motivated partly by strategic advantages from free trade pacts with Latin America, partly by an increasingly inward-looking Europe, and partly by Southeast Asia's economic and currency upheavals during the last two decades, a tidal wave of U.S. companies have already diverted their trade and investment away from Europe and Asia and toward the Western Hemisphere. As we saw in Chapter 1, U.S. exports to Latin America have increased 22 percent over the last five years. One-fifth of all U.S. exports go to Latin America. It's safe to say that Western Hemisphere free trade agreements, those already enacted and those awaiting ratification, have been a major contributor to this explosive export growth.

Such rapid growth is creating a marked shift in regional trading patterns that will inevitably affect corporate business strategies for many years to come. To dispel any doubts about the seriousness of these new patterns,

> Whether we like it or not, and notwithstanding the efforts of the WTO, we could be heading toward a tripolar world—a world comprising three massive trading blocs.

consider for a moment a few of the possible negative scenarios that could emerge over the next 10 years to the detriment of the United States.

What if MERCOSUR, a trade agreement among Brazil, Argentina, Uruguay, and Paraguay (plus a hoard of South American nations as associate members) with a combined population of 250 million (83 percent of the population of the United States) and a GDP of close to $1 trillion, struck a free trade agreement with the European Union, as member countries have talked about doing for the last decade? What if such a pact included external tariffs, quotas, licenses, and other regulations designed to discourage U.S. companies from tapping South American markets and resources? Or what if MERCOSUR members were to receive financial aid from the European Union in exchange for a monopoly on the region's exports of natural resources?

From a strategic perspective, positioning your company in one or more of the world's trading blocs will probably be the only way to effectively compete for the long term, not only overseas but in U.S. markets as well.

What if, for reasons unfathomable at this time, China joined with South Korea, Japan, and Singapore to develop industrial, agricultural, and mining bases among themselves and then turned isolationist, erecting barriers to trade with the outside world, similar to those being considered by the European Union?

What if, after shunning membership in the European Union, Turkey became a member of GAFTA (the Greater Arab Free Trade Area), and negotiated a free trade agreement with the EU that made American imports noncompetitive with those from the European Union? Or banned U.S. companies from owning national businesses while permitting EU firms ready access? Or prohibited U.S. companies from exploiting the region's natural resources while permitting EU firms to do so?

We already know that the EU is trying mightily to corner trade with Latin America before the United States can forge through the Free Trade Area of the Americas—which now appears to be a dead issue anyway. European leaders understand that if the Americans are the first to achieve a Western Hemisphere free trade agreement (or more bilateral agreements) any hope of competing effectively in major Latin markets would be remote. Similarly, China is attempting to entice several African countries, along with India, into free trade agreements that would effectively exclude American companies from lucrative natural resources and cheap labor. And it won't be long before India and China join forces in some form of free trade agreement, possibly making the majority of Western imports noncompetitive.

Region wide free trade blocs cast a dark shadow over any hope of limiting worldwide protectionism. From a strategic perspective, positioning your company in one or more of the world's trading blocs will probably be the only way to effectively compete for the long term, not only overseas but in U.S. markets as well. It may also be the only way to gain enough clout to penetrate newly formed trans-Atlantic and trans-Pacific pacts.

Clearly, developments in free trade agreements will bear close scrutiny over the next few years. There can be little doubt that they will have a major impact on the market strategies of companies of all sizes and in all industries—manufacturing, distribution, retail, services, and the professions.

COMPETITIVE LIBERALIZATION

Often overlooked by a media preoccupied with the Middle East and China, the U.S. Trade Representative has been busy with what Washington calls "competitive liberalization," a fancy term for the negotiation of bilateral trade pacts. In addition to the raft of free trade pacts already negotiated or planned for the future, many more will likely be born. Although such a flurry is certainly uncharacteristic of administrations during the past two decades, the American business community welcomes this new thrust. I should mention, however, that with the exception of NAFTA and other Latin American free trade agreements, bilateral accords negotiated to date are all with countries who take very few U.S. exports, so far a measly 4 percent. That isn't going to help many U.S. exporters. Moreover, as we have seen, Congress is increasingly antagonistic toward the ratification of any more free trade agreements—with anyone.

Critics of Washington's trade-pact fever are quick to point out that bilateral agreements are already beginning to overlap and eventually will end up costing more to comply with than the original tariffs they were designed to reduce.

Critics of Washington's trade pact fever are quick to point out that bilateral agreements are already beginning to overlap and eventually will end up costing more to comply with than the original tariffs they were designed to reduce. Also, a bilateral trade pact with one country may very well steal business that an agreement with another country was designed to enhance. This would happen if the United States enacted a trade pact with, say, Vietnam, an exporter of clothing, undercutting the benefits of DR-CAFTA.

When this emphasis on bilateral accords will end is uncertain. Perhaps it has already run its course. Perhaps Latin America has had enough of free trade pacts with the United States. Perhaps accords with South Korea, Malaysia, Oman, Kenya, the U.A.E., and all the rest of them will never transpire. Perhaps new administrations will turn their backs on new trade agreements of any type with anyone. It has happened before. It can happen again.

EXPANDING YOUR HORIZONS

When one considers the implications of regional free trade pacts, it seems clear that long-term strategies restricting your company to just exporting won't suffice to keep you competitive. You will have to develop marketing plans to source materials, parts, or labor-intensive assemblies from foreign countries. You must position yourself within the key trade groups to benefit in the same way as in-country companies.

Whether yours is a small business, a midsize company, or a Fortune 100 corporation, your future success surely lies in global trade. To ensure a competitive position in these markets you have to be there with manufacturing plants, distribution centers, retail stores, service centers, or sales and administrative offices. The days of relying exclusively on U.S. markets are drawing to a close. Regardless of your industry, it is no longer possible to ignore the rest of the world. Your competitors recognize this. It's only sound logic that you should, too.

Assuming your company is not a Fortune 100 corporation and that you are not already involved in global trade, your logical first questions are probably: (1) Where should I begin?, (2) Which countries offer the greatest opportunities?, and (3) Which countries entail the greatest risks?

I'll try to answer those questions as we progress through this book. Meanwhile, here are a few broad suggestions for you to mull over:

1. If you have little or no experience in international trade or if you do not have personnel with a good command of a foreign language, your best

bet is to learn the ropes in nearby English-speaking countries, perhaps Canada, Trinidad and Tobago, or Jamaica.

2. If your home office is in Texas, Southern California, or the Southwest, Mexico might be a good beginning. Maquiladora facilities are an excellent way to get your feet wet.

3. Central America offers reasonably good opportunities for offshore sourcing, especially with maquila plants. However, the inherent political and social instability there adds an amount of risk to the equation.

4. Markets in the BRIC nations—Brazil, Russia, India, and China—are far and away the most difficult for newcomers, but they also hold the most promise. After honing your international expertise in English-speaking countries, you will probably want to explore one of these more difficult but substantially more lucrative high-growth markets.

Whatever country you choose, be sure to do sufficient research to understand not only the risks you will encounter, but also the position of that country on free trade pacts. Trade agreements around the world are expanding rapidly. If part of your strategy is to take advantage of one or more of the many bilateral or multilateral agreements, it only makes sense to clearly understand how cross-border trade within a trade pact and relationships of that trade pact with others will influence your business.

chapter four
Public and Private Information and Assistance Resources

WITHOUT QUESTION, THE SHEER AMOUNT OF INFORMATION AND resources available to help you get started in global trade can be overwhelming. Still, the only way to become informed about what's going on in the world is to start digging. But I caution you to be alert about what you read and hear. Much of the data from government agencies and trade bureaus will be dated and information from private organizations, such as multinational accounting firms and universities, will be slanted. Nevertheless, information from these sources is better than nothing. You'll waste a lot of time and money unless you arm yourself with as many facts and opinions as possible about market characteristics, cultural barriers, tariffs, quotas, licenses, costs, competition (both local and foreign), distribution aberrations, financing, and other topics that impact either getting the order, delivering the shipment, or getting paid.

Seminars and conferences are a good place to begin. A variety of federal agencies hold briefing seminars on everything from soup to nuts. Several private sector seminar producers hold one-day and two-day seminars and conferences ranging from abysmally elementary to politically insufferable (although if you pick and choose carefully you can find a few good ones). If you are interested in Latin America, I recommend the annual Miami Conference on the Caribbean and Latin America sponsored by the Washington-based Caribbean/Latin American Action. For many years, this Miami Conference has been the most informative—albeit politically inspired—conference and trade show on Latin America available in this country. Seminars and conferences provide you with an opportunity to learn about various aspects of doing business in foreign lands from experts in their respective fields. I encourage you to attend one or more a year.

Reading is also an essential part of market research. The more you read, the better prepared you'll be. This book is a good start, and you'll get a pretty good sense about what it takes to do business worldwide. But don't stop with this book. International trade periodicals are another important resource. There aren't many worth subscribing to, so your expenditures will be modest. But subscribe to a select few, and then read them regularly. The following are my top picks:

➡ The Economist, a must read every week (www.economist.com).
➡ Journal of Commerce, also a must read (www.joc.com).
➡ World Trade (www.worldtrademag.com).
➡ Global Finance (www.gfmag.com).

If you have time, *Current History* magazine (www.currenthistory.com) contains good political and economic background material, as does *Foreign Affairs* (www.foreignaffairs.com).

Here are a few other periodicals that can be helpful:

➡ Background News from the Bureau of Public Affairs. (www.state.gov/r/pa), Department of State.
➡ United Nations Development Business included in the business edition of the Development Forum (www.un.org).
➡ International Business Outlook from the World Bank (www.worldbank.org).

If you have time, read through or at least skim all this material on a regular basis. Only through diligent market research can you be reasonably confident that your entry into global trade will be profitable.

Seminars and reading aren't the only ways to get information. Once you get started, you'll find it almost impossible to digest the barrage of information about specific export markets, distribution channels, sales financing options, and trade barriers and incentives coming your way from a conglomeration of sources. Federal and state agencies, trade associations, trade promotion bureaus, and private organizations all collect and distribute a flood of data about exporting and foreign direct investment. These same organizations—plus many more—are ready to assist you with locating joint venture partners, negotiating contracts, and analyzing market demographics. To avoid being overwhelmed, it helps to first restrict your search to the most obvious sources. If additional information or assistance is needed, contact some of the less publicized sources. The balance of this chapter outlines resources from public as well as private organizations that can be tapped into on relatively short notice.

As your wealth of data accumulates, you will eventually want to include information about specific countries, such as current and projected political stability, advantages resulting from trade agreements, local business climates, the status of U.S. government trade policies, and so on. Most likely you will want to take a fairly comprehensive look at cultural peculiarities that affect your particular market, its banking system, infrastructure, income distribution, educational standards, and a variety of other matters. However, most of this data can only be obtained from within the host country and that means performing an in-country survey as detailed in Chapter 15.

U.S. GOVERNMENT AGENCIES

The federal government collects, collates, and distributes international trade data from a variety of foreign and domestic sources. Much of it is free, although some reports, pamphlets, and booklets carry a nominal price tag. Many federal agencies compile data for specific purposes. Some, like several of those within the Department of Commerce (DOC), provide rather general information that might be of universal interest to U.S. exporters. Others concentrate on specific industries, certain areas of the world, or types of data, such as demographics, sales representatives, joint venture partners, and so on. The DOC supports U.S. business interests domestically and internationally with a wealth of resources. The following is organizational hierarchy within the DOC.

ABBREVIATED ORGANIZATION CHART—DEPARTMENT OF COMMERCE
Office of the Secretary, Department of Commerce
1. Bureau of Industry and Security (BIS)
2. Economics and Statistics Administration (ESA)
   a. Bureau of the Census (BC)
   b. Bureau of Economic Analysis (BEA)
3. Economic Development Administration (EDA)
4. International Trade Administration (ITA)
5. Minority Business Development Agency (MBDA)
6. National Oceanic and Atmospheric Administration (NOAA)
7. National Telecommunications and Information Administration (NTIA)
8. Patent and Trademark Office (PTO)
9. Technology Administration (TA)
   a. National Institute of Standards and Technology (NIST)
   b. National Technical Information Service (NTIS)
   c. Office of Technology Policy (OTP)

 U.S. Department of Commerce; 1401 Constitution Ave., NW, Washington, DC 20230; 202-482-2000; www.commerce.gov

As you weave your way through the maze of federal websites you will soon see a plethora of duplication. Like any government bureaucracy, federal agencies thrive on titles. This stems from the belief that all problems can be solved and all obstacles overcome merely by adding another layer of people with a director or a deputy secretary in charge. When a new or revised subject comes up, instead of changing or deleting an existing department or agency, an entirely new one is formed. This very quickly leads to a duplication of effort.

For example, instead of going directly to one of the offices listed go to two new websites (www.export.gov and www.buyusa.gov), which were established presumably to be the primary sites for all federal agencies. Export.gov "helps American exporters navigate the international sales process and avoid pitfalls such as nonpayment and intellectual property misappropriation." Buyusa.gov, the U.S. Commercial Service site, contains a wealth of valuable information about foreign markets, financial and resource aids for U.S. companies, and a variety of other information. As it turns out, these sites are good starting points and will give you links to almost every conceivable government site dealing with international trade. One very helpful link goes directly to the DOC trade library called the National Trade Data Bank (NTDB) (www.stat-usa.gov).

The NTDB, which falls administratively under the ITA, was established by the Omnibus Trade and Competitiveness Act of 1988. It provides reasonable access to export promotion and international economic information. This library of information offers international trade and export data from 15 federal agencies. It contains more than 100,000 documents in the form of books, pamphlets, bulletins, and reports including:

➡ The Basic Guide to Exporting, which summarizes basic export information.
➡ The CIA World Fact Book, which contains country specific statistics and other data.
➡ The Industrial Outlook, which contains industry specific statistics and data.
➡ Market Research Reports, which relates market and economic trends from combined industry country data.

Within the NTDB, the Globus and NTDB site offers a "comprehensive source for credible trade leads and timely market research." This is a catchall site has excellent links that actually work. If you only look at one site in your search for informative data, this is it. If you can't find what you are looking for here, you probably won't find it on any U.S. government site.

Trade Promotion Coordinating Committee (TPCC)

The TPCC is billed as a one-stop shop for information on government programs and activities that support U.S. exporters. It tells you where to get information on a whole range of support services relating to exporting, including counseling, seminars and conferences, sources of overseas buyers and sales representatives, locations and dates of overseas trade fairs and trade missions, export financing, and organizations that provide technical assistance. The TPCC also publishes an invaluable directory called *Export Programs: A Business Directory of U.S. Government Resources*.

 Trade Information Center; 800-872-8723; fax 202-482-4473; www.export.gov/exportbasics/ticredirect.asp

World Trader Data Reports

Of all the reports coming out of the federal government *World Trader Data Report* (WTDR) seems to be the most popular source of usable information. WTDR are customized reports, either hard copy or computer download, that contain business information about potential foreign customers. These reports include background information on the foreign company (which may be either public or private sector), its reputation in the business community, its creditworthiness, and its overall reliability and suitability as a customer for U.S. businesses. Although the reports do not include financial information they do: (1) identify the company's type of organization (e.g., corporation, partnership, single owner, government) and the year it was established, (2) give its relative size and number of employees, and (3) specify its market reach, product lines, and trade references (including bank references in some cases).

Trade Opportunities Program

Through the Trade Opportunities Program (TOP), exporters can obtain current sales leads on foreign customers seeking to buy their products or services. TOP also keeps a current listing of foreign sales agents seeking to represent U.S. exporters. This can be a very valuable resource for companies beginning an export program who require local distribution.

Agent/Distributor Service

The Agent/Distributor Service (ADS) offers a customized search for qualified foreign representatives. The process involves distributing your company's sales literature and then choosing six foreign prospects that express an interest in representing your lines. If sufficient information isn't available through the TOP, try going this route even though there is a nominal charge.

In addition to providing sales leads and contacts with potential sales representatives, the ITA sponsors a series of matchmaker events, overseas trade missions, overseas catalog and video shows, foreign buyer programs, and overseas trade fairs aimed at bringing together U.S. exporters and potential foreign buyers.

Matchmaker Events

Matchmaker events are specifically designed for small business executives. These events are inexpensive, short trips that bring you together with prospective foreign sales representatives and/or joint venture partners who are specifically interested in handling your product line.

Overseas Trade Missions

Trade missions are groups of U.S. executives who travel together to one or more countries to pursue sales or joint venture leads. Participants meet with local business and government leaders who can help in the development of local marketing programs. Staff personnel from the DOC travel with the delegation and, if desired, arrange a full schedule of local appointments.

Overseas Catalog and Video Shows

Catalog and video shows are promotions prepared by ITA industry experts and are then distributed to select foreign audiences. At your request, they will include sales promotion literature and videos of your product lines. This can be an excellent way to promote export products without incurring the cost or time of overseas travel.

Foreign Buyer Programs

Periodically, the ITA conducts trade shows in the United States specifically for foreign buyers. This is another chance to display your wares without going overseas. The shows are promoted worldwide and usually attract a sizable audience.

U.S. COMMERCIAL SERVICE

The U.S. Commercial Service (USCS) is the liaison with the U.S. businesses arm of the ITA and is responsible for a vast number of export aids. Primarily geared to U.S. smaller and midsize companies, its services are grouped under four headings: counseling and advocacy, market research, searching for a partner, and trade events and related services. The best way to find out about everything offered by the USCS is to visit your local Export Assistance Center (see Appendix).

Counseling and Advocacy

Counseling and advocacy covers three types of services. Counseling involves working with one of the USCS personnel in more than 100 U.S. cities to get your export program moving. They are supposed to be able to communicate with their counterparts stationed in worldwide offices to get the information you need to begin exporting.

The glitzy title of platinum key service is tailored to your specific needs. In-country USCS employees will presumably help you identify markets, launch your products, develop major project opportunities, resolve market-entry questions, and advise you about regulatory hurdles. This is not a free service, however. It is priced according to the expected work to be performed as outlined in the scope of your agreement.

As residents in U.S. embassies throughout the world, USCS employees serve as strong advocates for U.S. companies and are in excellent positions to promote American made products in the business community. Although USCS personnel in some embassies are very helpful, I'm sorry to report that in other offices they are virtually invisible. The official line claims that these folks will help you resolve payment issues, settles disputes, win contracts, and overcome regulatory hurdles. Well, maybe. But I haven't found any who were that helpful.

Market Research

The USCS maintains an extensive library that covers doing business in 110 industries for more than 120 countries. It carries updates on new regulations, business trends, and U.S. government financed projects. The USCS will also customize its research efforts to match your requirements. And lastly, it provides a Business Facilitation Service in which in-country personnel can help you or your local representative organize a product launch, technical seminar, cocktail reception, or other similar event. At some U.S. embassies they will even help set up a videoconferencing arrangement. This service is tailored to meet your specific needs, and the price varies depending on the venue and services requested. Although all this help certainly supplements your own survey work, don't substitute government supplied information for your own hands-on research.

Searching for a Partner

Although the amount of involvement by USCS in a partner search varies considerably from country to country, some staff personnel are extremely helpful and certainly worth a try. These folks promise to deliver detailed company information on up to five prescreened potential partners, distributors, or sales representatives who have expressed interest in your products.

The Gold Key Matchup Service is a customized search effort whereby in-country USCS employees actually help you find a buyer, partner, representative, or distributor. They will set up appointments for you to interview prospects and help verify each one's credentials against your specific requirements. None of these customized services are free, however.

Commercial News USA

Commercial News USA is a product catalog distributed through U.S. embassies and consulates to more than 400,000 international buyers in 145 countries. It is also available online. The main purpose of this publication is to promote the products and services of small U.S. exporters. Your advertisement in it could bring a significant number of sales leads.

The catalog contains three sections:

1. Service promotions, which advertise a broad range of services for sale.
2. New product promotions, which advertise new product offerings (including product pictures and descriptions) along with business addresses for more information.
3. Special industry promotions, which push the technologies and products of a single industry.

 As of this writing, the price for a black-and-white, full-page ad for one issue is $6,420. A full-page color ad is $7,800. You can also run a website listing for $295.

The USCS also maintains a trade leads database. It includes announcements from qualified international companies looking for U.S. products and services and advertisements of foreign government tender projects. All trade leads are prescreened by in-country USCS personnel and are provided as a free service for U.S. exporters.

International Company Profile (ICP) (www.icpcredit.com) reports are low cost—usually less than $1,000—credit checks or due diligence reports on international companies. Order an ICP on all prospective representatives, distributors, or partners as well as on large or questionable customers.

Trade Events and Related Services

One of the best and least expensive ways to promote your company and its products is at in-country trade shows certified by USCS personnel. Such certification is very helpful in eliminating those shows that do not reach your type of customer. Let USCS check out which ones are best for you. It will save you a lot of money and aggravation.

Trade shows in the United States are also a great way to promote your products and company. USCS invites more than 125,000 foreign buyers and distributors to 32 top U.S. trade shows every year. By and large, these shows draw more from Europe and Asia than anywhere else, unless they are held in Miami or Houston, in which case they draw heavily from Latin America.

Another excellent way to get started in a new country is through USCS sponsored trade missions. These meetings with key customers, in-country representatives, and government officials are organized and led by state economic organizations, chambers of commerce, and industry associations. It's a great way to meet prescreened business contacts face-to-face.

The USCS also offers the International Catalog Exhibition Program in which in-country personnel will translate your company profile into the local language and dialect, display your marketing materials, collect sales leads, and then help you follow-up with local contacts. However, I have not used this service, so I cannot vouch for its effectiveness.

DISTRICT EXPORT COUNCILS

In addition to direct assistance from ITA and USCS staff, you might also check out the experiences of veteran U.S. exporters that ship to a country in which you are interested or who have experience with a specific foreign agency. This can be accomplished through Department of Commerce sponsored District Export Councils (DECs). DEC member firms represent a cross section of U.S. businesses whose employees volunteer their time to counsel and assist new-to-export companies. Of all the services offered by the DOC, this can easily be the most beneficial, provided you are truly serious about making an export commitment. And it's free.

ITA PUBLICATIONS

The International Trade Administration also publishes a variety of periodicals, reports, and bulletins. *Business America*, a biweekly magazine, is probably the ITA's best-known publication. It includes a wide range of information including trade leads, export tips, individual country marketing reports and economic analyses, and advance notice of trade fairs and exhibitions. The inclusion of actual company success stories makes it a more lively read than most government publications. Annual subscriptions and single copies are available from the Government Printing Office (GPO).

International Trade Administration, U.S. Department of Commerce
1401 Constitution Ave., NW, Washington, DC 20230;
202-377-5494 or 202-482-3809; www.trade.gov

BUREAU OF EXPORT ADMINISTRATION

The Bureau of Export Administration (BXA), which falls under the DOC, has as it's mission: (1) to direct U.S. export policy, (2) to investigate breaches of federal export control laws, and (3) to administer antiboycott laws. The bureau's main interface with exporters is that it facilitates the application of export licenses through two systems:

➥ Export Application and Information Network (ELAIN). This is a computer-based system used to file export license applications directly with the DOC. When applications are approved, the computer issues the license to the applicant. The computer access telephone number is 203-377-4811.

➥ System for Tracking Export License Applications (STELA). This system enables applicants to trace the status of their export license application by telephone (203-377-2753).

 Bureau of Export Administration, Exporter Assistance Staff, Room 1099D; 202-377-1455; www.bis.doc.gov

INTERNATIONAL PROGRAMS CENTER

The International Programs Center is a section in the Bureau of the Census. It maintains a computer database of worldwide demographic, economic, and social data. This database, called quite naturally the International Data Base (IDB), is especially helpful for developing strategic analyses of potential markets and projected market trends. See the following for the database's categories:

➥ Population, by urban/rural location, age, and sex.
➥ Vital statistics, including infant mortality rates and life expectancy tables.
➥ Health and nutrition data.
➥ Fertility and child survivorship.
➥ Migration/foreign-born and refugee data.
➥ Provinces and cities.
➥ Marital status and marriage/family planning statistics.

➡ Ethnic, religious, and language groups.

➡ Literacy and education.

➡ Labor force, employment, income, and gross national product statistics.

➡ Household size and housing indicators.

International Programs Center, U.S. Census Bureau, Washington, DC 20233; 301-763-2870; www.census.gov

FOREIGN AGRICULTURAL SERVICE

The Foreign Agricultural Service (FAS) of the Department of Agriculture is the principal agency involved in promoting U.S. agricultural exports. Its main contribution to exporters is to arrange international trade shows and trade missions with the help of a network of counselors, attaches, trade officers, commodity analysts, and marketing specialists.

FAS has trade offices in 15 major market countries that function as service centers for U.S. exporters and foreign buyers. Furthermore, agricultural affairs offices are located in U.S. embassies throughout the world. Export marketing support is offered through the Targeted Export Assistance program, which helps industry trade groups finance promotional activities for agricultural exports that may be disadvantaged because of unfair foreign trade practices.

Also within the FAS, the Minority and Small Business Export Program, which can be reached by telephone at 202-382-9498, provides a mechanism for small and minority-owned agricultural businesses to get started in international trade. The Agricultural Information and Marketing Services program provides information on foreign trade contacts and buyer identification and advertises U.S. exports. In addition to providing information and financial services to exporters, the FAS publishes reports and periodicals that can sometimes be helpful.

U.S. Department of Agriculture, Foreign Agricultural Service, 1400 Independence Ave., SW, Washington, DC 20250; 202-447-7937; www.fas.usda.gov

MARKET ACCESS AND COMPLIANCE

The Market Access and Compliance office (MAC) is the watchdog arm of the ITA. MAC identifies and helps resolve trade issues and verifies that our trading partners fully meet their obligations under free trade agreements. By doing this, MAC attempts to ensure that American companies have access to foreign markets, enabling them to compete on a level playing field.

The MAC office in Washington has a cadre of country desk officers who claim to be experts on political, commercial, and economic climates in each of their respective counties. These people need to be experts because their sole reason for existence is to ensure that U.S. companies filing trade complaints and market access issues are treated fairly. They are concerned with matters, such as customs, quotas, sanitary standards, and intellectual property piracy. To resolve issues, MAC coordinates with in-country USCS staff and other federal agencies as the occasion warrants.

Personnel from the Trade Compliance Center (TCC) who work in the MAC office also monitor foreign compliance with trade agreements to ensure that U.S. firms get the maximum benefits from these agreements. If you have trouble resolving trade issues or are subjected to what you consider to be unfair treatment in a foreign country the TCC is the place to go.

 Trade Compliance Center, Market Access and Compliance/ITA
U.S. Department of Commerce, 1401 Constitution Ave., NW,
Washington, DC 20230; www.tcc.export.gov

UNITED STATES AGENCY FOR INTERNATIONAL DEVELOPMENT

The U.S. Agency for International Development (USAID) programs are administered by the U.S. Department of State in more than 60 qualified countries. USAID field offices include private sector departments that coordinate their activities with USAID's Office of Trade and Investment.

This agency is only involved with government-to-government programs and not the private sector, although it does indirectly help U.S. companies. When USAID finances a project, one of its requirements is that the recipient government or its contracted agencies purchase from U.S. exporters a percentage of the products and services needed to complete the project. Not only does this result in excellent buyer contacts in new markets, it also assures you of getting paid in U.S. dollars.

As an aside, USAID has been very supportive of U.S. firms who participate in private sector economic development projects throughout the world, especially those companies that are involved in infrastructure projects, either as a subcontractor or in supplying materials and equipment. In that case, be sure to contact USAID to get the maximum exposure in your bidding process. See the following for a few examples of the types of projects supported by USAID:

➡ Privatization of government owned or managed enterprises.
➡ Project feasibility studies.
➡ Infrastructure development such as roads, port facilities, irrigation projects, and free zone facilities.
➡ Establishment of trading companies.

USAID has a specific department set up to act as an advocate for small and disadvantaged exporters. It is called the Office of Small and Disadvantaged Business Utilization/Minority Resource Center and offers the following services:

➡ Acts as an information clearinghouse for American businesses, organizations, and institutions interested in participating in the procurement and contracting process for USAID financed goods and services.
➡ Maintains a USAID Consultant Registry Information System, a computer database of more than 2,000 companies, organizations, institutions, and individual consultants that have the capabilities to match USAID project requirements.
➡ Counsels U.S. businesses, organizations, and institutions on how to do business with USAID.
➡ Negotiates USAID procurement and contracting goals for small, disadvantaged, and women-owned firms in conjunction with the SBA.

 Office of Small and Disadvantaged Business, Utilization/Minority Resource Center, U.S. Agency for International Development, 320 21st St., NW, Washington, DC 20523-1000; www.usaid.gov

Overseas, USAID offices are located in U.S. embassies. If you want to meet a representative face-to-face, your best bet is to go the U.S. embassy in the country of your choice.

EX-IM BANK

Ex-Im Bank offers comprehensive financing and insurance assistance for U.S. exporters as described in Chapter 22. In addition, Ex-Im Bank maintains a special office whose mission is to encourage U.S. businesses to sell internationally. This office provides information on the availability and use of export credit insurance, guarantees, and direct and intermediary loans.

SMALL BUSINESS ADMINISTRATION

Several regional offices of the SBA have a very active counseling service available through the Service Corps of Retired Executives. Although part of the SBA's mandate includes assisting small businesses in the development and financing of exports, budgetary constraints and a lack of qualified personnel severely limit the agency's involvement in international trade. Nevertheless, since a few offices do have personnel sufficiently versed in overseas protocols to be of some assistance, the SBA should not be totally ignored. Your best bet is to work directly through the SBA's Washington office, although you might get speedier results from an SBA regional office. (See Appendix for the addresses and phone numbers of all 10 regional offices.) Officially, the SBA offers the following types of assistance:

➡ Export counseling.
➡ Export training cosponsored with other federal agencies.
➡ Legal advice through the Export Legal Assistance Network staffed by lawyers from the International Law Council of the Federal Bar Association.
➡ Data reports from the Export Information System, classified by the UN's Standard International Trade Classification codes.
➡ Matchmaker events, trade delegations organized to meet prospective foreign sales representatives and joint venture partners, similar to the matchmaker events sponsored directly by the Department of Commerce.

The wide range of publications distributed by the SBA are a major contribution to small business exporters. These reports, guides, and booklets disclose basic information about the fundamentals of exporting.

 SBA Publications, Office of International Trade, Room 501A, Small Business Administration, 1441 L St., NW, Washington, DC, 20416; www.sba.gov

DEPARTMENT OF STATE

Private businesses usually don't have much contact with the Department of State except in unusual circumstances related to expropriation of foreign shipments or other matters that involve government-to-government coordination. However, three Department of State services can be very helpful in supplying commercial information.

Regional bureau country desk officers are one of the best sources of current information about a country's political and economic status. Desk officers remain in day-to-day communication with all overseas diplomatic posts. So when you plan to enter an export market, it can't hurt to check with the appropriate desk officer to make sure no unusual political or economic events are occurring. In addition, the Office of Commercial, Legislative, and Public Affairs (202-647-1942) is a good resource for specialized assistance in dealing with unusual problems. And finally, before you board a plane to a less developed country, be sure to check the Department of State's Travel Advisory. When even the slightest chance of trouble or action against foreigners arises, the local U.S. Embassy issues a Travel Advisory detailing the problem or problems.

 U.S. Department of State; 2201 C St., NW, Washington, DC 20520; 202-647-4000; www.state.gov

STATE AND LOCAL FOREIGN TRADE ASSISTANCE

Every state and many cities maintain active foreign trade commissions to assist local companies who want to get started in exporting. Although each offers slightly different incentives and assistance, these trade bureaus generally offer export counseling, coordination with federal export assistance programs, statistical data on the experience of local exporting firms, a modest amount of foreign market research information, technical assistance, and financing advice. Many states and some cities also participate in Ex-Im Bank's City-State Partnership Initiative program to help finance exports.

In addition, state and city trade commissions assist industry trade associations and private trade groups identify appropriate freight forwarders, export trading companies, and export management firms. Although some trade associations and trade groups seem to be invisible, the more active ones sponsor trade shows, trade missions, industry symposiums on foreign trade, and a wealth of other export assistance programs. Furthermore, in some states foreign trade bureaus help companies set up new foreign trade zones and provide listings and descriptions of zones currently operating in the state. It can't hurt to check out what's available in your area.

AMERICAN CHAMBERS OF COMMERCE

The primary objective of American Chambers of Commerce (AmCham) offices located in countries around the world is to "promote trade and investment between those countries and the United States." Although affiliated with the U.S. Chamber of Commerce, AmCham offices are independently owned, private sector organizations.

AmCham provides a unique link between U.S. companies and local governments. As such, these offices are able to successfully lobby for favorable treatment of U.S. companies interested in investing in local projects. AmCham personnel also provide a number of beneficial services to expatriates of U.S. companies. When doing your country surveys, the local AmCham office should be your first stop. (See Appendix for a complete listing of all AmCham offices.)

PROFESSIONAL FIRMS AND BANKS

Regardless of the volume of data supplied by federal, state, and local government agencies or the involvement of industry trade associations and private trade groups, nothing beats doing your own market research. It will become obvious when you start gathering public data that much of it has been sifted through and diluted to meet the objectives of the particular agency or trade bureau that compiled it. Furthermore, in many cases the data may be six months to a year old. International trade is very dynamic and decisions should be made based on current information, untainted by the supplier's mission or objectives. And the only way to get current, clean data is by gathering it yourself.

Most professional firms, especially the large public accounting firms and international consultants, have a wealth of relatively current information gathered from clients in addition to their own research. The Miami offices of Ernst & Young and PricewaterhouseCoopers in particular have proven to be excellent sources of information relayed from their Latin American branches and affiliates. Contact their New York offices for information about Russia, Eastern Europe, and the Middle East and their Los Angeles offices for Asia.

Multinational banks are also valuable resources. Citibank, JPMorgan Chase, Bank of America (BankBoston in Latin America), and many British and Canadian banks have foreign branches that compile local economic, business, and political data. Depending on your choice of market, local managers of these banks can be helpful in leading you to joint venture partners, influential bureaucrats, or even potential customers.

These accounting firms, consulting firms, and banks all produce newsletters and other publications about foreign trade for their clients. Most are happy to include your company on their mailing list if they think they might get business from you in the future.

RESEARCHING ONLINE

The internet has added a whole new dimension to market research. Not that the information available through computer databases is any more current, accurate, or comprehensive than that which is available through periodicals, books, hard copy reports, or other written medium. It's just easier and faster to access. For instance, the DOC's National Trade Data Bank described earlier. Now instead of requesting hard copy reports you can tap into the database directly (www.stat-usa.gov).

Commercial databases can also be helpful in locating specific information. Dialog (telephone 800-334-2564; www.dialog.com), a Thomson

company, is the granddaddy of all commercial databases and includes everything imaginable about virtually any subject. Many other internet commercial databases can also give you vital information, but there are far too many to discuss in this book. Once you get into the swing of Googling these services, you'll find more available data than you could ever use.

In conclusion, the more information you can gather about your particular market and its business environment before soliciting orders or committing to local facilities the better your chances of success. And, in the end, it makes more sense to seek assistance in matters that you may not be confident of handling yourself than to go it alone and perhaps stumble along the way.

PART II
ANALYSIS OF KEY COUNTRIES AND REGIONS

chapter five
Competitiveness and Barriers to Market Entry

I N 2003, MR. JAMES O'NEILL, A GLOBAL ECONOMIST AT GOLDMAN SACHS, COINED the term BRIC, in his paper Dreaming with BRICs: The Path to 2050, as a shorthand designation of a specific group of countries—Brazil, Russia, India, and China. His thesis was that these four countries will become the world's most dominant economies by 2050. By that year, they are forecasted to have more than 39 percent of the world's population and a combined GDP (PPP) of $15.435 trillion. They will form the largest entity in the world. I must quickly point out, however, that neither Goldman

Sachs nor Mr. O'Neil predict that the BRIC countries will be involved in any type of political alliance, such as the European Union, or any formal trade association, such as ASEAN, MERCOSUR, or NAFTA.

Mr. O'Neil predicts that China and India will be the "dominant global suppliers of manufactured goods and services" while Brazil and Russia will "become similarly dominant as suppliers of raw materials." From this hypothesis, it follows that the logical next step for the BRIC countries would be to form a powerful trade alliance to the exclusion of the modern day G8 nations, Mr. O'Neil's denial notwithstanding. This scenario, of course, differs from the tripartite power blocs that I hypothesized in Chapter 3.

Many uncertainties arise in conjunction with the BRIC prognostication. The disregard of human rights by China and Russia is problematic as is the possibility of conflict between China and Taiwan and Russia's steadily declining population. Other problematic issues include Brazil's failure to live up to investor expectations; India's continuing antagonism toward its neighbors and its debilitating caste system; the gigantic number of people who live below the poverty line; a seeming disregard for the environment; unstable political regimes; terrorism; social uprisings; and the spread of infectious diseases. These are the barriers the BRIC countries face while reaching the pot of gold that rich nation status brings.

Still, these emerging giants pose a force to be reckoned with. The wealth of raw materials, enormous consumer populations, dynamic industrial bases, and desperate need for rehabilitated infrastructures beckon U.S. companies of all sizes and industries. Clearly, these potential benefits outweigh the advantages smaller countries offer. For this reason, plus fierce competition from giant transnational corporations that limit the participation of smaller companies in the G8 and other rich nation markets, we will focus primarily on opportunities and barriers proffered by the four BRIC countries. However, to complete our panorama of global trade, we will also look at a relatively small number of other countries that feed off the BRIC countries. Unfortunately, lack of space prohibits a thorough critique of every country in the four major regions of emerging nations.

I want to quickly point out that I do not mean to infer a lack of opportunities in these smaller countries. In fact, excluding the BRIC nations, the rest of Eastern Europe, Latin America, Southeast Asia, and Israel offer enormous potential for smaller U.S. companies to carve out outstanding profits and high returns on investment. When combined with the economic growth expected of the BRIC nations, the range of profitable possibilities is staggering.

Yes, global trade offers significant opportunities for smaller companies but barriers need to be overcome. No one should think of today's world as orderly, predictable, or secure. It is anything but that. On the contrary, the world of emerging nations is a composite of wealthy pockets, abominable poverty, vibrant cities, horrendous slums, glorious vacation spots, and dangerous crime.

> No one should think of today's world as orderly, predictable, or secure.

Despite enormous improvements in the availability of consumer goods, electricity, cell phones, the internet, and primary school education for a vast number of children, a conglomeration of debilitating issues have still not been addressed. A widening wealth gap heightens the evils of poverty, especially in countries with large indigenous populations. Healthcare in rural areas is abysmal. Air pollution and water contamination continue to be major health hazards. Sanitary waste disposal remains an elusive concept. Standards of secondary and tertiary education fall well below those of rich countries. And with a few exceptions, women are still treated as second-class citizens.

Although the middle class and the elite class have shown remarkable growth over the last 10 years, the working classes have decreased. Despite the remarkable economic resilience of the masses and the vast number of economic reforms that have been developed over the last decade, the lack of attention by governments to finding a resolution to the enormous economic inequalities has begun to cause political unrest in countries previously immune from such turmoil. In China, India, and many other less developed countries, blue-collar men and women have begun to rebel. Several countries in Latin America have seen this working class rise up and replace moderate presidents with populist left-wing radicals. While the Russian working class has yet to be heard, the swords of unrest are beginning to rattle in Romania, the Balkans, and even Poland.

It's only natural that the blame for shoddy efforts to reduce poverty, repair collapsing infrastructures, alleviate healthcare shortages, and raise education standards has fallen on rich countries. In fact, economic liberalization is felt by many to be the single overriding factor that has caused the widening of the wealth gap. It is certainly easy to blame the "haves" of the world but that begs the question. The United States, Western Europe, and Japan cannot be held responsible for decisions made by duly elected governments or traditional family despots. No one forced these governments and families to adhere to democratic principals or to be part of the 21st century world economy. No one coerced them into ignoring their own people. No one goaded them into abrogating their responsibility, silencing corrupt police and judges, or supporting terrorism. Neither rich country governments nor their citizens had anything to do with the sliding decline of education and healthcare systems. Certainly, no one outside a country's borders advocated the widening income inequalities so prevalent throughout the world. To blame Europe, the United States, or Japan for these maladies is purely a cop-out. If anyone is to blame for the mess of the world's social structures it must be the citizens of those countries. Fortunately, the global business community stands ready to help emerging nations dig their way out of this morass, provided, of course, that they want assistance.

The United States, Western Europe, and Japan cannot be held responsible for decisions made by duly elected governments or traditional family despots.

COMPETITIVENESS

Wouldn't it be great to have the option of picking which country you'd like to focus on? Unfortunately, that may not be possible. A top executive in your company might have a personal preference, presumptions might be made about the benefits of specific markets, a distributor might exert undue influence, or a marketing manager might fall for media pronouncements about thriving markets in one country or another. Although any of these reasons may lead to the right choice, increasing competition and changing business environments encourage a more disciplined approach.

The World Economic Forum (www.weforum.com), an organization that brings together the world's top government and business leaders to discuss the state of the world's economy, meets annually in Davos, Switzerland. For 20 years, the Forum has published its annual competitiveness report comparing the economic, political, and business climates of countries throughout the world. Since 2001, the methodology used in this report has been based on a model developed for the World Economic Forum by noted economists Jeffrey Sachs and John McArthur. It is called the Global Competitiveness Index (GCI). The World Economic Forum's definition of competitiveness is the "collection of factors, policies, and institutions which determine the level of productivity of a country and that, therefore, determine the level of prosperity that can be attained by an economy." Its basic premise is that "a more competitive economy is one that is likely to grow faster over the medium- to long-term." If you have a choice about which country to devote resources and energy to it just makes sense that you give serious consideration to one ranked near the top of the GCI.

The GCI is composed of three separate indexes: the technology index, the macroeconomic environment index, and the public institutions index. The 2007 survey consists of 122 countries divided into two groups: innovator countries and all others. Innovator countries are those that have more than 15 U.S. patents registered per million population. For innovator countries, the weighting of the three subindexes is that GCI equals one-half of the technology index, plus one-fourth of the macroeconomic index, plus one-fourth of the public institutions index. For all other countries, each subindex is given an equal one-third weighting.

The technology index consists of several pieces of hard data plus answers to a survey of 11 subjective questions. The hard data are:

➥ U.S. patents granted per 1 million population.
➥ Gross tertiary school enrollment rate.
➥ Cellular mobile subscribers per 100 inhabitants.
➥ Internet users per 10,000 inhabitants.
➥ Internet hosts per 10,000 inhabitants.
➥ Main telephone lines per 100 inhabitants.
➥ Personal computers per 100 inhabitants.

The macroeconomic index survey asked, "Is your country's economy likely to be in a recession next year?" and "Has obtaining credit for your company become easier or more difficult over the past year?" The additional hard data are:

➥ Government surplus/deficit.

➡ National savings rate.

➡ Inflation rate.

➡ Real effective exchange rate.

➡ Lending/borrowing interest rate spread.

➡ Government debt.

The public institutions index consists of a survey of seven subjective questions dealing with judiciary independence, crime, public contracts, financial assets, and bribes paid to public officials. Figure 5-1 shows how 10 countries in each of the four emerging regions of the world ranked against the 122 countries included in the world index.

The purpose of the GCI is to alert businesses who are considering either exporting, foreign sourcing, or opening a plant, warehouse, or retail establishment in one or more of the 122 countries to the potential benefits and difficulties of choosing one country over another. This is a valuable tool and should be incorporated into your strategic marketing program. But this doesn't mean that everyone should choose Singapore, Hong Kong, Taiwan, or Israel merely because they are the top four on the ladder. Any of the other countries might have better markets, distribution channels, or less competition that would make them a more logical choice. But at least with the GCI, you have more information with which to make a decision.

It's interesting to note how some of the world's rich countries did against these emerging nations. Switzerland ranked 1st, then came Finland, followed by Sweden and Denmark. Other major rich nations include the United States (6th), Japan (7th), Germany (8th), the Netherlands (9th), and the United Kingdom (10th).

In addition to the GCI, the World Economic Forum publishes an annual Business Competitive Index (BCI). Instead of looking at countries from the macroeconomic level, the BCI looks at microeconomic factors to determine sustainable levels of productivity and competitiveness. The underlying concept of the BCI is that "while macroeconomic and institutional factors are critical for national competitiveness, these are necessary but not sufficient factors for creating wealth." The BCI specifically measures two areas for each country: (1) the sophistication of private sector company operations and strategy and (2) the quality of the overall national business environment in which companies operate.

FIGURE 5-1 Global Competitiveness Index Ranking (122 Countries)	
Country	World Rank
Singapore	5
Hong Kong	11
Taiwan	14
Israel	15
Estonia	25
Malaysia	26
Chile	27
Czech Republic	29
United Arab Emirates	32
Thailand	35
Latvia	36
Slovakia	37
Qatar	38
Lithuania	40
Hungary	41
India	43
Kuwait	44
Poland	48
Indonesia	50
Costa Rica	53
China	54
Mexico	58
Turkey	59
El Salvador	61
Russia	62
Egypt	63
Colombia	65
Brazil	66
Trinidad and Tobago	67

FIGURE 5-1 continued	
Country	World Rank
Romania	68
Argentina	69
Morocco	70
Philippines	71
Bulgaria	72
Peru	74
Algeria	76
Sri Lanka	79
Dominican Republic	83
Pakistan	91
Source: The Global Competitiveness Index Ranking 2006–2007, World Economic Forum	

The BCI is an important adjunct to the GCI in that it is a fairly good measure of what to expect from local businesses in a given country. This will give you a feel as to the amount of resources you will probably have to commit to be successful. Figure 5-2 shows the BCI rankings for each of the 10 countries in the four regions.

Once again, comparison with the rankings of rich countries yields interesting results. The United States ranked 1-1-2, then came Finland (2-9-1), followed by Germany (3-2-4), Denmark (4-4-3), United Kingdom (6-6-6), and Switzerland (7-5-7). Other major rich nations were ranked as follows: Japan (8-3-10), the Netherlands (9-8-8), Austria (10-11-9), France (11-10-11), and Canada (13-18-13). Although neither of these indexes tells the whole story about a country, both should be included in your analysis as relevant statistics but not necessarily deal makers or deal breakers.

GOVERNMENT INTERVENTION

Without a doubt, government intervention in the form of regulatory barriers to trade and foreign investment is one of the most difficult obstacles you'll

FIGURE 5-2 Business Competitiveness Index (116 Countries)			
	World Rank	Company Operations and Strategy	National Business Environment Quality
Singapore	5	14	5
Taiwan	14	13	15
Hong Kong	20	20	19
Israel	22	19	22
Malaysia	23	24	23
Estonia	26	33	25
Czech Republic	27	29	27
Chile	29	31	29
India	31	30	31
United Arab Emirates	33	36	33
Hungary	34	40	32
Thailand	37	35	37
Slovakia	39	47	38
Lithuania	41	41	41
Poland	42	43	46
Qatar	44	64	43
Kuwait	47	63	45
Latvia	48	51	48
Brazil	49	32	52
Costa Rica	50	34	53
Turkey	51	38	51
Colombia	56	49	57
China	57	53	58
El Salvador	58	57	56
Indonesia	59	50	59
Mexico	60	55	62
Argentina	64	52	64
Pakistan	66	68	65
Trinidad and Tobago	65	62	63

	World Rank	Company Operations and Strategy	National Business Environment Quality
FIGURE 5-2 continued			
Romania	67	69	67
Philippines	69	44	78
Egypt	71	58	74
Sri Lanka	72	73	73
Russia	74	77	70
Ukraine	75	71	76
Morocco	79	80	75
Bulgaria	80	81	77
Peru	81	66	82
Venezuela	92	85	97
Algeria	95	111	88
Dominican Republic	101	88	103

Source: The Business Competitiveness Index 2006–2007, World Economic Forum

face when choosing a country in which to do business. Yet, in any country, developing a strategy to deal with these regulations has to be a primary goal in your marketing plan. Although coming up with such a strategy may seem a daunting task, with detailed planning and preparation, there is no reason why you cannot succeed.

It might help to look at which countries tend to be the easiest to do business in from the perspective of government regulations. Such a ranking will also give you a feel for which countries are more difficult to enter. The World Bank Group publishes an annual report, the latest edition of which is *Doing Business in 2008,* that measures the impact of government business regulations in 178 countries. Rankings are based on 10 criteria:

1. The ease of starting a business.
2. The ease of dealing with licenses.
3. The ease of hiring and firing workers.
4. The ease of registering property.
5. The ease of getting credit.

6. The ease of protecting investors.
7. The ease of paying taxes.
8. The ease of trading across borders.
9. The ease of enforcing contracts.
10. The ease of closing a business.

The results of this study show that out of 178 countries, Singapore, New Zealand, and the United States, in that order, are the top three "easiest to do business in" countries. This means that overall, government regulations are less onerous in those three countries than anywhere else. In Latin America, Chile (33rd) is the easiest in which to do business. In Asia, Singapore followed by Hong Kong (4th) are the easiest. In Eastern Europe, Lithuania (26th) is the easiest, and in the Middle East, Saudi Arabia (23rd) is easiest. In all four BRIC countries, government regulations pose a serious obstacle to doing business with Brazil ranked 122nd, Russia ranked 106th, India ranked 120th, and China ranked 83rd. Figure 5-3 shows the rankings by country.

This index should be helpful in determining which market to go after and, equally important, which countries require extra effort to maneuver around government regulations. However, the ease of doing business index does not take into consideration economic and social factors such as macro-economic policy, quality of infrastructure, currency volatility, investor perceptions, or major social issues such as crime rates and joblessness. For your purposes, these factors may be more important than onerous government regulations.

In addition to managing government intervention, you'll have to decide how to deal with the impact of crime and corruption on your business in all emerging nations. Let's look at crime first.

CRIME AND THE BUSINESS COMMUNITY

The overall crime rate in Latin America is double the world average, making this region one of the most violent places on earth, virtually equal to the war torn regions of sub-Saharan Africa. The Inter-American Development Bank estimates that Latin America's GDP per capita would be 25 percent higher if the region's crime rates were equal to the world average. Eastern Europe is almost as violent. Respondents to several recent trade association surveys

FIGURE 5-3 Ease of Doing Business Ranking 2008 (178 Countries)	
Country	World Rank
Singapore	1
Hong Kong	4
Thailand	15
Estonia	17
Latvia	22
Saudi Arabia	23
Malaysia	24
Lithuania	26
Israel	29
Slovakia	32
Chile	33
Kuwait	40
Mexico	44
Hungary	45
Bulgaria	46
Romania	48
Oman	49
Taiwan	50
Czech Republic	56
Turkey	57
Peru	58
Colombia	66
Trinidad and Tobago	67
United Arab Emirates	68
El Salvador	69
Poland	74
Pakistan	76
China	83

FIGURE 5-3 continued	
Country	World Rank
Dominican Republic	99
Russia	106
Argentina	109
Costa Rica	115
India	120
Brazil	122
Indonesia	123
Algeria	125
Egypt	126
Morocco	129
Philippines	133
Source: Ease of Doing Business Report 2008, World Bank Group	

overwhelmingly rank crime as the number one issue holding back increased trade and infrastructure investment.

Although difficult to believe, the World Bank estimates that worldwide violence (not counting wars) claims more lives per year than HIV/AIDS. Such mayhem undermines the public's faith in democracy and creates the impression that governments cannot provide public security.

Two types of crime impact the business community worldwide—street crime and organized crime. Most street crime is against individuals, foreigners as well as nationals. Organized crime (e.g., Mafias and Triads) is usually but not always directed against businesses and business transactions.

The UN's survey of crime trends ranked countries by the number of total crimes per 1,000 people (Figure 5-4). Unfortunately, this survey covers only 62 countries out of nearly 200 worldwide, so in effect, it only represents a sample. And it does not distinguish between street crime and organized crime.

When you do your country surveys, you will probably be mostly concerned with street crime. Pickpocketing, robberies, burglaries, and crimes against persons are the more common forms of crime throughout the world. However, transnational organized crime has begun to play a major role in the economies of several countries. One facet of organized crime's participation in the world economy is that it makes illicit businesses look very legal. These gangs even form strategic alliances, just like legitimate companies. For example, the Japanese Yakuza and the Hong Kong-based Triads joined forces to tap worldwide markets for synthetic drugs and to traffic women and children for sexual slavery. Powerful drug cartels in Colombia joined with the Russian Mafia and Eastern Europe crime groups to do the same.

One facet of organized crime's participation in the world economy is that it makes illicit businesses look very legal.

The tentacles of organized crime reach every bureaucratic layer. Worldwide networks lean on government officials of all ranks to pass goods, money, and people through their countries. According to the UN's *Global Report on Crime and Justice*, the world's largest transnational crime group is the Japanese Yakuza. This gang operates worldwide in drugs, prostitution, and smuggling. It corrupts customs officials, law enforcement officers, judges, and even state ministers to turn a blind eye to their operations. Every year the Yakuza and other gangs launder billions of dollars, distorting the world financial system. As the UN report states, "From the perspective of organized crime in the 1990s [and the 2000s as well] Al Capone was a small-time hoodlum with restricted horizons, limited ambitions, and merely a local fiefdom."

Don't be surprised if you run into one of the Russian, Japanese, Chinese, or Eastern European transnational gangs when you try to get licenses, permits, or recruit labor in emerging nations. I'm not saying you will have to deal with these people. I'm merely saying that you *might* have to do so and that you should be prepared. This is when you need a well-connected local partner who knows how to handle such a situation.

Various governments have responded to this crime wave with methods equally as horrific as those used by organized gangs. As happened when the United States reduced personal freedoms in the name of the war on terrorism, governments in Latin America and Eastern Europe have sacrificed civil liberties in the name of stopping violent crime. Torture is a common weapon used to solicit confessions. Vigilante justice, including mob lynching,

FIGURE 5-4
Total Crimes Committed per 1,000 People (60 Countries)

Country	Total Crimes per 1,000 People
Chile	88.2
Hungary	45.0
Estonia	43.3
Czech Republic	38.2
Poland	32.9
Lithuania	22.9
Russia	20.5
Romania	16.5
Slovakia	16.4
Mexico	14.3
Costa Rica	12.0
Ukraine	11.8
Hong Kong	11.7
Venezuela	9.3
Thailand	8.8
Qatar	6.8
Colombia	5.0
Turkey	4.1
India	1.6

Source: Survey of Crime Trends and Operations of Criminal Justice Systems, UN Office on Drugs and Crime

is rising in rural areas where police are either ineffective or corrupt. In any event, nothing is being done to stop crime.

Youth gangs are becoming increasingly violent and reportedly get involved in human trafficking, drugs, auto theft, weapons smuggling, and kidnapping in Jamaica, Mexico, Brazil, and Colombia. Violent crime has become endemic in Brazil. Rio de Janeiro is one of the world's most violent cities. Come nightfall, gangs roam the streets. Foreigner's being robbed is common.

Now terrorist type attacks on Brazil's upper class have started. These gangs are mostly young men, many not even into their teens. The city's police aren't much better. As reported by the research firm Pelton & Associates, retail shopkeepers pay police to "pick off the toddlers like coyotes on a Wyoming sheep farm." According to the University of São Paulo, five children are murdered every day. Many are involved in the drug trade as couriers. Estimates claim that 7 million kids live on the streets of Brazil.

The U.S. State Department warns in its travel advisory that "crime throughout Brazil has reached very high levels." Brazilian police report that the number of crimes continues to rise, especially in the urban centers where the murder rate is four times that of the United States. And the majority crimes go unsolved. Brazil's President, Luiz Inácio Lula da Silva sees this crime wave as an expression of a social problem, specifically the widening gap between the rich and the poor.

In Russia, organized crime is more prevalent than street crime. According to the report *Russia's Road to Corruption*, from the Speaker's Advisory Group on Russia, "the continuing and pervasive role of government in the economy has provided an enormous impetus for organized crime." Here's one way organized crime infiltrates the Russian economy. The Russian Mafia provides a means for businesses to evade high taxes and overly restrictive regulations. Rather than pay outrageous fees to the government to get licenses and permits for anything and everything, a business may opt to pay less costly bribes to government bureaucrats. The Mafia acts as a middleman or broker for these transactions by arranging transactions between business executives and corrupt government officials—for a fee of course. Such a system adds to the cost of doing business thereby increasing the prices of products and services.

Russian officials estimate that 50 percent of the nation's economy is connected one way or another to organized crime. Ten years ago the Ministry of Internal Affairs reported that organized criminals owned or controlled 40 percent of Russia's private businesses, 60 percent of state enterprises, and 50 to 85 percent of the banks. Typically, Russian businesses pay 10 percent or more of their revenues each year in protection money. Illegal drug traffic in Russia is valued at approximately $7 billion per year. If you are thinking of exporting to or investing in this huge country be prepared for this rather un-

American way of doing business. And be sure to engage an effective, well-connected local partner.

Officially, China reports a low crime rate. Apparently, that's one of the few benefits of a communist government. Still, crime does exist. In 2006, police reported 1,130 bombings, 10,087 cases of arson, and 36,175 cases of rape. Eighty percent of all reported crime involved theft, fraud, or robbery. For some undefined reason, either murder is generally unacceptable in the Chinese culture, or more likely, it goes unreported. Contrary to the method Westerners use to resolve disputes, namely with guns, Chinese prefer to settle grievances between parties, either personal or business, with bombs. Why? Because guns are illegal, but explosives are readily available.

Contrary to the method Westerners use to resolve disputes, namely with guns, Chinese prefer to settle grievances between parties, either personal or business, with bombs.

As the number of pockets of capitalism increase and the flow of money accelerates, commercial centers such as Shanghai, Guangzhou, and Shenzhen can expect to see a significant rise in crime against property and persons. Also, organized crime under the Triads has primarily moved from Hong Kong to Mainland China. These Triad societies are similar to the Russian Mafia but are much more subtle in their dealings. Although officials know that Triad business enterprises cross over with legitimate companies, the lack of definitive laws and moral standards makes it virtually impossible to separate legal businesses from illegal ones. So beware. China holds forth a maze of contradictions and to do business there you need patience, courage, a strong local partner, and a bit of luck.

In all countries, crime breeds violence, which in turn breeds corruption. Crime, violence, and corruption are the three witches of emerging societies. Each of the BRIC countries as well as most other less developed countries pay the penalty by allowing these witches to stir the cauldrons of their economies.

INSIDIOUS CORRUPTION

Forty years after its enactment, the Foreign Corrupt Practices Act still prohibits U.S. companies from paying bribes to foreign bureaucrats and must be known by every American business person. A second bit of legislation, the Sarbanes-Oxley Act of 2002, originally enacted to attack accounting fraud (including off-the-books bribes), gives the U.S. Department of Justice a new weapon against corruption. Every American company—large or small—must have policies on its books to be certain that employees abide by these laws. Yet in any emerging nation, bribes are a way of life. If you want to do business in one of these countries you better be ready to pay up.

The World Bank estimates that illegal transactions cost the world economy about 1 trillion dollars a year. So although the U.S. Congress would like to prohibit Americans from being a part of this worldwide problem, the fact is that we are all party to it. I must point out, however, that the two U.S. laws referred to above pertain only to large bribes or kickbacks given to *foreign government officials*. Fortunately, the U.S. Congress recognizes the need of American businesses to pay bribes to lower echelon officials and local suppliers to remain competitive. This is known as grease, as in greasing the skids.

But corruption is more than paying bribes. Transparency International (TI) (www.transparency.org) defines itself as "a global civil society organization leading the fight against corruption, bringing people together in a powerful worldwide coalition to end the devastating impact of corruption on men, women, and children around the world." TI defines corruption as "the abuse of entrusted power for private gain." It hurts everyone whose life, livelihood, or happiness depends on the integrity of people in a position of authority.

TI publishes an annual Corruption Perceptions Index (CPI), which reflects the perceptions of the degree of corruption as seen by business people and country analysts from around the world. CPI scores range between 10 (squeaky clean) and zero (highly corrupt). Figure 5-5 shows the results of this survey.

In Figure 5-5, Brazil, India, and China all have scores of 3.6, significantly less than the average of 5.0. Russia's 2.5 is even worse. Even though the BRIC countries offer the best, largest, and fastest growing markets, be prepared to deal with the high level of corruption in each of these countries.

For informational purposes, the three least corrupt countries are Denmark, Finland, and New Zealand, each with a CPI of 9.4. The five most corrupt are Uzbekistan (1.7), Haiti (1.6), Iraq (1.5), Myanmar (1.4), and Somalia (1.4).

FIGURE 5-5
Corruption Perception Index 2007 (179 Countries)
(10 is squeaky clean, 0 is awful)

Country	CPI Score
Singapore	9.3
Hong Kong	8.3
Chile	7.0
Estonia	6.7
Israel	6.1
Qatar	6.0
Taiwan	5.9
United Arab Emirates	5.7
Hungary	5.3
Czech Republic	5.2
Malaysia	5.1
Costa Rica	5.0
Latvia	4.7
Slovakia	4.9
Lithuania	4.8
Oman	4.7
Kuwait	4.3
Poland	4.2
Bulgaria	4.1
Turkey	4.1
Colombia	3.8
Romania	3.7
Brazil	3.6
China	3.6
India	3.6
Mexico	3.6
Morocco	3.6
Peru	3.6

FIGURE 5-5 continued	
Country	CPI Score
Saudi Arabia	3.4
Trinidad and Tobago	3.4
Thailand	3.3
Algeria	3.1
Sri Lanka	3.1
Dominican Republic	3.0
Argentina	2.9
Egypt	2.9
Philippines	2.5
Indonesia	2.3
Russia	2.3
Pakistan	2.2
FOR COMPARISON	
Canada	8.7
United Kingdom	8.4
Japan	7.5
United States	7.2
Source: Corruption Perception Index 2007, Transparency International	

Another TI report, written in conjunction with the World Bank Development Indicators, the *Global Corruption Barometer 2007*, tries to express how corruption affects the daily lives of ordinary people. The survey included interviews with 63,199 people in 60 countries, emerging nations, and rich countries. The results of the survey follow:

➥ The poor suffer the most from corruption and are most pessimistic about the prospects for less corruption in the future.
➥ About 1 out of 10 people worldwide had to pay a bribe last year with the largest amounts paid in Asia and Eastern European.

➥ Bribery is most prevalent in interaction with the police, the judiciary, and the registry and permit/license services.

➥ The general public believes that political parties, legislative bodies, and the judiciary/legal system are the most corrupt institutions in their societies.

➥ Half of those interviewed expect corruption in their countries to increase in the next three years and also deem their governments' efforts to fight corruption to be ineffective.

The most shocking statistics are that 23 percent of Latin American and 15 percent of Asian respondents stated that their governments actually encouraged corruption. Nineteen percent of Canadians and Americans believed their governments encouraged corruption. However, 89 percent thought their governments were corrupt, and 85 percent thought that the business community was corrupt.

It goes without saying that corruption is a major problem worldwide, siphoning off a significant amount of money from the formal economy. It also seems obvious that this is not going to stop any time soon, regardless of laws passed by the U.S. Congress. Huguette Labelle, Chairman of Transparency International states that, "The worldwide poll shows that corruption has a dramatic effect on the lives of individuals. Its power is enormous. When basic services like electricity are denied to the poor because they cannot afford a small bribe, there is no light in the home, no warmth for the children, and no escape for the government from the responsibility to take action."

One might add that the effects of corruption are also felt in the business community, forcing increased prices and endangering the well-being and even the lives of employees.

INSIGHT... The general manager of Felowset Electric, a small business client, had to pay more than $50,000 in bribes just to get his distributorship set up in Jakarta, Indonesia. Thugs threatened him with physical harm and blocked his employees from entering the building unless he paid up.

Crime and corruption block emerging nations from achieving their full potential by infecting the lives of everyone—the rich, the middle class, the poor, business people, farmers, bureaucrats, academics, the elderly, and even children, women as well as men.

So much for corruption. Now we'll switch gears and look at barriers to trade that affect specific groups of citizens and hence specific markets. They are:

➡ Education shortfalls.
➡ The evils of joblessness.
➡ Poverty and the wealth gap.
➡ Broken healthcare systems.

As you will see throughout this book, the enigma of emerging nations is that while economies continue to grow handsomely, generating and increasing income and new jobs, almost unbearable social conditions go virtually untouched. Yes, several governments now recognize that they will never join the ranks of rich countries if they cannot resolve their social dilemmas. And yes, some are beginning to take a few tentative steps. However, by and large, they are merely scratching the surface. Inferior education, extreme poverty, unemployment, and virtually invisible healthcare systems persistently plague every emerging nation. It's important to grasp the risks that these shortfalls bring to your company and how they impact your choice of countries and market-entry options. We'll begin with education.

EDUCATION SHORTFALLS

While it is true that nearly all school age boys and, to a lesser extent, school age girls now have a primary school education (except perhaps in India, where official statistics are suspect or nonexistent), the education systems in virtually all less developed countries are still in dire need of restructuring.

A good indication of the level of education in a country is the percent of an age group that is actually enrolled in school. If you sell products for which buyers need at least a secondary school education to use effectively, such as those that require the use of chemistry, physics, biology, mathematics, or other subjects not taught at the primary level, this becomes a valuable statistic. If only 50 percent of men or 50 percent of women have a secondary school education, products that tap those markets will not sell well. Educational services are another group of products that assume buyers have a formal education through secondary school. Figure 5-6 shows the ranking of secondary school enrollment by country.

As might be expected, the Eastern European countries did better as a whole than any other region. This probably reflects the more or less universal attitude of Europeans toward education. Latin America didn't fare well. Unfortunately, out of the four BRIC countries, Brazil is the only one included in this survey. It would be helpful to see the results of a survey that included Russia, India, and China.

These statistics do not tell the whole story. They neither reflect the number of students that graduate from secondary schools nor the number of students who repeat a grade. One of the main reasons students leave school early is because they need to produce income to support their families. Severe poverty often forces young children to be the only breadwinners in the family. This is evident in Latin America, Asia, and the Middle East, where many students never graduate.

Overall, educators seem to agree that even with so many negative conditions, the heart of the education problem throughout the world is a result of the very low quality of teaching. People are less educated, not only because they leave school early, but also because the education they receive is inferior. The real problem is not the lack of access to education, but the poor quality of teachers, as reflected in the very small percentage of an emerging country's GDP that is allocated to education. Military arsenals yes. Education no. This is especially true in Latin America, as shown in the performance of school children in science. In 2006, the Organization for Economic Cooperation and Development (OECD), which includes rich countries, reported an average score of 500 out of a possible 800 on the science exam. Chile was the top performer in Latin America with an average score of 440. Uruguay had a score of 425, Mexico scored 410, and Argentina, Brazil, and Colombia each had scores of 390.

Unfortunately, boys and girls are not always given the same opportunities, even at the primary school level. This is especially true in China where a strong prejudice against girls still exists and India where girls tend to be

FIGURE 5-6
Secondary School Enrollment as Percent of Population (150 Countries)

Country	Females Enrolled (Percent)
Lithuania	93.69
Poland	91.51
Hungary	90.25
Qatar	89.25
Israel	89.21
Bulgaria	87.39
Argentina	81.91
Romania	81.89
Jordan	81.80
Malaysia	80.75
Kuwait	79.59
Hong Kong	78.28
Brazil	78.13
Trinidad and Tobago	77.39
Egypt	76.69
Oman	75.93
Peru	68.67
Saudi Arabia	68.35
Philippines	66.68
United Arab Emirates	59.24
Dominican Republic	58.75
Colombia	57.85
Chile	57.36
Indonesia	56.67
Costa Rica	39.33
Morocco	32.36

Note: Percent of female population in female's secondary school age group
Source: World Development Indicators Database 2007, World Bank Group

kept home to help with family chores. The almost universal discrimination against women and girls in less developed countries prevents girls from ever catching up with the schooling given to boys. Don't overlook such gender bias in your marketing plans. The gender gap remains an eyesore on the facade of emerging nations. It inevitably diminishes the opportunity for market growth and may be reason enough to dissuade you from pursuing certain markets. Unemployment is also a serious worldwide problem that needs to be reflected in your market-entry strategies.

> The gender gap remains an eyesore on the facade of emerging nations.

THE EVILS OF JOBLESSNESS

Despite a plethora of foreign direct investment and the abolition of runaway inflation, unemployment remains at unacceptable levels in emerging nations. The UN Economic Commission on Latin America and the Caribbean judges that unemployment throughout that region jumped 10 percent in the last 10 years. Some countries, notably Argentina and Venezuela, of the major economies, and Honduras and the Dominican Republic, of the minor economies, have seen unemployment rates accelerate even more.

In Brazil, economic inequality is very pronounced. High migration to and widespread poverty in its cities means that approximately 20 percent of Brazil's urban population lives in shanty towns called *favelas* that are controlled by drug gangs. Although it has many flourishing industries, this country reports an overall unemployment rate of nearly 10 percent. In major urban centers like São Paulo, Belo Horizonte, and Rio de Janeiro, however, at least 25 percent of able adults are out of work. Children looking for work are not counted. Illiteracy prevents at least 15 percent of the nation's population from getting work. Meanwhile, the crime rate in these same urban centers continues its never ending rise.

In Colombia, with a reported unemployment rate of 10.2 percent, 1 out of 5 children from the ages of 5 to 17 are forced to work to support their families, mostly in the informal economy. Although the minimum wage in Colombia is the equivalent of $41 per month, close to 2.5 million Colombian children toil for less. No one knows how much kids earn in the informal economy.

In China, more than 1 million people have lost their jobs in Shanghai over the last 10 years. This is mainly because old core industries, such as the textile industry, died off or moved to inland areas, leaving a large swath of unemployment along the southern coast. The prosperity of capitalism encouraged new, high- and low-tech companies to move to Shanghai and other commercial centers, but this was not enough to offset the huge number of lost jobs from the old industries. Prime Minister Zhu warns that increased foreign competition will double the official unemployment rate in the next few years, driving 30 million people to the unemployment lines. He blames the substitution of new, more efficient factories for old, labor-intensive ones. The government's official unemployment rate is 4.2 percent, but the Beijing-based think tank Development Research Center estimates that joblessness in industrial rust belt is closer to 20 percent.

India's official unemployment rate of 7.8 percent is meaningless. Sixty percent of India's official workforce is self-employed and many of these entrepreneurs continue to live in extreme poverty. Unofficial estimates place more than 90 percent of the country's labor force in the "unorganized sector," which to most of us means the underground or black-market economy. Officials report that the total labor force is growing at an annual rate of 2.5 percent. With the number of jobs growing at only 2.3 percent, joblessness will inevitably increase.

Of the four BRIC countries, Russia faces what could conceivably be the most severe case of joblessness. The Russian Federation State Statistics Committee reports that economic reforms planed for the state owned public utility, railway, and metallurgic industries will throw hundreds of thousands of people out of work. The committee also reports that 21.6 percent of Russians (30.6 million people) already have an income lower than the official living wage of 1,893 rubles ($50) per month. However, private research firms indicate the number is closer to 53 million or nearly 40 percent of the population. Women take the brunt of this unemployment problem. On average, women represent about two-thirds of all unemployed, while in some provinces they account for 90 percent. Moscow's women represent 78 percent of all the unemployed in the city. Figure 5-7 shows the country rankings and related unemployment percentages.

FIGURE 5-7 Unemployment Rate (124 Countries)	
Country	Unemployment Rate (Percent)
Dominican Republic	16.0
Algeria	15.7
Sri Lanka	15.6
Oman	15.0
Poland	14.9
Saudi Arabia	13.0
Indonesia	12.5
Colombia	11.1
Egypt	10.3
Turkey	10.2
Argentina	10.2
Slovakia	10.2
Brazil	9.6
Bulgaria	9.6
Israel	8.5
Philippines	8.4
Chile	8.3
India	7.8
Morocco	7.7
Peru	7.2
Trinidad and Tobago	7.0
Russia	6.6
Pakistan	6.5
El Salvador	6.2
Romania	6.1
Hong Kong	4.9
Estonia	4.7
Lithuania	4.5

FIGURE 5-7 continued	
Country	Unemployment Rate (Percent)
China	4.2
Taiwan	3.9
Malaysia	3.5
Mexico	3.2
Qatar	3.2
Singapore	3.1
United Arab Emirates	2.4
Kuwait	2.2
Thailand	2.1
Source: CIA Fact Book 2007	

These are dismal statistics. While professionals, government bureaucrats, and many business owners and executives drive Mercedes and vacation in New York, Miami, Paris, or Rome, most of the working class in emerging nations swelter in pitiable poverty. As you begin to do business in one of these less developed countries you will quickly see that all is not right.

You will soon be asking yourself, how can businesses flourish while such large groups of adults and children live in poverty? The answer lies with underground or informal economies.

In several countries, the informal economy generates as much or more income than the formal economy—in some, as much as 80 percent of GDP. This represents an enormous amount of uncounted effort, time, and, skill, causing a very large distortion in the official statistics. Unfortunately, as long as unemployment in the formal economy remains high, an increasing number of people will look to the informal economy for their income. Moreover, high unemployment breeds poverty. With high unemployment in the formal economy and gross uncer-

While professionals, government bureaucrats, and many business owners and executives drive Mercedes and vacation in New York, Miami, Paris, or Rome, most of the working class in emerging nations swelter in pitiable poverty.

tainties in the informal economy, a great many working age people will, by necessity, live below the poverty line and more than a few will live in extreme poverty.

POVERTY AND THE WEALTH GAP

The inequity in wealth is beginning to change the composition of governments all over the world. From Buenos Aires to Moscow, from Mumbai to Ankara, politicians who promise more jobs and less poverty are winning election after election. Left leaning politicians seem to be the best at answering the populist call. One only has to look at Latin America to see leaders like Hugo Chavez (Venezuela), Eva Morales (Bolivia), and Rafael Corea (Ecuador) echo doctrines promising the moon, which have been so effectively enunciated by Fidel Castro (Cuba) for the last 50 years.

Most economies of the world are humming along. Local businesses are doing better than they have in decades. In such circumstances, why do citizens turn away from the very market reforms and elected leaders who have brought their countries out of the doldrums? There is one simple reason. The wealth that these reforms create has not trickled down to the populace. Too many people are worse off now than they were 10 years ago. Huge indigenous populations continue to live in squalor. Persistent poverty, the widening gap between the rich and poor and, above all, joblessness, are taking their toll.

The UN has done a variety of studies of the world's poor trying to decipher not only the causes of the wealth gap but possible corrective measures that might help people climb out of this impoverished state and begin living a normal life. The poverty line or poverty threshold is the minimum level of income deemed necessary to achieve an adequate standard of living in a given country. The UN defines this poverty line as living on less than $2 per day. Its definition of *extreme* poverty is living on less than $1 per day.

Poverty is the most pervasive factor that keeps citizens from reaping the benefits of market economies.

Of all the shortcomings of emerging nations, poverty is the most pervasive factor that keeps citizens from reaping the benefits of market economies. As long as people are oppressed by poverty, nothing is as important to them as surviving another day with bread on the table. Figure 5-8 shows each country's

FIGURE 5-8 Population Living in Poverty (75 Countries)		
Country	Percent Living Less than $1/day	Percent Living Less than $2/day
Slovakia	N/A	2.9
Latvia	N/A	4.7
Ukraine	N/A	4.9
Chile	N/A	5.6
Bulgaria	N/A	6.1
Estonia	N/A	7.5
Lithuania	N/A	7.8
Costa Rica	7.3	9.8
Mexico	3.0	11.6
Russia	N/A	12.1
Romania	N/A	12.9
Morocco	N/A	14.3
Algeria	N/A	15.1
Dominican Republic	2.8	16.2
Argentina	6.6	17.4
Columbia	7.0	17.8
Turkey	3.4	18.7
Brazil	7.5	21.2
Peru	10.5	30.6
China	9.9	34.9
Trinidad and Tobago	12.4	39.0
Philippines	14.8	43.0
Egypt	3.1	43.9
Indonesia	7.5	52.4
Pakistan	17.0	73.6
India	34.3	80.4

Note: N/A = not available
Source: Human Development Report 2007/2008, United Nations; CIA Fact Book 2007

percent of the population who live on less than $2 per day and, where statistics are available, those who live on less than $1 per day.

I don't know why the Eastern European countries do not report the percentage of their populations living below $1 per day—perhaps because none of their citizens live on such a small amount. Also, with a few exceptions, half of the top 10 countries with the least poverty are in Eastern Europe.

In a country as huge as Russia, one would expect wide ranges in poverty levels, and that's exactly what we find. More than 73 percent of all Russians live in urban areas, and 58 percent of the poor live there. Moreover, wide variations of poverty exist among Russian districts. In some districts, only 3.1 percent of the people live on less than $2 per day. In other districts, 55.6 percent live in poverty. That's quite a range.

Although Brazil has become a major power in the group of emerging nations, with a large number of industrial and commercial enterprises, poverty is still widespread throughout the country. Brazilian economists concede that more than 50 percent of the population of 188 million people live on less than $2 per day, although the official statistic is 21.2 percent. Rural areas suffer the most. Estimates place 80 percent of rural Brazilians or about 30 million people as living on below $2 per day.

Parts of China are actually doing much better than they were 10 years ago. The wealth gap has narrowed significantly in the country's commercial centers. Even in a few of the rural regions citizens are earning more than they were in the past. Overall, however, China's wealth gap is widening. In China's rapid race to become the world's fourth largest economy, an increasing number of its citizens are being left behind. Government reports indicate that the richest 10 percent of Chinese families now own more than 40 percent of all private assets, while the poorest 10 percent own less than 2 percent. If any single hurdle stops China from achieving its growth goals, this widening income inequality will certainly do it.

Of the four BRIC countries, India has by far the largest percentage of people living in poverty. The changes that have taken place over the last 10 years are indeed profound, bringing opportunities and hope to millions of people. However, the 650 million Indians who live in 500,000 rural villages and the 150 million who live in urban slums are mostly spectators with little hope of improving their fate in the future. With 34 percent of its citizens living on less than $1 per day, many on less than $0.50 per day, the Indian government has a long way to go if it hopes to convert a larger slice of the country's population into eager consumers. The top 10 percent of Indians earn 33 percent of the total country's income while 25 percent of the nation's population lives on less than $0.40 per day. Children suffer the most. India's rate of malnutrition among children is 46 percent, the highest in the entire world, including Africa.

It goes without saying that poverty has a major impact on the economy of any nation. Markets that should flourish, stagnate under the yoke of intense poverty. Countries that could provide excellent potential for exports and direct investment, lock out vast rural areas because no one has the income to spend. Still, even in countries like India and China, both of which have high poverty rates, enormous opportunities can be found. But you have to sort them out, separate the wheat from the chaff. Many governments have, in fact, begun a wide range of social programs designed to ameliorate the uneven distribution of wealth. Certainly these programs will, over the long-term, help to alleviate poverty. However, they don't always reach the indigenous peoples and other segregated groups who are, in fact, the poorest.

Countries that could provide excellent potential for exports and direct investment, lock out vast rural areas because no one has the income to spend.

For some countries, indigenous and other segregated groups account for an enormous slice of the population (more than 50 percent of Guatemala's population). They seldom have schools in their villages. Healthcare professionals are unknown. Mothers seldom, if ever, receive reproductive care. Food is grown and hunted, not purchased in stores. The following are some findings of a World Bank study, *Indigenous Peoples, Poverty, and Human Development: 1994–2004*:

➥ Few gains were made in poverty reduction among indigenous people during the decade 1994–2004.

➥ During the 1990s, the indigenous poverty gap deepened and the number of indigenous peoples living below $1 per day shrank more slowly than ever before.

➥ Being indigenous increases an individual's probability of being poor and this was as true at the end of the decade as it was at the beginning.

➡ Indigenous peoples continue to have fewer years of education and the quality of education they do receive is substandard.

➡ Indigenous peoples, and especially women and children, have less access to basic healthcare.

This situation is analogous to the Native Americans of the 21st century who continue to live on reservations in decrepit housing without professional healthcare or adequate schools. Until solutions can be found to bring indigenous peoples the basic necessities of life, no government programs are going to be successful in lifting them out of extreme poverty.

Except for dealing with indigenous and other segregated groups, many governments have made strides in alleviating poverty. Surely, if governments across the board are successful in their efforts, eventually peoples around the world will work their way out of the poverty trap.

A WASTING ENVIRONMENT

Many experts believe that the three most serious environmental issues facing the world are: (1) climate change, (2) air and water pollution in urban centers, and (3) deforestation that threatens biodiversity. If your products or services relate in any way to these three issues—either the prevention of further degradation or the cleanup of the mess we already have—you can look forward to dynamic expanding markets in all four BRIC countries and most other emerging nations, too.

Anyone who has spent time in the mega cities of the world is well aware of the choking fumes spewed forth from industrial smokestacks and broken down buses, trucks, and automobiles. Air pollution is so obvious that further discussion is unnecessary. Water pollution is also an obvious problem. I can't think of one city in an emerging nation that I have visited where I would drink the tap water. Of course, this is great news for bottled water companies. Waste disposal is another obvious environmental problem. Waste disposal plants are scarce and most waste gets dumped into rivers, lakes, or oceans. If a body of water isn't handy, it just gets dumped on vacant land.

The ranking of countries according to their environmental performance, as shown in Figure 5-9, is the result of studies done at Yale University during 2006 and 2007. The phrase *environmental performance* means how effective a country's environmental protection measures are.

The low rankings of China and India show how far they have to go to begin changing the environmental destruction in their respective countries. On the other hand, a much higher ranking for Russia and Brazil gives hope that even the worst degradation can be stopped and corrected.

The destruction of the Amazon Rainforest has received an enormous amount of media attention over the last two decades. Although the Brazilian government has tried many times to institute laws that would alleviate this destruction, lumbering in the rain forest continues, as does the clearing of land for farms and ranches. Despite cries of anguish from world observers, this debasement goes on and on—seemingly without end—and impervious to government decrees.

In China, environmental bureaucrats readily admit that pollution is poisoning the country's water resources, air, and soil. They admit that carbon emissions are soaring. Fearful of contaminated local foodstuffs, *The New York Times* reported that U.S. athletes brought tons of food with them to the Beijing Olympics. And many athletes from around the world were seriously concerned about how China's horrific air pollution would affect their performance. More than a few of these athletes found breathing masks to be a partial solution. Global warming is also having an effect in northern China where rivers are beginning to dry up, eventually causing this old manufacturing region to run out of water.

If only the government would funnel some money their way, China's environmental bureaucrats complain, they could do something about the pollution problems. An environmental watchdog agency reports that the cost of China's pollution ranges upward of 10 percent of GDP. That's an enormous amount of money.

Apparently the government is listening—at least a bit. A State Environmental Protection Administration has been set up and, hopefully, will begin taking action to mitigate pollution problems. Officials claim that China will spend $180 billion from 2006 to 2010 on environmental protection and cleanup. But that's a pittance compared with what needs to be done. For

FIGURE 5-9
Environmental Performance Index 2008 (149 Countries)
(scored on a base of 100 for the best)

Country	World Rank	Environmental Score
Costa Rica	5	90.5
Colombia	9	88.0
Lithuania	16	86.2
Slovakia	17	86.0
Estonia	19	85.2
Hungary	23	84.2
Malaysia	27	84.0
Russia	28	83.9
Chile	29	83.4
Dominican Republic	33	83.0
Brazil	34	82.7
Argentina	38	81.8
Poland	43	80.3
Mexico	47	79.8
Israel	49	79.6
Thailand	53	79.2
Bulgaria	56	78.5
Peru	59	78.1
Philippines	61	77.9
Czech Republic	68	76.8
Egypt	71	76.3
Turkey	72	75.9
Saudi Arabia	78	72.8
Morocco	81	72.1
Romania	83	71.9
Trinidad and Tobago	89	70.4
Oman	91	70.3
Indonesia	102	66.2

FIGURE 5-9 Environmental Performance Index 2008 (149 Countries) (scored on a base of 100 for the best)		
Country	World Rank	Environmental Score
China	104	65.1
Kuwait	111	64.5
United Arab Emirates	112	64.0
India	120	60.3
Source: Yale University		

example, disposing of electronics waste is big business in China. Unfortunately, most reclamation is done by peasants from their homes, polluting air, and, in some cases, water supplies. As reported in the village of Guiyu in the south of China, acrid air hovers over small gas burners outside the doors of many homes where melting wires and cooking computer motherboards reclaim gold. Meanwhile, migrant workers smash picture tubes by hand to recover glass and electronic parts, releasing as much as 6.5 pounds of lead dust.

China burns more coal than any country in the world, accounting for 15.1 percent of the world's sulphur dioxide and 9.6 percent of carbon dioxide emissions. Smokestacks of old, dilapidated factories bellow toxic fumes across the north of China. Unfortunately, the lack of an independent media and very limited accountability prevent the central government from knowing how or if its environmental protection polices are getting implemented at the grass roots level. So even if the government had stringent regulations, which it does not yet have, little improvement would likely be seen in the countryside or in the cities. And so it goes. Pollution accelerates even as the government increases its efforts at pollution control.

Cigarette smoke also contributes to air pollution. The World Health Organization reports that 30 percent of the world's smokers live in China. Another 11 percent come from India and another 5 percent from Indonesian. That's almost half the world's smokers—nearly 1.3 billion people—who live in those three countries. China now has more citizens who smoke than the entire population of the United States. One reason there are so many Chinese smokers is that the state owns the largest tobacco company in the world, China National Tobacco Corporation, whose cigarette sales feed billions of dollars into government coffers. All emerging nations combined account for 70 percent of the world's smokers, and by 2030, these countries are projected to account for 77 percent or 135 million tobacco related deaths.

India's enormous population that lives below the poverty line contributes mightily to air, water, and soil pollution. As in Haiti, very poor Indians are more concerned with surviving day-to-day than with saving the environment, so they burn forest woods for heat, wash clothes and their bodies in ponds and streams, and use fertile pastures for fodder. The result translates into the deforestation of thousands of acres and water resources drying up from overexploitation. Rivers and lakes are becoming sewage dumps. Such deterioration of natural resources accelerates the process of impoverishment and everyone loses.

For 70 years in the old Soviet Union, environmental officials were subservient to the military who ran the utilities, mines, and chemical and metalworking industries. No thought was given to the environment. Natural resources were pillaged. Vast swaths of land were stripped of nutrients. Huge bodies of water and rivers were contaminated with industrial toxics. Today, the Russian government is making an honest effort to resurrect environmental protection measures and is making some progress, although much of the land and water supplies are already wasted for many decades to come.

Now is the time for any company who has the products or services to help save or cleanup the environment of any country to step up and move ahead to tap the huge market potential of emerging nations worldwide.

Environmental degradation is a major concern throughout the world. With so much political turmoil and wars that have been going on for so many years, it's not surprising that the environment has been short shifted. While people are trying to kill each other with bullets and bombs, the protection of woodlands, mountain streams, and fertile land and the reduction of industrial, auto, and truck emissions are bound to play second fiddle. Nevertheless, such hazards create enormous opportunities for the business community. Now is the time for any company who has the products or services to help save or cleanup the environment of any country to step up and move ahead to tap the huge market potential of emerging nations worldwide.

Although environmental degradation is certainly a very serious problem, in the short term it doesn't directly affect the everyday lives of ordinary citizens nearly as much as the lack of adequate healthcare.

BROKEN HEALTHCARE SYSTEMS

The World Health Organization predicts that each year 11 million children under the age of five years will die from largely preventable causes. Among these children will be 4 million babies dying in the first month of life. More than 500,000 women will die in pregnancy, childbirth, or shortly thereafter. Yes, these statistics relate to the world, and yes, we all know that Africa has more cases of HIV/AIDS than any other region. However, Latin America is right behind Africa and gaining ground.

Although crime, joblessness, and poverty suppress the economic growth of all emerging countries, HIV/AIDS is a most insidious social malady. Healthcare throughout the emerging world has taken second place to economic progress. However, without adequate healthcare, consumers will not reach their full potential, businesses will not master markets, and governments will not function effectively. The lack of adequate reproductive care for women and the lack of any meaningful effort to fight HIV/AIDS are two of the most destructive parts of broken healthcare systems.

Figure 5-10 shows that 9.5 million people have been infected with HIV/AIDS. About 300,000 new cases are reported each year. The Caribbean is the second most infected area in the world, surpassed only by sub-Saharan Africa. In all of Latin America, Haiti is the worst with 5.6 percent of the population infected.

India alone accounts for 5.1 million people with HIV/AIDS. That's more than half of the world's carriers. HIV/AIDS isn't the only health issue suppressing economic growth in emerging nations, however. In most of these countries, healthcare for all but the elite class is well below the standards of rich countries. Health insurance is seldom available. Reproductive care for women is nonexistent among poor and indigenous peoples.

The World Health Organization also ranks countries according to how well their healthcare systems are functioning. Figure 5-11 shows the somewhat surprising results.

FIGURE 5-10 People Living with HIV/AIDS 2007 (115 Countries) (descending from most people infected to least infected)			
Country	World Rank	People Living with HIV/AIDS	Percent of Population
India	2	5,100,000	0.4
Russia	13	860,000	0.6
China	14	840,000	(*)
Brazil	15	660,000	0.3
Thailand	16	570,000	0.9
Colombia	32	190,000	0.4
Mexico	34	160,000	0.1
Argentina	36	130,000	0.3
Indonesia	38	110,000	(*)
Dominican Republic	41	88,000	1.0
Peru	42	82,000	0.3
Pakistan	44	74,000	(*)
Malaysia	51	52,000	0.2
Trinidad and Tobago	57	29,000	2.6
Chile	58	26,000	0.2
Poland	66	14,000	(*)
Costa Rica	68	12,000	0.3
Philippines	73	9,000	(*)
Romania	79	6,500	(*)
Singapore	88	4,100	(*)
Hungary	94	2,800	(*)
Hong Kong	95	2,600	(*)
Czech Republic	96	2,500	(*)
Lithuania	101	1,300	(*)

Note(*): Less than 0.1 percent of the population
Note: Less than 0.1 percent of the populations of all Middle East countries are infected
Source: UNAIDS 2007 Report, World Health Organization; AVERT (www.avert.org); CIA Fact Book 2007; International Trade Administration, U.S. Department of Commerce

FIGURE 5-11
Working Healthcare Systems (190 Countries)

Country	World Rank
Singapore	6
Oman	8
Colombia	22
Saudi Arabia	26
United Arab Emirates	27
Israel	28
Morocco	29
Chile	33
Costa Rica	36
Qatar	44
Kuwait	45
Thailand	47
Czech Republic	48
Malaysia	49
Poland	50
Dominican Republic	51
Philippines	60
Mexico	61
Slovakia	62
Egypt	63
Hungary	66
Trinidad and Tobago	67
Turkey	70
Lithuania	73
Argentina	75
Estonia	77
Indonesia	92
Romania	99

FIGURE 5-11 continued	
Country	World Rank
Bulgaria	102
Latvia	105
India	112
Pakistan	122
Brazil	125
Peru	129
Russia	130
China	144
Source: World Health Report 2007, World Health Organization	

In rich countries, some with universal health coverage, out-of-pocket healthcare costs run about 25 percent of household income (except in the United States where it is 56 percent). However, in India, people typically pay 80 percent of their income for healthcare. This, of course, is why so many families treat themselves instead of using a physician, which in turn, increases the death rate for many diseases. The World Health Organization reports that the main failings of many health systems are:

➥ Many health ministries focus on the public sector, disregarding the much larger private healthcare sector.
➥ Many physicians work simultaneously for both sectors, making the public sector subsidize the private sector.
➥ Many governments fail to prevent a "black market" in healthcare where widespread corruption, bribery, moonlighting, and other illegal practices flourish, thereby causing official healthcare systems to malfunction.
➥ Many ministries fail to enforce regulations covering healthcare systems already in place.

All in all, healthcare is another social inequity that prevents emerging nations from achieving their rightful places in the world's economic spectrum.

SUMMARY

The competitive and social issues discussed in this chapter point to the long road emerging nations must travel to reach rich nation status. Like the other less developed regions of Africa, and to some extent Asia, Latin America's extensive background of political upheaval has prevented it from making much progress in the very difficult task of dealing with these issues. Unlike much of Africa, however, Latin America has at least evolved to mostly democratically elected governments. Eventually, one hopes that these governments will find the will to seriously address their nations's social inadequacies.

Poland, Hungary, the Czech Republic, and other Eastern European nations are certainly the closest to achieving rich nation status. Their industrial bases, education systems, consumer sophistication, and minimum poverty levels bode well for the future. If you're looking for the most developed region, Eastern Europe may be it. Also, certain Arab states, plus Israel, Singapore, Malaysia, and Thailand offer interesting possibilities. In Latin America, Chile, Colombia, Costa Rica, and Trinidad and Tobago have the least problems and the highest overall future growth potential.

As long as these emerging economies continue to improve like they have done for the last 10 years, eventually many of their nefarious shortcomings will be thrown off, and they will gain entrance to the developed world of the 21st century. If the American business community continues to support these efforts, the time it takes these countries to reach that plateau will be immeasurably shortened. Now let's turn to a more detailed look at specific countries in each of the four regions.

chapter six
Market Opportunities in Brazil and Latin America

P OVERTY REMAINS A CONTINUING PROBLEM THROUGHOUT LATIN AMERICA, A
region that lags behind the rest of the world in
improving the plight of its impoverished citizens.
A recent UN report places the income inequality—
that is the spread between the haves and the have-
nots—in this region as one of the worst in the
world, comparable to India and sub-Saharan
Africa. About 205 million or 40 percent of the
region's population lives below the poverty line. Of
that number, 79 million live on less than $1 per day.

The poorest one-fifth of the population accounts for only about 3 percent of national consumption. Obviously, this group can be eliminated from the ranks of active consumers.

Despite these startling statistics, 29 Latin American countries have made significant progress during the last two decades. Since 1990, the number of children receiving a primary education has increased from 87 percent to 97 percent, and nonagricultural female employment rose from 37 percent to 42 percent. Today, two countries have elected women as president, and women hold 20 percent of parliamentary seats, except in Costa Rica where 39 percent of the legislature are women. Child mortality per 1,000 births dropped from 54 to 31. Nearly all Latin American governments have implemented programs to fight poverty and most plan on enacting more during the next five years.

Economically, the region has done even better. All Latin American nations are now moving toward their rightful place in the global economy. It is no longer a backwater region. Its citizens are no longer wrestling with military rule, state controlled economies, and unworkable democratic administrations. Political institutions, financial systems, and environmental and social awareness have matured. In fact, it's safe to say that some Latin American countries have evolved well beyond what many call less developed economies.

Financial institutions in most countries are relatively stable. Every nation has weathered the storm of currency devaluations. In Mexico, Argentina, Brazil, Colombia, and Chile the capital markets and banking systems are on more solid footing than in recent memory. At the macroeconomic level, hyperinflation has disappeared, although inflation is still too high in two-thirds of the region.

You could do a lot worse than trying Latin America as your first shot at exporting. Distances are much shorter than to any other emerging region. Despite the ranting of President Hugo Chavez of Venezuela and a few other Latin leaders, most people like Americans and American products. The English language is spoken in the business community of several countries, although it is not predominant. Governments are relatively stable. And plenty of smaller businesses have done extremely well there. Of course, Brazil is by far the largest economy in the region.

BRAZIL

With a population of 188 million and a landmass equivalent to the continental United States, Brazil has the largest and certainly the most complex markets in Latin America. It has 10 metropolitan areas where populations each exceed 1 million people. Brazil's industrial base is very similar to the United States. Manufacturing, retail, and service industries are all healthy and growing. The country's large, diversified consumer base exhibits a wide range of tastes.

Brazil has the 12th largest economy and is the fifth most populous country in the world. It encompasses about half of South America's geography and economy. The United States is Brazil's second largest trading partner after the EU, with exports totaling about $19 billion in 2007. Rich in a variety of agricultural products and natural resources, Brazil also has a world renowned industrial base. Automobiles, steel, petrochemicals, and computers are major industries. Large shopping malls in the metropolises of Rio de Janeiro, São Paulo, Belo Horizonte, Brasilia, San Salvador, and Recife attract consumers of all ages.

Recognizing the need to improve its education and healthcare systems, the Brazilian government came up with a creation called the *Bolsa Família* (Family Fund). Modeled partly on a similar scheme in Mexico, this fund is the largest anti-poverty program of its kind in the world. Eleven million families now participate in the program. The plan has been so successful that a refined version was recently tried in New York City. This is how it works. If a family earns less than 120 reais ($68) per month, mothers receive up to 95 reais with the proviso that their children attend school and participate in the government's vaccination programs. Each beneficiary receives a debit card, which is charged every month as long as the conditions of the program are met. If the family fails to comply, the stipend stops.

Brazilians want American goods in their shopping malls. Consumers clamor for the same products that do well in American stores, except for cold weather gear. Vibrant import markets include virtually all healthcare products, education supplies (including textbooks), electronic appliances, and American designer clothes. If Brazilian shoppers can't find the American products they want in the mall, they turn to a very large, very active underground economy. The best commercial/industrial product lines for export to Brazil are: (1) computer software, especially programs related to internet security, education, and telecommunications, (2) medical equipment, especially radiological and diagnostic imaging equipment, laboratory equipment, dental equipment and supplies, implants and components, and disposables, (3) safety and security equipment, (4) pharmaceuticals, (5) electric power equipment and supplies, and (6) construction equipment and parts.

Trade shows are the best way to enter a new market in Brazil. Many trade shows are offered throughout the year in all major cities. You will need a Brazilian partner, however. Joint ventures are very popular, although you can get by with a local sales representative or distributor. Brazil's business culture is based on personal relationships. If you don't have an in-country presence, at least a sales office, you will not be able to communicate personally with bureaucrats, customers, and suppliers. By all means, open a sales office and, if possible, form a joint venture with your representative or distributor. This will show Brazilians that you are a permanent fixture in the business community and not merely another American company testing the waters

Although no one can dispute that Brazil offers the largest and most varied markets in Latin America, there are also some negatives you need to recognize. The local business base is firmly entrenched. Competition from U.S. and European companies as well as from a thriving underground economy is fierce. Markets in São Paulo, Rio de Janeiro, Recife, Fortaleza, and other metropolitan areas are very dissimilar. Urban markets differ from rural markets. The country's commercial laws are changing so rapidly that it's difficult to plan anything.

Corruption in government seems to be increasing. In 2006, Transparência Brasil (www.transparencia.org.br) reported that nearly 20 percent of congressional representatives in the lower house were implicated in either a cash for votes scandal or a scheme to buy overpriced ambulances (ambulances?). The report also claims that 39 percent of the 496 members of this lower house face legal proceedings.

Rural Brazilians continue to migrate to the cities causing, among other ills, a large base of unemployed, unskilled workers, which adds to one of the most unequal distributions of wealth in the world. This results in significant crime, drug abuse, health epidemics, and poor public education. Brazil also suffers from appreciable environmental degradation, especially in its rain forest, although the government has now passed legislation to control logging. See Statistical Facts for Brazil's summarized statistics.

STATISTICAL FACTS

Ease of doing business (out of 178 countries)	122nd
GDP per capita (PPP)	$8,600
Population	188.1 million
Inflation rate	4.2%
Unemployment rate	9.6%
Global competitiveness index world ranking (out of 122 countries)	66th
Business competitiveness index world ranking (out of 116 countries)	49th
Total crimes per 1,000 population	N/A
Corruption perception index score world ranking (out of 179 countries) (10 is squeaky clean, zero is awful)	3.6
Internet users	25.9 million
Percent of population living on less than $2 per day	21.2%
Working healthcare system index world ranking (out of 190 countries)	125th
U.S. exports	$19.2 billion

In the ease of doing business ranking, Brazil was 122nd out of 178 countries surveyed. In all of Latin America, only Venezuela, which ranked 172nd, has more onerous government regulations to deal with. But the business competitiveness ranking, which includes nonregulatory factors, puts Brazil in the 49th slot, which is about average. The corruption score of 3.6 is not good and indicates one of the more onerous problems facing U.S. exporters.

Nearly 40 million Brazilians live on less than $2 per day in the slums of large cities and in the rural north and west. Many rural dwellers are indigenous and will probably not rise above this level for many years to come. Therefore, they should be excluded from your country analysis. Moreover, the nation's healthcare system is barely working, holding a rank of 125th out of 190 countries. Although a pitiful statistic for the citizens of this great country, it rings dollar signs for U.S. exporters of medical equipment and supplies and pharmaceuticals. Brazil's size makes it a tempting morsel. Such large markets encourage U.S. companies to continue exporting to this country and investing in its commercial/industrial base, despite the many barriers they encounter.

MEXICO

NAFTA gave Mexico a new lease on life. Imports from the United States skyrocketed in 2006 to a whopping $134 billion. In fact, the United States now accounts for 75 percent of Mexico's total trade, making this country the second largest trading partner of the United States, after Canada. Many reforms aimed at increasing the transparency and accountability of the Mexican government have been pushed through in the last five years.

The maquiladora industry has thousands of assembly plants near the U.S. border, producing assemblies for export back to the United States. A large number of U.S. companies find these maquiladoras an excellent way to produce goods at a much lower labor cost than in the States without incurring long-distance shipping costs. And with NAFTA reduced tariffs, the movement of goods back and forth across the border is easily and economically accomplished.

If you're considering Mexico remember that this is a huge country has many different regions. Each region—north, south, tourist centers, rural areas, and bordering states—has entirely different needs for products and services. My best advice is go to Mexico, not once, but several times. Visit the various regions. Do abbreviated country surveys in each region. Talk to the AmCham offices and U.S. Commercial Service personnel in each region. You may be surprised that Mexico's many diverse regions make it seem like you're dealing with several separate countries.

There is no list of best products for export to Mexico. Indeed, the diverse markets in this large country demand everything that Americans buy in our supermarkets and shopping malls. Be aware, however, that Mexicans are very price conscious and appreciate good service. Take your time learning the ways of this vast country, and before long, you'll be doing business like a native.

The education system cries out for U.S. goods and services. Mexico is the most populous Spanish speaking country in the world and the second most populous country in Latin America after Brazil. About 70 percent of its nonindigenous citizens live in urban areas. One result of this demographic is that the Mexican government has given education its highest priority, significantly increasing the education budget each year for several years running.

In fact, education expenditures rose more than 25 percent over the last decade. See Statistical Facts for Mexico's summarized statistics.

		STATISTICAL FACTS
Ease of doing business (out of 178 countries)	44th	
GDP per capita (PPP)	$10,600	
Population	107.5 million	
Inflation rate	3.4%	
Unemployment rate	3.2%	
Global competitiveness index world ranking (out of 122 countries)	58th	
Business competitiveness index world ranking (out of 116 countries)	60th	
Total crimes per 1,000 population	14.3	
Corruption perception index score world ranking (out of 179 countries) (10 is squeaky clean, zero is awful)	3.6	
Internet users	18.6 million	
Percent of population living on less than $2 per day	11.6%	
Working healthcare system index world ranking (out of 190 countries)	61st	
U.S. exports	$133.9 billion	

As the ease of doing business and the business competitiveness rankings indicate, doing business in Mexico is fairly easy. If you take your time, establish personal relationships, and pay attention to your competition, you should do all right. A corruption perception score of 3.6 is not great; however, corruption shouldn't cause you too many headaches as long as you're aware of its presence. Also, the high number of internet users makes e-commerce a viable alternative for in-country marketing.

On the downside, almost 12 percent of Mexicans live on less than $2 per day. This is a catastrophe. Clearly, the government hasn't paid enough attention to this large segment of the population, especially to the 30 million indigenous peoples.

ARGENTINA

Yes, Argentines speak Spanish, but that's about the only thing they have in common with the rest of Latin America. Historically, Argentina became home to thousands of European émigrés before, during, and after World War II.

These émigrés brought their European cultures along, and Argentina became a melting pot, much like the United States. This, plus a long line of dictators, has left Argentina with a complex culture and business community. Doing business there is not easy. It's certainly less complex than in Brazil but more difficult than in Colombia, Chile, or Mexico. On the plus side, Argentine consumers are probably the most sophisticated in Latin America and the infrastructure is in pretty good shape. European traditions predominate and influence product design, advertising, and sales promotions.

Some of the hottest consumer exports to Argentina are sports oriented and include equipment, clothing, and accessories for soccer, water polo, horse racing, backpacking, yachting, and water sports. American made computers, peripherals, software, and state-of-the-art electronic appliances are also in high demand. Drugs and healthcare supplies sell very well there, as they do throughout Latin America. Brand name apparel, fast food chains, physical fitness centers, compact discs, cellular phones, and all tourist related products also do well. The best commercial/industrial markets are telecommunications equipment and services, IT products and services, agriculture machinery and parts, medical equipment and supplies, and industrial chemicals.

There are also plenty of negatives to doing business in Argentina. Thanks to MERCOSUR, most imports from nonmember countries like the United States carry a common external tariff of up to 22 percent. Travel and shipping distances from the United States are very long. Local business cartels are hard to beat. And labor unions still have a high degree of control over both the workplace and the social fabric of the country.

Argentina is one of the strictest countries on imports in all of Latin America. Government regulations proliferate, and you need approval to import virtually anything. Such extensive government interference is the main reason Argentina ranks as low as it does in the ease of doing business index. See Statistical Facts for Argentina's summarized statistics.

STATISTICAL FACTS

Ease of doing business (out of 178 countries)	109th
GDP per capita (PPP)	$15,000
Population	39.9 million
Inflation rate	10.0%

Unemployment rate	10.2%
Global competitiveness index world ranking (out of 122 countries)	69th
Business competitiveness index world ranking (out of 116 countries)	64th
Total crimes per 1,000 population	N/A
Corruption perception index score world ranking (out of 179 countries) (10 is squeaky clean, zero is awful)	2.9
Internet users	10.0 million
Percent of population living on less than $2 per day	17.4%
Working healthcare system index world ranking (out of 190 countries)	75th
U.S. exports	$4.8 billion

With a ranking of 69th and 64th in the two competitive indexes, Argentina is a little worse than average. Although it has come down, an inflation rate of 10 percent is still much too high, making pricing especially difficult. The corruption index of 2.9 is bad, much worse than most other Latin countries, and it prevents foreign exporters and investors from making straightforward business deals. The poverty rate is also unacceptable with 17 percent of Argentines living on less than $2 per day. For a country with as sophisticated a business base as Argentina, this is very disappointing. On the plus side, with one out of four Argentines using the internet, e-commerce might be a viable alternative sales strategy.

Local sales representatives or distributors are the way to go. The business community is based on personal relationships, and you certainly cannot be in-country all the time. However, you must take the time to be there and socialize with your representatives and distributors, not once, but several times during the year. Doing business in Argentina requires a very high level of participation by a U.S. exporter, including a lot of research, preparation, and personal involvement.

CHILE

Chile is the darling of many U.S. companies because it offers far and away the most open markets and is the farthest along out of all Latin American countries in its economic reforms. Regulations are easy to comply with, and as a beginning exporter, you will find Chile a relatively easy place to cut your teeth. You do need a local presence, however, either a distributor or a partner. Consumer tastes run pro-American. Shopping malls are very popular. And credit card use is increasing daily. Chile's markets are growing fast, and its consumers are avid shoppers. Chileans are relatively well-educated, at least those who live in the cities. Its political climate remains as stable as any in the region, and its corruption perception score is the best in Latin America. Chile and the United States have a free trade agreement that allows U.S. companies to export to Chile with low or no tariffs.

The biggest problem faced by new U.S. exporters to Chile is competition, not only from in-country businesses, but also from European, Asian, and U.S. companies. Hundreds of U.S. companies have already taken advantage of Chile's open business climate and are vigorously pursuing increased shares of various markets.

I believe that everyone who has done business in this country would agree that the key to success is finding a Chilean partner with the right connections. A Chilean sales representative or distributor can open government doors and make the business and social connections necessary to move your products smoothly and efficiently to market. See Statistical Facts for Chile's summarized statistics.

STATISTICAL FACTS	
Ease of doing business (out of 178 countries)	33rd
GDP per capita (PPP)	$12,600
Population	16.1 million
Inflation rate	2.1%
Unemployment rate	8.3%
Global competitiveness index world ranking (out of 122 countries)	27th
Business competitiveness index world ranking (out of 116 countries)	29th
Total crimes per 1,000 population	N/A
Corruption perception index score world ranking (out of 179 countries) (10 is squeaky clean, zero is awful)	7.3
Internet users	6.7 million
Percent of population living on less than $2 per day	5.6%
Working healthcare system index world ranking (out of 190 countries)	33rd
U.S. exports	$6.7 billion

Chile's rank of 33rd in the ease of doing business index is the best in Latin America. Chile is also ranked high in global competitiveness (27th), business competitiveness (29th), and healthcare system (33rd). The fact that 5 percent of the population lives in extreme poverty indicates that the government has its work cut out to increase jobs and income for the lower class. You will also find that marine shipping routes from the United States are very long and that Chile's geography makes reaching markets other than Santiago difficult. For the record, this long, thin country is 4,000 miles long and 100 miles wide.

Chileans are modern consumers, demanding a wide range of imports, especially goods made in America. The list includes but is certainly not limited to cosmetics, women's work and dress clothes, leather goods, dried and frozen foods, low priced toys, furniture of all types, healthcare and personal care products, electronic and electric appliances, personal security and safety devices, costume jewelry, and sporting equipment and accessories. According to the U.S. Commercial Service, the best commercial and industrial products for export to Chile are computer hardware and software, food processing and packaging equipment, medical equipment, construction equipment, and mining equipment.

COLOMBIA

Colombia is the third most populous country in Latin America after Brazil and Mexico. Thirty cities are each home to 100,000 or more citizens. Unlike the rest of Latin America, Colombia has not suffered any dramatic economic collapses or fiscal panics. It boasts a stable government and close business ties to the United States.

Nevertheless, Colombia tends to be overlooked by U.S. companies because of the extensive publicity given to gangland type killings, nefarious drug trafficking, and kidnappings. Fortunately, these activities only occasionally touch foreigners. With recent changes in trade and foreign direct investment laws and the potential of a new free trade agreement with the United States, opportunities in Colombia for smaller U.S. companies look promising. Upper- and middle-class markets are expanding rapidly. U.S. dollars are in plentiful supply to pay for American imports. Shipping distances from the United States are not much greater than to Trinidad and Tobago or Panama. And Colombia continues to be the most fiscally sound country in the region.

But there are risks. Cartels or *sindicatos* flourish. (Sindicatos are firms linked through a tight web of cross holdings, in the same vein as the Japanese *keiretsu*.) Thirty-five percent of Colombia population live in rural areas with incomes too low to purchase imported goods. Travel and shipping lanes among the six urban centers can be difficult to navigate. And, although the government encourages foreign trade, Colombian consumers are not yet totally sold on American made goods in preference to locally produced products.

Although Colombia's population of 46 million is greater than that of Argentina's, consumer markets have not traditionally been favorite targets of U.S. exporters. But regional pressures to open the economy are causing this to change. The best prospects for consumer exports include automotive parts and accessories; healthcare and personal care products; processed foods; computers, peripherals, and software; cellular phones; travel and tourism products and services; and dress apparel. The best prospects for commercial/industrial products and services are information technology products and services, oil and gas machinery and services, plastic materials and supplies, construction and mining equipment and supplies, electric power systems, and processed food packaging equipment.

Several major projects that will require foreign direct investment and imported goods and services are in the works. The following is a very abbreviated list: road, port, and airport construction; oil and gas exploration; railways; water treatment and supply facilities; electric power generation; mass transit systems; security and defense products and services. The government is the main customer for these projects, and to sell to the government, you must have a local presence or an agent who can legally bind your company to contracts. This is a very dangerous strategy unless you also have your own supervisor on the premises.

Colombians demand efficient after-sales customer service. If you don't warrant your products, do not go to Colombia. See Statistical Facts for Columbia's summarized statistics.

Ease of doing business (out of 178 countries)	66th
GDP per capita (PPP)	$8,400
Population	43.6 million
Inflation rate	4.3%
Unemployment rate	11.1%
Global competitiveness index world ranking (out of 122 countries)	65th
Business competitiveness index world ranking (out of 116 countries)	56th
Total crimes per 1,000 population	5.0
Corruption perception index score world ranking (out of 179 countries) (10 is squeaky clean, zero is awful)	3.8
Internet users	4.7 million
Percent of population living on less than $2 per day	17.8%
Working healthcare system index world ranking (out of 190 countries)	22nd
U.S. exports	$6.7 billion

Colombia's ranking of 66th on the ease of doing business scale speaks well for the changes that have occurred in the business community during the last 10 years. When gangs of thugs roamed the roads and city streets and drug lords ruled the day, doing business in Colombia was anything but easy. Now that has changed. The business community is flourishing and the government did what had to be done to get the gangs under control. Colombia's global competitiveness (65th) and business competitiveness (56th) are about average. However, its healthcare system is the best in the region. That's a lot of positives for a country that was all but written off by American business several times in the past.

DOMINICAN REPUBLIC

The Dominican Republic (fondly referred to as the DR) has by far the largest population of the Caribbean nations and is the second most heavily populated country between Mexico and South America. (Guatemala tops the list.) The nation's primary industries are tourism, which accounts for 48 percent of its GDP, and agriculture, which employs 40 percent of the total workforce.

But the DR is also the Caribbean home of more than 400 American, European, South American, and Asian businesses, most of which are engaged in the assembly of apparel, footwear, and electronics. Nearly all of the plants are located in export processing zones, the Dominican Republic's version of duty-free foreign trade zones. The DR is also a participant in the DR-CAFTA free trade agreement. See Statistical Facts for the Dominican Republic's summarized statistics.

STATISTICAL FACTS

Ease of doing business (out of 178 countries)	99th
GDP per capita (PPP)	$8,000
Population	9.2 million
Inflation rate	8.2%
Unemployment rate	16.0%
Global competitiveness index world ranking (out of 122 countries)	82nd
Business competitiveness index world ranking (out of 116 countries)	101st
Total crimes per 1,000 population	N/A
Corruption perception index score world ranking (out of 179 countries) (10 is squeaky clean, zero is awful)	3.0
Internet users	0.9 million
Percent of population living on less than $2 per day	16.2%
Working healthcare system index world ranking (out of 190 countries)	51st
U.S. exports	$5.4 billion

This country is worth looking at if you are interested in establishing a maquila plant. It is also a good export bet if your products or services relate in any way to the tourism industry, including construction equipment and building products needed to build resorts and roads. In 2006, 232,000 tourists visited the DR, of which more than 90 percent were Americans. Recently, the DR has seen about a 5 percent increase in visitors each year.

The products most needed to supply the booming tourist industry are air travel and ground transportation products, parts, and services; car rentals and auto parts; and everything used in hotels from napkins to food, from liquor to table cloths, and from bar soap to kitchen equipment. Products to build and maintain amusement and theme parks are also in high demand. Convention facilities, visitor bureau services, wholesale travel products and services, and just about anything you can imagine that tourists need or want will do well there. You don't have to use representatives and distributors in the Dominican Republic, but it's a good idea.

The first time I did business in the DR 38 years ago everyone used backup generators because electricity would shut off four to five times a day. Nothing changes. Today, the DR still has the most unreliable electric power system in all of Latin America. Most businesses and many homes continue to use backup generators, which creates another interesting market. More than a million Dominicans live in the United States, so its not surprising that consumer tastes run the same as Americans, and 70 percent of imported goods come from the States.

The Dominican government, law enforcement, and the business community are rife with corruption, as the score of 3.0 indicates. Bribery and influence peddling are major headaches across all markets throughout the country. Such a culture of corruption, when coupled with a high poverty and unemployment rate, gives birth to vicious street gangs, especially in and around Santo Domingo and causes a severe social dilemma for the government and the business community.

PERU

Peru's economy is one of the most dynamic in Latin America. Market reforms and privatizations, along with a relatively stable banking system, have enabled this country to progress as fast or faster than most other Latin countries. According to International Trade Administration standards, Peru's economy is well managed. Now with better tax collections and sustained growth, the government has begun to realize significantly greater revenue flows. This country is three times the size of California, home to 26 million people, and the fifth largest country in Latin America, behind Brazil, Mexico, Colombia, and Argentina. American goods are welcomed at Lima's shopping malls, provided they offer high-quality, competitive prices, and a wide selection.

Clothing of all types, jewelry, cosmetics, electronics, processed foods, pet foods, computers, healthcare products, and anything having to do with music are especially well received.

Both the public sector and the private sector desperately need American industrial goods. In 2005, the U.S.–Peru Free Trade Agreement was negotiated and has now been ratified. This opened Peru's borders to even more trade and FDI than the country previously enjoyed. Although most Peruvian markets are fairly small, they are worth looking at.

Strategic alliances with sales representatives or distributors will open the right bureaucratic and market doors. Also, it's imperative to retain an in-country attorney. Much of Peru's business community operates informally, and government bureaucracy can be a devil to break into. Unpredictable variations in distribution patterns, energy generation, media advertising, and transportation make it almost impossible to do business there without well-connected legal counsel. See Statistical Facts for Peru's summarized statistics.

STATISTICAL FACTS

Ease of doing business (out of 178 countries)	58th
GDP per capita (PPP)	$6,400
Population	28.3 million
Inflation rate	2.1%
Unemployment rate	7.2%
Global competitiveness index world ranking (out of 122 countries)	74th
Business competitiveness index world ranking (out of 116 countries)	81st
Total crimes per 1,000 population	N/A
Corruption perception index score world ranking (out of 179 countries) (10 is squeaky clean, zero is awful)	3.6
Internet users	4.6 million
Percent of population living on less than $2 per day	30.6%
Working healthcare system index world ranking (out of 190 countries)	129th
U.S. exports	$2.9 billion

A reasonably high ease of doing business ranking of 58th indicates that, although government regulations are relatively complex, they are not as onerous as in some other countries. Also, the business competitiveness ranking of 81st puts this nation squarely in the middle of those countries surveyed. The corruption rating of 3.6 could stand improvement, although it isn't a deal killer. The biggest negative is that more than 30 percent of the population lives on less than $2 per day. Since indigenous peoples represent

45 percent of the total population, one can assume that the bulk of the very poor are indigenous.

The government is facing strong social pressure to raise the living standards of the very poor. Fortunately, there does seem to be a light at the end of the tunnel. Economic reforms are beginning to work, creating a broader job base and greater funding for the education of the poverty stricken. But these positives are partially offset by seething ethnic and class resentments that deeply divide this Andean nation.

Most Peruvian markets are fairly small, but this could be a real advantage for smaller U.S. exporters. Without large markets, you can count on U.S. transnationals looking elsewhere for their profits.

TRINIDAD AND TOBAGO

Trinidad and Tobago (T&T), a two island nation located seven miles off the north coast of Venezuela, is a treasure trove of gas, mineral fuels, lubricants, and chemicals. Its GDP per capita (PPP) of $19,700 is the highest in the Caribbean. Reserves of oil and natural gas provide the foundation for a thriving economy, and best of all, the government welcomes foreign investment and foreign products.

This English-speaking nation has, by Caribbean standards, an excellent education system. A literacy rate of nearly 100 percent means its consumers and workforce meet the best modern day standards in Latin America. Oil production and refining and liquified natural gas are the main industries, although petrochemicals and steel are becoming increasingly important exports. Trinidad and Tobago is one of the world's leaders in the production of ammonia and methanol. Tourism is also a major industry, especially on Tobago. T&T has zero investment barriers and welcomes American FDI. And you do not need a local partner—although you may want one.

With strong cultural ties to the United States, T&T is an excellent starting point for beginning exporters. It boasts a legitimately elected democratic government, a respected rule of law, and a rapidly growing economy. See the Statistical Facts for Trinidad and Tobago's summarized statistics.

STATISTICAL FACTS

Ease of doing business (out of 178 countries)	67th
GDP per capita (PPP)	$19,700
Population	1.1 million
Inflation rate	8.0%
Unemployment rate	7.0%
Global competitiveness index world ranking (out of 122 countries)	67th
Business competitiveness index world ranking (out of 116 countries)	65th
Total crimes per 1,000 population	N/A
Corruption perception index score world ranking (out of 179 countries) (10 is squeaky clean, zero is awful)	3.2
Internet users	160,000
Percent of population living on less than $2 per day	39%
Working healthcare system index world ranking (out of 190 countries)	67th
U.S. exports	$1.6 billion

The best products for export to T&T are construction equipment and services, hotel and restaurant equipment and supplies, automotive parts and accessories, computer hardware and software, and petrochemical equipment, supplies, and services. Yes, markets are small, but the government is stable and financially prudent and the economy is on the upswing. Add in Tobago's tourist spots, and that's not a bad combination as an investment location for smaller U.S. companies.

CENTRAL AMERICA—COSTA RICA, EL SALVADOR, GUATEMALA

While its neighbors struggle for political and economic stability, Costa Rica stands like a beacon in the night as a shining example of how a tiny country can—with determination—withstand the winds of turmoil and become a model to be emulated by the rest of the Caribbean Basin. Unfortunately, as if to demonstrate that no country is immune from the drug scourge, modern day international narcotics traffickers have increasingly used the Costa Rican territory as a stopover between South America and the United States (although it isn't as severe a problem as it is in Guatemala). Costa Rica has a very small industrial base, so nearly all its commercial and industrial products must be imported. The best lines for U.S. exports are paper and paperboard products, agricultural chemicals, automobile parts and accessories, plastic materials and resins, information technology equipment and software, and telecommunications equipment and supplies.

El Salvador has the second most open economy in Latin America, surpassed only by Chile. It has small, dynamic markets and the most transparent business climate in Central America. There are virtually no import restrictions and the few tariffs that exist are being phased down to comply with the new DR-CAFTA trade agreement. This nation also has free trade agreements with Chile, Mexico, Dominican Republic, and Panama. The capitol of San Salvador is only a two-hour flight from Miami or Houston. Cross-border travel within Central America is very easy and relatively inexpensive. Using local representatives and distributors is the easiest way to open new Salvadoran markets. Fortunately, El Salvador is so small that a single representative based in San Salvador can easily cover the entire country.

Although El Salvador has easy market-entry requirements and a thriving, Americanized consumer base, the fact that 22 percent of the population lives on less than $2 per day bespeaks of underlying social problems. Corruption ranked at 4.2 is certainly manageable, but a street crime hangover from the violent 1980s won't go away. The nation's healthcare system is also very weak, lacking both doctors and modern hospital facilities. El Salvador has virtually no manufacturing, so nearly everything must be imported. However, markets for most industrial and commercial good are very small. Healthcare products, cosmetics, electronics, and virtually anything sold in the United States are good prospects, provided you can deal with small markets.

Guatemala is the largest Central American country. It is also a hotbed of U.S.-owned maquila factories. As part of DR-CAFTA, U.S. companies enjoy duty-free exports to this country. In fact, 50 percent of Guatemala's imports come from the United States. Americans can also expect a warm welcome from Guatemalans, many of whom travel to the States regularly. English is widely spoken in the business community.

Security concerns, corruption, workers' rights violations, and intellectual property piracy are the most serious barriers, along with an ineffective and bloated bureaucracy. Security is a major problem for foreigners. Muggings in Guatemala City, *banditos* who attack buses, trucks, and automobiles on the highways and gangs of soldiers who harass anyone they can find, all contribute to an inhospitable environment for visitors. Still, tourism is big business, especially in the old capital of Antigua and around the Mayan ruins hot spots—Tikal in the north and Copan just across the Honduran border in the south.

Practically all consumer products sold in the States do well there. However, the elite class tends to do its shopping in the U.S. The following for the combined summarized statistics of these three Central American countries.

STATISTICAL FACTS

	Costa Rica	El Salvador	Guatemala
Ease of doing business (out of 178 countries)	115th	69th	114th
GDP per capita (PPP)	$12,000	$5,200	$5,400
Population	4.1 million	6.9 million	12.8 million
Inflation rate	12.1%	4.3%	6.6%
Unemployment rate	6.6%	6.2%	3.2%
Global competitiveness index world ranking (out of 122 countries)	53rd	61st	75th
Total crimes per 1,000 population	12.0	N/A	N/A
Corruption perception index score world ranking (out of 179 countries) (10 is squeaky clean, zero is awful)	N/A	N/A	2.6
Internet users	1.0 million	737,000	756,000
Percent of population living on less than $2 per day	9.8%	N/A	31.9%
Working healthcare system index world ranking (out of 190 countries)	36th	N/A	78th
U.S. exports	$4.1 billion	$2.1 billion	$3.5 billion

For small exporters, any Central American country might be a good first step. The governments are relatively stable, American goods are in demand, most business people know enough English to get by, consumers are fairly sophisticated, and with a few exceptions, all of these countries are easy to do business in. Moreover, the rest of Latin America is a lot closer than Europe, the Middle East, or Asia.

CONCLUSION

Latin America's turbulent past has created a surfeit of market risks that must be recognized and dealt with by any foreign company wishing to do business in this region. Market risks in a specific country or a particular region or city within that country are not always transparent, however. While some conditions are glaringly obvious, others are more subtle. Hopefully the preceding discussions will help you decide where to focus your efforts. I'll leave you with four points to keep in mind when you develop your Latin American marketing strategies:

1. During your country survey, dig deep enough to uncover the unique characteristics of each country.
2. Although middle-class consumers may not be as sophisticated and demanding as those from the upper class, they still want high-quality goods at reasonable prices.
3. Host country producers, underground market dealers, and European and Asian companies all offer stiff competition.
4. A wide range of political, social, and economic forces that are not encountered in U.S. markets, may, in the end, separate those marketing policies that will work from those that will not work.

chapter seven
Market Opportunities in Russia and Eastern Europe

ALTHOUGH U.S. COMPANIES DO NOT EXPORT MUCH TO ANY EASTERN European market, Russia is clearly the winner with $4.7 billion. All the other countries combined only receive $6.6 billion in U.S. exports. Most exports to Russia as well as to Poland the Czech Republic, Hungary, and the rest come from Western European companies, making the competition for these growing markets very intense. Still, opportunities do exist for smaller U.S. companies, and you shouldn't be dissuaded merely because of history.

The countries in this region comprise three separate and very distinct markets: Russia, first tier countries, and second tier countries. Of the non-Russian countries, Poland, Hungary, and the Czech Republic are considered first tier and have the most dynamic economies. Poland, with several very vibrant cities and manufacturing and shipbuilding bases rehabilitated after years of decay, is fighting hard to be taken seriously as a modern day economy. The Czech Republic, a heavily manufacturing-oriented economy that needs a whole list of industrial products, is also a viable destination for American products. Hungary was one of the first Eastern European countries to shine after the fall of communism and welcomes U.S. products, management know-how, and advanced technology. Remember, each of these countries was well on its way to becoming a modern day nation when first the Nazis invaded and then the communists took over.

Romania, Bulgaria, Turkey, and the tiny Baltic states comprise a second tier of Eastern European countries. Romania boasts one of the largest populations in the region and is beginning to emerge from its cocoon of social and environmental devastation under a viciously insensitive government. It needs everything imaginable for rebuilding factories and infrastructures. Consumers are also receptive to many American made goods. Bulgaria, often overlooked as just another misbegotten Balkan country, shows signs of awakening to advanced technology imports and services as well as replacements for worn-out, Soviet-era factories and equipment. And Turkey, the biggest country in the region, has opened its door to American imports in support of an increasingly sophisticated consumer base.

RUSSIA

The Russian bear stands alone as the largest, most varied market in Eastern Europe and one of the more difficult ones in which to do business. Without question, U.S. companies will find the widest range of opportunities in this huge country, provided they have the resources and product lines to compete against European and Asian transnationals. Although the Russian landscape was severely denigrated under the Soviet Union, this period also saw the advent of substantial investment in manufacturing, engineering, and science. Don't forget—Russia was the first to put a man into space. The great distance from the United States and many Russian markets does present a significant challenge, however. You might be better off tackling smaller markets first.

The economy still relies heavily on natural resources, mainly extractive industries, such as oil, timber, precious metals, steel, and nonferrous metals, which account for about 80 percent of all Russian exports. This is despite the government's intense effort to get its manufacturing base moving. At one time under the Soviet Union, Russian factories buzzed with output. But they wore out and, now, most are ready for the scrap heap.

Internally, the economy is gathering steam, backed by a multi-year trend of consumer spending and a construction boom. Although Moscow and St. Petersburg have benefited most from this surge, both construction and spending seem to be spreading to smaller regional centers, too. Strong competition from major European and Asian companies that have done business in Russia for many decades filters through most industries, so be on the lookout for collusive arrangements and stiff price competition. On the plus side, Russian consumers love Western products—especially American goods; however, they are very price conscious and expect reasonable after-sales service, too.

The main barriers to market-entry are (1) the extreme distance from the United States to the major markets and (2) the continued erratic transition from a communist planned economy to a market oriented one. Success depends to a large extent on your local partner. You must have a physical presence in Russia—an office, a warehouse, a retail store, or a manufacturing plant. It's impossible to do business there without one. I strongly suggest forming a joint venture with a local partner already established in the Russian business community. Unfortunately, finding a Russian partner who understands Western business practices and accounting is very difficult. Finding one who speaks English is even harder. Try the U.S. Commercial Service at the U.S. Embassy or the American Chamber of Commerce, both in Moscow. Personnel in both of those organizations should be able to point you in the right direction. Incidentally, the Moscow AmCham office has more than 800 members, which tells you that a lot of American companies have a local presence there.

Any Russian venture must be considered a long-term commitment, whether you set up a facility there or stick to exporting. It always takes a while to catch on to the Russian way of doing things, which in many respects, is the exact opposite of the American way. See Statistical Facts for Russia's summarized statistics.

STATISTICAL FACTS

Ease of doing business index world ranking (out of 178 countries)	106th
GDP per capita (PPP)	$12,100
Population	142.9 million
Inflation rate	9.8%
Unemployment rate	6.6%
Global competitiveness index world ranking (out of 122 countries)	62nd
Business competitiveness index world ranking (out of 116 countries)	74th
Total crimes per 1,000 population	20.5
Corruption perception index score world ranking (out of 179 countries) (10 is squeaky clean, zero is awful)	2.3
Internet users	23.7 million
Percent of population living on less than $2 per day	12.2%
Working healthcare system index world ranking (out of 190 countries)	130th
U.S. exports	$4.7 billion

A ranking of 106th out of 178 countries in the ease of doing business index shows how difficult Russia's convoluted business regulations are. This is a major barrier, especially for smaller companies without clout. The corruption score of 2.3 is abominable. Such a high level of corruption makes doing business in any straightforward way impossible. Everyone has his hand out, and you can't get anything done without dispensing a pocket full of rubles. Inflation of nearly 10 percent is very high, making prices fluid and subject to constant change. Compared with the other Eastern European countries, Russia's GDP per capita of $12,100 is low, reflecting the millions of Russians in rural areas, especially in the north, who live below the poverty level. Also, be alert to organized crime. The Russian Mafia has its tentacles in companies of various sizes in many industries. You can't do much about this. However, if you sense that you may be running into one of these gangs, let your partner handle it. The Russia Mafia is not to be toyed with.

Intense competition from very large European and Asian transnationals as well as an increasing number of U.S. companies, most of which have production facilities on Russian soil, makes breaking into these markets a definite challenge for smaller U.S. companies. This doesn't mean you can't do it. It just means you will have to be more astute in choosing a local partner—one with clout in Moscow—and in structuring your marketing plan to compensate for a widely dispersed customer base. But it can be done, and with the Russian economy growing at a fairly good clip, these markets may seem too tempting to pass up. Some of the best market-entry product lines are industrial, with a few consumer goods thrown in, as in the following:

	Market Size ($ millions)	U.S. Imports ($ millions)
Telecommunications equipment and services	28.00	0
Construction equipment/building products	11.50	0.70
Drugs and pharmaceuticals	9.15	0.50
Auto and truck parts	6.50	0.85
Agricultural machinery	2.46	0.25
Medical equipment and supplies	2.50	0.35

As you can see, exports from U.S. companies represent only a small percentage of each market. However, if you can live with a small market share in the beginning, chances are good that you could make some money over time.

I would be remiss if I didn't comment on the political winds that seem to be blowing across this vast nation. Russian President Vladimir Putin of the ex-KGB appears to be leading his country down a dangerous path, reverting to many Cold War tactics internally as well as in relations with the West. I don't pretend to be an insider, privy to Russia's political machinations; however, I do have Russian friends and business contacts in Moscow and St. Petersburg who have experiences and opinions that indicate a dark shadow hovering over future U.S.–Russia relations. None of my contacts will talk about this subject on the phone, some are afraid to use e-mail.

I am told that harassment from the police and minor bureaucrats—many of whom served in the intelligence community in one facet or another—is increasing. I am told that the clutches of the Kremlin seem to be getting tighter with each passing week. I am told that the fear of being imprisoned for a minor offense or even no offense—a practice thought to have been eradicated after the end of the Cold War—is back in all its horror. I am told that inflation is much worse than the official line admits, eating away at earnings. And I am told that an increasing number of working people believe that the return of Cold War methods is inevitable. When considering doing business in Russia, ask around, visit the country, and talk to Westerners who do business there now. If Russia is indeed heading down the Cold War road, you may want to reconsider your market strategy.

On the other hand, perhaps these signs have been interpreted incorrectly. Perhaps what these folks see is merely a strong central government. Perhaps Russia is, in fact, moving more toward a Westernization of market policies with a government learning as it goes, instead of retreating toward a renewed Cold War. Perhaps harassment is mistaken for concern by the authorities for the welfare of working Russians. You decide the correct interpretation. At least one Western reporter, Edward Lucas who writes for *The Economist*, professes the same concerns as my contacts in his book *The New Cold War: Putin's Russia and the Threat to the West*. Even if you don't believe that the internal and external maneuvering by Russian politicians points to a renewed Cold War, I strongly recommend this book as an example of enlightened reporting.

POLAND

A country of 38 million citizens, Poland joined the European Union in 2004. It has an extraordinarily close relationship with the United States, contributing troops to UN-approved and U.S.-led military incursions. EU and local companies offer very strong competition, allowing U.S. companies only 3 percent of Poland's total imports. However, excellent opportunities do exist, especially for smaller companies serving niche markets. To seriously compete in Polish markets, you must have a local presence. Although pricing is the most critical competitive factor, a local distributor must be available to provide prompt after-sales service and competitive prices. Moreover, since financing is hard to come by, commercial customers usually need financial help. See Statistical Facts for Poland's summarized statistics.

		STATISTICAL FACTS
Ease of doing business (out of 178 countries)	74th	
GDP per capita (PPP)	$14,100	
Population	38.5 million	
Inflation rate	1.3%	
Unemployment rate	14.9%	
Global competitiveness index world ranking (out of 122 countries)	48th	
Business competitiveness index world ranking (out of 116 countries)	42nd	
Total crimes per 1,000 population	32.9	
Corruption perception index score world ranking (out of 179 countries) (10 is squeaky clean, zero is awful)	4.2	
Internet users	10.6 million	
Percent of population living on less than $2 per day	N/A	
Working healthcare system index world ranking (out of 190 countries)	50th	
U.S. exports	$2.0 billion	

Poland's regulatory ease of doing business ranking is about midway relative to other countries. This should not scare anyone off, although it isn't as good as it could be. The Polish government is still working to reduce the regulatory burden, some of which holds over from communist days. The GDP per capita of $14,100 is certainly adequate to provide a reasonably solid consumer market, and an inflation of 1.3 percent is remarkably low. Although total U.S. exports to Poland are relatively small, this is a vibrant economy with over 10 million internet users (nearly one-third of the population).

America is the third largest foreign direct investor in Poland. Strong sales opportunities exist in aerospace, automotive products, environmental technologies, safety/security products, defense equipment, IT products and services, financial services, and a whole flock of consumer goods. Poles love American products. Because Polish citizens have good educations and a definite knack for languages, this country has become a significant player in the business processing center industry, including call centers, back office operations, and research centers. Wage rates are the lowest in the region. The state still controls nearly one-third of the economy, mainly in the chemicals, shipbuilding, and minerals extraction industries.

About 25 percent of Poles live in rural areas. As in most countries, these folks are a lot poorer than their city cousins and have less purchasing power.

In fact, the rural landscape is dotted with one factory towns, a holdover from pre-communist and communist days. Unemployment is particularly high in these areas.

HUNGARY

Hungary is about one-third the size of Poland and also joined the EU in 2004. The United States is the fourth largest foreign investor, behind Germany, Austria, and the Netherlands, investing more than $9 billion in the Hungarian economy. FDI has been an extremely important factor in Hungary's economic growth. Originally, foreign firms invested in manufacturing companies, most of which had been state run and were in a dilapidated condition. U.S. and EU firms upgraded these factories and installed modern production methods. Now foreign firms are investing in business processing centers, much like they are in Poland. Budapest has become a leading center for this service industry. As with other Eastern European countries, U.S. exports are dwarfed by those from EU countries and, recently, Asia. However, the smaller size of Hungary's markets and the definite attraction for U.S. technology and products makes these markets very viable for exports from smaller U.S. firms. See Statistical Facts for Hungry's summarized statistics.

STATISTICAL FACTS

Ease of doing business (out of 178 countries)	45th
GDP per capita (PPP)	$17,200
Population	10.0 million
Inflation rate	4.7%
Unemployment rate	7.4%
Global competitiveness index world ranking (out of 122 countries)	41st
Business competitiveness index world ranking (out of 116 countries)	34th
Total crimes per 1,000 population	45.0
Corruption perception index score world ranking (out of 179 countries) (10 is squeaky clean, zero is awful)	5.3
Internet users	3.1 million
Percent of population living on less than $2 per day	N/A
Working healthcare system index world ranking (out of 190 countries)	66th
U.S. exports	$1.2 billion

Trying to do business in Hungary without a local presence is almost impossible. The language is very difficult to learn, Hungarian purchasing habits lean toward one-on-one relationships, and transportation within the country is, at best, medieval. You need a local partner to manage these hurdles. The ease of doing business there is about the same as in Poland and the Czech Republic. Not easy, but not impossible. Hungarian crime statistics are not encouraging, however. Forty-five crimes per 1,000 persons is a high ratio. Also, a convoluted tax structure eats away at profits. To conform to EU requirements, Hungary boosted its tax rates well beyond the original 16 percent. To that a 20 percent national value-added tax and municipal levies from Hungary's cities and towns must be added.

Competition in Hungary is fierce, both from EU companies and from local Hungarian firms. Many well-known American companies operate there. General Motors, IBM, AIG, Dow, Citibank, Ernst & Young, AES, Coca-Cola, PepsiCo, Procter & Gamble, Sara Lee, ExxonMobil, and Morgan Stanley are a few major transnationals with a local presence. This should give you some idea of how successful U.S. companies have been. And if they can do it, so can you.

Hungary is a good place to do business. It has a low overall cost structure and low labor rates. Information technology and healthcare are two of the most lucrative industries. Automotive parts, biotechnology products and services, computer software, education supplies, pollution control equipment, and call centers are the hottest sectors for U.S. companies.

CZECH REPUBLIC

Entering the EU in 2004, along with Poland and Hungary, the Czech Republic is known as the Detroit of Europe because of its very large automobile industry. Many models are made there including Škoda and Tatra, which are sold all over the world. Moreover, Prague is one of the world's premier tourist destinations with new hotels springing up in several parts of the city to compete with the older, more traditional ones. For U.S. companies who sell to the hotel and other tourist industries, the Czech Republic offers several good markets.

Intense competition from close relationships with EU companies, especially German ones, plus a fair amount of corruption in government pro-

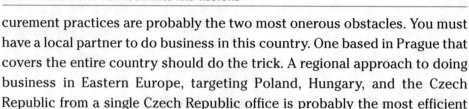

curement practices are probably the two most onerous obstacles. You must have a local partner to do business in this country. One based in Prague that covers the entire country should do the trick. A regional approach to doing business in Eastern Europe, targeting Poland, Hungary, and the Czech Republic from a single Czech Republic office is probably the most efficient way to tap markets in all three countries.

Business in the Czech Republic is very personal. One-on-one relationships must be established with customers, distributors, and to a lesser extent, government bureaucrats. In Prague, everyone seems to know everyone else. See Statistical Facts for the Czech Republic's summarized statistics.

STATISTICAL FACTS

Ease of doing business (out of 178 countries)	56th
GDP per capita (PPP)	$21,600
Population	10.2 million
Inflation rate	2.7%
Unemployment rate	8.4%
Global competitiveness index world ranking (out of 122 countries)	29th
Business competitiveness index world ranking (out of 116 countries)	27th
Total crimes per 1,000 population	38.2
Corruption perception index score world ranking (out of 179 countries) (10 is squeaky clean, zero is awful)	5.2
Internet users	5.1 million
Percent of population living on less than $2 per day	N/A
Working healthcare system index world ranking (out of 190 countries)	48th
U.S. exports	$1.1 billion

Direct marketing proves very effective for certain products. Avon, Amway, Lux, Mary Kay, Poriflame, Tupperware, Vorwerk, and WS International all do well there. Ninety-six percent of the 200,000 registered direct marketing dealers are women. That says something about the type of products suitable for direct marketing in this country.

The ease of doing business ranking of 56th closely matches that of Poland and Hungary. Indeed, all three countries are ranked very similarly in several surveys. The internet is big in the Czech Republic, with 50 percent of the population having access. Although U.S. companies do not export large quantities to these markets, they have made substantial FDI over the last 15 years and are a major presence. And American style supermarkets and shopping malls are taking over from the traditional small shops lining the narrow streets of Prague.

The key product lines to consider for export to the Czech Republic are automotive parts and accessories, electronic components, and medical equipment. Be aware, however, that although 65 percent of all medical equipment is imported, Germany dominates this market. Still, good markets exist for imports of dental equipment, catheters, x-ray and mammography systems, edoscopes, and so on. The IT and telecom markets are also growing rapidly. If you have products that serve niche markets, such as voice service equipment, network equipment, video conferencing, and wireless equipment, you should do well. Major players in the IT and telecom markets include Oracle, Microsoft, Hewlett-Packard, IBM, Sun Microsystems, Unisys, Novell, Symantec, and Citrix, to mention only a handful of American companies.

SLOVAKIA

Slovakia is the other half of the old Czechoslovakia. The economy is increasingly dominated by the automotive, electronics, engineering, and tourism industries. Slovak plants make Volkswagens and Audi SUVs for export to the United States and other countries. The government is very business friendly and welcomes foreign made products and foreign companies looking for a place to make a FDI. It plans to adopt the euro in 2009, making cross-border trade even easier and more transparent.

Hot product lines for U.S. export to Slovakia include electrical machinery, medical and other measuring instruments, auto parts and aftermarket accessories, chemical products, and plastics of various forms. The country is also in need of several technologies related to its energy and alternative fuels industries. The most urgent need is for biomass, biofuel, waste to energy, and hydro technologies. Slovak industry is more than capable of producing products in these fields but needs to license the technologies to do so. If you can fill that need, you could enjoy a very low-cost market entry into this small but growing economy.

Slovakia is currently in the process of making significant upgrades to its tourism industry. It is looking for foreign investment and products for new hotels, restaurants, and sports venues. It also needs advertising and public relations services to promote tourism. And finally, Slovakia needs products and services to rebuild its road system, including a route between the eastern and western parts of the country.

You definitely need a local partner in Slovakia. The business community and contract language quirks are too difficult to master alone. But don't get taken in by the small distributors. Many are one person businesses that can be there today and gone tomorrow. Go after the big boys, and you'll be safe. And be sure to join with a local partner. You'll also need a lawyer who can interpret the legal ramifications of any contract as well as handle the disbursing of grease.

On the downside Slovaks as well as foreign companies doing business there rank corruption, austere living conditions, high unemployment, and poor healthcare as the main drawbacks. Bribery is prevalent in the healthcare industry, the court system, and law enforcement. See Statistical Facts for Slovakia's summarized statistics.

STATISTICAL FACTS

Ease of doing business (out of 178 countries)	32nd
GDP per capita (PPP)	$17,700
Population	5.4 million
Inflation rate	4.4%
Unemployment rate	10.2%
Global competitiveness index world ranking (out of 122 countries)	37th
Business competitiveness index world ranking (out of 116 countries)	39th
Total crimes per 1,000 population	16.4
Corruption perception index score world ranking (out of 179 countries) (10 is squeaky clean, zero is awful)	4.9
Internet users	2.5 million
Percent of population living on less than $2 per day	N/A
Working healthcare system index world ranking (out of 190 countries)	62nd
U.S. exports	$510 million

Competitiveness rankings of 37th and 39th make this country a highly desirable target for both exports and FDI. And the ease of doing business score of 32nd indicates very workable government regulations.

TURKEY

Strategically positioned between Europe, Asia, and the Middle East, Turkey's economy is a complicated mix of modern industry and commerce on the one hand and traditional bazaars on the other hand. However, many American companies have successfully negotiated the maze of regulations and government restrictions.

You must have a local presence in Turkey to handle the constantly changing regulations coming out of Ankara. One office that handles the entire country is sufficient. You also need a local partner, one who can navigate the labyrinth of bureaucratic agencies. See the Statistical Facts for Turkey's summarized statistics.

		STATISTICAL FACTS
Ease of doing business (out of 178 countries)	57th	
GDP per capita (PPP)	$8,900	
Population	70.4 million	
Inflation rate	9.8%	
Unemployment rate	10.2%	
Global competitiveness index world ranking (out of 122 countries)	59th	
Business competitiveness index world ranking (out of 116 countries)	51st	
Total crimes per 1,000 population	4.1	
Corruption perception index score world ranking (out of 179 countries) (10 is squeaky clean, zero is awful)	4.1	
Internet users	16.0 million	
Percent of population living on less than $2 per day	18.7%	
Working healthcare system index world ranking (out of 190 countries)	70th	
U.S. exports	$5.7 billion	

To succeed in this sometimes medieval and sometimes modern country, you need a lot of persistence. Turkey's ever changing markets and regulations present a flock of confusing and often contradictory options, especially for the newcomer. You can get what you need, but it takes patience. And you must keep pushing, pushing, pushing. You'll find contradictory policies and a lack of transparency from the government, plus an inconsistent judiciary. The ease of doing business and the two competitiveness indexes place

Turkey about in the middle. It's corruption perception score is not too bad, about average. These measures ensure that at a minimum, you won't be hamstrung by failing or falling markets.

BULGARIA

Bulgaria is also strategically located for selling to Western Europe, Turkey, and Russia. However, this is one of the poorest countries in the EU, to which it was admitted in 2006.

Bulgaria has the lowest tax rates in the region plus some of the lowest wage rates. It also has a talented work force, making FDI a viable alternative to exporting. The government and the Bulgarian people are very pro-American, welcoming American made products, tourists, and business people.

Unfortunately, several barriers hurt the country's growth potential. Among the worst are an inefficient bureaucracy, a slow moving court system, organized crime that has infiltrated several sectors of the economy, corruption, and the piracy of intellectual property. See Statistical Facts for Bulgaria's summarized statistics.

STATISTICAL FACTS

Ease of doing business (out of 178 countries)	46th
GDP per capita (PPP)	$10,400
Population	7.4 million
Inflation rate	7.2%
Unemployment rate	9.6%
Global competitiveness index world ranking (out of 122 countries)	72nd
Business competitiveness index world ranking (out of 116 countries)	80th
Total crimes per 1,000 population	N/A
Corruption perception index score world ranking (out of 179 countries) (10 is squeaky clean, zero is awful)	4.1
Internet users	2.2 million
Percent of population living on less than $2 per day	6.1%
Working healthcare system index world ranking (out of 190 countries)	102nd
U.S. exports	$293 million

This is a small country with just over 7 million people. Its global competitiveness ranking and business competitiveness ranking are both relatively low, indicating that the institutions and infrastructure necessary to run efficient business operations are lacking. The healthcare system is a disaster. This is good, of course, if you are in the medical equipment or supplies business.

Unlike other Eastern European countries, you don't need a major local presence, although you do need to have local representation, either a distributor or a sales representative. Your best export prospects are automobile parts, healthcare products and equipment, power generation equipment and supplies, and safety and security equipment.

ROMANIA

Since the fall of communism, Romania has changed more than any other Eastern European country. What was once a state run economy with decrepit, smokestack factories, abominable social services, and bizarre policies toward its citizens, has turned into a market driven, mostly private sector economy. Its 22 million citizens comprise the largest market in the region, with consumers clamoring for more American goods. Romania has excellent maritime and river navigation for moving goods, a national fiber optics telecommunication system, a large and highly skilled labor force, and well-trained science and engineering managers.

There are some drawbacks, however. Very low wages create a lack of disposable income. Byzantine laws and regulatory procedures are backed by an inefficient judicial system. And government corruption diminishes the authority of contracts. See Statistical Facts for Romania's summarized statistics.

		STATISTICAL FACTS
Ease of doing business (out of 178 countries)	48th	
GDP per capita (PPP)	$8,800	
Population	22.3 million	
Inflation rate	6.8%	
Unemployment rate	6.1%	

Global competitiveness index world ranking (out of 122 countries)	68th
Business competitiveness index world ranking (out of 116 countries)	67th
Total crimes per 1,000 population	16.5
Corruption perception index score world ranking (out of 179 countries) (10 is squeaky clean, zero is awful)	3.7
Internet users	4.9 million
Percent of population living on less than $2 per day	12.9%
Working healthcare system index world ranking (out of 190 countries)	99th
U.S. exports	$554 million

GDP per capita is quite low for Eastern Europe, indicating a lack of disposable income. The corruption index of 3.7 is not good and reflects the high level of corruption in the government and business community. The healthcare system ranking is also very low. Romania has not been a significant recipient of U.S. exports.

The best product lines for export to this country are IT products and services, electricity generating equipment, construction services and supplies, environmental products, and automobile parts. A competent local partner will be the key to your success.

THE BALTIC STATES—LITHUANIA, LATVIA, ESTONIA

Lithuania boasts an open, growing economy eager for foreign investment. It has an educated, skilled workforce, excellent infrastructure, and competitive living and operating costs. Like the rest of Eastern Europe, the business climate in Lithuania is extremely competitive with very active companies from the EU and Russia forming the backbone of the economy. The government is enthusiastic about expanding, however, and welcomes foreign companies of all sizes and nationalities.

Together with its Baltic neighbors, Estonia and Latvia, this country could be an ideal stepping stone to the EU, Scandinavian, and Russian markets. Lithuania has not completely thrown off the yoke of the old Soviet Union, however. Corruption, an inefficient bureaucracy, and lack of regulatory transparency continue to plague newcomers. If you are interested in the Baltic states, I advise you to start with some type of joint venture either in Lithuania or Latvia.

Latvia is a very stable country that welcomes American exports of medical equipment and supplies, IT equipment and supplies, and machinery of a variety of types. The government is friendly toward foreign investment and looks to FDI from the EU, Russia, and America to build and rebuild its next phase of infrastructure development. The economy is primarily service oriented—transportation, information technology, and financial services. U.S. companies rank Latvia as the best business environment in Central and Eastern Europe.

As you would expect, EU and Russian companies provide strong competition. Moreover, the layers of government bureaucracy and corruption are seen as the two most damaging obstacles to free markets.

The third Baltic state, Estonia, is the smallest of the three with a population of only 1.3 million. It is very business oriented and welcomes American products and companies. As one would expect, competition (mainly from Finnish, Swedish, and other EU companies) is fierce, and unless you have products that are unique in some respect, I can't recommend Estonia or any Baltic state for that matter. However, if you can manage the competition, this is another good country to use as a distribution staging area for Russia, the EU, and the Scandinavian countries.

Hundreds of foreign companies have invested in Estonia, including many American transnationals. The main exports from U.S. companies are electrical apparatus, measuring and testing instruments, telecommunications equipment, automobiles and auto parts, pharmaceuticals, and cosmetics. Relationships between Estonia and the United States have always been positive. In addition to these products, future growth will come in tourism, financial services, and transportation of various kinds. See Statistical Facts for the combined summarized statistics of Lithuania, Latvia, and Estonia.

	Lithuania	Latvia	Estonia	**STATISTICAL FACTS**
Ease of doing business (out of 178 countries)	26th	22nd	17th	
GDP per capita (PPP)	$15,100	$17,700	$21,800	
Population	3.6 million	2.3 million	1.3 million	
Inflation rate	3.6%	6.3%	4.4%	
Unemployment rate	4.5%	5.9%	4.7%	

Global competitiveness index world ranking (out of 122 countries)	40th	36th	25th
Business competitiveness index world ranking (out of 116 countries)	41st	48th	26th
Total crimes per 1,000 population	22.9	N/A	43.3
Corruption perception index score world ranking (out of 179 countries) (10 is squeaky clean, zero is awful)	4.8	4.7	6.7
Internet users	1.2 million	1.0 million	690,000
Percent of population living on less than $2 per day	7.8%	4.7%	7.5%
Working healthcare system index world ranking (out of 190 countries)	73rd	105th	77th
U.S. exports	$566 million	$245 million	$510 million

Although corruption was called out as a major problem in Lithuania and Latvia, scores of 4.8 and 4.7 respectively, aren't bad. Estonia's 6.7 is very good. Also, English is widely spoken in the government and business circles of all three Baltic states. The three ease of doing business rankings pretty much tell the whole story. Each of these countries offers excellent opportunities for smaller U.S. companies, with competition being the only significant drawback.

chapter eight
Market Opportunities in India, China, and South and East Asia

NO ONE CAN ARGUE THAT CHINA AND INDIA ARE THE KING AND QUEEN OF Asia. But don't forget the countries in the South and East. Taiwan, Malaysia, Thailand, Indonesia, and the Philippines sport thriving markets that cry out for a wide variety of imported goods and services, as do Pakistan and Sri Lanka to a lesser extent. Infrastructure projects provide enormous opportunities for small U.S. companies that supply parts and services for building or renovating roads, ports, electric power generation and distribution, water supplies, waste disposal, hospital and school construction, and a variety of other projects.

In 2006, U.S. companies exported $12.5 billion to Malaysia alone, plus another $8.1 billion to Thai customers. Although constantly in the shadow of China, Taiwan boasts a booming economy with a rousing $23 billion in U.S. exports. The Philippines, long considered the poor boy of Southeast Asia, enjoyed substantial economic growth with $7.6 billion in U.S. exports. Although several of these smaller countries offer excellent market-entry options for newcomers to global trade, it's hard to beat the king and queen.

INDIA

India's enormous population tends to cloud one's thinking, particularly regarding market size and future potential. A population of more than 1 billion sounds like a goldmine of opportunity. But beware. In India, all is never as it seems. Of India's 1 billion citizens, 375 million live on less than $1 per day, many on less than $0.50 per day. An additional 505 million live on an income of between $1 and $2 per day. That leaves only 215 million who live on more than $2 per day as potential consumers. That's still a healthy number, more than the total population of Brazil or Russia. But it doesn't make India the marketing nirvana that media types would like us to believe.

Having said that, I don't mean to downplay India's importance in the world economy. This mammoth country has too many positives. A study by Goldman Sachs claims that the Indian economy is growing by 8 percent per year. That's truly remarkable. The report also claims that this growth will continue until 2020, so that by the year 2050, India will be the world's second largest economy next to China. Another study by the consulting firm McKinsey & Company reports that India will be the world's fifth largest consumer market by 2025. But the nation's infrastructure is in such drastic need of upgrading that the Indian government will be lucky to have roads, ports, electric power supplies, and water supplies ready to support such rapid economic growth. Clearly, market opportunities abound for U.S. exporting companies as well as for those interested in a FDI.

Only 30 percent of India's population lives in towns and cities. The rest make their homes in more than half a million tiny villages. One might assume that these folks account for a fairly large proportion of those who live in poverty. That's true. But the huge slums of Mumbai, Kolkata (Calcutta), and Chennai (Madras) also account for a good share.

It's important to approach India as several separate markets, by and large defined by its major cities (Mumbai [Bombay] with a population of 16.4 million, Klkata [Calcutta] with 13.2 million people, Delhi with 12.8 million, Channai [Madras] with 6.4 million, Bangalore with 5.7 million, Hyderabad with 5.5 million, Ahmedabad with 5 million, and Pune with 4 million people). Each of these markets has different characteristics and even different cultural quirks. One local representative cannot cover the entire country, so you need one partner for each region. Unless you already have extensive experience in India, I strongly suggest joint ventures with Indian companies as your primary market-entry strategy. See the following for advice on how to keep out of trouble when searching for the right local partner.

➡ When interviewing a representative or potential partner, do not believe the long list of foreign clients that he says he represents. It is probably grossly outdated.

➡ Don't trust the interviewee to tell you the truth about his organization; his tendency will be to project a professional staff and many clients when he may have no staff and a one room office.

➡ Keep in mind that small distributors might be better than large ones. They charge less and tend to be more flexible in following your directions.

➡ Be very careful when doing your due diligence. Indian records are not known for their completeness or authenticity. It pays to hire experts, such as Kroll, to check out a representative's reputation, customer base, and longevity.

➡ Do an extensive check on a prospective representative's technical qualifications, assuming you sell technical products. Many profess to be experts, when they are not.

Bear in mind that the way you handle religion, the caste system, and language peculiarities determines how successful you'll be. One or more of the three influences every transaction. Hindi is the national language, however, each state has the authority to set its own official language, resulting in more than 1,000 separate and distinct languages in use throughout the country. English is also granted official status by Delhi and used extensively by business types. But—and this is a big but—English words and phrases can have very different meanings from their use in the United States and even different meanings from one district or part of the country to another. See Statistical Facts for India's summarized statistics.

STATISTICAL FACTS

Ease of doing business (out of 178 countries)	120th
GDP per capita (PPP)	$3,700
Population	1.1 billion
Inflation rate	5.3%
Unemployment rate	7.8%
Global competitiveness index world ranking (out of 122 countries)	43rd
Business competitiveness index world ranking (out of 116 countries)	31st
Total crimes per 1,000 population	1.6
Corruption perception index score world ranking (out of 179 countries) (10 is squeaky clean, zero is awful)	3.6
Internet users	60 million
Percent of population living on less than $2 per day	80.4%
Working healthcare system index world ranking (out of 190 countries)	112th
U.S. exports	$10.1 billion

Don't let anyone convince you that doing business in India is easy. It definitely is not, and a ranking of 120th out of 178 countries in the ease of doing business index indicates this. India is a very difficult country and not the place for the faint of heart.

 U.S. exports to India of only $10.1 billion does not make this country a key destination. Several countries in Southeast Asia draw significantly more.

The global competitiveness ranking and the business competitiveness ranking at 43rd and 34th respectively, places India a little above average. A 3.6 corruption perception score is not good, however. This is well below the average and indicates serious obstacles in government circles that must be dealt with. Just one more hurdle to get over. The world health ranking of

112th shows how bad overall healthcare is and also that this might be a good market in the future.

India is such a diverse nation with so many different cultural traits and regional buying habits that any list of preferred export products would be meaningless. Almost anything related to infrastructure development would be a good bet. The same consumer goods demanded by U.S. consumers also sell well to the Indian middle- and upper-class.

The keys to success in India are strategic planning, thorough market research, and well-connected local partners who know the markets and bureaucrats. Most important of all, you have to make a long-term commitment and have plenty of patience. Nothing happens fast in India. Staying power is a prerequisite to success.

CHINA

Like India, China is a huge country. Diverse sections of the country have different customs and market structures. The nation even has two official languages—Mandarin in the north and Cantonese in the Guangdong Province in the south—as well as a basket of dialects. Also, like India, China's enormous population (1.3 billion) cannot be viewed as one consumer base. Of the 1.3 billion people, 128 million live on less than $1 per day (many of these folks live on less than $0.50 per day). Another 325 million live on an income of between $1 per day and $2 per day. That means about 860 million people live on income of more than $2 per day—much better than India where only 215 million meet that standard. China's edge results from its agrarian base and steamroller economy.

China is the world's third largest market for luxury goods, after the United States and Japan. However, disposable income for each of its 860 million potential consumers is only about $1,700 per year. Also, many of those folks live in rural areas in the north and west, regions that are generally inaccessible for imported consumer products. Income distribution is very uneven throughout China. Beijing's citizens, for example, have twice as much disposable income as citizens of other provinces. Some China watchers estimate that more than 200 million people have a disposable income of over $8,000 per year, a significant difference from $1,700. Conversely, millions of farmers have hardly any income and live off the land.

With China's exceptional economic growth, many expect disposable income to escalate rapidly in the years to come.

However, beware of the sirens of hope. Although the red hot Chinese economy shines like a flaming torch, dangers loom on the horizon. In many respects, China replicates Japan after Word War II. For more than two decades, Japanese industry fed low wage produced products of every variety to U.S. markets. Then as costs rose and the economy faltered, many foreign run companies left Japan for South Korea and Taiwan.

China's myth of a global industrial powerhouse is also cracking like brittle glass. A tough new law passed in January 2008 requires companies to guarantee collective bargaining rights, provide employee benefits including pensions, and hire for the long term. This has increased the cost of labor between 7 and 10 percent. Energy prices have gone through the roof. Beijing has abandoned preferred policies for exporters. The Chinese yuan soars against the dollar. Factories run at only 50 to 60 percent of capacity. Margins are crumbling. Manufacturing companies that make toys, shoes, furniture, automobiles, and variety of other consumer and industrial products are shutting down. The Federation of Hong Kong Industries predicts that more than 6,000 Hong Kong run factories in China will close this year. According to the Asian Footwear Association, 150 shoe factories have already shuttered their doors.

The *2007 Chinese Business Report* issued by the American Chamber of Commerce in Shanghai showed that most U.S. companies doing business in China were bullish about the future. It also reported that the majority of U.S. firms have operations in Shanghai, although an increasing number are moving to the inland cities of Chengdo, Nanjing, Dalian, Wuhan, and Xian in an effort to reduce costs. The report also contained a survey by Booz Allen Hamilton entitled *China Manufacturing Competitiveness 2007–2008*. Respondents indicated that margins are being squeezed by increased competition, pressure from major customers, high material costs, higher distribution costs, taxes, and rising inflation. They also ranked the top five challenges to their business success as:

1. Inability to attract and retain qualified personnel
2. Confusing regulations and inconsistent interpretation of regulations
3. Lack of bureaucratic transparency and bureaucratic meddling

4. Visa difficulties
5. Intellectual property infringements

Additionally, the stronger yuan, high employee turnover, and rising wages dim China's allure as a manufacturing hub. And China has a very, very serious pollution problem. The World Bank's Development Research Group estimated that China has the ignominious honor of qualifying for 11 out of the top 20 worst polluted cities in the world. They are Tianjin, Chongging, Shenyang, Zhengzhou, Jinan, Lanzhou, Taiyuan, Beijing, Chengdu, Anshan, and Wuhan. (India had five cities [Delhi, Kolkata, Kampur, Ahmadabad, and Lucknow].)

Nevertheless, companies remain buoyant about China's long-term potential. Many American companies of all sizes have ventured into this thriving market. Some have been eminently successful. Others have failed. Observers claim that to be successful, you need to thoroughly investigate your markets, obey official product standards, prequalify prospective partners, and draft contracts that minimize differences between the parties and can be enforced. The U.S. Department of Commerce lists four categories of problems you will likely face:

1. A lack of predictability. This evolves because of the lack of a transparent and consistent body of laws and regulations pertaining to business transactions.
2. Mercantile government policies. Many sectors of the economy are protected by state laws against competition from imports. This is the same protectionism that has been prevalent in Brazil for several decades and is still prominent in several sectors of the U.S. economy (e.g., sugar, steel, farm products, textiles, and so on).
3. A government controlled, planned economy. The state controls the only labor union. A five-year plan dictates policies, government strategies, and national goals. The Chinese do not understand the concept of competition or free markets.
4. Foreign companies almost always underestimate the difficulties of doing business here, especially the legal issues and the constraints imposed by a communist regime.

If you plan to export to China or to make a FDI here, you must have local partners. More than one is necessary if you plan to cover this huge landmass. These partners will need to have good connections in Beijing, have a firm grasp of the rules and regulations for doing business, and know how to deal with the Triads.

Furthermore, the Chinese love face-to-face meetings, not phone calls or e-mail. This means you'll have to make several trips to China and get to know as many people as you can. A well-connected partner can make the difference. I also strongly suggest you travel with a competent interpreter, even if you think you know the Chinese language. See Statistical Facts for China's summarized statistics.

STATISTICAL FACTS

Ease of doing business (out of 178 countries)	83rd
GDP per capita (PPP)	$7,600
Population	1.3 billion
Inflation rate	1.5%
Unemployment rate	4.2%
Global competitiveness index world ranking (out of 122 countries)	54th
Business competitiveness index world ranking (out of 116 countries)	57th
Total crimes per 1,000 population	N/A
Corruption perception index score world ranking (out of 179 countries) (10 is squeaky clean, zero is awful)	3.6
Internet users	123.0 million
Percent of population living on less than $2 per day	34.9%
Working healthcare system index world ranking (out of 190 countries)	144th
U.S. exports	$55.2 billion

The low ranking in the ease of doing business index underscores how difficult this country is. The two midrange competitiveness indexes, however, give it relatively high marks in terms of market growth. A score of 3.6 in the corruption perception survey is the same as India's and equally unacceptable. Corruption is very prevalent in all levels of government, not only in Beijing, but also with local municipal governors and law enforcement officers. For those businesses that have a hard grip on the activities of a town or city, corruption can be especially worrisome, particularly if they are state run companies. The Triads infiltration of legitimate businesses yields an added complexity. If you are uneasy about handing out bribes, don't understand how to do it, or if you worry about the Triads, China is not the place for you.

In terms of market growth, the best products for the ensuing four or five years seem to be power equipment, industrial chemicals, agricultural machinery, medical supplies and diagnostic equipment, construction equipment, parts and supplies, and financial services. Computer programs, computer hardware, and especially internet technology are in high demand. These markets are changing rapidly, and you should see for yourself, rather than merely accept a list of products. What is true today may be out of fashion tomorrow.

Agents seem to be the thing in China, although I repeat, this can be a very dangerous road to travel unless you have your own supervisor on the premises. You'll need permits to conduct trade, distribute, and do practically everything else. Do not try to get these permits on your own. Either have a local partner do it or hire an attorney to make the arrangements.

MALAYSIA

Malaysia has morphed from an agrarian society into an economy where manufacturing and services account for 80 percent of GDP. Surprisingly, Malaysia is the 10th largest export partner for the United States and purchases more U.S. exports than Germany, France, or Japan. Moreover, American companies represent the largest group of foreign investors.

The piracy of intellectual property continues to be a thorn in the side of Malaysian importers. This country has a significant amount of counterfeiting and a lack of effective patent and data protection for pharmaceutical products. Moreover, the government is very lax about enforcing the antipiracy laws that are on the books.

Kuala Lumpur boasts a strong middle-class consumer market where U.S. products are sought after, and U.S. franchises are very popular. In fact, the United States accounts for 70 percent of foreign franchises.

A local distributor will give you the easiest and fastest way to enter this market. The country is small, so one office should suffice. Be sure to do a thorough background check of your potential partner, however. See Statistical Facts for Malaysia's summarized statistics.

Ease of doing business (out of 178 countries)	24th
GDP per capita (PPP)	$12,700
Population	24.4 million
Inflation rate	3.8%
Unemployment rate	3.5%
Global competitiveness index world ranking (out of 122 countries)	26th
Business competitiveness index world ranking (out of 116 countries)	28th
Total crimes per 1,000 population	N/A
Corruption perception index score world ranking (out of 179 countries) (10 is squeaky clean, zero is awful)	5.1
Internet users	11.0 million
Percent of population living on less than $2 per day	N/A
Working healthcare system index world ranking (out of 190 countries)	49th
U.S. exports	$12.5 billion

It's surprisingly easy to do business in Malaysia, as evidenced by the ease of doing business ranking of 24th, the best in the region. The two competitiveness rankings are also very positive. A corruption perception score of 5.1 is average and nothing to worry about. GDP per capita of $12,700 indicates that consumers do have disposable income to purchase imported products. Typical middle-class consumer goods do well there, as do computer hardware and software. The internet is now beginning to catch on as a commercial tool.

TAIWAN

Taiwan is America's 10th largest export partner and has a red hot high-tech market. Taiwanese firms make more than 70 percent of the world's wireless communications products. This island nation is also a world leader in the production of thin-film liquid crystal flat panel displays. High-tech firms rely heavily on American imports of specialty components and technology licensing. Looking to the future, the government plans to build world class industries in biotechnology, optoelectronics, and nanotechnology.

Taiwanese consumers are very sophisticated. An average GDP per capita of $29,000 affords plenty of middle-class purchasing power for personal care and luxury items. The Taiwanese get more than enough commodity type consumer goods produced in low-cost Southeast Asia countries, so don't bother with that kind of product. From U.S. companies, Taiwanese consumers want high-quality, differentiated merchandise at competitive prices.

You will do best in Taiwan with a local agent or representative. Plenty of them are around, and they all want to do business with the Americans. One rather unique feature of the Taiwanese business community is the very high number of smaller firms. This island nation is dominated by small businesses, each employing less than 200 people. See Statistical Facts for Taiwan's summarized statistics.

		STATISTICAL FACTS
Ease of doing business (out of 178 countries)	50th	
GDP per capita (PPP)	$29,000	
Population	23.0 million	
Inflation rate	1.0%	
Unemployment rate	3.9%	
Global competitiveness index world ranking (out of 122 countries)	14th	
Business competitiveness index world ranking (out of 116 countries)	14th	
Total crimes per 1,000 population	N/A	
Corruption perception index score world ranking (out of 179 countries) (10 is squeaky clean, zero is awful)	5.9	
Internet users	13.2 million	
Percent of population living on less than $2 per day	N/A	
Working healthcare system index world ranking (out of 190 countries)	N/A	
U.S. exports	$23.0 billion	

The two competitiveness rankings of 14th are phenomenal. Taiwan can hold a competitive edge with anyone. Functioning infrastructure and institutions, less than average corruption, educated consumers, an aggressive workforce, and a business-oriented government make Taiwan an ideal place to do business. The downside is that being such a great place means intense competition from U.S. firms and companies from all over the world.

THAILAND

Thailand is the fifth largest Asian trading partner for U.S. companies after China, Japan, Taiwan, and Malaysia. However, for the first time in many years, the political regime looks unstable. The previous government was overthrown in September 2006 and replaced by a military junta. This interim government has enacted a number of policies that are counterproductive to a free market economy. They include (1) currency controls, (2) foreign business ownership restrictions, (3) compulsory licensing of pharmaceuticals, and (4) restrictions on the expansion of foreign owned retail operations. These constraints smack of an antibusiness fervor that has been missing from Thailand for decades.

Unfortunately, until the military gives up control and free elections can be held, it seems unlikely that conditions will change. Corruption throughout the government and law enforcement is widespread and the piracy of intellectual property continues to flourish. If it seems that such an environment poses market-entry barriers for you, it might be better to wait until conditions change or turn to another country altogether.

If you do decide to proceed with Thailand, arrange with a local partner to handle distribution. Also, be aware that consumers are extremely price conscious, preferring lower prices to higher quality. Medical products, cosmetics, food supplements, and, somewhat surprisingly, pet food are in high demand. On the commercial side, imports of automobile accessories, defense equipment, educational services, food processing and packaging equipment, and laboratory and scientific instruments are needed. See Statistical Facts for Thailand's summarized statistics.

STATISTICAL FACTS

Ease of doing business (out of 178 countries)	15th
GDP per capita (PPP)	$9,100
Population	64.6 million
Inflation rate	5.1%
Unemployment rate	2.1%
Global competitiveness index world ranking (out of 122 countries)	35th
Business competitiveness index world ranking (out of 116 countries)	37th
Total crimes per 1,000 population	8.8

Corruption perception index score world ranking (out of 179 countries)	
(10 is squeaky clean, zero is awful)	3.3
Internet users	8.4 million
Percent of population living on less than $2 per day	N/A
Working healthcare system index world ranking (out of 190 countries)	47th
U.S. exports	$8.1 billion

Despite the military takeover, Thailand still ranks a hefty 15th in the ease of doing business index. However, I question the validity of this statistic. Thailand has always been a fairly easy country to do business in, but I can't envision that continuing with the military in control. Still, it is possible. The crime rate of 8.8 crimes per 1,000 people is fairly high, and you should take precautions personally as well as with business property. Also, the corruption rating of 3.3 is not good.

INDONESIA

With a population of 245 million, Indonesia is the largest country in Southeast Asia and the fourth most populous country in the world. It is also the world's largest archipelago, comprising 17,508 islands. Java is the largest island and the home of Jakarta, the country's capital.

Although this heavily populated Muslim nation is richly endowed with natural resources, more than half the population lives on less than $2 per day. Indonesia's major industries are petroleum (it is a member of OPEC), natural gas, textiles, apparel, and mining. It has very little manufacturing and plenty of imported equipment is needed for virtually all industries. Japan, China, and Singapore supply most of Indonesia's imports. See Statistical Facts for Indonesia's summarized statistics.

STATISTICAL FACTS

Ease of doing business (out of 178 countries)	123rd
GDP per capita (PPP)	$3,800
Population	245.4 million
Inflation rate	13.2%
Unemployment rate	12.5%
Global competitiveness index world ranking (out of 122 countries)	50th

Business competitiveness index world ranking (out of 116 countries)	59th
Total crimes per 1,000 population	N/A
Corruption perception index score world ranking (out of 179 countries) (10 is squeaky clean, zero is awful)	2.3
Internet users	14.7 million
Percent of population living on less than $2 per day	52.4%
Working healthcare system index world ranking (out of 190 countries)	92nd
U.S. exports	$3.0 billion

Obviously, any country ranked 123rd in the ease of doing business index is very difficult. Government regulations stymie the business community and encourage corruption. With a corruption score of 2.3, that much is obvious. When antibusiness regulations and an impossibly corrupt judiciary are added to political instability, this nation is best left to the transnationals. I cannot recommend Indonesia as a viable country for smaller U.S. companies.

PHILIPPINES

The Philippines is a poor country (GDP per capita of $5,000) with a large population (89.5 million). Comprised of many islands, a good share of the country's citizens are very hard to reach. U.S. products constitute 13 percent of all Philippines' imports. The U.S. government continues to support the Philippines with substantial financial aid and development assistance, and the economy is moving ahead at a steady pace, growing more than 5 percent per year. Most Filipinos like Americans and American made products, remembering the close association of the two countries before, during, and after World War II. Almost any consumer products you ship to the Philippines will be welcome.

On the downside, terrorist groups still flourish on the outer islands and corruption remains a major stumbling block to increased business, as the corruption perception ranking of 2.5 clearly shows. The judicial system is only partially functional and IP piracy thrives. Moreover, a VAT tax of 12 percent attaches to all imports, driving prices up.

Pharmaceuticals, IT hardware and software, medical supplies and equipment, pollution control equipment, and telecom equipment are high-demand product lines. Be sure to use a local agent or distributor, however. See Statistical Facts for Philippines's summarized statistics.

Ease of doing business (out of 178 countries)	133rd	STATISTICAL FACTS
GDP per capita (PPP)	$5,000	
Population	89.5 million	
Inflation rate	6.6%	
Unemployment rate	8.8%	
Global competitiveness index world ranking (out of 122 countries)	71st	
Business competitiveness index world ranking (out of 116 countries)	69th	
Total crimes per 1,000 population	N/A	
Corruption perception index score world ranking (out of 179 countries) (10 is squeaky clean, zero is awful)	2.5	
Internet users	7.8 million	
Percent of population living on less than $2 per day	43%	
Working healthcare system index world ranking (out of 190 countries)	60th	
U.S. exports	$7.6 billion	

The horrible ease of doing business ranking of 133rd says it all. Despite the country's pro-American attitude, the geographic terrain, corruption in both the government and business community, terrorist uprisings, and a very high poverty rate make the Philippines a difficult place for newcomers. With nearly half the population living on less than $2 per day, your consumer market is about 45 million, not 89 million. An inflation rate of 6.6 percent is still too high, although it is decreasing. If you do have an interest in the Phillippines, products and services related to infrastructure development will likely be your best bet.

SINGAPORE

The 4.5 million citizens do not offer much of a market for consumer goods, and Singapore's state-of-the-art infrastructure doesn't need much in the way of industrial and commercial products. Nevertheless, Singapore is the ninth largest export market for U.S. companies. How can this be? Because of its ideal location and its virtual tariff free import policy. Singapore is one of the world's key transhipment locations. It is the perfect spot for distributing your products throughout Asia. You can ship finished goods, parts, or subassemblies to Singapore, complete the manufacturing process, repackage the goods, and then ship them off to all of South and East Asian markets. If you choose to distribute some of the goods in Singapore markets, well that's OK too.

Singapore's internet connections are state-of-the-art. Its population is highly educated. And every convenience you have in your hometown can be found in Singapore. There are really only two significant problems in this island state: (1) credit card fraud, especially when someone asks for immediate delivery and (2) arcane laws. Singapore has very strict laws against such minor offenses as jaywalking, littering, and spitting. Commit any of these infractions and you'll likely be looking out from behind jail cell bars. Also, you cannot chew gum, use firecrackers, or handcuffs, and you must not have in your possession any shell casings, gun silencers, or cigarette lighters in the shape of a gun. Obviously, guns are strictly prohibited.

Singapore imposes a compulsory caning sentence on males caught vandalizing anything. Caning may also be imposed for immigration violations and other offenses. Any use or sale of illegal drugs demands a jail sentence, and a mandatory death sentence will be imposed for many narcotics offenses. No juries muddy the waters in Singapore. Judges hear cases and decide punishment.

If you can live with these strange rules, Singapore offers a great opportunity. See Statistical Facts for Singapore's summarized statistics.

STATISTICAL FACTS

Ease of doing business (out of 178 countries)	1st
GDP per capita (PPP)	$30,900
Population	4.5 million
Inflation rate	1.0%
Unemployment rate	3.1%
Global competitiveness index world ranking (out of 122 countries)	5th
Business competitiveness index world ranking (out of 116 countries)	5th
Total crimes per 1,000 population	N/A
Corruption perception index score world ranking (out of 179 countries) (10 is squeaky clean, zero is awful)	9.3
Internet users	2.4 million
Percent of population living on less than $2 per day	N/A
Working healthcare system index world ranking (out of 190 countries)	6th
U.S. exports	$24.7 billion

It's hard to imagine any negatives about Singapore—other than its obtuse laws. Out of 178 countries, Singapore ranks at the top of the ease of doing business index. At fifth place in both competitiveness indexes, this nation is number one of the 40 countries included in this book. A corruption score of 9.3 out of 10 shows zero corruption for all practical purposes. Its healthcare system also ranks at the top of our 40 countries. To top off these positive attributes, there are no import tariffs, and English is widely spoken. Before you get carried away with all this good news, remember that all these positives bring an enormous number of transnational competitors from America, Japan, China, India, and the EU.

PAKISTAN

Pakistan and the United States have been on friendly terms for many years. More than 61 American companies do business here, including Citibank, Pepsi-Cola, Proctor & Gamble, NCR, Pfizer, Abbot Labs, 3M, IBM, Eli Lilly, Wyeth, Oracle, Microsoft, Cisco, Intel, Chevron, AIG and many others. For several years, the government has been implementing stringent macroeconomic reforms, and the country now reaps the benefits of strong economic growth. As you can tell from the diverse selection of U.S. companies, most products that sell in the states also do well there. However, competition from European, Chinese, Japanese, and South Korean firms is intense. If you go there you must be persistent, very patient, and willing to adapt to new circumstances as they develop.

American franchises do very well. McDonald's, KFC, and Dominos Pizza, for example, have been successful in Pakistan for some time. These and several other American franchises have learned to cope with the capricious turns of a volatile government.

Forecasts call for telecommunications, information technology products and services, thermal and hydroelectric power generation, airports and ancillary equipment and services, the oil and gas industry, and the construction of roads, bridges, ports, and buildings to grow handsomely over the next 5 to 10 years.

The political situation in Pakistan remains unsettled. Areas along the border with Afghanistan are brutal with Taliban fighters and bandits roaming freely. Obviously, stay away from the border. Corruption is also very pronounced throughout the country. Nothing gets done without a bribe. You definitely need a local representative. Someone who knows the ins and outs of the political scene would be the most beneficial. See Statistical Facts for Pakistan's summarized statistics.

STATISTICAL FACTS

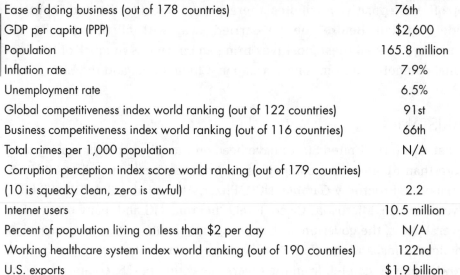

Ease of doing business (out of 178 countries)	76th
GDP per capita (PPP)	$2,600
Population	165.8 million
Inflation rate	7.9%
Unemployment rate	6.5%
Global competitiveness index world ranking (out of 122 countries)	91st
Business competitiveness index world ranking (out of 116 countries)	66th
Total crimes per 1,000 population	N/A
Corruption perception index score world ranking (out of 179 countries) (10 is squeaky clean, zero is awful)	2.2
Internet users	10.5 million
Percent of population living on less than $2 per day	N/A
Working healthcare system index world ranking (out of 190 countries)	122nd
U.S. exports	$1.9 billion

The statistic that stands out above all others is the corruption score of 2.2. This indicates how difficult it is to do business there, not because of regulations, but because you have to bribe everyone to get anything done, and then it seldom gets done right the first time—or so it seems. The fact that less than 10 percent of the population has internet access, gives you an idea of how rural and backward much of the country is. Also, remember that Pakistan is basically a Muslim country with close ties to the Arab states.

This is a tough place for smaller U.S. companies. I suggest you begin your global venture in an easier, less corrupt country closer to home.

SRI LANKA

Sri Lanka is a lot different from Pakistan. This country is open to FDI and has a workable financial system, moderately good infrastructure (except where it has been destroyed by Tamil rebels in the north and east), and for a small war torn country, relatively capable workers. At one time, the capital of Colombo was the European playground of the rich and famous jet-setters. I can remember watching several English and German movie stars cavorting by the hotel pool while reporters flashed their cameras. Unfortunately, civil war has changed that. Still, Colombo is a fascinating place whose citizens come from the far corners of the globe and are eager for American and European goods.

Tourism is still a major industry in Sri Lanka, despite the civil war. The country has a fascinating history and several unique archeological sites. It is also about midway between Bahrain (an airlines refueling stop from London) and Hong Kong. If you have to travel to Hong Kong or Taiwan, return via the eastern route and stop off in Colombo for a couple days. Sri Lanka is almost exactly half way around the world from New York.

Narrow roads continue to make cross-country transport difficult. Also, electricity is very erratic where several failures a day is a normal occurrence. Qualified workers and partners who speak English are hard to come by, and the Sri Lankan education system is badly deteriorated. Anyone with enough money goes to school in England or America. All types of food, cosmetics, healthcare products, and auto and truck parts are desperately needed, as are equipment, machinery, and supplies for construction and electricity generation.

The Sri Lankan bureaucracy is very corrupt. This, plus slow decision making and broken government promises, makes doing business there difficult. A population of 20 million, however, offers some intriguing potential. See Statistical Facts for Sri Lanka's summarized statistics.

STATISTICAL FACTS

Ease of doing business (out of 178 countries)	101st
GDP per capita (PPP)	$4,100
Population	20.9 million
Inflation rate	15.6%
Unemployment rate	6.3%
Global competitiveness index world ranking (out of 122 countries)	79th
Business competitiveness index world ranking (out of 116 countries)	72nd
Total crimes per 1,000 population	N/A

Corruption perception index score world ranking (out of 179 countries) (10 is squeaky clean, zero is awful)	3.1
Internet users	280,000
Percent of population living on less than $2 per day	N/A
Working healthcare system index world ranking (out of 190 countries)	76th
U.S. exports	$227 million

The low volume of U.S. exports to Sri Lanka reflects the 25 years of civil war with the Tamil. It also indicates that the government is still too opaque for most U.S. companies.

chapter nine
Market Opportunities in Israel and the Arab States

ISRAEL IS THE MOST STABLE, DYNAMIC MARKET IN THE MIDDLE EAST. FOR SMALLER U.S. exporters, it might be an excellent place to begin. On the other hand, the Arab countries, with the possible exception of Egypt, are very difficult places to do business. Antiquated laws that apply to companies as well as persons permeate each Arab country's culture. For example, firing a local agent is nearly impossible, despite proof of incompetence or other transgressions.

When I speak of Arab states or Arab countries, I am referring specifically to those eight countries included in this book. However, the Arab world is much larger, comprising 22 nations. The glue holding this menagerie together is the Arabic language and the Islamic religion. The following countries are considered to be part of the Arab world: Algeria, Bahrain, Comoros, Djibouti, Egypt, Iraq, Jordan, Kuwait, Lebanon, Libya, Mauritania, Morocco, Oman, Qatar, Saudi Arabia, Somalia, Sudan, Syria, Tunisia, United Arab Emirates, Western Sahara, and Yemen. Iran is not considered part of the Arab world even though 65 percent its population of is Shia Islamic.

No Arab state has much of a consumer base. Indigenous tribes and others living in remote, desert villages distort official population numbers. Infrastructure conveniences like electricity and running water are hard to find in these rural areas. Most tribes and villagers live off the land, and when they do shop, it's for the basics, not luxury items. Other than products they need for survival, these folks are not going to buy imported goods. Even in cities like Riyadh, Abu Dhabi, Algiers, or Doha the majority of the population is quite poor. Yes, the elite class has oil money by the carload, but they are a minority in all countries.

The greatest demand for imported products, aside from all types of Western style goods for the royal families and others of the elite class, is for construction equipment and materials and infrastructure products and services. Each of the Gulf states continues to build new roads, ports, office buildings, hospitals, schools, government buildings, desalinization plants, and electricity generators but only in the cities. A growing elite class demands better education facilities, hospitals, shopping malls, and entertainment complexes. Supplying products and services for these outlets could be very rewarding. Be aware, however, that nonGulf states do not have the abundant oil revenues of their Gulf state brethren and, therefore, are much less interested in imported products. All told, the Arab states do offer some intriguing possibilities, but doing business is difficult. And the Middle East is a lot different from any other place in the world.

ISRAEL

In 1985, Israel and the United States executed a Free Trade Area Agreement that has allowed the commercial relationship to expand sevenfold. Today, the United States is Israel's largest trade partner, despite intense European competition. And over the years, many Americans have immigrated to the motherland. This strong traditional relationship between countries tends to make Americans feel very much at home walking the streets of Tel Aviv and shopping in its malls. English is widely spoken, and the Israeli business protocol is about the same as in the States. A dark shadow overhangs this apparent tranquility, however. There seems to be a constant tension in the air, a sense of fear that an unknown Palestinian terrorist will walk up and bomb you, your car, or the mall you are shopping in. This creates a strain on American business dealings that is not often acknowledged by Israelis, probably because they are so accustomed to the fear.

Israel is a hot spot for high-tech design. In fact, its position as a global powerhouse in research and development places Israel at the center of outsourcing from the States. The types of imported products most wanted at the commercial and industrial level are safety and security equipment, defense equipment (including all types of armaments), medical technologies, biotechnology products and educational supplies, equipment, and services. Cogeneration plants, solar and wind driven turbine generators, and road construction equipment are also in high demand.

From the consumer's perspective, virtually all the typically shopping mall products found in the States are wanted in Israel. European firms also know this, however, and are fiercely protective of their market shares.

Four types of distribution avenues are used: commissioned agents for industrial equipment, raw materials, and commodities; nonstocking agents for manufacturers; stocking agents for high volume products; and importer/ distributors for most consumer goods.

Franchising is very popular in Israel and most U.S. fast food franchises are represented there. Additionally, ACE Hardware, Office Depot, Re/MAX, and Toys-R-Us, to name a few well-known U.S. companies, have franchises there.

Direct marketing is fairly common, although Israeli's dislike door-to-door sales calls. Both cable and satellite TV have shopping channels. Mail order catalogs are popular but telemarketing is not. The internet is fast becoming the most successful marketing media. See Statistical Facts for Israel's summarized statistics.

Ease of doing business (out of 178 countries)	29th
GDP per capita (PPP)	$26,000
Population	6.4 million
Inflation rate	1.9%
Unemployment rate	8.5%
Global competitiveness index world ranking (out of 122 countries)	15th
Business competitiveness index world ranking (out of 116 countries)	22nd
Total crimes per 1,000 population	N/A
Corruption perception index score world ranking (out of 179 countries) (10 is squeaky clean, zero is awful)	6.1
Internet users	3.7 million
Percent of population living on less than $2 per day	N/A
Working healthcare system index world ranking (out of 190 countries)	28th
U.S. exports	$10.9 billion

GDP per capita of $26,000 is proof that Israeli's have plenty of money to spend on imported items, although there is plenty of competition. Some corruption has crept into government circles but not as much as in most other countries and not enough to worry about. Half the country's population has access to the internet, making it not only a viable advertising and commerce media but also a steady stream in need of replacement equipment and programs. The healthcare system rank of 28th, while not superb, is at least adequate; however, regular deliveries of medical supplies and replacement equipment are sorely needed. The nearly $11 billion in imports from U.S. companies—about the same as Russia and Eastern Europe combined (excluding Turkey)—is ample evidence of the importance of Israel as a trading partner.

UNITED ARAB EMIRATES

The United Arab Emirates, or simply U.A.E. as it is normally referred to, is a composite of seven sedately governed emirates or states, of which Dubai and Abu Dhabi (which holds most of the U.A.E. oil and gas reserves and is the seat of the capital) are the two most progressive and aggressive states. The

U.A.E. is very, very rich. It has 10 percent of the world's oil reserves and 5 percent of the world's gas reserves.

The U.A.E. is the commercial and business hub of the Persian Gulf. There are no corporate or individual income taxes and only a 5 percent import duty. The internet is king in this country. The U.A.E. has more mobile phones and PCs than any other country in the Middle East. Dubai's Jebel Ali Free Zone is home to 2,500 foreign companies, including 150 American firms. Why? Because Dubai and Abu Dhabi are both excellent spots for distribution centers to service the entire Gulf region and Pakistan.

One of the more interesting developments in the Middle East is that the government of Abu Dhabi has announced plans to build a new city in the desert called Masdar City. It will cost $22 billion, take eight years to build, and "be home to 50,000 people and 1,500 businesses." Masdar City will be a solar powered "green" city with wind powered air conditioning. Residents will move about in pods running on magnetic tracks. Water will come from a solar powered desalinization plant. This city is part of a plan by Abu Dhabi to develop clean energy technologies, which it hopes to commercialize. Although this certainly sounds like a page out of a sci-fi magazine, officials are very serious about it and convincingly argue that such development efforts will revolutionize the energy, transportation, and water industries.

Obviously, as these plans come to fruition and the government of Abu Dhabi begins to offer construction tenders to foreign contractors, enormous markets will open to U.S. companies to supply everything from lumber to fasteners, from kitchen appliances to roofing and construction services. It will be well worth keeping a sharp eye on developments in this Gulf state.

Although the U.A.E. is a very attractive market and will be even more so in the future, a convoluted legal system still protects local firms and discriminates against foreigners. Without question, a local agent is a necessity. You can't do business here without an agent; however, it's almost impossible to fire one without a protracted court trial. Larger transnational companies get along OK, but this is not the place for first time exporters. For now, less resource rich smaller firms will find much better opportunities in other countries in Latin America, Southeast Asia, Eastern Europe, and even Israel or Egypt. See the Statistical Facts for the U.A.E.'s summarized statistics.

Ease of doing business (out of 178 countries)	68th
GDP per capita (PPP)	$49,700
Population	2.6 million
Inflation rate	10.0%
Unemployment rate	2.4%
Global competitiveness index world ranking (out of 122 countries)	32nd
Business competitiveness index world ranking (out of 116 countries)	33rd
Total crimes per 1,000 population	N/A
Corruption perception index score world ranking (out of 179 countries) (10 is squeaky clean, zero is awful)	5.7
Internet users	1.4 million
Percent of population living on less than $2 per day	N/A
Working healthcare system index world ranking (out of 190 countries)	27th
U.S. exports	$11.6 billion

A GDP per capita of almost $50,000 for a population of 2.9 million shows exactly how rich this country is. Although it is not especially corrupt with a score of 5.1, its obtuse business laws make the U.A.E. a difficult place in which to do business.

SAUDI ARABIA

Saudi Arabia is slightly easier to do business in than the U.A.E., but it too has arcane, antiquated laws based mainly on the royal family's interpretation of the Koran. The basic problem with Saudi Arabia is that to do business there you must—by law—have a local agent, only Saudi nationals can be registered agents, and only Saudi nationals can engage in trading activities. If you have to go to court and then to arbitration, be aware that no arbitration award has ever been granted in Saudi Arabia. To top off these strange Saudi laws, all business visitors to the Kingdom must have a local sponsor. You cannot get a visa without one. And local sponsors cost a fair amount of money. I should also add that intellectual piracy is rampant.

The Saudi government filters the internet. This means that when authorities do not like a particular website, they merely filter it out so no one can see it. News information is screened to delete anything that might be even remotely critical of the Saudi government or its dictums. Tens of thousands of sites are routinely blocked ostensibly to protect public morality. TV programming is just as censored. If authorities do not like a particular program—for any reason—they merely block its broadcast. And if reporters are deemed to have criticized the royal family, they can be imprisoned or even put to death. If you are still determined to do business in Saudi Arabia, your local partner better be well connected to the Riyadh government and to the Saudi banking community.

Everything must be imported in this country. There are no manufacturing companies of any significance and very little agriculture. However, infrastructure projects are still blossoming even after nearly 40 years of activity. And a whole new city is being planned for the southern area around Jizan, about 10 miles north of the Yemen border. See Statistical Facts for the Saudi Arabia's summarized statistics.

		STATISTICAL FACTS
Ease of doing business (out of 178 countries)	23rd	
GDP per capita (PPP)	$13,800	
Population	27.0 million	
Inflation rate	1.9%	
Unemployment rate	13.0%	
Global competitiveness index world ranking (out of 122 countries)	N/A	
Business competitiveness index world ranking (out of 116 countries)	N/A	
Total crimes per 1,000 population	N/A	
Corruption perception index score world ranking (out of 179 countries) (10 is squeaky clean, zero is awful)	3.4	
Internet users	2.5 million	
Percent of population living on less than $2 per day	N/A	
Working healthcare system index world ranking (out of 190 countries)	26th	
U.S. exports	$7.6 billion	

One fallout from the secretive nature of the Saudi government is the exclusion of that country from World Economic Forum surveys. The government opted not to be included because it did not want to reveal the type of information the pollsters needed to come up with their various indexes. None of the questions related to competitiveness were answered. Quite naturally, the same secrecy applies to people living under the poverty line and crimes committed. The only two relevant statistics were the corruption perception score of 3.5, which is quite a bit worse than average and the healthcare ranking of 26th, which is good. I can't believe the ease of doing business rank of 23rd. I have found Saudi business regulations nearly impossible to live with.

EGYPT

Egypt is clearly the most liberal of all Arab states. Perhaps because of its heritage of British occupation; because the Suez Canal attracts ships and business people of all nationalities; because of its booming tourist trade with visitors from all over the world; or perhaps because it is geographically distant from the more Islamic-oriented Persian Gulf nations. Whatever the reason, Egypt holds far more promise for America's smaller companies than any other Arab state.

The government, newly elected in 2004, has done wonders to open Egypt to Western businesses, and the country's rapid economic growth—6 percent—shows it. Tourism, a major industry in this country, is booming. New resorts along the Red Sea are built every day. Egypt is the sixth largest gas exporter in the world and more than 10 percent of Egyptian workers are employed in this industry.

Major infrastructure projects are about ready to begin. New airports, telecommunications projects, TV broadcasting systems, and seaport renovations will start in a year or so. If you sell products or services to the construction industry, this might be a terrific time to check out Egypt.

On the downside, red tape remains a horrendous problem. Getting through customs and dealing with arbitrary government decisions are guaranteed to slow down any business transaction and create massive headaches. A local partner can help, however, and you'll need one anyway. Try to locate someone with strong connections to key bureaucrats and who understands Western business protocol, although that may be too much to hope for. See Statistical Facts for Eygpt's summarized statistics.

Ease of doing business (out of 178 countries)	126th
GDP per capita (PPP)	$4,200
Population	78.9 million
Inflation rate	6.5%
Unemployment rate	10.3%
Global competitiveness index world ranking (out of 122 countries)	63rd
Business competitiveness index world ranking (out of 116 countries)	71st
Total crimes per 1,000 population	N/A
Corruption perception index score world ranking (out of 179 countries) (10 is squeaky clean, zero is awful)	2.9
Internet users	5.0 million
Percent of population living on less than $2 per day	43.9%
Working healthcare system index world ranking (out of 190 countries)	63rd
U.S. exports	$4.1 billion

A corruption perception score of 2.9 is very bad. And corruption is pervasive, stretching across government bureaus, businesses, and law enforcement. It's hard enough to do business in a country ranked 126th in the ease of doing business index without also dealing with abundant corruption. However, I don't believe the 126th ranking. I have done a lot of business in Egypt with little difficulty. Of course, I have always had strong local partners. Without question, Egypt offers some outstanding opportunities, but to succeed, you'll have to master the labyrinth of regulations and extensive corruption.

KUWAIT

After the first Gulf war in the early 1990s, Kuwait became very pro-American. This, plus the country's small geographic size, make doing business there relatively easy compared with other Persian Gulf states. Eighty percent of the Kuwaiti economy depends on the oil industry. Only very small light manufacturing companies operate there, making it necessary to import practically all manufactured products. About one-third of imports from U.S. companies relate to automobiles and auto parts and accessories.

Foreigners make up about 90 percent of the Kuwaiti workforce with most laborers coming from Pakistan and managers from Europe and America. Massive infrastructure projects are planned, including major highways, urban shopping centers, and a new container and transportation terminal. Environmental cleanup projects and upgraded electricity generating plants round out the largest undertakings. See Statistical Facts for Kuwait's summarized statistics.

STATISTICAL FACTS

Ease of doing business (out of 178 countries)	40th
GDP per capita (PPP)	$21,600
Population	2.4 million
Inflation rate	3.0%
Unemployment rate	2.2%
Global competitiveness index world ranking (out of 122 countries)	44th
Business competitiveness index world ranking (out of 116 countries)	47th
Total crimes per 1,000 population	N/A
Corruption perception index score world ranking (out of 179 countries) (10 is squeaky clean, zero is awful)	4.3
Internet users	700,000
Percent of population living on less than $2 per day	N/A
Working healthcare system index world ranking (out of 190 countries)	45th
U.S. exports	$2.1 billion

Marketing in Kuwait requires an inordinate amount of persistence and adaptability. Opaque regulations, an inconsistent judiciary, and a lack of consistency in decision making (especially by bureaucrats) means you'll face obstacles at every turn. The only way to cope is to have a strong local partner interpret what's happening and guide you through the maze.

The ease of doing business and the competitiveness rankings are well above average and reflect the pro-American attitude and the massive rebuilding effort still under way. English is widely spoken and most middle mangers in the business world as well as the government are American or European educated. The corruption score is not good, but it could be worse. All things considered, Kuwait is probably a better choice for smaller U.S. firms than other Gulf states.

QATAR

Qatar is a very small country with less than 1 million people. Like other Gulf states, oil and gas are the predominant industries. Infrastructure projects are the main attraction for foreigners. Over the next 10 years or so, Qatar expects investments of more than $120 billion in roads, housing and commercial buildings, hospitals and schools, and sanitation projects.

Food of all types is another good export prospect. Qatar imports more than 90 of all foodstuffs and processed food. To date, the main suppliers are from Australia, the EU, and Saudi Arabia, but smaller U.S. firms should be able to gain a foothold. Retail supermarkets are rapidly being developed, resulting in another possibility for U.S. firms that can export construction materials, supplies, equipment, and services. There are no import duties in Qatar.

A local partner is a practical necessity; it's also required by law. Additionally, most U.S. companies already doing business there recommend the hiring of a good local attorney who can speak English. This is especially important after you begin making a profit. That's when you can run into trouble with your local Qatari partner who suddenly wants a bigger split. See Statistical Facts for Qatar's summarized statistics.

		STATISTICAL FACTS
Ease of doing business (out of 178 countries)	N/A	
GDP per capita (PPP)	$29,400	
Population	900,000	
Inflation rate	7.2%	
Unemployment rate	3.2%	
Global competitiveness index world ranking (out of 122 countries)	38th	
Business competitiveness index world ranking (out of 116 countries)	44th	
Total crimes per 1,000 population	6.8	
Corruption perception index score world ranking (out of 179 countries) (10 is squeaky clean, zero is awful)	6.0	
Internet users	219,000	
Percent of population living on less than $2 per day	N/A	
Working healthcare system index world ranking (out of 190 countries)	44th	
U.S. exports	$1.3 billion	

The crimes per 1,000 population statistic of 6.8 is somewhat surprising. This is a relatively high number, and in such a small country, one would expect less crime. Inflation of 7.2% is much too high and distorts pricing structures. On the plus side, a corruption score of 6.0 indicates much less corruption than anywhere else in the Persian Gulf.

MOROCCO

Currently, 120 American businesses operate in Morocco, creating 90,000 direct and indirect jobs. Both Fruit of the Loom and Dell have operations there and are pleased with the results. The U.S.–Morocco Free Trade Agreement is now in effect, permitting about 95 percent of U.S. imports to enter Morocco duty-free. The Moroccan government looks to this trade pact to stimulate the economy and support the many economic reforms currently underway. This is a good example of how Morocco is moving toward modernization and globalization. The government desperately wants Morocco to become the regional hub of North Africa and is committed to economic and social reforms that will bring this nation into the modern world as quickly as feasible. Major reforms have also occurred within the monarchal government itself. For instance, at last count, the Moroccan Parliament seated 35 women. This is truly a remarkable occurrence, unheard of in the history of the Arab states.

Morocco is moving rapidly to upgrade its infrastructure and modernize business laws and regulations. It also encourages further development of its nascent tourist industry. Upgraded seaports, hotels, and restaurants augment its attractive 2,750 miles of coastline. Moreover, Morocco is not the sparsely populated desert country of several other Arab states. In a country the size of California, it has adequate rainfall and thriving agriculture on a very modest 20 percent of arable land.

The main competition in Morocco comes from France, which colonized this country and gave it its French language. Other EU companies are also very active there. If you want to do business in Morocco, you should plan to visit the country at least four or five times before beginning. And be patient. As with all Arab countries, time means nothing to Moroccans.

Although not required by law, a local distributor or partner is highly desirable. See Statistical Facts for Morocco's summarized statistics.

Ease of doing business (out of 178 countries)	129th	STATISTICAL FACTS
GDP per capita (PPP)	$4,400	
Population	33.2 million	
Inflation rate	2.8%	
Unemployment rate	7.7%	
Global competitiveness index world ranking (out of 122 countries)	70th	
Business competitiveness index world ranking (out of 116 countries)	79th	
Total crimes per 1,000 population	14.3%	
Corruption perception index score world ranking (out of 179 countries) (10 is squeaky clean, zero is awful)	3.6	
Internet users	4.6 million	
Percent of population living on less than $2 per day	20%	
Working healthcare system index world ranking (out of 190 countries)	29th	
U.S. exports	$878 million	

Despite the government's avowed interest in attracting foreign companies, its business regulations are stringent and difficult to cope with, hence an ease of doing business rank of 129th. For a country with a population of 33 million, about the same as California or Canada, the GDP per capita of $4,400 is quite low. This reflects the large number of people living in rural areas who will not be good consumers of imported goods. The corruption score of 3.6 places Morocco with most other Arab states. This is not good and retards economic growth. On the plus side, about 14 percent of the population has access to the internet.

OMAN

Oman is a tiny country with very limited oil reserves. This fact is encouraging the Sultanate to diversify the country's economic base, which means more business for foreign companies. Oman has virtually no manufacturing, so everything must be imported. Also, tourism is flourishing. This means an increased demand for imported food, equipment, and supplies. Construction equipment, supplies, and services are also needed for the building of new resorts. The Omani government is actively seeking foreign investors for light industry, the tourism sector, and power generation. Healthcare and medical equipment and supplies, water resource technology, and a vast array of consumer products are all viable choices for U.S. export.

Nationalization is unheard of in Oman. In fact, Oman has privatized its power, air transport, and telecommunications industries. In 2001, it become the first Gulf state to allow a private firm to build, own, and operate a major power project. A thriving shipping port, Port Salalah was built as a joint venture between the Omani government, private investors, and two American shipping companies, Sea-Land Service and Maersk. The government has announced that it intends to expand this port into a free trade zone and has already signed a letter of intent with a Houston-based developer.

The Sultanate of Oman is a free market economy, and Muskat is one of the most pleasant Gulf coast places to visit. Hotel accommodations are magnificent, the people are friendly toward Americans, and English is widely understood. If you are at all interested in doing business in the Gulf region, I suggest you give Oman a shot. See Statistical Facts for Oman's summarized statistics.

STATISTICAL FACTS

Ease of doing business (out of 178 countries)	49th
GDP per capita (PPP)	$14,100
Population	3.1 million
Inflation rate	2.0%
Unemployment rate	15.0%
Global competitiveness index world ranking (out of 122 countries)	N/A
Business competitiveness index world ranking (out of 116 countries)	N/A
Total crimes per 1,000 population	N/A
Corruption perception index score world ranking (out of 179 countries) (10 is squeaky clean, zero is awful)	4.7
Internet users	245,000
Percent of population living on less than $2 per day	N/A
Working healthcare system index world ranking (out of 190 countries)	N/A
U.S. exports	$829 million

The corruption score of 4.7 is about average and better than Morocco's. The ease of doing business rank of 49th bespeaks well of the efforts by the government to limit unnecessary constraints on business. This is a business friendly country trying hard to modernize. The very high unemployment rate of 15% relates primarily to the large number of Oman who live outside the only major city, Muskat.

ALGERIA

Algeria, like Oman and Morocco, is not a prominent export destination for U.S. products or services, although they did exceed $1 billion in 2007. The threat of terrorism remains the biggest problem for U.S. companies. Also, Algeria has arcane laws related to the repatriation of royalties and profits, stopping most American franchisers from entering this market.

The main export markets for U.S. companies relate to the construction of the country's road and rail infrastructures. In addition, healthcare products and services, basic consumer goods, power generation equipment, telecommunications, banking and financial services, hydrocarbon products and services for oil and gas, and water resources equipment and services are industries that require imported products and services.

The Algerian government has announced a series of projects for the coming years, all of which will be supplied by imported products and services. These projects include:

➡ A $110 billion social spending plan to upgrade housing.
➡ An east–west highway project in the high plains to connect Oran and Constantine.
➡ A north–south rail project, including high-speed trains.
➡ Hospital construction in nonmetropolitan areas.
➡ Hydrocarbons projects to develop natural gas resources.

Although these projects offer a significant opportunity for U.S. companies, the business climate in Algeria is anything but friendly. In fact, it can be downright unfriendly. For this reason, I cannot recommend Algeria for smaller U.S. exporters. See Statistical Facts for Algeria's summarized statistics.

Ease of doing business (survey of 178 countries)	125th
GDP per capita (PPP)	$7,700
Population	32.9 million
Inflation rate	15.0%
Unemployment rate	15.7%
Global competitiveness index world ranking (out of 122 countries)	76th
Business competitiveness index world ranking (out of 116 countries)	95th
Total crimes per 1,000 population	N/A
Corruption perception index score world ranking (out of 179 countries) (10 is squeaky clean, zero is awful)	3.0
Internet users	1.9 million
Percent of population living on less than $2 per day	N/A
Working healthcare system index world ranking (out of 190 countries)	81st
U.S. exports	$1.1 billion

Most of these statistics bear out my conclusion that Algeria is too tough an environment for beginning U.S. exporters. Corruption of 3.0, inflation of 15 percent, and an ease of doing business rank of 125th show very clearly the difficulties you would encounter there. It's more reasonable to choose a country where your chances of success are better.

PART III
INTERCULTURAL RELATIONSHIPS

chapter ten
American Habits that Drive Foreigners Up a Wall

Americans are basically considerate people. Yes, we get a bit raucous watching our favorite sports team; we fire off a few volleys when a rotten driver almost sideswipes our car; we fly off the handle when the electricity goes out in a storm; or we lose it when the bank turns down our request for a loan or our property taxes go up 30 percent. By and large, however, we're a rather calm people compared with other nationalities. We don't jail people for littering like they do in Singapore. We don't hang people for criticizing our government like they do in

Saudi Arabia. We don't shoot orphans on the street like they do in Brazil. When you think about it, compared to the rest of the world, we Americans are actually pretty careful to protect the rights of others.

That's not to say that we always behave like ladies and gentlemen. We definitely do not. Or that we don't have any bad habits. We most assuredly do. Or that we don't offend others, because that happens quite frequently—intentionally or unintentionally. And that's what this chapter is about—the cultural traits that cause us to behave poorly in foreign lands and ignore the idiosyncrasies of host country cultures.

To succeed in global trade, we need to be cognizant of our own behavior—how we talk, act, and dress. We must be aware of the things we say and do that may confuse or violate the cultural mores of our hosts. Our behavioral characteristics (or habits) emerge over a lifetime, partly in reaction to those around us, partly in response to media and government proclamations, and partly as a result of our upbringing and schooling. Each of us is infected by traits that are uniquely American. They show up in our actions and speech in business meetings, at cocktail parties, and at vacation haunts. We can't shake them, but we can learn to control them. And control them we must if we expect to be successful anywhere beyond our borders.

To succeed in global trade, we need to be cognizant of our own behavior—how we talk, act, and dress.

In addition to individual behavioral characteristics, our American society as a whole follows rules dictated by our government, churches, and other institutions. Some of these rules contradict individual traits, adding confusion and frustration to foreigners who try to understand the American way. We have no control over these contradictions, yet we must stand ready to explain how and why our lives are shaped by them. And if necessary, justify them to foreigners.

One of the by-products of globalization is that business people from all over the world travel all over the world meeting other business people. We absorb their traits, accents, and words, causing our customs and habits to change. Conversely, the people we meet absorb our traits and customs—the same ones that seemed uniquely American a few years ago—and their behavior changes. Global travel inevitably results in a merging of cultures, obliterating or at least shading national and regional differences and moving us toward one world, one peoples, a large melting pot not dissimilar from New York City as it entered the 20th century.

Having said that, let me be perfectly clear. Even with all the changes globalization has brought, the Ugly American (remember the book and movie by that title?) can still be found, making a nuisance of himself in foreign lands. All too often, our good behavior does not show through in everyday interactions with foreigners. I believe this is mainly because some of our not so gracious habits overshadow our good traits. Before we finish with this chapter, we will, hopefully, have zeroed in on most of the those typically American habits that are still unaffected by globalization and continue to drive foreigners up a wall. Dealing with language differences should be one of the easiest hurdles to get over but it never seems to be.

INSIGHT ... A few years ago I owned a manufacturing company that made metal fasteners—chrome plated rivets, high tensile bolts, stainless steel screws, and so on—and specialized batteries for natural gas drilling applications. My vice president of operations was a man named Jake Waslowski. Jake was young when I hired him, about 31 years old, but a whiz with computer controlled machine tools. We had a small export program selling batteries to customers in Quito and Guayaquil, Ecuador. Following complaints from a Guayaquil customer about our quality assurance program, I got Jake a passport, a plane ticket, and briefed him on this customer's idiosyncracies.

While Jake was still in the air on the way home, I received a call from our customer. He was furious and threatened never to order from us again. On Jake's return, I asked him what happened, expecting a lengthy discourse covering all of our customer's current headaches. Instead, Jake's only observation was that hardly anyone in Guayaquil spoke English. "I don't understand why they can't learn English. They've been buying from us for three years now and certainly could have learned in that time. I'm afraid I lost my temper and told Espocia that if he couldn't hire people who spoke English by the next time I came down, we had no interest in doing business with him."

Needless to say, within five minutes Jake was on the street looking for work. Never before, or since, have I been that embarrassed to deal with a customer. I quickly hopped a plane to Guayaquil. The next morning I pleaded with Sr. Espocia to forgive Jake and promised that he would never see Jake or anyone like him from my company ever again.

As we all know, one of the primary ingredients for success in any business endeavor is to know our customers—know how they think, where they're coming from, what turns them on, and what turns them off. But cultural dissimilarities tend to blur our vision. Therefore, to be successful in global trade, you must understand at least the obvious cultural differences long before you meet a customer, distributor, or sales representative.

Unfamiliar languages always cause problems. No one denies that. But putting those obstacles aside, the typically American characteristic that seems to cause the biggest problem when we meet foreigners for the first time is our hurry-up attitude, our frenetic speed in everything we do.

FRENETIC SPEED

Have you noticed how much we live by the clock? We spend our days running for trains or planes, always in a hurry to get somewhere or to accomplish something. Speed is crucial. Start meetings on time, finish them on schedule. Close the order and get on to the next customer. Don't waste time with small talk. Get to the point quickly. Work in the evening. Return to the office on weekends. Work 60-hour weeks. Hurry, hurry, hurry. Time is money. Do you recognize yourself or any of your associates? This frenzied search for more time, trying to squeeze 28 hours into a 24-hour day, drives foreigners nuts.

It's not only at work that we race against the clock. We do the same thing in our personal lives. Americans can't wait for anything. We hate to stand in line. Being put on hold for a phone call is maddening. Traffic jams lead to road rage. Let's get on with it. Why waste time waiting when there are so many places to go, so many things to do, and so little time. We seem to have an unending need to keep moving. However, citizens of most less developed countries have a laid-back attitude. They focus on the event, not the clock. Time isn't as important as enjoying the moment. Establishing personal relationships is far more important than signing an order or a contract right now. Why push it, they ask? You'll eventually get into the theater. I'll answer your call in a few minutes when I finish my break. Traffic is always heavy, just relax, you'll get there. We can always do tomorrow what we can't finish today, and no one loses. Don't let this laid-back attitude fool you. Your host will be as eager as you are to get things done. But not necessarily to your schedule.

INSIGHT... A case in point occurred when I was consulting for an off-shore HVAC contractor. My client was a subcontractor for a new central air conditioning system that the prime contractor was installing in a Caracas hospital. The project manager, a fast-talking native New Yorker on his first Latin American assignment, arrived at the job site intent on meeting predetermined deadlines. All the workers and the crew boss were Venezuelans. One month to the day after the job began, the project manager quit. "I've never been so frustrated," he told me. "No one wanted to work. Not even the crew boss. Tools kept disappearing or breaking. Workers didn't show up when they were supposed to. We were way behind schedule. I knew we had to work weekends to catch up, but the entire crew refused to do so. That was the final straw."

Damage control Plan A went into effect. I flew to Caracas and met with the crew boss. "What happened?" I asked. But I already knew the answer. "Señor Tuller, why all the rush? My men have families. They have things to do on weekends. But don't worry. We'll finish the job. Just keep Flanagan away from here!" I recruited a new project manager with extensive Latin American experience and the job was finished, albeit, three months late. But the prime contractor was satisfied, the hospital board was satisfied, and my client was paid in full.

Wearing the wrong clothes or displaying the wrong mannerisms are two other American traits that cause us grief overseas.

THE WRONG DRESS, THE WRONG MANNERISMS

I don't know exactly when dressing-down became a fad, but I think it was during the dot-com era of the 1990s when very young entrepreneurs made their fortunes under the California sun. First, the office dress code changed to casual on Friday. Then it evolved to casual every day. Then this dressing-down habit overflowed to other public places—the theater, air travel, restaurants, vacation spots, and even the Metropolitan Opera. Pants overtook dresses as women's preferred mode of dress. Men cast aside suits, ties, and dress shirts for open neck sport shirts. Summer shorts became the norm in hot weather, for men and women alike, whether in public places or private backyards.

All this casualness is well and good as long as you remain in your hotel room. However, when in public settings, more often than not casual dress will be offensive and contrary to local norms. Men do not usually wear shorts in public. It may be over 100 degrees, as it usually is in the Arab states, but Arab men do not wear shorts in public. Outside the Arab world America's influence is beginning to show, and I have seen a few exceptions. Last year while visiting a large Latin American city, I was surprised to see for the first time about 1 in 100 men wearing shorts in public, albeit on a weekend. That's not a huge number. But compared to five years ago when no Latin man would be caught dead wearing shorts in public, it was a massive change.

You'll be much happier if you leave your pants and shorts at home when you travel to these places.

I have yet to see women wear shorts in public. As far as I know, no emerging nation dress code sanctions such a display. At beach resorts its OK but definitely not in restaurants, public transport, government or business offices, shopping malls, or even strolling down the street. And ladies, I know many of you love to wear pants at the office and other public places. So does my wife. That's fine in America. It's even OK overseas in countries that have accepted this American custom. But in many less developed countries it raises questions of propriety. You'll be much happier if you leave your pants and shorts at home when you travel to these places. Wear a dress and I guarantee you will be treated like a lady, anyplace in the world, which reminds me of a recent trip.

INSIGHT... Not long ago I traveled to Mexico with a lovely lady in her fifties. She was aggressive, technically competent, and a very successful executive for my U.S. client. Before leaving the States, I persuaded her (with some difficulty, I might add) to leave her leisure clothes at home, even though part of our stay would be at an Acapulco resort. She argued that I was bringing shorts, why couldn't she? Or at least a pair of comfortable pants?

After our first day of meetings my lady friend was flabbergasted. Flushed in the face, she called me aside, "I have never been treated so well by any of our American customers. These Mexican guys bent over backward to be courteous and gracious to me. The young man even asked me to have lunch with him." During our return flight home she went a step further. "Our last meeting at the resort took the cake. You were right about the dress code. Who wants to wear shorts when you can dress up a little and be treated like a queen. I love Mexico and Mexicans."

I don't expect every American business woman to receive this great of a reception, but I'm certain you will feel more at ease and be able to accomplish your business more expeditiously by dressing up, not down. And that's true anyplace in the world. Once again, however, American customs are breeding changes. Designer jeans for women and work jeans for men are becoming an increasingly acceptable way to dress—especially in Latin America. But until you know for sure what is acceptable and what is not acceptable, leave your jeans at home.

Although it seems like a minor point, I feel obliged to comment on the lackadaisical way we Americans hold ourselves. Have you ever looked around your office to see how your compatriots are standing, sitting, holding themselves? If not, take a look, and I think you'll be surprised. Joe will be talking with his hands in his pockets. Joan will be draping an arm over a nearby chair. Peter will be slouching in his chair with his legs apart or perhaps with his feet up on the desk. Mary has her legs crossed, showing the sole of her shoe (which, by the way needs resoling).

We are all guilty of these mannerism at one time or another. When we are by ourselves, its OK to get comfortable, take our shoes off, stretch our legs, lounge in our chairs. It is definitely not acceptable to do these things in public places overseas. In fact, your host will consider these mannerisms not only rude but uncultured and uncouth. That's an easy way to lose an order or to alienate a bureaucrat.

COARSENESS, ARROGANCE, AND SELF-CRITICISM

Fortunately, not all Americans are coarse in their speech and mannerisms. But enough of us are to make it appear like everyone is a bit rough around the edges. Particularly when overseas, too many Americans are ill at ease and cover up their uneasiness with coarse language, off-color jokes, and snide remarks. To even the most uneducated person anywhere in the world, this smacks of rudeness and a lack of concern for the feelings of others.

If you are ill at ease in a foreign land, uncomfortable with the local culture, and stymied by an unfamiliar language or dialect, go out of your way to be pleasant, congenial, and respectful of your host's culture—even if you don't understand what's going on. And stay away from attempts at humor, especially off-color jokes. Most people will not understand your punch line anyway.

INSIGHT... One of the most uncomfortable moments I can recall from my many overseas adventures occurred several years ago during a preliminary meeting with two well-educated, courteous, Omani business men. My vice president of sales accompanied me to Muscat where we tried to nail down a fairly large order for diesel engine fasteners. We were about to conclude the meeting when my associate felt obliged to tell an off-color joke that ridiculed the sexual prowess of our American president. The Omanis were not only shocked, embarrassed, and indignant at such denigration of the leader of the most powerful nation in the world, they were angry enough to call off the meeting and cancel further discussions. Needless to say, we lost the order.

Why is it that we Americans tend to give the impression that we believe we are always right and that our way is the only way, leaving no room for an opposing opinion? It seems that because we live in a competitive society with opposing viewpoints thrust on us from all media, we have become so opinionated that we find it difficult to accept the position of others as anything but controversial and, therefore, wrong. Such arrogance will not get us anywhere. No one will put up with it. And why should they? After all, we are doing business in their countries. We are their guests. Nine times out of 10, foreigners will not argue with Americans about matters they consider to be either personal or of no consequence. Instead, they will merely ignore us and stop doing business with us.

Americans are taught from an early age that in a democracy politics is everyone's business. We think nothing of expressing our opinions about the antics of a president or a new law passed by Congress. We do this at the office, at cocktail parties, during athletic events, and even in church. But people in other cultures don't understand this. Many of them have never experienced true democracy. As with any new concept, they have trouble grasping what it is all about. They have yet to learn the value of good-natured criticism of those in authority. In fact, in Saudi Arabia or China you could be imprisoned or even hanged for criticizing the government. It wasn't too many years ago that this was also true in Russia and Eastern Europe. When we start expressing our opinions about politics, 9 times out of 10 our foreign counterparts will quickly change the subject. Best to stay away from this sensitive subject right from the onset.

Foreigners regard the distinctly American capacity for self-criticism as one of our strangest traits.

Foreigners regard the distinctly American capacity for self-criticism as one of our strangest traits. We often don't realize we're doing it, but by and large, most Americans love to criticize anything and anybody, mostly in good humor. We poke fun at our leaders, our institutions, ourselves, and just about anyone or anything we can think of.

Rodney Dangerfield became a celebrity by deprecating himself. Mark Russell made a living satirizing government leaders. Don Rickles insulted his audience, and they laughed. Jon Stewart takes on anyone from the president to the pope on downward with his sharp wit. Listen to the rhetoric in any political campaign. Criticizing friend and foe alike has become the American way.

From time to time most of us voice disapproval of our president, our church, corporate giants, labor unions, state and federal laws and legislators, social welfare, our local sports teams, lawyers, and so on. We even make cracks about our democratic system. Yes, we love to criticize ourselves, our leaders, and our institutions. But it's all done internally. Americans criticizing Americans. All in the family. And we want to keep it that way. We take strong offense when outsiders criticize us, our way of life, or our leaders.

Foreigners can't understand this strange trait. How we can be so self-critical yet get madder than hell when they voice the same opinions as us. I don't know of any nationality that has a similar sense of humor. In all my travels, I have never heard anyone engage in this type of good-natured criticism directed toward their own institutions, country, governments, or churches. When you are in country, you'll be farther ahead if you don't criticize anyone or anything—not ours, not theirs. Compliment rather than criticize your host country's mores. And be proud of America as well.

LACK OF COURTESY

Another American habit that causes problems is our lack of courtesy in day-to-day relationships. It is unfortunate that many of us seem to have forgotten most of the manners we were brought up with. Civility has become a lost art. When in the heat of battle, striving for individual achievement, and combating all the forces that seem to work against us, we tend to ignore common courtesies toward others. I don't mean garden-variety manners that most of us practice intuitively day in and day out, such as saying thank you, please, and excuse me or standard table manners. I am talking about more blatant discourtesies. For example:

➡ How often do we interrupt others when they speak?
➡ How often do we let our minds wander and forget to listen to others?
➡ How often do we take an action for our own benefit, knowing that such an action will harm others?
➡ How often do we say things, intentionally or unintentionally, that hurt others?

➡ How often do we lie, cheat, or even steal to gain personal advantage over customers, suppliers, employees, peers, and bosses without regard to the harm inflicted?

The advent of cell phones has taught us how to communicate anytime, anyplace for as long as we want. This enables us to ignore those around us. They are not part of the conversation, so we just forget they are there. We certainly do not care whether everyone within hearing distance listens to our conversation. After all, isn't the main purpose in using a cell phone in a public place to show everyone how important we are?

How annoying that is. Using cell phones in public has to be one of the most discourteous acts ever conceived. It didn't start in the United States, but Americans have definitely caught up to the Europeans in the time spent on the phone. Numerous studies have proven that talking on a cell phone while driving a car is very dangerous. Yet Americans are so addicted that they ignore laws in those states that prohibit the use of cell phones while driving.

Americans aren't totally to blame for the spread of cell phones. These devices enable people who live in remote locations and who do not have landlines to communicate with each other. And that's fine. Cell phones are extremely beneficial when used properly. It's their discourteous use that is so annoying. Unfortunately, we seem to have exported this discourtesy to every corner of the globe.

Speaking of telephoning, another American discourtesy that has caught on in other countries is the belief by business people that voice mail relieves them of any obligation to return phone calls. Just as in the United States, when confronted they will claim they haven't received the call or they forgot to check their calls or the message was so garbled they couldn't understand it. It is indeed unfortunate that we have become so entranced with our own importance, so fascinated with our own routines, that we cannot even follow the common courtesy of returning phone calls. I always return calls, and you probably do the same. But I must admit that in the course of everyday activities most of my calls are never returned, or if they are returned, it's many days or even a week later. By and large, this habit has not, in the past, been

> **Another American habit that causes problems is our lack of courtesy in day-to-day relationships.**

common worldwide, but it is rapidly becoming so. The more we indulge in this very discourteous practice, the more our friends emulate us. If your customer or distributor or anyone else calls your hotel room or in-country office, please return that call as soon as you can.

Another typically American habit that has become so commonplace, we don't even recognize it as being discourteous, is the use of familiar first names when addressing complete strangers, in both oral and written communications. We say Mike, Sally, Ester, and Joe rather than Mr. Jones, Ms. Patrick, or Mrs. Smith. Such familiarity is totally unacceptable anywhere in the world. If you don't speak the local language use Mr., Miss, or Mrs. If you can muster the courage to use the local form of address so much the better.

These discourtesies alienate foreigners and foster the image of the Ugly America. Anywhere in the world a kind word, smile, or small favor will get you much farther than aggressive behavior, or worse, offensive habits. Yes, everyone wants our dollars and our technologies. And yes, to achieve that people will continue to put up with Ugly Americans. But for a long-term, profitable relationship, we need to put aside our discourteous habits and practice the good manners we were brought up with.

DIVORCE AND FAMILY VIOLENCE

Statistics show that 60 percent of U.S. marriages end in divorce. Headlines about child abuse, domestic violence, and the abdication of responsibility for the family blaze across big city dailies. To outsiders, such national mayhem bespeaks of a troubled society. Why do so many Americans get married and have children when they clearly have no intention of assuming the responsibility that goes along with such an act?

When you have the opportunity emphasize how important your family is to you.

Yes, the world has many violent regions. Latin America is one of the worst—but not against the family. Except for non-Latin countries such as Guyana and Trinidad and Tobago, families throughout Latin America are still a sacred institution mostly immune from random violence. While it is true that Brazilian police slaughter innocent orphan children on the street, Guatemalan militiamen plunder peasant villages indiscriminately murdering women and children, and people of all ages get caught in the cross fire of

Colombian thugs, there is very little violence directed exclusively at family members. Few mothers would think of driving a car into a lake to drown two innocent children. Infants are seldom left to starve on doorsteps. And fathers don't throw their children out fifth floor windows because they cry too much.

When you have the opportunity emphasize how important your family is to you. If you have children, don't be afraid to show their pictures. You will never go wrong by praising family values. Even if you're not married, heaping kudos on the family institution will bring good feelings from your host.

INAPPROPRIATE USE OF THE ENGLISH LANGUAGE

Have you noticed how very intense we Americans are when we are in a business setting, whether it a meeting, an interview, a negotiation, a sales call, or any gathering where we must interface with others? I don't know anyone who has mastered the art of relaxation when trying to make a point or win a business challenge. I certainly have not. One way we cope with stressful situations is to use buzzwords. I don't know why, but we do. And many of these words are new to foreigners, although those who deal regularly with Americans are beginning to incorporate these same slang words in their own vocabularies, whether or not they understand their meaning.

Maybe you haven't noticed, but I guarantee you that foreigners do notice and become very confused by our desecration of the Queen's English.

Even if you don't suffer such stress, chances are good that you practice corporate speak, the special language evolved from corporate America, or legalese, the language developed by the legal profession, or computerese, the language that comes from the dot-com gurus. Maybe you haven't noticed, but I guarantee you that foreigners do notice and become very confused by our desecration of the Queen's English.

It seems that we constantly come up with new buzzwords to describe an event, an action, a person, or an object. We are peppered with politically correct expressions that expand simple one word adjectives and nouns into compound words and milk-toast phrases. We get so carried away with improper English that we pick up from our workplace friends and, of course from television programs and newscasts as well as movies, that we don't even realize what we are doing. As far as I know, our colloquialisms are not taught in any English-language class anywhere in the world. So how could our friends in other lands possibly know what we mean when we use buzz-words that even Americans have a hard time deciphering. Just for fun, here are a few catchy words that I have recently read or heard. Most are corporate speak (love that buzzword) with some politically correct phrases thrown in. See how many you recognize. By the way, to conserve space, I have intentionally excluded computerese, a subject for an entire book.

Here are the buzzwords: action items, African- or Asian-American, sales associate, corporate speak, customer relationship management, deferred success, Enronitis, going forward, insourcing or onshoring, intellectual infrastructure, learning opportunity, mentally challenged, mission critical, negative profit, PDFing, physically impaired, RIF, silver bullet, spin, telephonically communicable, variable staff, and value added.

The one that sends me up a wall is the now common use of the word "ton" to describe a quantity of items (e.g., a ton of people attended the event). The word ton describes a weight—2000 pounds—not a quantity of anything.

Some words are concocted to describe specific conditions or arrangements. Still others make derogatory or complimentary statements. Certainly, some of them can be found in English dictionaries but with definitions completely different from those intended in the business world. Foreigners who have dealt with U.S. companies over the years will generally figure out what you mean by these buzzwords. Those who have not had such experience or who have had only casual brushes with American business people will be lost.

I thank John Walston, buzzwacker-in-chief and author of the marvelous book, *The Buzzword Dictionary* for shaking my memory and inspiring my plunge into buzzwords. Mr. Walston and his army of contributors have provided me with an uproarious journey into the art of wordology (how's that for a buzzword). I strongly recommend his book for anyone with a sense of humor.

Big words are also a no-no. We all have pet words that we use to impress people or express a particular situation when no other word will do. This is fine on our home turf. But overseas, unless the person you are addressing has an American university education, chances are very good that you will be badly misunderstood. I find the following to be a helpful reminder, "When promulgating your esoteric cogitations, eschew all conglomerations of flatulent garrulity." (When speaking, don't use big words.)

The moral, of course, is to be very careful about what you say and how you say it. Be precise. Clarify any phrases that could be misunderstood. And by all means, let it be known that you want the other party to ask for clarification of any words that seem confusing or contradictory.

Also, be aware that many American clichés and idioms will only translate into a host country language literally. And the literal translation may connote an entirely different meaning from that which you intended. For example, here are a few advertisements that I clipped from newspapers and trade magazines:

➡ "Dow tanks 184 on high oil"—headline in Philadelphia Inquirer
   Did they really mean "thinks" or perhaps "thanks"?
➡ "The King of Cash makes cash work harder for you"—E*Trade Financial
   Who is the king? How does cash work, on a throne?"
➡ "Charting Your Course for Export Success?"—Reed Exhibition Companies
   To Brazilians, charting your course implies preparing a map for a boat trip.
➡ "Realize Making Your City Fly"—Verizon
   How can a telephone company make a city fly? Is this something new in telecommunications?
➡ "First Cut Sale Starts Today"—Saks Fifth Avenue
   Does that mean you have to bring your knife to the store or perhaps scissors?
➡ "Be Locked and Loaded"—E*Trade Financial
   This one loses me completely.
➡ The coup d'grace comes from Soloflex WBV Exercise Machine:
   "God does the healing. We collect the fee."
   Oh, really?

While we're on the subject of language, I should answer a question that I have been asked many times by clients thinking about entering global trade: Do you have to be fluent in the host country language to succeed? Yes and no. Being bilingual will make your job a lot easier and you will get things accomplished much faster. Speaking the language is definitely a huge advantage. But no, you do not have to be fluent in any host country language to do business there. Interpreters are always available. And be sure to use them if you have any doubt about your ability to correctly use the local dialect. I learned that lesson the hard way.

INSIGHT... Linguistics has never been my strong suit. Nevertheless, several years ago I thought I had mastered Spanish sufficiently to get by without an interpreter. My client was building a facility in the Colombian mountains near Buccaramunga. One of my assignments was to negotiate for the overland transport of several pieces of heavy equipment that my client was shipping to the port of entry, Barranquilla. In Cartegena, I negotiated with a hauler for three lowboys to meet the ship in two months, or at least I thought that's what I had negotiated. When the shipment arrived at the docks in Barranquilla it was met by three school buses and two taxis but no lowboy trucks. Needless to say, I had some explaining to do. That was the last time I negotiated a contract any place in the world without an interpreter present.

⟩ OBSESSIVE CONTROL

At an early age we learn that we can do anything, be anyone, accomplish any project, and we can control our lives. In addition to our own lives, we become infested with an overwhelming need to control other people's lives as well as events. This propensity to control manifests itself in our relationship with everything and everybody we touch—our children, our spouse, our subordinates, our health, our work pace, our commuting schedules, how we do our jobs, even how we choose our elected officials. And when this control is wrested from us, by other individuals, events, or legislated rules and regulations, we rebel. Rebellion takes the form of anger, stubbornness, withdrawal, and sometimes violence. Some people get so mad when they lose control that they damage relationships, seek refuge in alcohol or drugs, turn out poor work, or even lose jobs. Several human relations studies have discovered that one of the main reasons underlying divorces is that one or both partners could not control the other.

Most business people from around the world have a hard time understanding why we get so uptight about everything we do.

Most business people from around the world have a hard time understanding why we get so uptight about everything we do. Is it really necessary, they wonder, to be the master of every situation? Why not let things happen as they will? And for goodness sake, our foreign friends imply, don't infringe on my personal life just because you're a control freak.

INSIGHT... When a person who needs to control does business with or has a relationship with one who won't be controlled, sparks are bound to fly. A good example of this occurred when a very successful West Coast publisher of a women's travel magazine came out with an Asian version, to be printed in Taipei and distributed throughout China and Southeast Asia. This dynamic, outspoken publisher decided she needed a partner to cut through the red tape and manage complex Chinese distribution channels, so she teamed up with an equally dynamic Taiwanese cosmetics distributor.

The two parties agreed that the Taiwanese partner's distribution network would more than compensate for his lack of experience in magazine publishing. But unanimity was not to be. The Taiwanese partner claimed the American wanted to control his business. And, conversely, the publisher claimed her partner was totally unreasonable in his demands for autonomy. Not surprisingly, the partnership broke up in six months. Our obsessive need to control everything that touches our daily lives is seen by foreigners as a very destructive American habit.

The land of the free is supposed to mean a country free of government control over individual actions. Yet many other nations seem to have far fewer restrictions on their citizens than the United States. This not only confuses our friends, it makes them wonder if we Americans know what we are about. Do we really believe we are free to pursue our own lives, they wonder? Do we really practice the sanctity of the individual? Do we really have a freer society than Brazil, China, Russia, or India? Or are we merely parroting propaganda from our leaders? Be prepared to cautiously debate this point because it certainly will come up.

COMPETITIVENESS AND INDIVIDUALITY

Competition is as American as apple pie and baseball. We seem to have an innate drive to compete. Practically since birth, we are taught that we live in a competitive world and to accomplish our goals we must compete as fiercely as the next person. We learn the virtues of competitiveness in schools, on playgrounds, in athletic contests, and most of all, in our business schools and business media. The more competitive we are the better. We must do whatever it takes to win, the consequences be damned.

> This intense competitive drive conflicts with the laid-back attitude in most emerging nations. It is not part of their culture—not that people in other lands do not like to compete. World class soccer teams and rugby teams from Brazil, Argentina, Cameroon, and South Africa; beauty contestants from Venezuela; and the massive appeal of baseball in Venezuela and the Dominican Republic belie any lack of a competitive nature. But citizens of less developed nations do not feel compelled to compete in business matters the way Americans do. Other than the Chinese, Israelis, and a few other nationalities, hardly anyone takes business that seriously. Although you will find advertising and sales promotions proclaiming this or that product more reliable, lower priced, or more up-to-date than those of other companies and you will certainly see public officials vying for favor like it is a national pastime, you will not find the acute competitiveness in business that we are accustomed to. I suggest that you tone down your competitiveness when in a meeting or negotiation with foreign associates. Stay cool. You may lose the battle but win the war.

I suggest that you tone down your competitiveness when in a meeting or negotiation with foreign associates. Stay cool. You may lose the battle but win the war.

> The main building block of our competitiveness is our individuality. The primacy of the individual is the backbone of our free enterprise system. We constantly strive for individual achievement, a better paying job, a higher position in our company, the acquisition of material goods that signify our social standing, the accumulation of wealth. These are our ultimate goals. Our democratic system and social standards stress the worth of the individual over the group. During this competitive drive for more power, wealth,

and social standing, we tend to relegate family, friends, religion, and community to the back burner, focusing our attention on our own gains. This really drives foreigners up a wall, especially those from emerging nations. The cultures of less developed nations place primary importance on the betterment of the group, not the individual. Individuality is a foreign concept not practiced anywhere except in rich nations. You won't win friends in China, Russia, the Arab states, or anywhere else for that matter, by charging ahead with an intense drive to succeed.

A corollary to our society's emphasis on individuality is the belief, now common in management philosophy, that empowering the individual with certain freedoms and responsibilities causes that person to strive ever more diligently to do a better job, rise in stature, and contribute more to the organization whether it be a company, the military, the government, educational institutions, or charitable organizations. One byproduct of this emphasis on individual freedom and personal responsibility is the lack of loyalty toward the companies we work for. The company needs us more than we need the company, seems to be the mantra of today's workers and managers. The high management turnover in virtually every industry is a good indication of how far the sense of individuality has come. Of course, the lack of loyalty works in reverse as well. Companies give little thought to the effect that cost-cutting layoffs and plant closings have on the individuals being laid off, their families and communities, or the workers remaining on the job. Contrast these philosophies with Russia or China where the primacy of the state supercedes any position of the individual, and workers seldom get fired.

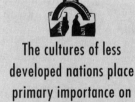

The cultures of less developed nations place primary importance on the betterment of the group, not the individual.

In those cultures that stress the betterment of the state, the family, and the community over the achievement of individual goals, empowerment of the individual is not part of the value system. Employees expect to be told what to do and most would be afraid to offer suggestions. Rewards are associated with loyalty and following orders, not with showing individual initiative. Attending state rallies, sporting events, and family gatherings is far more important than working long hours and taking on special projects to achieve a job promotion. The impact of this lack of individuality on manufacturing productivity, employee motivation, and managerial consistency is very pronounced, and you need to cope with it when you set up your in-country facility.

One offshoot of the American belief in the empowerment of the individual is that we love to negotiate. We negotiate prices, contractual agreements, wages, advancement opportunities, benefit packages, and a host of other matters with a vengeance. And of course, the corollary to negotiation is compromise. We consider a confrontation successful only when compromise is reached and neither party gets what was originally sought. Labor contract negotiations are a prime example.

Now I'm not saying that negotiating is unique to Americans. Try getting anything accomplished in the Arab states without negotiating and you'll soon throw in the towel. The same goes for Russia, Israel, and most Asian countries. What is uniquely American, however, is the willingness to end negotiations with a compromise. The will to compromise is not a common trait in other cultures and falls on deaf ears almost everywhere, except in the Arab states. Negotiating tactics are so important to success in global trade and so convoluted in many parts of the world, that I have devoted the entire Chapter 14 to offering a few tips for smoothing the negotiating trail.

GUNS AND VIOLENCE

One behavioral trait that causes an enormous amount of concern and misunderstanding is our predilection toward guns and violent acts. It seems so un-American. We all know that our movies, television shows, and TV news reports saturated with violence are seen around the world and music is listened to by millions on every continent. The violent use of guns peppers the consciousness of every watcher and listener. Quite naturally, they believe that such entertainment media portrays the American way.

Many foreigners that I have done business with have been aghast at America's fascination with guns.

Many foreigners that I have done business with have been aghast at America's fascination with guns. "In a society that has one of the most prolific law enforcement regimes in the world, why," they ask, "must every citizen keep a loaded revolver in his home? Why are mentally deranged lunatics permitted to purchase automatic weapons, grenades, even bazookas that are then used to massacre innocent bystanders? How can a society that prides itself on law and order employ police officers and federal agents who shoot first and ask questions later?" How you debate this is beyond me. Maybe you will have an answer if, and when, it comes up.

Our legal system also mystifies nearly everyone—with the exception, perhaps of the British. "How can a country with three levels of courts—municipal, state, and federal—and a judicial system that is the envy of the world, allow convicted rapists, thieves, and murderers to walk the streets a second, third, or even a fourth time?" Good question.

Now I don't mean to infer that other countries are not just as violent. They most assuredly are. What I am saying is that as U.S. citizens we are in no position to criticize this violence. More often than not I have heard the comment, "Yes, we have violence in our country. That we cannot deny. But what right do you as an American have to point fingers at us when your country has more than its share of violence?" A valid point. It's very dangerous to throw stones when we live in a glass house.

To conclude this chapter, let's turn to a few contradictions that seem to contradict all the good things foreigners have learned about our country and our behavior.

When you think about it, the American culture is full of contradictions. And this baffles the rest of the world.

CONTRADICTIONS

When you think about it, the American culture is full of contradictions. And this baffles the rest of the world. What do I mean by contradictions? Here are a few of the more prominent ones.

Although we pride ourselves on being individualistic, self-confident, strong, and able to conquer every obstacle in life, we insist that our government enact policy after policy to protect us from everything—from secondhand smoke to automobile crashes to fireworks to speeding motorists to illnesses to cheap medicines to airplane terrorists to drowning in the ocean to breaking a leg while skiing to the sky falling. The obsession of our elected leaders to control our daily lives under the guise of protecting us from ourselves often takes the form of waving the public good flag. Our elected representatives pass laws to forbid racial, age, and gender discrimination; define product labeling; reduce environmental hazards; limit highway speed; guarantee a minimum wage; enforce surveillance of our private lives; push for occupational safety; and a host of other matters, many of which are best left to an individual's initiative. In most cases, we buy into these regulations because we believe that sacrificing control over our own lives for the good of society is a beneficial trade-off.

This is very confusing to foreigners. Why do Americans demand that their government protect them from everything under the sun, yet they risk every dollar they have to start a business?

Americans love to help people in distress. When hurricanes, earthquakes, snowstorms, or floods hit, people from all over our country rush to give assistance. If they can't physically help, they send money. Hurricane Katrina was a good example when untold millions poured in from individuals, businesses, churches, and other organizations. Our government rushes troops to such far-flung places as Afghanistan, Iraq, Bosnia, and Somalia to protect the citizens of those countries from danger—but simultaneously refuses to intercede in the Sudan, eastern Congo, northern Uganda, Indonesia, Northern Ireland, East Timor, and dozens of other countries. This is very confusing to foreigners.

Millions and millions of political campaign funds are spent on TV commercials, plane transport, newspaper ads, and various other expenses, which everyone agrees is an unproductive use of money. Additionally, according to the Deloitte Center for Banking Solutions (www.deloitte.com) banks spend more than $83 million annually just to comply with new government regulations, an obviously unproductive use of cash. At the same time, our inner cities rot away, succumbing to dirt, grime, and the drug scourge. City and national parks deteriorate because of a lack of maintenance. Prisons hold three times the number of inmates for which they were designed. Veterans who have given their limbs and hearts to follow our government's direction pack VA hospitals, clamoring for medical attention and medicines that are unavailable because of a lack of federal funding. Bureaucrats at the federal, state, and municipal levels all agree that solutions to these problems won't be forthcoming until more money becomes available. Foreigners look at this dilemma and think, "Its strange that there seems to be plenty of money for political campaigns and government compliance but not enough to meet the needs of America's citizens."

Most Americans live in relatively clean accommodations—clean houses, condos, or apartments. We send our children to clean schools, work in clean environments, eat in clean restaurants, attend sporting events in clean stadiums, and pray in clean churches. We demand that our restaurant kitchens pass rigid health inspections. We insist that our hospitals and doctors offices are as free of germs as possible. On the other hand, Americans are probably some of the worst litterbugs in the world. We think nothing of dropping cigarette butts on the sidewalk or ground. We toss trash out of our car windows. We allow garbage to pile up on street curbs for days on end. We permit local governments, businesses, and transport companies to pollute our air and water. This is very confusing to foreigners. On one the hand, we demand cleanliness. On the other hand, we pollute our streets, parks, air, and water supplies with toxic chemicals and trash. Too many times foreigners have complained to me that Americans are unclean, messy, and inconsiderate of others, especially when it comes to disposing of their cigarette butts.

Although Latin American smokers outnumber American smokers by a wide margin, and for many years cigarette butts were a common sight, conditions have changed. During a recent visit to the downtown area of Guayaquil, Ecuador, a city of 3 million people, I walked four city blocks of the Malecón 2000 and did not see one cigarette butt on the sidewalk or ground. By the way, didn't I see any cigarette receptacles either. Compare this to the littered downtown areas of Philadelphia or Boston or Chicago. That comparison explains why foreigners are confused about our demand for cleanliness.

So much for American habits. In the next chapter, we'll take a look at some of the most unusual cultural traits of the BRIC nations and the Arab states.

chapter eleven
Beware of Cultural Risks

A few years ago, I was asked to give the keynote address at the annual conference of a large trade association. The audience was comprised of 800 people, many of whom have been involved in global trade for a long time. After dinner, one member asked me, "What do you mean by cultural risks? I know about culture clash, cultural differences, and cultural traits, but I've never heard of cultural risks?" My rather long-winded explanation was approximately as follows.

Anyone doing business in a foreign land must adjust his or her behavior to local customs and protocol. We all know that. However, more and more, it seems that Americans abroad tend to believe that everyone, all over the world, should accept their behavior as typically American and take no offense when their words or actions differ from local customs. With all the publicity international trade has had in the last 15 years, this surprises me. Yet my experience has been that once American business people step on foreign soil, they forget about any cross-cultural training they've had and jump right into a business situation with the same vigor and lack of courtesy they exhibit at home. This creates conflicts. Either we do not understand the customs and business protocol of our hosts, or we do not respect our differences. After all, and this we must always remember, we are guests in another country. As guests, we should honor the cultural diversity of our host as we would honor the desires of our host at a dinner party back home.

Anyone doing business in a foreign land must adjust his or her behavior to local customs and protocol.

At any rate, when we venture into a new overseas market, we face a cauldron of external market risks. We also face significant challenges from peculiar, and at times, bizarre local customs that jeopardize our success as much as corruption, street crime, or government interference. That's what I mean by cultural risks.

The four BRIC countries are excellent examples of the wide variances in cultures. Brazil, Russia, India, and China have significantly different cultures that emanate from a combination of tradition, religion, and politics. Moreover, they are all at variance with our American culture. Except for Brazil, these countries are much, much older than the United States, and as such, have had many more generations to develop their cultures. Although the Arab states do not hold the business potential of the BRIC countries, cultural anomalies are so pronounced that I would be remiss in ignoring that part of the world in this discussion. Keep in mind as we look at each of these cultures, globalization has narrowed the differences among the BRIC countries, the Arab states, and the United States. We are constantly absorbing many of each other's cultural traits, leading eventually to a single, one-world society.

BRAZIL

Most traits common to Portuguese-speaking Brazil are also present throughout Spanish-speaking Latin American, making it reasonably safe to juxtapose most of Brazil's cultural characteristics on the rest of the region.

All Latin countries, whether of Portuguese or Spanish heritage, place a high value on family. Daily life centers on the family, not the individual. Some people define the family as immediate relatives—mother, father, and children. But Brazilian families often extend well beyond this close-knit group to include distant relatives, such as grandparents, cousins, nieces, and nephews plus, of course, everyone's spouses. The term family also refers to neighborhoods and entire communities. Athletic teams, churches, and small businesses may include members from several families living in close proximity. The bonds that hold this type of extended family together are as strong as those that bind mother, father, and children.

Nearly all activities, including shopping, focus on one aspect or another of family life. For example, TV sets are purchased under the assumption that family and friends will gather to watch their favorite programs. Cars are purchased knowing that all family members will drive them or ride in them. In lower income families, clothing, shoes, and accessories are purchased under the assumption that they will be handed down from one family member to another. With such a strong emphasis on family life, it's vitally important to frame marketing strategies that show how families will benefit from your products. Emphasize their value to the entire family, not just the individual.

With such a strong emphasis on family life, it's vitally important to frame marketing strategies that show how families will benefit from your products.

Brazilians teach their children that they need adult protection and guidance. They are expected to accept the judgment of their parents about what is good for them and what is not. Contrary to American culture, children are not considered little adults, able to make up their own minds as consumers.

Life is a lot slower in Brazil than in the States. Yes, streets are jammed with traffic in Rio de Janeiro, São Paulo, Belo Horizonte, and the other large

Brazilian cities. (This seems to be the case in metropolitan areas the world over.) However, fewer media distractions, slower and more difficult transportation, and the warmer climate slows the pace of everyday life. This more relaxed lifestyle, plus the natural Latin affinity for leisure pursuits, leads to a laid-back attitude about virtually everything.

In any Latin American country, but especially Brazil, business dealings are based on personal, one-on-one relationships. Your counterparts want to get to know you. They want to know how your family is, the acceptability of your hotel accommodations, and most importantly, your reaction to their lovely country. Conversely, Brazilians expect you to have the same interest in them. They expect you to ask about their health, their family, and their interpretation of events occurring in their country. Brazilians are a very proud people. And that pride begins a strong nationalistic bias, regardless of the difficulties their country may have encountered in the past.

Brazilians look kindly on the elderly. Undoubtedly, such reverence for the elderly is an offshoot of strong family values. I should mention that most Latin American family groups are ruled by the eldest male member. In other words, they are patriarchal. This doesn't mean that the eldest female member doesn't have a say in family decisions. On the contrary, males may be the titular heads, but women normally rule the roost and must be consulted about decisions affecting the everyday lives of family members.

Age also refers to companies. Relatively new companies that do not have longevity in their home markets will have a harder time doing business anywhere in Latin America than companies that have been around a long time. No one wants to do business with the new kid on the block. In what were the early days of expanded regional trade, too many unknown American companies jumped into the fray. What were perceived as terrific growth markets turned out to be too difficult to enter, with margins too meager and external market forces too strong to make the venture pay off. A quick evacuation by the Americans soured many Brazilian business people and bureaucrats and added fuel to the already blazing fire of public opinion that the United States regarded Brazil and its Latin American cousins as third-rate business partners.

Community involvement is a mainstay of Latin life. Years of political violence, runaway inflation, and economic depredation have forced people even closer to their community church as the focal point. A little later we'll take a look at the strong role religion plays in everyday life. For now, however, suffice to say that as a cohesive force that draws people together into a practicing community, the church stands tall. Most Americans have probably not experienced community to this context. We live in apartment or condo complexes, suburban developments, or neighborhoods of single-family homes for years without knowing our neighbors beyond saying hello now and then. We explain this by saying we value our privacy. We would help if anyone needed it, but otherwise, let us enjoy our quiet comfort.

Community in the Latin sense means a common goal, namely, the survival or betterment of the group as a whole without regard to individual desires. If the group survives or improves its economic standing so does each individual family in the community. It is this togetherness that stymies attempts to subdue indigenous villages, for example in Guatemala. When soldiers destroy one village, another one rises from the ashes. When mountain guerilla fighters are killed off, others from nearby villages take their places.

Community in the Latin sense means a common goal, namely, the survival or betterment of the group as a whole without regard to individual desires.

Brazilians are very class conscious. In the large metropolitan areas of São Paulo, Rio de Janeiro, San Salvador, and Belo Horizonte class lines are drawn according to job position, income, company or government affiliation, and the normal status symbols one finds in developed nations. However, in the far north, Amazonia, and other underdeveloped regions, race and gender seem to be the main determinants of class standing. As a general rule, the class ranking runs white Brazilians on top, then mestizos and Creoles, then indigenous Amerindians, and then blacks at the bottom of the ladder. Class rank is also determined by position of authority. In earlier times, Jesuit priests were held near the top of class strata. But that has changed. Now high government officials and military generals rank about even with them at the top of the ladder. Business leaders come next, followed by urban workers, church leaders, and peasants. Of course in rural areas heavily populated by indigenous peasants, church leaders hold a much more elevated position.

Brazilian class rank is also determined by gender. In rural areas, elder men hold the top ranking, followed by young men, elder women, boys, and then young women and girls. In other words, a young peasant girl can't get much lower on the totem pole. An elderly man, holding a high government or military position, who also happens to be white, is at the top of the ladder. As in most of Latin America, Brazilian women do not enjoy the same class ranking or social status as men. This inferior social status of women—this gender gap—must change if these countries are to ever be accepted in the world community as civilized, modern day nations and take their rightful places in the 21st century.

RUSSIA

Several American traits that we looked at in the last chapter are exactly the opposite in Russia. Take for instance our obsession with time. Americans thrive on being on time. We look at time in very short bytes—a few minutes, a few hours. We pride ourselves on being at a specific place when we say we will be there. Russians don't want to hear such nonsense. Dating from their agrarian heritage, Russians look at time through long-term glasses, just like the seasons—a time to sow, a time to reap, and nothing to do in between. Remember that Russians spent 70 years under communist rule. During this period, jobs were for life. Workers could not be fired. They could be killed, imprisoned, tortured, or banished—but not fired. This destroyed all incentive for accomplishing anything, including being on time. To this day, when you set up a meeting allow plenty of time at the end. Do not expect an evening meeting to end before midnight. Two or three in the morning is more likely, mainly because it won't begin until 10:00 p.m. or 11:00 p.m.—not the 7:30 p.m. or 8:00 p.m. you planned. But that's OK. Just be patient and everything will turn out right.

Russia and the United States do have a few similarities. In addition to being very large, both countries were settled by diverse groups, giving each a melting pot of cultures. The Russian people, like Americans, can be very blunt, dogmatic, and opinionated. Another similarity is that Christianity is the dominant religion in both countries. In America, Catholicism and Protestantism are the predominant denominations. In Russia, it's Russian (Eastern) Orthodox Church.

Although I have always felt welcome when doing business in Russia, other American business people have told me that they have encountered nothing but problems. I believe this stems from a cultural chasm between the two countries. The chasm is best signified by the value placed on individual initiative. In the United States, individuality is prized. As individuals we are encouraged to think for ourselves, take the bull by the horns, and solve our own problems—to act independently when a crisis hits. That is definitely not the Russian mentality. Russians believe that the central government knows best. That laws and regulations emanating from Moscow will benefit all Russians. This leads to abject obedience to the dictates of the state. If government officials at any level say something is good for everyone, then it must be good for everyone. I cannot imagine such a scenario playing out in America. Perhaps this belief in the sanctity of government, rather than the individual, comes from the hardships suffered by the Russia people. From the Vikings swooping down from the north to rule Rus, to the communal culture brought by Scandinavian settlers, to the mayhem wrought by Mongols from the east, to the overthrow of the Tsarist regime, to the devastating attacks by the Nazis, to the insanely cold winters, Russians have suffered greatly in the past and continue to suffer to an extent now, far beyond anything we Americans can comprehend.

Dating from their agrarian heritage, Russians look at time through long-term glasses, just like the seasons—a time to sow, a time to reap, and nothing to do in between.

Because of its geographic isolation, Russia has never been a trading nation. One characteristic that all traders possess is the desire and ability to compromise. When trading goods for goods, as during the American emigration West, the art of selling was compromise. The same goes for the British, French, Italians, and so on during the 18th and 19th centuries. This willingness to compromise has found its way into all Western cultures. For Russians, however, compromise is not part of their vocabulary. This makes negotiating any type of deal almost impossible. Unless you are willing to meet their demands—or most of their demands—you will never negotiate anything. I could go on and on about the Russian psyche, which I find fascinating. But this book isn't long enough for that. So I'll end this section with the caveat that Russians live in the past, with old ideologies, an old religion, and old forms of government. The status quo is supreme. Americans, on the other hand, live in the future, welcoming all things new. Tear down the old; build the new. That's the American way. And that's another major difference in our cultures.

The following are a few personal observations about doing business with the Russians:

➡ Russians believe their country is destined to be a great world power.
➡ Russians are very family oriented, including the extended family.
➡ Business meals take forever to end and toasts are common at any time.
➡ Vodka, king of alcohol, is a national vice, and Westerners are expected to join in.
➡ Women are a major part of the Russian workforce but hold very few decision-making positions.
➡ Lots of hand shaking is common practice among everyone, and bear hugs are the way between old friends.
➡ The Slavic-based Russian language with the Cyrillic alphabet is difficult to learn; however, you are at least expected to know a few words of greeting.

INDIA

India is a complex country with more than 1 billion people, spread over a small continent. It has several spoken languages, hundreds of dialects, and a business culture significantly different from ours or from any culture you may have experienced in other countries. The caste system is the overriding cultural anomaly that Westerners have difficulty understanding, and once understood, accepting. But the caste system is ingrained in the Indian culture. It is as old as India itself and is not going away, regardless of Western influences. I have no intention of delving into the details of this medieval social strata. Suffice to make two points. First, the caste that an Indian is born into remains with that person for a lifetime. Second, the lower caste, the untouchables, can only hold jobs that are considered dirty or unclean by those above them. One example would be garbage haulers. Another would be janitors. These jobs are specifically set aside for the lower caste.

The caste system is the overriding cultural anomaly that Westerners have difficulty understanding, and once understood, accepting.

Here are a few other Indian customs that Americans tend to have trouble grappling with.

- Indians are basically very shy. Aggressive Western behavior frightens them and is considered a sign of disrespect.
- Indians inherently have low self-esteem. They are constantly afraid of offending you. Criticizing their work must be done very subtly, or they will be decimated.
- Indians hate to say no. They are afraid they will offend. Also, when an Indian hesitates, it may mean that he worries about his competence to do the work.
- Women are welcome in the workplace, but mostly for lower echelon jobs. American women should be extremely careful how they dress. Be sure to be ultraconservative, or you will embarrass your male counterparts.
- The pecking order of a business hierarchy is extremely important. When in a group, always address the senior member first, just like in the U.S. military. And it's the senior Indian that speaks for the group, whether the rest agree with him or not.
- Humor is not part of the Indian culture, at least not in the workplace.
- Nearly all Indians, except the young Turks, are vegetarians.
- Indians do not understand the purpose of standing in line. Whether at sporting events, the theater, waiting for a bus, or getting into a restaurant, Indians will not stand in line, preferring instead to plow ahead, elbowing their way through, much like native New Yorkers. This surprises many Westerners because such a trait is in direct contrast to typical Indian timidity.

Indians are not known for their punctuality. Time means little to them. Therefore, plan on meetings that last well into the night and meals that seem to go on forever. On the other hand, every once in a while you'll run across an Indian who has spent time in the United States and has absorbed our addiction to time. Unless you know for certain, I suggest you arrive on schedule for whatever is planned, even though you may have to wait an interminable time for it to begin.

Do not ever use first names when addressing business people. This typically American obsession is considered uncouth and extremely disrespectful throughout the world, especially in India. Unless you are dealing with young men who have picked up the American habit, you will be very embarrassed using first name familiarity. Always use Mr., Mrs., or Ms., and you won't go wrong.

Indians do not like to be touched. Therefore, do not offer to shake hands, hug, put your arms around a person's shoulders, put your hands on that person's arms, or use any other touch as a sign of familiarity. Again, young Turks probably won't mind, but why take the chance?

Indians value the elderly. Not infrequently, a mother and father will live with their offspring. The Indian culture assumes that children will take care of all the needs of their parents in old age, whether they need healthcare, food, or shelter. Americans who have factories or other facilities in India need to understand this and make allowances for employees to take time off. An Indian's first allegiance is to parents—not jobs.

INSIGHT... I am reminded of an occasion when I met an Indian entrepreneur, who was interested in selling his business to my client, at his home. We ate lunch and then adjourned to his study to begin the small talk. By ten o'clock that evening I was bushed and excused myself to return to my hotel. I had a hard time believing it, but we had spent the entire afternoon and evening on small talk, covering every topic under the sun, including India's participation in the upcoming World Cup of Cricket.

Indians are very hospitable. If you get invited to a home for lunch or dinner by all means accept the invitation. And don't be surprised if it turns into a business meeting. Indians like to do business at home, the opposite of most Americans. While on the subject of informal meetings, I should mention that Indians love to make small talk preceding any serious discussion.

Polite Americans remember to say *please* when asking for something and *thank you* when it is delivered. These words are not part of the Indian culture. Yes, many Indians have picked them up from their American friends, but they are definitely not words an Indian would normally utter. This doesn't mean that they are impolite. On the contrary, the Indian business person is very quick to express his pleasure but with a nod of the head or a smile, not words.

India is the only country that I'm aware of that has 18 official languages plus a plethora of unofficial languages spoken by millions of people. Moreover, it has several hundred mother tongues. Each state legislature has the authority to determine that state's official language. Broadly speaking, the major families of languages are:

- ➡ In the north of India, Hindi/Urdu, Marathi, Punjabi, Bengali, and Oriya.
- ➡ In the south of India, a Dravidian group of languages; the major ones are Tamil, Telugu, Kannada, and Malayalam.
- ➡ Hindi in Devanagari script is the official language of the central government in Delhi, although English is also allowed.

For those of you who enjoy linguistics, languages in South Asia, which includes India, Pakistan, Nepal, Bangladesh, Bhutan, and Sri Lanka, are grouped into six very, very broad categories—Indo-Aryan, Iranian, Dravidian, Austro-Asiatic, Tibeto-Burman, and Huristari. And that's as far as a neophyte like me can go.

To conclude this segment, I'll quote an old Indian adage, "It takes two hands to generate applause." That means that it takes two parties to make a deal. When both parties understand and accept the idiosyncrasies of each other, deal making is a success. But when one or both act as if the other party is nuts, wrong, out of order simply because of cultural differences, chances are good that the deal will fail.

CHINA

China has traditionally been an agrarian society. Although 1.3 billion people populate this huge country and many of them work in the industrial and commercial centers of the East, the majority still till the land as they have done for centuries. One characteristic of agriculture is that it is relatively permanent, settled, and firmly fixed for generations. Farmers are not mobile. And being securely tied to the land, farmers are relatively free from adventure and the attendant risks. Perhaps that's why the Chinese appear to be so conservative. Being dependent on the whims of nature and agriculture breeds patience, something the Chinese have plenty of. This is radically different from the frenetic speed we Americans are accustomed to. No wonder we drive Chinese business people nuts when we insist on timely meetings and quick resolutions. The Chinese can dwell on a subject seemingly forever. Only after much meditation and conversation with compatriots are decisions made. Even then, it might take weeks or even months for the decision to be implemented.

Another characteristic that seems strange to Americans is the Chinese fixation on a naturalistic view of life. I have known several Chinese business men who would rather walk than drive or take a bus, simply because it is more natural. They also use natural herbs for medicinal purposes rather than over-the-counter drugs. At home they buy fresh meat daily for cooking rather than for storage in a refrigerator. And at one time or another, you will probably run into a Chinese who would rather keep milk, beer, vegetables, and dairy products at room temperature instead of cooled by ice or refrigeration. If you are invited to that person's home for refreshments or a meal, be sure you do not comment on the lack of air conditioning or refrigeration. It just isn't natural. This is changing, however. Western ways, especially American ways, are rapidly catching on in China, mainly because so many Chinese travel to the United States either to live and work for a short time or attend a university before returning to their homeland.

> Simplicity seems to be a reasonable offshoot of this naturalistic view. To the average Chinese, modern day life is far too complicated. Their guiding principle of life is, "Big things are to be reduced to small things and small things are to be reduced to nothing."

Simplicity seems to be a reasonable offshoot of this naturalistic view. To the average Chinese, modern day life is far too complicated. Their guiding principle of life is, "Big things are to be reduced to small things and small things are to be reduced to nothing." American business people have a terrible time with this trait. How can you negotiate a contract or even sell products if the recipient refuses to partake in normal modern conveniences? For instance, Chinese believe that air travel in the United States with the constant harassment at security checkpoints, rude employees, cattle car type airplane seats, and obnoxious fellow travelers is too much to bear. They will manage at great inconvenience to get to the West Coast or New York for meetings, but don't expect Chinese visitors to travel to Lexington, KY or Mobile, AL unless they feel compelled to do so to satisfy their American host. For important meetings, I strongly suggest you travel to China rather than insist on the Chinese coming to the States, much as they enjoy experiencing our Western ways.

As is true with other Asian cultures, Chinese revere the elderly. They consider old people wise and perceptive. Chinese are eager to learn from the elderly and give older men and women an honored place in a household. What a change from American society. As a wise American scholar once said, "In the United States, youth is a blast, middle-age is a struggle, old age is hell." That pretty much describes how Americans view aging. Ours is a youth oriented society, believing that big money is made and positions achieved during the middle years. By the time one reaches old age, America has become far too complex, too busy, and too frenetic to actively participate in. In the Chinese culture, however, people look forward to aging so that they too may be considered wise and held in high esteem.

Confucian ethics describe five human relationships that are critically important for a good life: sovereign–subject, father–son, elder brother–younger brother, husband–wife, and friend–friend. Note that three of the five are family oriented. In China, everything revolves around the family—everything good and everything bad—even more than in Latin America. Debts are not considered liabilities of an individual, as in the United States, but instead, are considered owed by the family. Not only debts. Honor, shame, privileges, crimes, and so on are equally shared by all members of a family, not borne by an individual. A good example of this characteristic is when a Chinese obtains an immigrant visa to the United States. This isn't just for him. No. It is assumed that once in the United States this new immigrant will take care of his entire family, either bringing them to the States or sending remittances home. Once relatives are in the States, they reach out to more relatives and friends. Larger U.S. cities, such as San Francisco, New York, Los Angeles, and Seattle sport Chinese communities that have expanded like waves on a beach.

Chinese make excellent business people. A strong entrepreneurial spirit that emanates from the agrarian tradition gives Chinese business owners a head start at home as well as in the world economy. Interestingly, this contrasts with the social status hierarchy of the Chinese culture. That hierarchy is scholars on top of the social ladder, farmers next, then craftsmen, and on the bottom, merchants. Politicians slip in wherever and whenever it fits their purpose. The high esteem granted scholars and teachers probably originates from Confucius who was a scholar and a teacher. In fact, he was the first teacher in the history of Chinese education. Don't misunderstand this emphasis on the scholar, however. Chinese do not disdain money and wealth. If they did, there wouldn't be so many successful Chinese entrepreneurs. However, for the Chinese, money has only instrumental value, while culture, education, and art have intrinsic value. A fine point but one worth remembering.

The Chinese strive to avoid extremes or one-sidedness. They are more than willing to consider all sides to an argument, taking as long as necessary to hear and weigh all points of view. This trait leads to a natural moderation in the way Chinese think. Extremes are to be avoided at all costs. Middle ground is always the best answer. This cultural trait is vital to remember when conducting business, either in China or with American-Chinese. Do your best to stay away from either being ultra conservative or ultra liberal in your thinking and in your arguments.

Chinese are a very interesting people. The more you do business with them the easier it will become. In the beginning, however, my best advice is to go slow. Try to understand where your adversary is coming from. Then try to agree with him, if possible.

ARAB STATES

Each of the Arab states stretching from the United Arab Emirates, Saudi Arabia, and Oman on the Persian Gulf to Morocco, Algeria, and Tunisia in western North Africa has somewhat different cultural traits. However, all are similar enough to speak of the Arab states of the Middle East and North Africa as having one culture.

Islam governs everything in the Arab states, every walk of life, every business transaction, every custom, every mode of behavior. Islam is more than a religion. It is the foundation on which an entire culture is based. Nowhere does religion play such a crucial role in the lives of every man, woman, and child. Oil rich Saudi Arabia, geographically the largest of the Arab states, is by far the most dictatorial of all Arab nations in demanding absolute obedience to a strict interpretation of Islamic law. More on the Islamic religion a little later in this chapter.

It's hard to get into Saudi Arabia. As we have previously seen, you need to be personally sponsored by a Saudi national. I have found that the best course is to get a Saudi lawyer to do this for a fee, of course—and at times, a handsome fee. Choose your lawyer carefully, however. Why? Because once you are in the Kingdom, your sponsor is completely responsible for your actions, and the payment of your debts. Speaking of debts, after you begin to do business in Saudi and incur the normal trade or bank debts, and for some reason, forget to pay them off before leaving the country, you will never get out of the airport. In fact, if you try, you will likely end up in jail. Oh, and by the way, you must advertise in a local newspaper the date you plan to leave the country.

The standard Arabic greeting is "As-salam alaikum," which means "peace be upon you." The standard reply is "Wa alaikum as-salam," which means "and upon you be peace." This common greeting and response are used over and over and over again whenever you meet someone. And by the way, be sure to take your shoes off before entering a carpeted room (most rooms are carpeted) and shake the hand of the most senior person, not necessarily your host.

Arabs place great emphasis on good manners. They are far too polite to embarrass a foreigner by pointing out his snafus. To make matters worse, most Westerners have no idea what most of the courteous Arab gestures, dress, comments, and body language mean, regardless of how many culture books they have read. The problem is that most Arab manners are the direct opposite of those of Westerners. I always hold the door for a lady and let her pass first. This is verboten in Arab lands. The man goes first. Following a lady allows a man to ogle her from behind.

Arabs place great emphasis on good manners.

Before the discovery of oil, the Kingdom of Saudi Arabia as well as the rest of the Arab states, had nothing practically to offer the world, certainly nothing of interest to the business world except dates and a few essences. The only significant exception were the antiquities of Egypt. The one contact Arab states had with the outside world was trade. They needed to import everything; therefore, they needed to trade. The epitome of the Arab trader was the Omani Sinbad the Sailor. All Arabs, those from Muscat in Oman to Abu Dhabi and Dubai in the U.A.E. to Alexandria in Egypt grew up learning how to trade. Negotiating deals was a national past time. This has made Arabs some of the shrewdest bargainers in the world. When negotiating a contract with anyone from the Arab states, hang onto your wallet because the odds are very good that you will be the loser. And remember, in the Arab states everything, and I do mean everything, is negotiable, including all airfares and hotel room rates.

While on the subject of negotiating, I should warn you that no deal is final until all parties have parted ways. You may have a signed contract, but changes can and will be made up until the time you leave. Saudi Arabia is one big "good ol' boy" club. Everyone knows everyone. As a foreigner, you will feel that you are alone against the entire business population. (Your lawyer may be your only friend.) There are about six or seven families who populate each region of the Kingdom, so everyone seems to be related to everyone else. In the U.A.E., the "good ol' buy" clubs are split according to nationality. The British, Germans, Italians, Chinese, Russians, and so on each has its own network to rely on. This reminds me of the way the Brits and the French managed segregation in their colonial empires, especially in Africa. You'll soon see that Americans haven't caught on to the "good ol' boy" method yet.

One characteristic that I found particularly difficult to get accustomed to was the Arab tendency to get in your face when they speak to you.

Also, the pace of business in the U.A.E. frustrates Westerners. There seems to be two paces—extremely slow, as in a snail's pace, or lightning fast. You may work for weeks trying to close a deal or manage a project only to find that, voila, you are now expected to reach a conclusion by morning.

The U.A.E. is an exception to all other Arab states—it actually encourages foreign enterprise. If you want to set up a distribution warehouse in the Middle East, the two city-states of Abu Dabai and Dubai are the places to do it. Both locations are eager for your business.

One characteristic that I found particularly difficult to get accustomed to was the Arab tendency to get in your face when they speak to you. Most of us like our space, maybe a foot or so around our bodies. Not the Arabs. They love to get right up in your face, practically touching your stomach and chest while talking to you. Backing off is considered very rude. Do this and they will believe that you find their close presence distasteful (they are right about that) or you are a very cold, unfeeling person.

The Egyptian culture is the easiest for Americans to grasp, probably because of the years of British occupation. In fact, Egyptians consider their country a bridge between the Arab East and the European-American West and are proud to act this out in business transactions. Business practices more closely resemble those that we are used to. Protocol and personal customs are much less stringent that in other Arab states. And not all Egyptians are practicing Muslims. In fact, Christianity has a firm grip on a minority of Egyptian citizens, again probably a playback to the years of British rule. To conclude this discussion of the Arab culture, Wa alaikum as-salam.

Those are the basic traits of the four BRIC powers and the Arab states that every business person who expects to do business in these countries must understand and accept. Obviously, the list is not complete. And obviously, globalization is changing national cultures very rapidly. Before too long you won't be able to see many cultural differences between Russia and Western Europe, between Brazil and the United States, and between India and China. Not in my lifetime, but maybe in yours. However, I suspect that you won't see many changes in the Arab states.

The cultural norms we have looked at are somewhat unique to specific countries, except for Brazil, whose cultural traits are fairly common throughout Latin America. Each country's culture is based on its unique ideology, religion, and politics. However, more universal traits also affect how and why people do things they way they do them. Although these traits vary somewhat among countries, to some extent they tend to be fairly common among emerging nations. The more important ones are (1) the power of the church, (2) racial and other biases, and (3) national pride.

POWER OF THE CHURCH

The influence of the church over individual lives, and the enormous impact it has on political, social, and business activities, puts dogmatic religious beliefs right up there at the apex of universal traits. In emerging nations, the church influences every aspect of daily life—family values, entertainment (e.g., music, art, literature, cinema, and athletics), conflict resolution, politics, the drive for economic improvement, travel preferences, business matters, and so on. In some countries this is more pronounced than in others. But in all cases, without a basic knowledge of how the pertinent religious influences shape a person's beliefs and actions, you will be lost.

Religion in Latin America

For hundreds of years, when one spoke of the church in Latin America one meant the Roman Catholic Church. An estimated 450 million Catholics, almost half the church's global population, lived in Latin America. But the power of the Catholic church is fading fast. In at least a dozen countries, including Argentina, Chile, Honduras, and Peru membership in the Catholic Church has dropped 10 to 25 percent in the last three decades. This decline is exemplified by Brazil, which has the largest congregation of Catholics in all of Latin America. In that country's 1970 census, 92 percent of the population claimed to be Catholic. By 1990, it dropped to 84 percent. In 2000, of the 170 million people in the census, 74 percent claimed to be Catholic. To grasp the meaning of this decline as well as the importance of the modern day church in Latin America, we have to understand its contradictions.

For generations, Catholic priests stayed clear of politics. Then liberation theology took hold. This was a school of thought that found in the gospel a call to free people from political, social, and material oppression. Liberation minded Jesuit priests turned the tables, focusing on social issues such as poverty, community development, and human rights, vociferously criticizing dictatorial rulers. Especially in outlying areas, the church became identified with social justice and structural change.

During the 1980s, in Guatemala, El Salvador, and many other regions of South America, liberation theology challenged the authority of military dictators and privileged one party rulers. In the outlying areas of Central America, bishops and Jesuit priests alike became such thorns in the side of government troops that they were sought out along with guerrilla fighters and murdered. After previously passive Jesuits morphed into vociferous human rights advocates, teaching the primacy of divine authority over secular governments, those living in extreme poverty were the first to rise up in open rebellion against strong-arm military governments.

This created a vacuum between liberation theology and traditional Catholic teachings. In step with Pentecostal fundamentalists from the United

States, teaching the belief that people should seek to be filled with the Holy Spirit in emulation of the Apostles at Pentecost. Translated into daily life, this eternal search for salvation in the hereafter meant that everyone should obey secular authority and docilely accept the often cruel and inhumane conditions of this life while waiting for a better tomorrow in the afterlife. If they couldn't improve conditions in this world, they could always look forward to a sublime future in the next world. The Pentecostal movement caught on like a wildfire, especially in areas dominated by abusive rulers. It has had a major impact on the relationship between governments and private sector businesses. Concentrating on the glorious hereafter, citizens can now face the cruel repression of right-wing and left-wing dictators, secure in the knowledge that after death their souls will reach glorious heights in salvation. The Pentecostal movement has also caught on in countries with duly elected governments. In Brazil, for example, the World Christian Database (www.worldchristiandatabase.org) reports a Pentecostal membership of 24 million (compared with only 5.7 million in the United States where the movement began).

By ceding secular authority to bureaucratic leadership, whether elected or not, Pentecostal theology became the right hand of tyrannical governments. And this new, unquestioned power of officialdom has resulted in much stronger enforcement of government regulations, both with regard to the participation of foreign companies in local businesses and with regard to the acceptance of foreign imports in preference to locally produced products. If you plan to open facilities in countries or regions with strong Pentecostal leanings, you would be wise to research the impact that a downplaying of secular gains may have on worker productivity and efficiency.

Religion in Russia

Of the several cultural traits that differ between Russia and the United States, one major departure stands out above all else—the role played by religion in everyday life. As Americans, we do not have a state church or anything resembling an official ideology. Just the opposite, we believe in a pluralistic society, a complete separation of church and state, and the right to be different. If anything, America is a pragmatic society, following the principle that if it works do it.

On the other hand, Russia has a state church, the Russian (Eastern) Orthodox Church. The nation's culture and fierce nationalism flow directly from the church. This state religion is very much like Pentecostal teachings in Latin America in that it preaches submission to the will of the state. The Russian Orthodox Church has molded the Russian culture for more than a thousand years, dictating a centralized government with authority flowing downward to the people. This is in contrast to the United States, where authority is vested in the people and flows upward to the government.

The Russian Orthodox Church has molded the Russian culture for more than a thousand years, dictating a centralized government with authority flowing downward to the people.

Dogmatic in its teachings, this ancient Christian religion defines the ethics, culture, and nationalism of the Russian people. Russians believe that their religion has solved all the basic problems of belief and worship. Changes in dogma, teachings, or phraseology will not be tolerated.

The Russian sense of community and egalitarianism has its roots in the Russian Orthodox religion. The church teaches a singular truth—the only truth—by which the Russian people must live. Neither religious nor political dissidents will be tolerated. With such a dogmatic underpinning is it any wonder that the Russian business scene is the exact reverse of American free enterprise? Not only do Russians have little interest in our system, they are prohibited by their national church from even suggesting that anything in their current economic or political system be changed.

Religion in China

Underlying all of China's primary cultural traits, Confucianism yields a belief structure so complex that I doubt whether any Westerner can ever understand it completely. K'ung Fu Tzu (Confucius) founded modern day Confucianism. Not quite a religion, it is a philosophical system that embodies moral, social, political, and a sort of quasi-religious teaching. Over the years Confucianism has become tainted by Taoism (teachings of community), Buddhism (teachings of an afterlife), and the Chinese version of Communism. In the doctrines of Chinese metaphysical cosmology, man is the cocreator of the universe. He takes part in the creation of all material things. He is in charge of his own destiny. Man is the measure of everything and everybody that exists. This anti-Christian doctrine manifests itself in the Chinese belief that instead of worshiping God as a supernatural force and creator of all things, they worship man in the form of their ancestors. Add to this, the communist doctrine of all righteous power vested in the state, and you have a dogmatic compendium of teaching that points to the Chinese man (non-generic) as the main determinant of how Chinese men and women should live their lives. (This in contrast to the Christian belief that Jesus Christ guides Christians in how to live their lives.)

This is a hard pill for many Westerners to swallow, especially those who follow the Judo-Christian tradition. Translated into its relationship with everyday business transactions, Chinese Confucianism borrows virtually all ideas and thoughts from the past. In other words, as far as the Chinese church is concerned there is nothing new under the sun. When we try to instill new business techniques, distribution systems, or manufacturing procedures, we often find ourselves talking to the wall. The Chinese will learn new tricks if we insist but only grudgingly. Moreover, they will take their time learning them, and when we're not looking, revert to their old ways.

Religion in India

The Constitution of India declares the nation to be a secular republic that must uphold the rights of citizens to freely worship and propagate any religion or faith. Having said that, I must quickly add that religious pundits who expect to find a Swami to lead them out of darkness into the light will be grossly disappointed. Partly because of the formalized education system introduced by the British, partly because of the rigid caste system that systematically separates Indians according to ancestral wealth, and partly for other reasons little understood by Westerners. India has inherited a strange mixture of religious fervor. Centuries of Muslim-Hindu conflict coupled with Christian beliefs inherited from the British have resulted in a deterioration of the collective psyche of the Indian masses. The majority of Indians claim to be Hindus, yet about 750 million souls (three-fourths of the population) do not understand, study, or practice the basic Hindu belief, Sanatana Dharma, which means eternal religion. In fact, most Indians have no clear conceptual idea about their own national philosophy or religion. Literate, middle-class

Indians much prefer to accept the materialistic practices of the West. Science, as depicted in technological advances, has become the karma of the rapidly growing class of young entrepreneurs.

Scientific progress has led to the decline in the importance of religion in the daily lives and social interactions of most of the upper class of Indians. In a very real sense, religion is believed to hinder social and economic progress. Even in the lowly untouchable class, the materialistic benefits of the scientific age have become the aim and driving force of life, provided these poor souls can find access to technical wonders.

India is smitten with cadres of soothsayers, more than anywhere else in the world.

India is smitten with cadres of soothsayers, more than anywhere else in the world. Famous scientific spiritual practitioners such as Sri Rama, Lord Buddha, Mahavir, and so on claim to have directly realized and experienced the Truth, that is the divinity of each soul, and brought to earth this truth for the benefit of all Indians.

That's as far as I intend to go with Indian religious beliefs. It is far too complex a subject for further discussion in this book. If you are interested in studying more about the Indian shift to more scientific religious mores while retaining the basic Hindu belief structure, I encourage you to speak to one of the hundreds of Indian gurus practicing throughout India and the United States.

As for the impact on business transactions brought by this somewhat strange approach to religion, suffice to say that an understanding of the other Indian cultural characteristics described elsewhere in this chapter and in other parts of this book will be far important than current day Indian religious beliefs.

Religion in the Arab States

Turning to the Middle East, we all know the role of religion in the Arab world. Islam has caught the attention of media the world over and in some quarters is blamed for the heinous terrorism acts that have disrupted vast swaths of our world for more than a decade. Perhaps there is some truth in that, although this not the place to argue the point.

Originating in the 7th century AD in the Arabian cities of Medina and Mecca, Islam is a major world religion alongside Christianity, Judaism, Hinduism, Buddhism, and Confucianism. It has spread from Saudi Arabia through the Middle East and North Africa to Southeast Asia (Pakistan, Indonesia, and Malaysia) and many other countries. According to Islam, the Qur'an (Westernized to read the Koran) wais the final word of God, and its message came from all the prophets, of which Allah was supreme. The story of Genesis is one of the few similarities between Islam and the Judo-Christian West. Muslims believe that a version of Genesis proclaims the lineal descent of Arabs from Abraham through Ishmael.

Saudi Arabia follows the Koran closer than any other Arab state. In fact, Islam controls everything Saudis do. Well, everything they do while at home in Saudi Arabia—but not necessarily when they travel abroad. I have witnessed several princes enjoying liquor and women at parties in London and Paris.

Some Islamic rules might seem a bit strange to Westerners. For instance, the Kingdom strictly forbids pork, alcohol, and pornography. The pornography prohibition is worth a chuckle. On my first trip to the Kingdom many years ago, I flew the Italian airline Alitalia from Rome to Jeddah. When going through Saudi customs, one of the armed guards dumped the contents of my briefcase on the counter. Right on top was the Alitalia Airlines in-flight magazine that had an article I planned to read. The Saudi official grabbed the magazine, stuck it in his pocket, and proceeded to give me a lecture in Arabic. Later I learned that the lecture was about how pornography could not be taken into the Kingdom. The pornography the official was so concerned about was a picture on the cover of the Alitalia magazine of a not-too-pretty model in a conservative swim suit.

The Saudi government run by the royal families protects its citizens from all kinds of scourges. The guardians of public morality are called the Mutawa. These vigilant protectors are not religious police, although they seem to think they are. Usually, a regular policeman patrols with the Mutawa to arrest you if they deem you to be morally offensive. I'm told that the main purpose of the patrolling Mutawa is to make sure that shops close, and people adhere to the five daily prayer times—Fajr, Dhuhr, Asr, Magrib, and Isha'. During your first visit to an Arab state, you will enjoy these five prayers times that take place every day and evening. All business stops, and all true believers kneel, face Mecca, and touch their foreheads to the ground. You'll know it's prayer time when you hear the wailing blasted out from loud speakers all over cities, towns, and villages.

Islamic states do not have civil codes of law. Shari'ah (Islamic law) is the only law permitted. As with other aspects of the Islamic religion, Saudi Arabia is far and away the strictest of any Arab state. For example, a bizarre interpretation of Islamic law calls for dealing with a murderer or a drug dealer by beheading him. Adulterers are stoned. Fornicators are flogged. A thief who has been caught before has his right hand cut off. None of these perpetrators face charges in a court. None are convicted on the basis of circumstantial evidence. If authorities deem someone guilty, he is guilty, and the prescribed penalty is dished out. Blood money for an accidental killing, as in a car accident, is enforceable. I have worked in Saudi many times, and I am always thankful beyond belief to get out in one piece. However, I do know several other Americans who think Saudi Arabia is the greatest place on earth to live and work. Certainly, Saudi society is orderly and relatively calm compared with the United States.

Change in the Arab world is in the air. For the business community, a change for the worse. From the secular-oriented Syria, Algeria, and Morocco to the devout Persian Gulf states to extremist Saudi Arabia, young people are boiling. Many have graduated from local colleges only to find no job openings. I should quickly add, however, that plenty of blue-collar jobs now filled by Pakistanis and other foreigners could be reserved for these disenfranchised youth. But with a college degree, they feel that such work is beneath them and that they would lose face by accepting blue-collar jobs. Hmmm . . .

These young men are up against a social wall. Islam dictates that they must have the means of supporting a wife before the two can marry. Without a job, the young men cannot support themselves, much less a wife. This, of course, adds fuel to the fire. What happens in such a tinderbox? Increasingly, young males turn to the radical side of Islam, much as the unemployed in Latin America turn to Pentecostal teachings, young unemployed German males turned to Nazism in the 1930s, and unemployed young Americans turn to religious cults. This is a serious development not only because young males expand the ranks of radical Islamic groups, but because they also encourage their governments to become much more active in enforcing strict Islamic teachings. Sixty percent of Arabs are under the age of 25, and this flood of discontented youth bodes ill wind for Westerners. Hopefully, conditions will change once again, and the governments of these countries will soon find jobs that these young people need and want.

In conclusion, be aware that a prevailing belief of Islam is that solutions to all problems will be found in the correct interpretation and application of Islamic law. Nothing else is relevant.

RACIAL AND OTHER BIASES

Americans have been legislated to ignore race in everything we do. We are told to be color blind. A person's national heritage must never be considered in hiring, firing, promotions, or any other aspect of business life. Federal and state laws protect everyone against discrimination for any reason but primarily because of race. This is not the case in other parts of the world. Racial bias is in full bloom in China, Russia, India, Southeast Asia, the Middle East, Eastern Europe, and throughout Latin America. It rears its ugly head in many ways—in business practices, in the granting of services, in military barracks, and in the halls of government. Skin color is not the only form of discrimination. Prejudice is also levied against nationality and religious and cultural anomalies.

> Racial bias is in full bloom in China, Russia, India, Southeast Asia, the Middle East, Eastern Europe, and throughout Latin America.

Most biases are partly inherited and partly a result of political, social, and economic events that have transpired over hundreds of years. Discrimination is manifested in several dimensions. Cultural heritage seems to be a very prominent prejudice in every country. The virtual genocide that the Guatemalan government perpetrated on the Mayan Indians and their supporters in the 1980s and 1990s is a good example of how the clash of cultures can bring about violent racial bias. At times, this racial extermination was as deadly as anything going on in the Middle East, Africa, or Eastern Europe. Murder and torture were commonplace. And why? The government would like us to believe that the military was merely trying to subdue guerrilla bands. Observers, including this writer, disagree, blaming instead an attempt by the government to systematically erase the entire indigenous population.

Racial bias caused by cultural differences goes beyond indigenous groups. In Malaysia, Indonesia, and Thailand unwarranted prejudice among

Muslim, Chinese, and European groups festers prominently. Extreme racial hatred of one group by the another has played a significant role in retarding the economic growth of Southeast Asia. Without cultural discrimination, a few of these countries could be knocking on the door of developed nations. Discrimination also rules sections of Eastern Europe. One has only to look at the horrors perpetrated during the recent breakup of Yugoslavia to see that.

Skin color definitely causes discrimination. I have not seen the intense prejudice against blacks in Latin America that was prevalent in the United States during the 1930s and 1940s, but it does exist. By and large, Latin Americans are mostly tolerant, perhaps because many nationalities with various skin colors settled in South America, just as they did in the United States. On the other hand, you will find very prominent prejudice based on skin color throughout the Caribbean. Except for Trinidad and Tobago and the Spanish-speaking islands, black West Indians run the Caribbean. In the islands, racial prejudice against people with white skin can be just as deadly as discrimination against people with black skin in other countries.

Cultural discrimination is quite evident in the business community of the Middle East. While Americans and Europeans are tolerated and sometimes wooed to get our technology or weaponry, at a social level, we are outsiders. This is patently obvious in restaurants, hotels, and other public places. For example, while working in Jeddah, Jizan, and Riyadh, I had many occasions to eat by myself and spend untold hours alone in hotels, waiting for phone calls from my clients' customers. I had traveled the world for many years and was quite aware of the dissimilarities between the Arab states and Western cultures, so I'm certain I did nothing to offend any Muslim. Yet in restaurants, I was always seated away from crowds. In hotels, although treated politely, I was always profoundly aware of the fear or prejudice that festered just beneath the surface. In business settings, my hosts remained as courteous as they thought necessary, but when they perceived I was unaware of their conversations in Arabic, I heard many, many references to the dumb, dirty American. I found this fascinating because Saudi Arabia is, without a doubt, the dirtiest country I had ever been in—with Egypt a close second.

In Asian cultures, and especially in China, the locals are far more subtle than Arabs. When prejudices arise you won't even know it. Chinese business people have become very adept at the smile, the polite bow, and the small-talk repartee aimed at making us relax. Any prejudices Chinese business people may have against Americans are put on the back burner until the business transactions are completely over. I have never seen overt discrimination against Westerners in China, although it certainly exists beneath the surface.

INSIGHT... Several years ago, a very good Chinese-American friend accompanied me on my first business trip to Shanghai. Ted and I had gone through school together, and he was in my wedding party. He graciously showed me around the city and then we spent a couple days touring the province. My purpose in going to China was to try to source a very scarce commodity for my client. The material owned by a truly ancient Chinese supplier was supposed to be the highest quality in the world. I met with this supplier, and with Ted's help, negotiated what I thought was a reasonable price and delivery schedule.

On the plane home, Ted explained to me that although he didn't think it wise to interfere with the ancient Chinese gentleman, he was certain I had paid about 50 percent more than I should have paid, had I understood the negotiating nuances. Ted then explained that it was an ancient Chinese custom to squeeze the last penny out of a transaction. He also explained that all Chinese thought Westerners had plenty of money and that every Chinese businessman knew how to get it. Discrimination? Well, yes. I was not treated the same as if I had been of Chinese descent and that is discrimination of a sort.

In most countries, you'll find less bias in the business community than in social settings, but it has its share as well. It is evident in hiring practices, work assignments, pay scales, promotion opportunities, preferential licensing, import restrictions, tax collection, and in many other areas. You can't do much about such prejudice except recognize its existence when dealing with authority figures. Although most Americans detest flagrant discrimination, and especially racism, you need to be very careful when setting up or managing a foreign operation. On the one hand, it won't do to practice overt racism. Few Americans would voluntarily sanction company polices that mistreat employees, suppliers, and others because of skin color, cultural heritage, or religious beliefs. Yet we must be careful not to violate local customs by completely ignoring such biases. Although tricky, racial and other differences can be acknowledged without flagrant adherence to discrimination policies.

NATIONAL PRIDE

National pride is very close to the surface in most countries. Notwithstanding the near chaotic conditions of political, social, or economic institutions, business people from every nation in the world will defend the honor of their country against all newcomers. This has led to a form of intense nationalism, not dissimilar to that felt by most patriotic Americans. It is the main reason that several logical groupings of nations have never been successful in forming cohesive common markets or free trade pacts, even though doing so would probably be the only feasible way they could create a strong enough front to deal with the United States and other G8 countries.

The intensity of nationalism varies from country to country. Generally speaking, the larger the country or the more advanced its institutions, the more prominent nationalism becomes. In any event, when visiting a foreign country, and especially one of the BRIC nations or Arab states, be sure that you do not make disparaging remarks about anything that could even remotely infringe on national pride. Doing so is a sure way to make enemies, land in jail, or get thrown out of the country. And remember that you are a guest. Honor all local customs, including national pride, and you will likely be invited to return another day.

chapter twelve
Overcoming Language Barriers

I am the perfect person to write about overcoming language barriers. Not that I'm a great linguist; I am probably the world's worst linguist. I'm sure that sounds strange, considering that I have spent more than 40 years of my life traveling and working in the far-flung corners of the globe. Not that I haven't tried. (In every country, I have listened carefully. I have participated in seminars and language classes both in country and in the United States. I have spent a good deal of money and time taking Berlitz courses in Spanish, German, French, and Norwegian. At one stage of my life, I even made an honest effort to learn Russian—to no avail. The only explanation I can give is that I must have a mental block against learning languages.

Notwithstanding my inability to converse in a foreign language, I have learned how to cope with the problem. Hopefully by the time you complete this chapter, you will also have some ideas about how to manage the language barrier.

I can't count the number of people who have told me they will not get involved in global trade because they don't know a foreign language. I always try to dissuade them. Contrary to popular belief, you don't need to know the language to do business. The following insight explains how the two of us managed to do business in China.

INSIGHT... A very good friend owned a distributorship that carried specialized women's cosmetics. Gene read about how markets for some of his lines were opening in the south of China. In the worst way, he wanted to set up a small warehouse there and stock it with a minimum amount of cosmetics to see if the market was as good as it appeared to be. We talked about how he could get the licenses, staff the facility, and manage the long shipping distance. I arranged with my Chinese contact to have someone meet us at the Beijing airport when we firmed up an arrival date. Everything was a go. That evening Gene and I had dinner to finalize the work he wanted me to do. Suddenly he stopped eating. He stared at me like a lost dog. "What am I doing?" he said. "How can I possibly start up a distributorship in China when I don't know one word of Chinese?"

Good question. I tried to calm my friend with assurances that I would be with him for the first week, plenty of time to arrange for a facility and hire a manager. "But you don't speak Chinese either," was all he could mutter. That gave me the opening I needed, and I proceeded to explain how we would handle the language problem.

LEARNING KEY WORDS

The first thing we had to do was learn a few key words, just enough to let our Chinese hosts know that we were trying to learn their language. Also, I felt it was necessary to have a few words on tap to get through customs and travel to our hotel. This was easer said than done. I couldn't read one word of Chinese from the script. We needed help in the worst way. I asked my friend John Chung for advice. He suggested two possibilities: (1) an online course in Chinese or (2) a small language school located in the Chinatown section of Philadelphia.

I have an aversion to internet courses, so I opted for the school. I set up a meeting for Gene and myself. I should add, however, that internet classes could be a viable alternative, especially if you live in an area where it is difficult or impossible to actually attend a school. If you happen to be in that situation, give the net a shot. It can't hurt, and it may work for you.

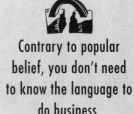

Contrary to popular belief, you don't need to know the language to do business.

As we explained what we were planning to do in China, the school's owner was happy to oblige. He compiled a list of words that hopefully would get us through the initial meetings. It doesn't make sense to repeat the entire list, but here area a few English words that he translated into phonetic Chinese for us: hello, goodbye, where is, what is, when is, man, woman, child, restaurant, hotel, taxi, car, truck, how do you say, going, planning, doing, meat, vegetable, chicken, a little bit, beautiful, how much money, one month's salary, rent, customs, big, small, hungry, thirsty, beer, whiskey, gin, tea, coffee, milk, time (e.g., one o'clock, ten o'clock, etc.), good, bad, I, you, your, he, she, his, hers, and theirs.

The full list was about three times this size, but you get the idea. I should add that the school's owner suggested that spoken Chinese was all we needed and that we should not be concerned with the script. Phonetic pronunciation was sufficient. After each English word, the director wrote the Chinese phonetic equivalent. The next week, Gene and I returned to the school to take our tests, and we both passed with flying colors.

As an aside, I have to admit one more shortcoming. In addition to being an awful linguist, my memory isn't as good as it should be. After a meeting is over, I have difficulty remembering the foreign words I learned. I don't think it's too surprising when you consider that I'm forever learning words from new languages for trips. Maybe if I stayed in one location long enough, I would remember, but that has never happened.

At any rate, once Gene and I mastered the word list, we had to practice pronunciation, and for me, this was harder than memorizing the words. In fact, I think it was the pronunciation that did me in for both French and German.

PRACTICE PRONUNCIATION

Chow wa nu. Nai rah be. Cha'a ros mu sai li. Don't ask your Chinese friend to interpret this. These are not Chinese words. They are merely how a few of the phonetic words on our list sounded. Unless you have a good ear, pronunciation of a foreign language can be a bearcat. Still, if you plan to use any of the words you learn, you'll have to be able to pronounce them.

Spanish is one of the easier languages for me to pronounce. Phonetics aren't necessary because 9 times out of 10 the words are spelled phonetically or close to it, and once you learn the basic accent strokes, it's a simple matter to hit the right pronunciation—not like English, and definitely not like Chinese.

Pronunciation is half the battle in coping with a new language. Conversely, if you don't pronounce correctly, no one will know what you are trying to say. One time during a seminar I produced for Latin America/ Caribbean Productions, we had a woman from Argentina who ran a language school in Miami make a presentation. She explained the difference in pronunciation between Spanish and Portuguese. "Spanish," she said "is always spoken with the tongue against the palate of the mouth whereas Portuguese is spoken the same as French, through the nose." That's fine. But knowing what to do and doing it are two different things.

Pronunciation is half the battle in coping with a new language.

I have found that an excellent way to practice pronunciation is to speak into a recorder while facing a mirror. To get the right sound you often need to twist your mouth or blow your cheeks or make any number of other strange facial expressions. Without a mirror, you can't tell whether you are doing it right, and without a voice recorder, you can't hear how you sound. I go through this exercise before every business trip.

Another trick that I've found helpful is to use one of those small phraseology books—English to Spanish, English to Arabic, English to Russian, and so on. Find English phrases that you normally use in your everyday speech. Write them on a notepad. Practice speaking in front of a mirror. You'll be surprised how quickly you pick up the pronunciation of your pet phrases. You may not remember the phrase, but it will help you remember how to pronounce.

Unless it is written or recorded in some manner, the spoken word quickly fades away. Written words are either script (pictures of one type or another) or alphabetical (letters). A revolution in communications occurred eons ago when ancient man learned how to write. Over the millennia, hundreds of different alphabets and scripts have been created, used, and lost. In the modern world, 19 alphabets and scripts are in daily use; they are Amharic, Arabic, Armenian, Bengali, Burmese, Cyrillic, Davenagan, Georgian, Greek, Hebrew, Khmer, Korean, Lao, Latin, Sinhala, Thai, and Tibetan—plus Chinese and Japanese scripts. In addition, the Persian language or Farsi is spoken in Iran, Afghanistan, and Tajikistan and by about two million people who live in the Gulf states. It uses the Arabic alphabet.

Linguists claim that the Latin alphabet (English, Spanish, Portuguese, French, etc.) is used by about two billion people, about 1.3 billion use the Chinese script, one billion use the Indian Davenagan alphabet, about a half billion use the Arabic alphabet, and about 300 million Russians use the Cyrillic alphabet.

Latin-based languages all use vowels and nouns. Once you learn the rules about which syllable to accent and which vowels and consonants are silent, pronunciation becomes a snap. Cyrillic is a little different. It takes about 10 percent longer to say anything in Russian compared to English. Pronunciation is very tricky, and to learn it properly, you need to immerse yourself within a Russian community or at least with a competent Russian instructor. It's not as difficult to learn or pronounce as Arabic or Chinese.

THE ART OF LISTENING

Anyone who is an accomplished linguist knows that listening is three-fourths of learning a new language. In the beginning, you won't understand what is being said, and that's OK. But you will be learning what that language sounds like (loud or soft), how it is spoken (fast or slow), and the use of intonation (raising or lowering the voice at the end of words or sentences). After you listen for a while, you will begin to grasp the general subject material and have at least some idea of what the person is talking about.

By now you're probably saying to yourself, of course I listen, doesn't everyone? No. Everyone doesn't listen. In fact, very few of us listen to anything. We hear, but we don't listen. This is probably because we are deluged with sound wherever we go—music blasting from iPods. TV blaring out commercials, soundtrack laughter, movies with deafening sound tracks, noise from speeding traffic, train whistles, children crying in shopping malls, bad acoustics in restaurants and bars, and so on, ad infinitum. This constant attack on our auricular cavities leaves us numb. To be heard, we shout. To show anger, we shout just as loud. To express joy, we laugh loudly.

Listening requires concentration. You must concentrate on what is being said. This means you have to block out all distractions and allow the speaker to absorb your full being. This is hard to do. In fact, my experience has shown that very few people are capable of truly listening to others, which might explain why only a few people are expert linguists.

Have you ever been at a large gathering, say for lunch or dinner, and the keynote speaker speaks in a foreign language and a simultaneous interpreter translates to English? Everyone wears headphones to hear the translation. But hearing the translation doesn't tell you what the speaker is talking about. You hear the words, but you don't associate them with concepts or the subject matter. To do that, you need to concentrate. You need to give the speaker your undivided attention. You can't allow whispering at your table, waiters serving dessert, or faulty sound equipment to distract you.

Not long ago, I had the opportunity to listen to a high-level government official from Saudi Arabia give a speech at a Foreign Affairs luncheon. Simultaneous interpreters were used. Just for fun, and cognizant of my linguistic limitations, I concentrated as hard as I could on the speech. I was surprised to find that by the end of the luncheon, I actually picked up a few Arabic words, at least the pronunciation of them. To this day, however, I'm not sure what they meant.

The moral is to practice pronunciation as often as you can. But unless you listen to others speak the language, I guarantee you won't get it right. Now lets return to how Gene and I managed to start up a Chinese warehouse.

INSIGHT...

After spending a good bit of time practicing the pronunciation of the words our Chinese instructor had given us, we decided to try them out on an actual Chinese citizen. At the time, I was fortunate to live next door to a Chinese family that was here on a work visa. The husband had a professorship in chemical engineering at the University of Pennsylvania. Wu was a likeable person and always had something pleasant to say. Gene and I knocked on his door, and when he answered, we gave him our best Chinese "hello, how are you." Wu had a good laugh and then proceeded to help us correct our pronunciation. He explained that the official Chinese language was Mandarin, which was spoken primarily in the north and the inland provinces of the west and south. The other widely known language was Cantonese, spoken in the coastal south, mainly in Guangdong Province, Hong Kong, and Macau. Then there were hundreds of dialects or offshoots of Mandarin used throughout China as well as Taiwan. One of the four languages spoken in Singapore was yet another dialect of Mandarin. And another one was used in Malaysia. We were learning the Cantonese variety because Gene wanted to set up his warehouse in Guangzhou, the capital of Guangdong Province.

Over the next several weekends, Gene and I spent many hours with Wu and his wife, listening to them speak Cantonese and participating as much as we could. Wu encouraged us to try to express our wishes in Chinese, even though we fractured the pronunciation. We carried around our list of words in two small notebooks, constantly referring to them. While we would never pass for Chinese, by the end of the month, both Gene and I had gained enough confidence to buy plane tickets to China.

My friend Wu was a gracious, patient host, as most Chinese are. He convinced us that we had to keep trying our new words again and again. "They won't do you any good on a list in a drawer," he told us. If we ever hoped to be able to use them, we had to practice. We should not be afraid to experiment, he said. We should try to speak the words even if we aren't sure of the pronunciation. Fortunately, with two of us trying to learn, we could practice speaking to each other and try out different pronunciations for some of the more difficult words.

Before leaving on our trip, we had dinner at a local Cantonese restaurant. The menu was in Cantonese with English subtitles. Most of the items were not on our list, but brimming with confidence we ordered in Chinese. The bilingual waiter was very patient, explaining which words we had not pronounced correctly. Even with the many mistakes, we were able to convey exactly what we wanted for a starter, entree, and dessert. Not bad for a couple white-skinned gringos. After dinner, we decided to experiment some more and went on a mini-shopping spree in Chinatown, restricting our purchases to those items with names that we could pronounce.

If I have learned anything during my 40 years of international trade, it is that you cannot be afraid to experiment. Your host will welcome your effort to understand his language. In-country business people will, by and large, think you are a lot more confident than you probably are. And you will have more fun learning what the host country is all about.

While I certainly encourage you to experiment, I must also add a caveat—be very careful what you say. If you may be even close to saying something controversial or that might cause offense, stop and rethink your comments.

BE CAREFUL WHAT YOU SAY

Before going any farther, I suggest you review the previous two chapters covering offensive or confusing American habits and the specific cultural anomalies of your host country. This will help you remember what not to do or say. However, if you focus on major metropolitan hubs, you'll find that a fair number of American traits have rubbed off. The worldwide business community is rapidly throwing off the yoke of traditionalism and beginning to grapple with many Western sayings and idiosyncrasies, so don't be surprised if your host shelves some local customs during your visit, especially if you are dealing with customers or bureaucrats who desperately want or need your products.

Even when you have carefully studied a host country's customs and successfully stayed away from saying anything that might be construed as offensive, in the heat of a negotiation or a sales pitch, you could easily slip into American slang. Although this may not be offensive, it will certainly confuse your audience.

If you remember, in Chapter 10 I mentioned a group of buzzwords. Very few—if any—are translatable into a foreign language. You might find something similar in a Latin language, but I doubt it. Certainly none are translatable into Cyrillic, Chinese, or Davenagan. Just for fun, take a few of the following words and phrases and try to translate them from a Russian-English, Chinese-English, or Indian-English dictionary. I bet it can't be done with phrases such as corporate speak, computerese, customer relationship management, Enronitis, insourcing or onshoring, intellectual infrastructure, legalese, mission critical, negative profit, PDFing, RIF, spin, telephonically communicable, or variable staff.

Even when you have carefully studied a host country's customs and successfully stayed away from saying anything that might be construed as offensive, in the heat of a negotiation or a sales pitch, you could easily slip into American slang.

Since American buzzwords cannot be translated, it seems obvious that you should never use them because no one will know what you're talking about—even your interpreter. Lacking American idiomatic knowledge, the interpreter will merely repeat the English word, which I guarantee will doubly confuse your host. Buzzwords are not the only words to avoid. Other words can also be offensive or translated incorrectly.

Here's a trick I learned some time ago. Before boarding your plane, make an effort to search out words that might have double meanings in the host country language. These are words that may be perfectly acceptable in English but translate into something with an entirely different meaning in the host country. Also, find out if two or more languages or radically different dialects are spoken in the host country. I'm thinking of China, for example, with Mandarin and Cantonese. India is another country with hundreds of dialects. I couldn't even begin to list their names. Also many people speak an Indian version of English, so check this out too.

Finally, here are a few words or topics to avoid like the plague, whether you are fluent in a foreign language or not:

➥ Anything related to or that could be associated with any type of religion.

➥ Politics, either U.S. politics or host country politics.

➥ Sports that your host may not be familiar with, such as nearly every. American sport except soccer, rugby, and cricket (except in British Commonwealth countries and India).

➥ Colors of any type, although this is easy since we rarely mention colors in a business setting.

➥ Exploits of your own, your spouse, or your children which you may be proud of, or conversely, ashamed of.

➥ Deprecating anyone or anything (e.g., yourself, your country, or your leaders [business or government]).

➥ Jokes of any type because no one will have your sense of humor.

INSIGHT... Now I will return to the exploits of Gene and myself in China. As I said earlier, we finally felt secure enough with the Chinese language to make arrangements for our first meeting in China. Fourteen hours after boarding our plane, we landed in Beijing where our host met us. The first item of business after clearing customs was to hire a driver. We could have done this from the States, but I prefer to see who I hire rather than rely on a service. Our host quickly alerted us to two driving services he knew about. One of them agreed to meet with us at our hotel in the morning.

I know that some people enjoy driving in strange countries. Why, I cannot fathom, but they do. If you are such a person, go for it. Rent a car and have a ball. For the rest of us, I recommend hiring a driver for the duration of your stay. Your life will be a lot easier if you can find someone who speaks at least a little English. Also, it helps to have a driver who knows the tourist sites. You can't work all the time, so you might as well see the sites while you're there.

In addition to a driver, I suggest you consider hiring an interpreter, even if you feel relatively comfortable with the language. Depending on the type of business you expect to conduct, you may need a *consecutive* interpreter or a *simultaneous* interpreter. A consecutive interpreter is ideal for small groups or one-on-one business meetings. Consecutive means the interpreter listens to what is said, the speaker pauses, and the interpreter verbally translates into English or vice versa. Simultaneous interpreters work in real time, parroting what the speaker says in English or the host language. This is the way it is done at the United Nations and other large gatherings. The problem with simultaneous interpretation is that it requires audio equipment and headphones for the interpreter and for each person in the audience. With all that equipment, simultaneous interpreting is much more expensive than consecutive interpreting.

China. Gene was exuberant that she understood the nuances of cosmetics and could easily translate English names into recognizable Mandarin. But we had one problem. Gene planned to open his warehouse in Guangdong Province, so we still had to find a Cantonese interpreter—but that was a decision for another day.

Having hired several interpreters over the years, I have deduced a list of qualifications that might help you in your search. They are as follows:

➡ If possible, find an interpreter that has experience in your industry, just as we did in Beijing.

➡ Remember that hiring an interpreter is the same as hiring any new employee—that person will inject his or her own acronyms, idiosyncrasies, and biases, making it very important that you spend time teaching the interpreter the technical terms and acronyms used by your company.

➡ Before the meeting, provide the interpreter with as much background as possible about your company and the goals you are trying to achieve at your meeting.

➡ Do a thorough check of the interpreter's background and experience including contacts with American clients.

➡ Be sure the interpreter is security conscious and will keep everything learned about your business confidential.

➡ Execute a contract that spells out the specific duties of the interpreter and the results you expect to receive.

➡ Insist on a guarantee from the interpreter, spelling out that if you are not satisfied you won't pay.

➡ Understand the cancellation policy in case of an emergency.

➡ Give the interpreter the names of the parties involved, the date and place of the meeting, and whether you want any kind of written follow-up report.

One final note on interpreters. There are several ways to locate qualified interpreters. Host country embassies located in Washington or New York usually have lists of acceptable ones. The American Chamber of Commerce located in the foreign city of your meeting should have similar lists, although not all AMCHAM offices do. The U.S. Embassy in your host country will seldom get involved in recommending interpreters, but sometimes they do, depending on how much political pull you have.

The easiest and fastest way to find an interpreter is through the internet. People I have worked with recommend two sites, although I do not have personal experience with these companies. They are as follows:

➡ www.translatorstown.com. This outfit claims to have contacts with freelance interpreters worldwide that can handle 119 languages. In addition to pure interpreting, they offer proofreading, voice recording, and subtitling skills.

➡ www.language-finders.co.uk. This firm is located in London. They claim to have 1,000 interpreters on staff plus an additional 1,500 part-timers. They also say they can handle 140 languages and dialects.

MAKING FRIENDS/MAKING ENEMIES

We've covered a lot of ground in this chapter. I hope it has proven helpful. Just for the record and to conclude the story of my friend Gene and his cosmetics warehouse in south China. He did, in fact, open it. We had some difficulty recruiting a qualified manager who spoke English, but with the help of the interpreter, we found one who had a degree from the University of Washington in Seattle. Gene still owns the distribution facility. Moreover, since his initial venture into China, he has set up two more centers, one in Pakistan and one in India, both profitable.

The primary objective in learning how to cope with a foreign language is to concentrate on making and keeping the friendship of your host. This is seldom necessary—or even desirable—when doing business in the United States. But in a foreign land, with strange laws, corrupt law enforcement, and unfamiliar customs, not to mention a peculiar language, it doesn't pay to make enemies. Imagine if you will, how difficult it would be to survive in a jail in Saudi Arabia or Venezuela. Think of how unhappy you would be stuck without a passport in Russia or Ukraine. Envision the difficulties you would have trying to persuade corrupt Turkish officials that your car accident was nothing more than a fender bender. Friends can help mitigate problems like these.

If you plan to do business overseas, and I can't imagine why you are reading this book if you aren't, try to make friends, not enemies, in your host country. In the long run, and in the short run too, friends will help you a lot. Enemies will not.

chapter thirteen
Woman Power in Global Trade

G reat news ladies. The business world may discriminate against you, but 13 countries think enough of your gender to elect a woman president. They are as follows: Chile, Michele Bacheler; New Zealand, Helen Clark; Mozambique, Luisa Diogo; Finland, Tarja Halonen; Liberia, Ellen Johnson-Sirleaf; Philippines, Gloria Macapagal-Arroyo; Ireland, Mary McAleese; Germany, Angela Merkel; Ukraine, Yulia Tymoshenko; Netherlands Antilles, Emily de Jongh-Elhage; India, Prattibha Pati; and Argentina, Chistina Fernandez de Kirchner.

No one can rightfully accuse me of being a do gooder or a champion of the downtrodden. As a businessman, nonproductive and mostly hopeless social welfare programs go against my firm belief in the profit motive as the driving force in free market enterprise. Having said that, I believe that one soft topic is so shameful and destructive of individual liberties and freedoms that I am compelled to speak out. I'm talking about the worldwide physical, emotional, and economic devaluation of women and girls. I realize that female readers will likely take issue with a man writing about women's rights. That's quite natural. I do ask, however, that you bear with me for one chapter. Perhaps you'll change your mind.

As Americans, we can help these nations recognize the valuable contribution of women in both business and politics by showing our foreign business associates the crucial role women play in every aspect of the American business community.

As we all know, the feminist movement of the 1970s opened the door of opportunity for American women. Although the number of women rising to top positions remains abysmally low, the mere fact that we now have several female CEOs of major corporations as well as presidents of universities and nonprofit organizations indicates that women are beginning to crack the glass ceiling. The same can be said of the political scene. Time and time again, women run for and are elected governors, mayors, and to the U.S. Congress. Women make up more than one-third of several state legislatures. And I wouldn't be too surprised to see a female president one of these days.

But such empowerment of women has not happened in emerging nations. With the possible exception of a few Eastern European countries and a handful of countries in Latin America, women are not offered the same opportunities as their male counterparts in either the workplace or the political sphere. As Americans, we can help these nations recognize the valuable contribution of women in both business and politics by showing our foreign business associates the crucial role women play in every aspect of the American business community. By observing the success of American women in dealing with complex business issues, perhaps our foreign customers and suppliers will eventually pressure their governments to close this nefarious gender gap.

Many cultures attribute a very low status to women and the roles they are required to perform. That we all know. Not only are their rights subjugated to the demands of men, but in many countries, they are denied the very basic rights of civilized humanity—adequate nutrition, education, healthcare, financial support, reproductive rights, ownership of property, family planning, and information about happenings in the world at large.

In some countries, one in six girls are sexually abused before the age of 16. An untold number of girls, but probably in the millions, are married by age 12 and bear children in their early teens. More than 15 million girls, aged 15 to 19, face pregnancy related complications while giving birth. Child prostitution is rampant in India, Thailand, and other countries in South and Southeast Asia. The Indian culture forces large dowries on families of female brides, which encourages prenatal feticide and post birth infanticide to reduce the number of female births, especially in poor families. Sexual harassment and molestation are common in the workplace. In India and China, mothers neglect and even kill their daughters in favor of sons. Widows are often ostracized. Why do these atrocities occur? Because they are not only sanctioned by political regimes but form an integral part of several world cultures. The feelings against women are so strong that men believe they will lose status and power as well as face in the community by granting women their due rights.

The UN Population Fund's *State of the World Population* report for 2005 shows that in Southeast Asia only two-thirds of girls complete primary education. Moreover, the World Bank's *World Development Indicator 2007* shows that in the majority of emerging nations, excluding Africa, less than 60 percent of girls of secondary school age are enrolled in secondary schools. In sub-Saharan Africa, the percentage is much lower. Although belatedly recognizing the seriousness of a lack of education for girls and women, the United Nations now includes in its *Millennium Development Goals 2000*, the following statement from former UN Secretary General Kofi Annan, "there is no tool for development more effective than the education of girls. No other policy is as likely to raise economic productivity, lower infant and maternal mortality, improve nutrition and promote health—including helping to prevent the spread of HIV/AIDS."

As one would expect, women comprise about 50 percent of the world's population. However, in many emerging nations, women make up more than 80 percent of agricultural labor and hold 90 percent of marginal jobs; that is, jobs that are very low paying and which men refuse to do. In rich countries, women fare much better. For instance, 9 percent of corporate boardroom seats across Europe are held by women; 15 percent of America's directorships have gone to women; and in Norway, according to the Center for Corporate Diversity (www.managementwomen.no), beginning in 2008 all public companies were required to have at least 40 percent of their board seats filled by women.

Staying with Norway for just a moment, the January 5, 2008 issue of *The Economist* reported that when Ms. Grace Reksten Skaugen and two other female directors forced the resignation of the Statoil chairman and CEO as a result of claims of possible illegal payments to a consultant. Ms. Skaugen said that, "Women feel more compelled than men to do their homework, and we can afford to ask the hard questions because women are not expected to know the answers." Now that's a positive story.

Nearly all international nongovernmental organizations (NGOs) and bilateral aid agencies advocate women's economic and political participation as the single most effective weapon against abject poverty.

Nearly all international nongovernmental organizations (NGOs) and bilateral aid agencies advocate women's economic and political participation as the single most effective weapon against abject poverty. Women not only focus more than men on family healthcare and nutrition, they are also more effective in conflict resolution and the human dimension in political decision making. I suspect that's the case because women and children suffer the most in wars and political upheavals and therefore are most concerned about avoiding confrontations.

India and China both have the populations, the manufacturing capabilities, and other assets necessary to become world powers. But will they reach that goal? That is certainly doubtful as long as the cultures and the politics of these two emerging giants continue to repress women and girls. Certainly, the most shameful infringements on women's rights are infanticide and feticide, which are practiced openly in both countries. Recent studies indicate that more than 10 percent of pregnancies in upper- and middle-class Delhi are aborted. China encourages parents to dispose of daughters both during pregnancy and post birth. Until these types of inhuman acts are done away with, it seems unlikely that either China or India will ever graduate to first-rate, rich-country status. Moreover, the ratio of girls to boys in both countries is estimated to be as low as 90 percent. This cultural abnormality, supported by political enforcement, reflects practices that continue to restrict the ability of women to reach equal status with men.

Other cultural mores also pose pernicious barriers to equality. In Latin America, India, and rural China, tradition dictates that girls should work in the home and fields rather than waste time in school. The fact that women do not acquire any property rights at marriage is also deeply entrenched in several societies. In Saudi Arabia, the U.A.E., Pakistan, and other countries that hold to the Sharia law governing the behavior of women, very few rights are vested on females. For instance, for nearly 30 years Islamic radicals in Pakistan fought the government's efforts to amend the ancient Hudood Ordinances that denied women the right to testify on their own behalf against a man they accused of rape. In fact, rape could not be proven unless four independent males witnessed the penetration. The Pakistan National Commission on the Status of Women reported that in 2003 about 80 percent of imprisoned women were in jail because they had "failed to prove rape charges and were consequently convicted of adultery" if married or fornication if unmarried. In 2006, amendments modified, but did not invalidate, the Hudood Ordinances.

Fortunately, not all followers of the Islamic code agree that such incongruous laws reflect the teachings of the Koran. Shirin Ebadi, the Iranian Nobel Laureate, is one who has spoken out against such a rigid interpretation.

EARNING A LIVELIHOOD

The lack of opportunity to earn a livelihood is another issue that deprives women of equal rights. Many rural areas in developing nations foster abject poverty. With men off fighting insurgencies, laboring in cities, or merely lounging around doing nothing, a woman is expected to do all those things necessary for her family to survive—from carrying firewood to toting water cans from central springs to tending livestock and plowing fields to managing food and shelter for extended families—all for no pay. When these women do manage to scrape together a few hours a day to work at paying jobs such as domestic help or even in factories, the meager pay they receive is practically meaningless. For instance, during a recent trip to South America, I witnessed maids, nannies, and gardeners working six to eight hour days in the homes of affluent Ecuadorians and expats for wages of $200 a month. After bus transportation to and from work, about $175 was left over to feed and cloth and house their families. And these women are considered very well off compared to women in many other countries, including India and rural China.

While offshore maquila assembly plants are a boon to U.S. consumers who buy clothing, food, electronics, and so on at prices significantly lower than similar goods produced Stateside, the earnings of women, and in some cases children, who work 8 to 10 hour days in these factories remain at the very bottom of the local wage scale. Although American civil rights proponents chastise U.S. companies who own these factories for employing what they call slave labor and call on Americans to boycott products made there, these altruistic advocates miss the point. Women and children work in these factories, not because some foreman stands over them with a whip, but because these jobs are the only ones they can get to earn a living. Yes, the income is low. But compared to no income, it's a fortune. Without maquila factories, these women and children would probably have no legal way to survive. In the slum, *favelas*, of Rio de Janeiro or the mean streets of Bangkok where maquilas do not exist, children earn an income by begging and running drugs while women, if young enough, earn an income by being prostitutes in the *tourista* gathering spots. Is this any better than working in U.S.-owned factories for low wages?

MICRO FINANCE

In many rural areas, especially in South Asia, a new breed of entrepreneur has emerged—the female micro business owner. Women tend to be excellent owners and managers of very small businesses. Street vending, fabric design and assembly, craftwork, and other micro businesses are mostly owned and managed by women, not only in Asia, but in Russia and Latin America as well. These micro business entrepreneurs have been able to start and run their businesses because small groups of financial people saw fit to lend them money for working capital. Micro finance lenders have found that the track record of women repaying these loans is far better than that of men.

Founded in 1997 and inspired by the work of the Grameen Bank of Bangladesh, the Grameen Foundation institutionalized the idea of micro finance. The foundation is now active in virtually every extreme poverty region of the world. In South Asia loans are made in India, Pakistan, and Bangladesh where 440 million people live on less than $1 per day. In East

Asia, the foundation makes loans in China (a very small number), the Philippines, East Timor (still trying to recover from its wars of independence), and Indonesia (mainly for survivors of the 2004 tsunami). Estimates suggest that 245 million East Asians live on less than $1 per day. In Latin America, where estimates hold that 50 million people live on less than $1 per day, the foundation lends to poor entrepreneurs in Haiti, Honduras, Bolivia, and Mexico. In the Arab World of the Middle East, where 10 million people live in extreme poverty of less than $1 per day, the foundation is active in Morocco, Tunisia, Egypt, and Saudi Arabia. It is inconceivable that Saudi Arabia, a country of 24 million citizens and with far and away the greatest amount of dollar

In many rural areas, especially in South Asia, a new breed of entrepreneur has emerged—the female micro business owner.

reserves in the world, is unable to raise the living standards of a mere 400,000 Saudis above $1 per day. Something seems terribly wrong with that.

GENDER EQUALITY/INEQUALITY

As defined by the World Economic Forum's 2007 report, *Women's Empowerment: Measuring the Global Gender Gap*, gender equality refers to that "stage of human social development at which the rights, responsibilities, and opportunities of individuals will not be determined by the fact of being born male or female; in other words, a stage when both men and women realize their full potential."

Unfortunately, achieving gender equality is an agonizingly slow process. Even in the United States where federal legislation prohibits gender discrimination, women have a difficult time matching the progression of men in nearly every profession or occupation, from business to the military to elected political office. Imagine how difficult it is to achieve gender equality in nations where the culture, national religion, historical precedent, labor laws, or other regulations brazenly dictate discrimination against women and girls. Most of the less developed countries continue to follow the custom of having male members of the family provide income and serve in the military while female members take care of the home, the well-being of the family, and tend to the livestock and crops as well. Some Islamic societies have a whole list of things that women are prohibited from doing, from swimming in a hotel pool at the same time as men to baring their heads or limbs in public to working at a long list of jobs.

Facing nutritional discrimination, many poor Indian women are anemic and malnourished. Custom dictates that within the family, women eat last and only get the leftovers. More than half of Indian women are illiterate and legally discriminated against by being denied ownership of land and property rights. Rape in India occurs once every 34 minutes.

If there is ever any hope of eliminating or even reducing discrimination against women, it must come from the heart and that requires changes in cultural mores.

In Russia, which has enacted legislation against gender discrimination, the biggest gender inequality occurs in the home where violence against women has reached epidemic proportions. More than 25 percent of married women are reported to have suffered family violence. Moreover, rape, attempted rape, and sexual harassment of women in the workplace has become a national issue.

As Americans have learned over the years, cultural gender discrimination cannot be legislated away. If there is ever any hope of eliminating or even reducing discrimination against women, it must come from the heart and that requires changes in cultural mores. Personally, I cannot see how that can possibly happen to any great extent in my lifetime.

The World Economic Forum attempts to quantify gender inequality by ranking 158 countries, according to five criteria:

1. Economic participation, equal remuneration for equal work.
2. Economic opportunity, access to the labor market that is not restricted to low-paid, unskilled jobs.
3. Political empowerment, representation of women in decision-making positions.
4. Educational attainment, access to education.
5. Health and well-being, access to reproductive healthcare.

Economic Participation

Economic participation is important, not only for lowering the disproportionate levels of poverty among women but also as a crucial step in raising household income, and hence, the economic growth of the entire country. Too many societies assume that women should be passive recipients of financial or physical help. In Western societies, this dates from the ancient days of Anglo chivalry. In Eastern societies, it comes from the belief that women are unable to contribute elsewhere. And in Islamic societies, the dependence of women is dictated by religious belief. Clearly, breaking the hold of custom, inadequacy, and religion is a massive task. Still, many emerging countries in Latin America have made significant strides in that direction, and if they can do it, other societies can, too. Economic participation by women is not only necessary for achieving gender equality, it is an integral part of any successful economic base.

Economic Opportunity

Economic opportunity follows closely on the heels of economic participation. It stresses the quality of women's participation in the job market over and above their mere presence in the workforce. In most countries, including the United States and Western Europe, the wage rates of women tend to be less than their male counterparts performing the same tasks.

The economic opportunity measure also analyzes the types of jobs common to each gender. In Western societies and nonagrarian nations, women tend to hold so-called soft jobs like nursing, elderly care, teaching, and office clerical work. The economic opportunity leg of the Gender Gap Index attempts to compare the type of jobs and the wage disparity among the 158 nations. For simplicity, it combines economic participation and economic opportunity into one ranking.

Educational Attainment

Without the educational opportunities afforded to boys, girls can never reach a level of either economic or political equality. They must have the same knowledge tools in order to compete. Illiteracy in women is a serious issue, especially in rural areas and in countries with large indigenous populations. Studies have shown that more than two-thirds of the world's female population is still illiterate.

The greatest majority of these women live in the poorest, least developed countries of Africa, Asia, and Latin America. New technologies, like cell phones and computers, have yet to reach them, further restraining women in those nations from achieving equal footing with men. The education attainment measure compares literacy rates, enrollment rates at various levels of schooling, and average years of schooling among the 158 countries.

Health and Well-Being

The health and well-being cone measures the disparity between men and women related to nutrition, healthcare and reproductive facilities, and issues of fundamental safety and integrity of persons. According to the World Health Organization, 585,000 women die every year, more than 1,600 per day, from causes related to pregnancy and childbirth. The Planned Parenthood Foundation reports that 46 million abortions are performed worldwide each year, resulting in the death of 80,000 women or 13 percent of maternal mortality.

Violence against women is part of this cone. Within the category of violence, the study includes mutilation of female genitalia. A very small percentage of these crimes are ever reported, so official statistics do not tell the whole story. However, the World Health Organization claims that primarily in Africa and the Middle East, each year two million girls aged four to eight are forcibly subjected to female genitalia mutilation, causing death or chronic infection and bleeding.

Political Empowerment

The political empowerment cone attempts to measure the involvement of women in structural decision-making positions of government and business. The Inter-Parliamentary Union reports that worldwide women only hold 15.6 percent of seats in combined houses of parliament. This ranges from 39.7 percent in the Nordic states, to 18.6 percent in the Americas, to only 6.8 percent in the Middle East and North Africa.

It seems obvious that a country's laws affecting the inequality of women will never change if women do not have a voice in government. The Americas, led by Canada and the United States, have made enormous strides in the makeup of representative bodies, at the provincial/state level as well as in the central government. Latin America has also recognized the important role of political empowerment for women, with no less than seven countries electing a woman president during the last decade. With that background, let's take a look at the results of the 2007 World Economic Forum's study in Figure 13-1.

	FIGURE 13-1 Gender Gap Index—Country Ranking—By Component (128 countries)				
Country	World Rank	Economic Participation	Education	Health and Survival	Political Empowerment
Philippines	6	2	1	1	14
Lithuania	14	7	29	37	18
Colombia	24	39	23	1	113
Bulgaria	25	30	62	37	32
Costa Rica	28	95	36	1	16
Argentina	33	75	33	1	25
Israel	36	45	38	92	41
Trinidad and Tobago	37	64	78	1	58
Russia	45	16	22	37	120
Romania	47	31	47	37	89
Thailand	52	21	81	1	110
Slovakia	54	50	37	1	86
Poland	60	74	1	37	63
Hungary	61	56	50	37	93
Czech Republic	64	71	53	37	78
Dominican Republic	65	88	68	110	65
China	73	60	91	124	59
Brazil	74	62	116	126	21
Peru	75	103	59	110	121
Singapore	77	55	98	115	71
Indonesia	81	82	93	81	70
Chile	86	105	78	1	58
Malaysia	92	93	71	97	10
Mexico	93	109	49	1	57
Kuwait	96	80	63	110	126
U.A.E.	105	119	68	110	65
Qatar	109	115	45	123	124

FIGURE 13-1 countinued					
Country	World Rank	Economic Participation	Education	Health and Survival	Political Empowerment
India	114	122	116	126	21
Oman	119	125	83	89	119
Egypt	120	120	101	83	123
Turkey	121	118	110	87	108
Saudi Arabia	124	127	87	60	128
Pakistan	126	126	123	121	43

Source: Gender Gap Report 2007, World Economic Forum

The following are a few interesting points not revealed in Figure 13-1:

➡ Sweden, Norway, and Finland filled the top three slots, followed by Iceland and New Zealand.
➡ Germany (8th), the United Kingdom (11th), and Canada (18th) all ranked higher than the United States (31st).
➡ Japan placed an abysmal 91st.
➡ The three lowest ranked countries in the survey were Pakistan (126th), Chad (127th), and Yemen (128th).

The report did reveal some interesting and rather surprising results. Of the four BRIC countries, Russia ranked 16th in the world in economic participation and opportunities (women work alongside men in many jobs), 22nd in educational attainment (legislation requires girls to have the same access to schooling as boys), and 37th in health and well-being (quite startling since the Russian healthcare system is ranked very low in worldwide studies), but 120th out of 158 countries in political empowerment (expected since women cannot run for political office in most districts).

China also achieved a relatively high ranking at 60th in economic participation and opportunities (in agrarian districts, women work alongside men) and 59th in political empowerment (surprising, since very few Chinese women hold elected posts except in villages). However, China did poorly in educational attainment ranking only 91st (expected with its avowed prejudice against girls) and in health and well-being with a rank of 124th (outside of the eastern cities, rural healthcare is virtually nonexistent).

Brazil ranked 62nd for economic participation and opportunities and did well in political empowerment, reaching 21st (both categories reflect the increasing number of women holding mid and high-level business and political positions in many of Brazil's large cities). This country did not do so well in educational attainment, however, ranking 116th (reflecting the abysmal record of girls completing secondary and tertiary schooling). It also did poorly in the health and well-being category, scoring only 126th (a result of subpar healthcare, especially reproductive care in rural settings).

India scored poorly in all categories except political empowerment. Much of India's gender inequality is a direct result of its caste system, which severely discriminates against poor Indians, many of whom are women.

It should also be noted that in the Middle East, only Israel scored high in most categories, with health and well-being the weakest leg. All Arab states scored poorly in nearly all categories, reflecting Islamic discrimination against women. Of the nine Arab states, however, the U.A.E. was about average with a score of 68th in educational attainment (reflecting the large number of girls from elite families sent to foreign schools) and 65th in political empowerment (a huge surprise given that women are permitted to hold only a very few public official positions).

When choosing which countries to become involved with for exporting, sourcing, or FDI, the position of women in the economic spectrum should be incorporated into your strategic marketing plans.

So much for the subject of equality—or inequality—for women. It is not a pretty picture. Too many countries have too far to go to equalize gender equality. Perhaps I'm being too harsh. Perhaps religious dogma, political preferences, and historical customs will someday change, allowing women to take their rightful places in decision-making positions of the world.

When choosing which countries to become involved with for exporting, sourcing, or FDI, the position of women in the economic spectrum should be incorporated into your strategic marketing plans. This is particularly important if you sell female oriented products or if you plan to open a facility that employs women. No sense trying to establish market share or staff a factory in a country that suppresses women to the extent that consumer imports are not in their economic purview.

Before leaving the subject of woman in global trade, we need to address a barbaric practice that increasingly affects the well-being and opportunities of women and girls— trafficking in persons. It indirectly influences the advisability of a FDI in what the U.S. government refers to as Tier 3 countries.

TRAFFICKING IN PERSONS

I cannot imagine how any man or woman who profits from trafficking in persons can sleep at night. Whether such trafficking results in slave labor, forced servitude, or sexual exploitation, people who engage in this crime are no better than the Arab slavers of 200 years ago or the Roman bullies in Mesopotamia. Most victims are young women and children, forced into performing unspeakable acts under threat of bodily harm or even death. For most Americans, trafficking in persons means Chinese stowaways aboard freighters or Latinos smuggled across the Rio Grande. But to the rest of the world, it means much more.

In the year 2000, the U.S. Congress passed a law called the Trafficking and Violence Protection Act that reports on the worldwide epidemic of trafficking in persons for sexual purposes, forced labor, or any other activity that compels a person to perform a deed contrary to that person's wishes. Originally, trafficking statistics were confined to the cross-border movement of persons. Now, in-country trafficking is also included. The U.S. State Department analyzes trafficking from information gathered at its embassies around the world. These studies reveal that slave labor and involuntary servitude are as appallingly common as sexual exploitation. It is not unusual for entire villages to work to pay off old debts passed down through generations.

The sixth annual Trafficking in Persons Report assigns each country to one of four tiers:

1. Tier 1. Countries whose governments fully comply with the act's minimum standards.

2. Tier 2. Countries whose governments do not fully comply with the act's minimum standards but are making significant efforts to bring themselves into compliance with those standards.

3. Tier 2—Special Watch List. Countries whose governments do not fully comply with the act's minimum standards but are making significant efforts to bring themselves into compliance with those standards and meet one of the following criteria:

➡ The absolute number of victims of severe forms of trafficking is very significant or is significantly increasing.

➡ There is a failure to provide evidence of increasing efforts to combat severe forms of trafficking in persons from the previous years.

➡ The determination that a country is making significant efforts to bring itself into compliance with minimum standards is based on commitments by that country to take additional steps over the next year.

4. Tier 3. Countries whose governments do not fully comply with the minimum standards and are not making significant efforts to do so.

Obviously, Tier 3 countries are the worst offenders. The governments of these countries aren't even trying to stop trafficking.

The report assigns the following countries to Tier 3: Algeria, Bahrain, Cuba, Equitorial Guinea, Iran, Kuwait, Malaysia, North Korea, Oman, Qatar, Saudi Arabia, Sudan, Syria, Uzbekistan, Venezuela, and Zimbabwe. Membership in this group is not something to be proud of. Hopefully, in the near future Venezuela, which is a reasonably civilized country, will undertake procedures to stop the horrific practice of trafficking in persons. Interestingly, out of the 16 countries assigned to Tier 3, half of them are Arab states. Such a dismal reputation has dissuaded many U.S. companies from even considering doing business in the Middle East. One would hope that at least some of these countries will recognize the harm their lack of diligence is causing. I would certainly not consider an FDI in Kuwait, Oman, Saudi Arabia, or Syria for fear that my employees might have been trafficked into the country.

Tier 2 Watch List countries are doing better but only by the narrowest of margins. The Tier 2 Watch List countries are: Argentina, Armenia, Belarus, Burundi, Cambodia, Central African Republic, Chad, China, Cyprus, Djibouti, Dominican Republic Egypt, Fiji, the Gambia, Guatemala, Guyana, Honduras

India, Kazakhstan, Kenya, Libya, Macau, Mauritania, Mexico, Moldova, Russia, South Africa, Sri Lanka, Ukraine, and the United Arab Emirates. The fact that three of the four BRIC countries are on this watch list is a disgrace. It is a shortcoming that must be corrected—soon—if these countries have any hope of becoming major players in the world economy.

This is what the State Department has to say about the three BRIC countries on the watch list.

1. Russia. This is a source, transit, and destination country for men, women, and children trafficked for various purposes. It is a significant source of women trafficked to more than 50 countries for sexual exploitation. Russia is also a transit country for men and women trafficked from Central Asia, Eastern Europe, and North Korea to Central and Western Europe and the Middle East for forced labor and sexual exploitation. Women are also trafficked from rural areas to cities for sexual exploitation and men are trafficked internally from Central Asia for forced labor in construction and agriculture. Debt bondage is common. Child sex tourism appears to be increasing.

2. India. India is a source, transit and destination country for men, women, and children used in forced labor and sexual exploitation. Well over one million of these souls are in debt bondage and face forced labor in brick kilns, rice mills, and embroidery factories. Children are forced into domestic servitude. Sexual exploitation and forced marriage also occur. The Indian government estimates that 90 percent of sex trafficking is internal. It should be noted that many U.S.-based advocacy groups believe that India should be in Tier 3 because of the enormous number of persons trafficked internally and externally. Some counts place the number of forced laborers at more than 65 million. As reported in the **Foreign Service Journal**, October 2007, Representative Christopher H. Smith, who sponsored the law requiring the tiered report, issued a statement speculating that the Tier 2 Watch List ranking was probably given to India instead of Tier 3 out of fear of alienating its government. Such is Washington's way.

3. China. The majority of trafficking in China is internal for sexual exploitation and forced labor. However, women are also trafficked to Taiwan, Thailand, Malaysia, and Japan for sexual exploitation. Women

and children are trafficked to Mongolia, Myanmar, North Korea, Russia, and Vietnam for forced labor and marriage. Men are forced to work in construction and agriculture. Officially, the Chinese government puts the trafficking in persons problem at about 20,000 persons per year, which must be a sick joke. Experts place the count in the high millions, which seems more likely. These same experts also believe that because of the male/female imbalance resulting from the preference for male babies, foreign girls and women are being trafficked into China to be brides.

CONCLUSION

By now, you probably agree with me that women and girls are severely discriminated against all over the world. Perhaps not as much in rich countries, but there, too. Is there any hope of women ever taking their rightful places in the world society? Or are they doomed to suffer these indignities forever? I certainly hope that the State Department's tier ratings penetrate the hearts and minds of those in power in the BRIC countries and elsewhere. Unfortunately, China has already dismissed the findings as "groundless." President Chavez of Venezuela has also snubbed the findings, claiming that the U.S. "simply wanted to damage [his] standing internationally." How callous.

But there is some light at the end of the tunnel. Women continue to make good headway in the United States, France, Germany, and Britain. Many Latin American countries have enacted radical reforms in education and reproductive healthcare that are now just beginning to take effect. Also, women are assuming increasingly important roles in the Latin American political scene with new female presidents in Argentina and Chile.

The Latin American labor gender gap is also shrinking. The spread in wages between men and women has narrowed considerably in Honduras, Brazil, Colombia, Argentina, and Mexico. Argentine women now earn 98 percent on average of the male wage. In Mexico, they earn 89 percent of the male wage. In Colombia it's 84 percent, Peru 80 percent, Brazil and Chile 77 percent each, El Salvador 74 percent, and Nicaragua 64 percent. These percentages are significantly higher than they were only 10 years ago. Also, women are now the principle wage earners in the service sector throughout Latin America.

This is one example of how much progress women have made, especially in Latin America. Sexual fantasy, long the purview of men, now attracts women in droves to a nightclub named Moria Restó y + in Buenos Aires. According to Alejandra Labanca of the *Miami Herald,* January 3, 2008, nude erotic dancers, men and women, perform sexual fantasies live on stage as the audience feasts on filet mignon and Argentine wine. Sex shops exclusively for women (no men allowed) dot the boulevards of Buenos Aires. In this cosmopolitan city of the south, women are in the forefront of a new sexual revolution that seems to reflect a general trend in cities throughout Latin America. Aleira Camilucci, an Argentine psychologist and sexologist, was quoted in the *Miami Herald* as saying, "Today women are reaching out to find out more about sex and pleasure and they are owning their sexuality."

Russian women are also breaking bonds. Legislation aimed at reducing gender discrimination, moving women closer to full status in the business community and perhaps even in government in the not too distant future, has already been enacted. A woman also heads the German government. While sex tourism continues unabated in Thailand, destroying the lives of countless young girls, women in the Philippines have a stronger role in politics than they had 20 years ago and women and girls in parts of Indonesia and Malaysia are beginning a gradual trend toward slightly more important and higher paying jobs.

Although the outlook today in many countries is dismal, it may be that global trade will, in the end, force many emerging nations to stop bullying and start appreciating women as integral players in their societies.

Although worldwide inequality continues to plague women and girls in many walks of life, there can be little question that their roles are gradually changing in many societies. Certainly, woman power is an integral part of global trade. Women form the backbone of consumer markets in nearly every emerging nation, except certain Arab states. Women account for approximately 50 percent of the population in most countries and therefore contribute about that same percentage to the well-being of the world. Women tend to be more concerned with the soft issues that plague society, such as healthcare, education, and nutrition and therefore are major contributors to resolving these issues worldwide.

Although the outlook today in many countries is dismal, it may be that global trade will, in the end, force many emerging nations to stop bullying and start appreciating women as integral players in their societies.

chapter fourteen
Winning Negotiations

Negotiating a contract in China, Russia, India, or Brazil is the same as negotiating one in New York, Chicago, or Los Angeles. Negotiating a contract in China, Russia, India, or Brazil is not at all like negotiating one in New York, Chicago, or Los Angeles. Which statement is correct? Both are correct. Both are incorrect.

Each contract you negotiate with a foreign buyer, bureaucrat, supplier, sales representative, distributor, potential joint venture partner, or anyone else is different. None have the same clauses. None of your adversaries will have similar likes and dislikes. Legal language in one country is not the same as it is in another. Nevertheless, successful negotiating strategy is very similar, regardless of the country. Tactics vary slightly, but strategies are similar.

The objective of any negotiation is to reach a compromise that satisfies both parties. It may be reached in a few hours, a few weeks, a few months, or even a few years. Negotiating is similar to playing poker. You bluff now and then, but to win the evening, you need the cards. You need to know when to bet, when to fold, and when to call it a night and walk away. You need to keep your wits about you at all times. You need to avoid being too friendly, too confrontational, or too emotional. Above all, regardless of the nationality of your adversaries, you need to be patient and extremely confident.

> Negotiating is similar to playing poker. You bluff now and then, but to win the evening, you need the cards. You need to know when to bet, when to fold, and when to call it a night and walk away.

PREPARING TO NEGOTIATE

Before sitting down at the negotiating table, you need to do some preparatory work. If the negotiation is to take place on foreign soil, you will have to bring all the documents, analyses, financial statements (if needed), and of course, a contract proposal. Bringing a proposed contract that reads the way you would like the final agreement to read is extremely important. When the meeting begins, it should land on the table before your adversary has time to do the same. Negotiating the terms and conditions of a contract that you have prepared is much easier than negotiating from a document prepared by your adversary. So get your proposal ready before leaving your office. Have your attorney approve the contract language. Make sure it says exactly what you want it to say in language that you understand. Don't worry about your adversary. If he doesn't understand English, it can be translated into his language once your arrive in country. From your position, it's much better to translate a contract from English to the foreign language than the other way around. This is a crucial negotiating tactic. Introduce your proposal in English right away. Don't hesitate for any reason, even if your adversary isn't quite ready. That's his problem—not yours.

Be sure to brief your negotiating team on how you want the meeting to proceed. Everyone must understand his or her role—when to be silent, when to interrupt, when to pull the good guy/bad guy stunt, or when to suggest a break. Also instruct everyone on body language. Hands on the table. No slouching or leaning on elbows. No opening shirt buttons or ties. No yawning or fidgeting. If your opponent smokes, that's OK. But tell your team to layoff. Leave all cigarettes, pipes, and cigars as well as matches at the hotel. That way no one will be tempted. And be sure to tell everyone to control their tempers. Negotiations are not the place to get angry, and in fact, most negotiators who do get angry, lose the war.

Decide before the meeting how long you want to go before a break. Also decide when you want to end the day's session. Your opponent may not agree, but that's OK. You should make the suggestions and let him turn them down. That way you're controlling the meeting, just like you did when you opened your contract proposal first.

Always do as much tactical planning ahead of time as possible. Get briefed on business protocol and any wildly dissimilar cultural traits. You'll never get everything right so don't worry about it. Making faux pas merely shows you're human. There must be dozens of books out there that claim to be the end all on cultural traits for any country you may visit. Go ahead and scan a few. It can't hurt, and you may pick up some pointers. Remember, however, that conditions change rapidly in international trade. What is correct today may be wrong tomorrow. That holds as true with cultural traits and business protocol as it does with trade topics.

Negotiating the terms and conditions of a contract that you have prepared is much easier than negotiating from a document prepared by your adversary.

To the extent that you can structure the meeting to your time schedule, you will have another leg up on your opponent. In China and India, mornings are a good time to begin. Russians like to work in the afternoon. Brazilians prefer evenings when it's cooler, except in São Paulo, where the pace is a lot faster and the weather temperate. For Chileans, Mexicans, and the rest of Latin America, meetings can begin at any time. Malaysians and Indonesians also opt for evening meetings whenever possible. Polish, Hungarian, and Czech business people prefer to start around noon and end before 7:00 p.m. Middle Easterners always meet in the evening. It's much too hot during the day to do anything that might require leaving an air-conditioned office.

BRAZIL

I don't intend to pop out a list of Brazilian cultural anomalies that might or might not affect your negotiating strategy. The world is changing too fast for that. However, we can discuss a few uniquely Latin behavioral characteristics that you should expect to see.

One characteristic is so crucial and so uniquely Brazilian that it demands special attention. Brazilians speak Portuguese and consider themselves apart from—and superior to—Spanish-speaking citizens. They do not consider themselves Hispanic and will be offended if you speak Spanish to them—unless you ask permission first. If you are more comfortable speaking Spanish, go ahead and ask your host if it is OK. Since most Brazilians understand and speak Spanish as well as Portuguese, you will probably be allowed to do so. Fortunately, English is widely spoken by the upper class and is rapidly becoming the language of choice for all international business matters.

> Once negotiations begin, do not under any circumstances change the members of your negotiating team.

Although Brazilians disavow their Hispanic heritage, they do have many characteristics common to Spanish-speaking Latin America. For instance, Brazilians do not make rapid decisions. They do not move with the frenetic speed of Americans. Hardly any negotiations are concluded in one session. Most will take at least three or four meetings spread over a period of a week to two or three. Don't try to hurry it along by staying in the country. This will annoy your hosts who will assume you are either too cheap to spring for another plane trip or pressuring them to finish the deal. Either way, you lose. Go home, wait a week or so, then phone your host to schedule the next meeting. The entire negotiation will probably require at least three or four trips.

Once negotiations begin, do not under any circumstances change the members of your negotiating team. This will offend your Brazilian opponents. Instead, spend a good deal of time convincing them how much you value your team, employees, and customers, and how much you want to establish good relations with your hosts. Build relationships first with lots of small talk. Then talk business. If you jump right in, you will be perceived as arrogant and unworthy of their trust.

You'll find that Brazilian managers are very well educated and well read. They can and will discuss almost anything with you—sports, books, international trade, the latest movies, classical music, the theater, and so on. They do not like to talk about their private lives. To Brazilians, that's personal and none of your business.

Brazilians tend to look at the whole picture, not the details. They base their judgments on the overall validity of the contract, not necessarily on how it is written. In other words, they want to negotiate the end result and not get hung up on the fine points. And they do not worry about possible laws or rules that the contract may infringe on. But you and your legal counsel better be concerned.

Bring lots of business cards printed in English on one side and Portuguese on the other side. Feel free to hand them out to everyone.

RUSSIA

Russians are a stoic lot. Their heritage requires them to leap one hurdle after another. They want to get on with business and the last thing they want to do is sit around a table for days arguing about contract details. The hierarchy of the Russian business culture is deeply entrenched in the bowels of these long suffering peoples. While it is true that the days of rigid state control and discipline are long gone, bosses still have an enormous amount of authority over workers and are ultimately responsible for all matters related to the business.

The country is still in the throes of replacing communist social and economic structures with something resembling free market democracy. Russian managers try hard to learn from the West, even though most will never admit it. Unfortunately, many Russian are still unfamiliar with the Western business culture. They want to learn, but they aren't there, yet. And this has a profound effect on your negotiating strategy. I'm certain that unless you deal with young managers who have been trained in the West, you will have to explain what you mean by such things as fair play, proprietary rights, sales motivation, goodwill, public relations, payroll bonuses, and individual accountability. You will also have to explain how these terms fit into your business logic, practices, and protocol. Finally, you need to persuade your Russian hosts that these concepts will benefit them—just as much as you.

You will likely have a fair amount of difficulty getting that message across. Russians are not very adept at processing new information. When they get frustrated, they act exactly the same as we would under the same circumstances; they revert to familiar patterns. The difference is that in Russia, those patterns are the old, state-directed and close-minded ones.

When you present your arguments, use visuals if possible. And be sure to translate any verbiage in the visuals to Cyrillic. Your arguments should be kept as simple as possible. Don't make it any more difficult to comprehend than you have to. Remember that you're dealing with people who are just now beginning to grasp the nuances of free market business. Although it is certainly important to make your arguments cohesive and factual, don't lose sight of the importance of conveying a good impression of yourself, your team, and your company.

Beware of vodka. It's all part of the Russian negotiating game.

You'll have to do your homework before you get on the plane. Be sure to decipher who your adversary's decision makers will be. Russians have a habit of sending lower echelon managers to greet newcomers. This is fine, as along as they do not participate in hands-on negotiations. Unfortunately, upper-level managers responsible for making decisions like to play the messenger game, inferring that their underlings have authority. It makes these managers feel important. Don't buy into this. It's only a ploy to throw you off balance. If you go along with it, you'll waste a lot of time at the negotiating table without getting results. The lower-level person will always take matters up the chain of command until he finally reaches the decision maker. This may take days away from the negotiating table. Don't let it happen. If it does, be alert to it in the beginning and excuse yourself from the meeting until the boss can be present. You may have to make a second or third trip, but keep trying until you get to the boss.

Make sure your counterpart gets to know you. Establishing this relationship is crucial to successful negotiations. It will also make you appear to be a regular guy or gal who thinks the same way as your new Russian friend.

One quick comment for the women. Very few Russian women hold positions of authority in the business world and male managers are not accustomed to treating women as equals. If you get stuck with a Russian negotiation, just dress your best, be feminine, and you'll do fine. I hate to admit it, but you will face considerably more challenges in Russia than your male counterparts.

Beware of vodka. Toasting at every turn with this national drink is customary. It's OK to join in the toast. In fact, you must join in or your host will feel insulted. Just remember to limit your intake to one. Your adversary may become a bit tipsy and run off at the mouth, but that's perfectly normal. Don't let it bother you. It's all part of the Russian negotiating game.

I strongly advise you to engage a Russian lawyer familiar with the convoluted system of that country's contract law. Constant changes are occurring in both contract law and other business regulations, and you need someone on your side who knows the ropes and can stay on top of these myriad variations. Also, don't forget to hire an interpreter. Try to make contact with one who resides in Russia, preferably in the city in which negotiations are to take place. Meet the interpreter a day or two before negotiations begin. Try to establish a relationship so that during negotiations, translations will be focused on your company, its products, its goals, and you personally. This will be a huge help when it comes to rewriting clauses in the contract.

Bring lots of business cards—English on one side and Cyrillic on the other side. Again, feel free to hand them out to everyone.

INDIA

I have negotiated more contracts than I can count in various countries around the globe, but I have never had more trouble doing so than in India. The Russian, Brazilian, even the Chinese business cultures are relatively easy to grasp. But India is so convoluted and the rules are so varied that I still don't completely understand all the nuances of their negotiating process. I wonder if any foreigner can be reasonably certain that he grasps the entire picture.

You might be surprised at the diversity of the Indian business culture. Protocol and practices vary from one region to another. No two states have the same contract laws. No two sectors of the country have the same customs. The citizens of one state do not look at things in the same way as citizens of another state. And no two companies have quite the same ownership and management structures. For instance, a large number of Indian businesses are family-owned or owned by members of different communities. Communities with names like Parsi, Marwari, Gujarati, and Chettiar keep popping up as owners of large and small businesses in a variety of industries. This community business culture sets India apart from the other three BRIC nations and from any Western nation.

Companies involved with advanced technology such as high-speed telecoms, Wii, computer games, and financial services tend to be more egalitarian and flexible, whereas the culture of old manufacturing companies is staid and traditional. Government-owned businesses will always be more hierarchal and bureaucratic than their private sector counterparts. Regional differences also come into play. Companies in the south of India are more conservative than their northern or western cousins. Employees in northern and western companies tend to be more individualistic and assertive than their eastern counterparts. The categories into which your adversary's company falls dictates how you should proceed with your negotiating strategy.

It's important to understand that Indians love anything old, including transnational corporations that have been doing business there for several decades. A negotiation between one of these giants and an Indian company usually goes very smoothly. However, Indians are prone to regard new entrants to their business community, especially smaller companies, with suspicion—if not outright disdain.

I suggest that before you begin a negotiation, you contract an Indian consultant or lawyer to be at your elbow at the negotiating table. Your lawyer can also be of immense help in explaining the myriad laws and bureaucracies, both of which are convoluted, cumbersome, and changing rapidly. Moreover, just like in the United States, each Indian state has its own set of laws that are enforceable in addition to laws coming from Delhi.

As in Russia, a lower echelon manager will try to be your negotiating adversary. Don't let this happen. If you can't deal with a decision maker, excuse yourself and wait in your hotel until he is available.

English is the language of business, but Indian English is like none other in the world. A host of strange words mean things entirely different from the way we use them. For example, when something is *deadly*, it is intense. *Godown* is a warehouse. Indians love the words *simply, obviously,* and *actually* and overuse them consistently—sometimes several times in the same sentence.

Pronunciation also varies from one part of the country to another, making negotiations difficult to manage unless you happen to be familiar with that dialect. I imagine Indians could say the same about Americans with peculiar dialects from New York City, Boston, Philadelphia, the deep South, and the Upper Midwest.

In the United States, common courtesy dictates that if you are a man, you stand when a women enters the room. Regardless of gender, you stand when the boss comes in and remain standing until he or she is seated. Follow these same rules in India. They are normal courtesies and if you ignore them, you'll get a black mark. Common courtesies between men and women, respect for the elderly, and loyalty to one's family and extended family or community are still very much in evidence. Also, although it may be hard for Americans to swallow, many Indians practice religious rituals in the workplace. If you notice this, just go with the flow. Do not comment.

> Relationships count for a lot in India. More than once, I've had my opponent acquiesce to a point simply because he liked me and trusted me.

You ladies will likely be uncomfortable during your first negotiation. Very few Indian women hold decision-making positions in the business world, although this is changing. Indian men will shy away from you. They will be very courteous but make you feel like an outsider. That's normal. There is nothing you can do about it. Just grit your teeth and bear it.

Relationships count for a lot in India. More than once, I've had my opponent acquiesce to a point simply because he liked me and trusted me. That's not bragging, it's just the way Indians are. They would much rather negotiate with someone who will share part of themselves than with a feisty, aggressive American whom they feel cannot be trusted.

One Indian characteristic that drives me nuts is their propensity to mul-titask by opting to discuss topics that have nothing to do with the subject at hand. For instance, it is not uncommon for your adversary to digress into a variety of unrelated topics right in the middle of intense negotiations. A secretary may enter the room with a note. Your adversary may take a cell phone call. The local cricket match may come up for discussion. Questions about how you like your hotel accommodations may be asked. And so on. None of which have any bearing on the subject being negotiated. But that's how Indians think. They bounce from one subject to another without a second thought, eventually—sometimes a day or two later—weaving their way back to the negotiation. Don't be upset with this ploy. It's a normal occurrence and has nothing to do with you or with how the negotiation is progressing.

Very seldom will Indians express their disapproval directly. I have never heard one say "no." That would be considered rude. Instead, they will circumvent a decision commenting, "I'll have to check with Mr. Raj on this" or "We will discuss that later." Once again, don't get frustrated. That's just the Indian way of handling things.

As with Russians, Brazilians, and as we'll see next, Chinese, every Indian loves to get business cards. I don't know what they do with the stacks they get. But if you don't hand them out to everyone, they will consider you unknowing and uncaring. Fortunately, cards only need to be printed in English.

CHINA

China is probably the only communist country you will deal with, at least for a few years. We hear about all the great opportunities in China, with its huge consumer base and cheap labor force. We hear about how many companies have ventured into China and come out huge winners. We hear about predictions that China will be the most powerful country on earth by the year 2050. There may be a grain of truth in all this, but China is still a communist country with all the horrific connotations that brings.

Chinese negotiating tactics reflect this addiction to a peoples state, as the Beijing leaders like to call their huge land. Objective facts, empirical evidence, and century old truisms will be accepted only if they do not conflict with the communist doctrine. Moreover, your adversary will believe that your facts are indeed facts only if he likes them. Such denial of truths makes negotiating a difficult task at best and a nightmare at worst. You can't resolve this dilemma. The only way to cope with it is to continue presenting your evidence and hope that eventually your adversary accepts it.

The age and education of your adversary makes an enormous difference in how you approach the negotiation. Chinese who are 35 years old or older will generally follow traditional Chinese and communist rules. Younger generations, and especially those educated in Western universities, prefer to just negotiate the deal. One of the oldest Chinese cultural quirks that effects every negotiation is the ancient belief of *saving face*. The worst affront a Westerner can make is to cause his adversary to be embarrassed in public and to lose face.

The decision-making process for older adversaries is very opaque and indirect. Nothing is said directly, every point, every decision, every conclusion is convoluted. Younger managers, on the other hand, are more concerned with getting the best possible price than with practicing the old Chinese custom of indirection. But saving face applies to everybody.

The age and education of your adversary makes an enormous difference in how you approach the negotiation.

While on the subject of age, I should mention that as more and more Chinese deal with Americans, they are beginning to learn how to whitewash their company, covering up practices that might be objectionable to us, and making their company look more American. They hire Western consultants who are adept at painting the company as a progressive-minded, modern-day business with open and caring managers. Underneath the facade, however, you'll find a traditional business with inbred communist managers who continue to follow all the old customs and practices. I mention this, not to suggest you that can do anything about it. You can't. However, you can be alert to signs that this is the case with your adversary. You may then want to back off and try a different tack. Or you might decide to move on to a different company. If you smell a rat, there is probably one rotting somewhere.

Be sure to hire your own interpreter, one who understands the nuances of the Mandarin or Cantonese language, whichever your adversary will be using. With all Western companies doing business in China, you won't have any trouble finding a good interpreter. If you can possibly find one who is not addicted to the communist ideology, you'll be miles ahead. Unfortunately, that may not always be possible or practical.

Decisions in this communist country are made collectively, not individually. Even in those businesses and sections of the country that are experimenting with the Chinese form of a free enterprise system, collective decisions predominate. Since your adversary must get a decision from his collective bosses, which could take several days or weeks, it's hard to know when negotiations have ended. Even after you return home, positive that you have reached an agreement, don't be surprised if you receive an e-mail or phone call demanding changes in language, price, or delivery. I don't have any suggestions for resolving this issue, which by the way, happens quite frequently. If you can make the contract changes without too much difficulty, by all means change them. If you can't, tell your opponent. If he insists, move on to another customer, supplier, or representative.

> Decisions in this communist country are made collectively, not individually.

Before closing, I want to reemphasize the importance of saving face. This is probably the most significant attribute that permeates the entire Chinese culture, regardless of a person's age, party status, business position, or education. Furthermore, it has nothing to do with communism. Personal reputation is so important that when denied or sullied, nothing else matters. In any Chinese walk of life, reputation and social standing are paramount to survival and acceptance by family, friends, business associates, and communist bureaucrats. Losing face means being embarrassed, and to the Chinese, this is a major blow to one's reputation. Even if you cause such loss of face unintentionally, you might as well close down your negotiation because nothing good will come of it.

Here are a few pointers you should find helpful:

➥ Only the senior member of your team leads discussions, junior members remain silent.

➥ As the senior member, you lead your team into the meeting room.

➥ Humility is a virtue, making grandiose claims raises suspicions.

➥ Chinese do not say "no," but if that's what they mean, they will say things like "We'll see," "I'm not sure," "Perhaps," and "I'll think about it." Each of these responses means "no."

➥ Never mention deadlines at a negotiation because the Chinese do not believe in them and will keep going forever until they decide they have had enough—even then, they may try to reopen discussions at a later date.

➡ When your adversary finally does conclude the negotiation, you leave the room first.

Of course, business cards are a prerequisite, just like they are in every other emerging nation. Carry plenty of them with you whether you're negotiating in Mandarin or Cantonese. One final bit of advice: Have your business cards embossed in gold ink. To the Chinese, the color gold means prestige. A gold card shows how important you must be in America.

PREVENTING NEGOTIATION FAILURES

From time to time, even with extensive planning and cautious exploration of cultural traits and business protocol, you will inevitably run into conflicts. This cannot be avoided. You try to do all the right things but occasionally an opponent will be looking for a fight, not a resolution. Or perhaps the negotiation stirs your emotions so much that you blow up and end the meeting prematurely. These things happen to the best of us. However, you can prepare to mitigate such a catastrophe.

There is a right way and a wrong way to deal with conflicts, regardless of the nationality of your adversary. I have experimented with several conflict resolution tactics proposed by self-appointed authorities and none have worked. I don't know of any magic formula, but I can give a few tips that have worked for me in warding off fractures in relationships that most likely would have been difficult or impossible to mend. Perhaps the best way to proceed with this delicate subject is to frame these methods in a series of do's and don'ts. By the way, these are universal suggestions, independent of specific cultural anomalies.

The Setting and Preliminaries
➡ Do encourage a neutral location, if possible, such as a restaurant, golf course, theater, athletic event, or even an airport lounge, but if that doesn't work, agree to meet on your adversary's turf and at your adversary's convenience.
➡ Don't force the issue by insisting you meet in an office or other formal location.

➡ Do let it be known that your company must abide by the U.S. Foreign Corrupt Practices Act, and as low-key as possible, offer to make a donation to a local hospital, school, or church instead of a payoff—but only when dealing with a high-ranking bureaucrat.

The Participants

➡ Do bring your boss if your adversary does the same. However, remember that your boss may then have to lead the negotiations, which most prefer not to do.

➡ Do bring a peace offering, preferably flowers, fine wine, or some other gift for your adversary's spouse.

➡ Do bring an interpreter, even if you are confident in the language.

➡ Do have your local sales representative/distributor/intermediary standing by in your hotel room or other location away from the meeting room in case they are needed.

➡ Don't bring lawyers, accountants, consultants, or other advisers to the meeting, unless your adversary does, with one exception—you may need a lawyer to interpret local laws.

➡ Don't bring business associates as negotiating team members unless your adversary does—in other words, keep the number of participants the same on both sides of the table.

The Meeting

➡ Do approach the meeting as a discussion, not a confrontation.

➡ Do take a positive position, but do not be offensive.

➡ Do engage in as much small talk as your adversary wants.

➡ Do work out a compromise in your mind before the meeting, determining exactly how much you are willing to concede.

➡ Do try to decipher your adversary's hot button and then push it.

➡ Do ask for a recess when you don't understand something or when you need assistance from your legal or other advisers.

➡ Do invite your adversary to visit you in the States.

➡ Do be gracious in victory or defeat.

➡ Don't negotiate for something that is impossible for your adversary to agree to.

➡ Don't lose your cool.

➡ Don't drink wine, beer, or liquor before or during the meeting, and do not smoke even if members of the other side do.

➡ Don't watch the clock—the negotiation may take hours, days, or weeks.

➡ Don't be defensive.

➡ Don't guess at local laws or regulations.

➡ Don't fight it if you can't resolve the conflict with one meeting. Instead, offer to come back tomorrow, next week, or some later mutually agreeable date.

➡ Don't let discussions finalize without a resolution, whether it takes hours or days and whether you have to return next week or next month.

Hopefully, these suggestions will stimulate your thinking process. However, everyone has his or her own subtle ways to resolve disputes, so if you have techniques that worked in the past, by all means use them. One thing you can count on—conflicts will arise whenever you do business overseas. Your success in negotiating your deal will depend on how well you master the intricacies of resolving them.

STRATEGIC TIPS FOR MALE/FEMALE NEGOTIATING PLOYS

Cultural barriers may make it necessary, or at least expedient, for women to remain out of the negotiation. Certainly Arab men, and very often Chinese and Russia men, would be embarrassed to have a woman sitting at the negotiating table. Arab or Chinese negotiators will never outwardly refuse to negotiate with a woman present, but they will vent their displeasure by refusing to allow the negotiation to reach a conclusion. In Russia, you will likely be able to participate, but beware of the Russian propensity for bluntness and vodka, either of which can reduce a negotiation to tatters and negotiators to tears.

Latin America is another story. Women are more than welcome to sit at the negotiating table in any Latin country—except, perhaps, modern day Venezuela. The same holds true in India. Unless you come across an old-time adversary with outdated ideas about the role of women in the business world, you shouldn't run into any gender problems in either location.

Assuming negotiations take place in an atmosphere devoid of gender barriers, here are a few ideas for increasing the odds of winning with a male/female negotiating team:

The Female Player
➡ Pass out business cards with your executive title clearly visible.
➡ Dress in feminine attire—dress or blouse and skirt.
➡ Carry yourself like a woman.
➡ Don't pretend to belong to a "good ol' boy" club.
➡ Speak gently and slowly.
➡ Defer to your adversary when tensions rise.
➡ Don't lose your cool under any circumstance.
➡ Don't tell your male partner what to do or how to negotiate—at least not in public.
➡ Don't smoke.
➡ Join your adversary in a toast, if offered, even if it's vodka—but only one.
➡ Don't let alcohol make you woozy or intoxicated.

The Male Player
➡ Treat your female partner with extreme and obvious courtesy.
➡ Let your adversary know that you consider your teammate's presence an honor.
➡ Don't forget your manners.
➡ Don't smoke.
➡ Join your host in a toast.
➡ Don't let alcohol make you woozy or intoxicated.
➡ Defer to your adversary when tensions rise.
➡ Don't lose your cool under any circumstance.
➡ Don't tell your female partner what to do or how to negotiate—at least not in public.

Good Guy/Bad Guy Tactic
➡ In the early stage of negotiations, the male should be the bad guy and the female the good guy.

➡ The male should struggle with language nuances, and the female should bail him out.

➡ When the male raises his voice in argument, the female quietly calms him down.

The Decision Point

➡ The female should take charge, becoming more forceful in her arguments.

➡ The male should gradually slip into a supporting role.

➡ The female should point out several soft-type benefits to the adversary of agreeing with her arguments (any contract has a few soft-type benefits, such as the beginning time or date or termination clauses).

The Signing

➡ Both team members should be humble but firm and very appreciative of your adversary's patience.

➡ Both team members should take part in a final toast, if offered.

➡ Before beginning negotiations, learn the proper protocol for leaving the room (e.g., before or after your adversary).

Always remember that the two of you are a team—not individuals. Also, I strongly advise you not to increase the number of team members beyond the two of you. You want your adversary to focus on the male/female polemic.

PART IV
MANAGING GLOBAL TRADE

chapter fifteen
Market Research:
Performing a Country Survey

MARKET RESEARCH IS THE STARTING POINT IN DECIDING WHICH COUNTRY
and markets to go after. It makes sense to do as much market research as
time and money allow. You'll be looking for
hard data to make intelligent marketing, financial, and
manufacturing decisions and also to calculate a
country risk assessment. Obviously, the more information you can pull together, the better chance you
have of avoiding costly mistakes.

You can get a fair amount of information without
leaving home, such as a country's business structure

requirements; audit, tax, legal, and licensing rules; potential communications bottlenecks; and types of insurance coverage. On the other hand, reliable political and economic data as well as market specific information can only be obtained within the host country. While several U.S. government agencies will give you a fairly good feel for current happenings in the political and economics spheres, to get the full scoop, you need to see for yourself and that means visiting the country. You'll have to go there to gather data on the following market specific matters anyway:

- ➡ Possible distribution channels.
- ➡ Sales representative/distributor arrangements.
- ➡ Business support activities (e.g., interpreters, safety and security features, banking, business permits, and informal trade barriers).
- ➡ Safety and security matters.
- ➡ Alternative advertising media.
- ➡ Exchange controls.

Moreover, if your current or future plans call for establishing a local manufacturing plant, distribution center, retail outlet, or sales office, you'll need information about labor availability, sources of materials and supplies, inland transport, infrastructure conditions, and expatriate living arrangements.

Reliable political and economic data as well as market specific information can only be obtained within the host country.

You may have the personnel within your organization who can perform country surveys, but why bother with such a tedious task? Extensive interviews must be conducted with government officials, in-country managers of U.S. companies, potential customers, likely sales representatives and distributors, transportation executives, and various other individuals. And that takes an enormous amount of time. Why not let a consultant separate the wheat from the chaff? I have performed any number of country surveys for clients in various countries around the world. No, I cannot take on any new clients, but there are lots of qualified consultants who can do the job for you. If you elect to use a consulting company, the following rules of the road can save you a significant amount of money.

1. Describe to the consultant in as much detail as possible exactly what you want done and what your strategic objectives are for entering a given market.
2. Arm the consultant with data about your company, its products, current markets, and personnel capabilities.
3. Ask the consultant to identify potential limitations in the scope of the assignment.
4. Find out how the consultant plans to get the information you want and be sure you're comfortable with its modus operandi.
5. Clearly define the level of detail you expect in each element of the survey.
6. Gather as much data as you can from U.S. sources first. Turn over the names, addresses, and telephone numbers of host country referrals you have already uncovered to the consultant. Don't hesitate to have the consultant help analyze pre-research data. The less time he spends in the field, the less your costs will be.

BUSINESS STRUCTURE

If you plan to export directly to end users, intermediary distributors, or trading companies that take immediate title of the goods, you don't have to worry about business structure requirements. However, if you plan to initiate a joint venture or local facility of any kind, the form and capitalization of the host country business entity must meet the legal requirements of that country.

Some countries require import licenses that can only be granted to registered businesses. Others forbid foreigners from holding a controlling interest in local companies. You may or may not be permitted to incorporate a business. You may have to operate out of a joint venture partnership, possibly with the government as a partner. Some countries insist on hybrid business structures that combine the characteristics of partnerships and corporations.

The host country's embassy or trade representative office in the United States is the best place to get the rules governing business structure and ownership. While you're at it, pick up copies of any regulations that apply to import licenses, tax clearances, business licenses, foreign exchange permits, and other operating approvals.

The following are a series of questions about business structure and ownership that need to be answered:

1. What laws relate to foreign business ownership?
2. Is there a required business form? Corporation? Partnership? Hybrid?
3. What are the restrictions on each form?
4. Can or should tiered corporations be used?
5. Do local laws require a host country partner in a joint venture or other strategic alliance?
6. If a local partner is required, what percentage of ownership must you give up?
7. Must the joint venture carry one of the partners' names or can its name be completely divorced from them?

AUDIT, TAX, LEGAL, AND LICENSING REQUIREMENTS

Many questions that relate to audit requirements, taxes, contract law, and licensing can only be answered by sources within the host country. You can get some information, however, from the U.S. offices of multinational accounting firms such as Ernst & Young, KPMG Peat Marwick, Pricewater-houseCoopers, and DTR International. Each of these firms publishes newsletters, special reports, and information pamphlets about broad changes in tax laws and reporting requirements. Each also prints booklets summarizing tax information for use by individuals and corporations in every country in which the firm has offices. Be sure to ask for a directory of the firm's worldwide offices. It will contain the names and telephone numbers of resident partners whom you can contact once you begin your in-country research.

Every country has an embassy in the United States. Many also have trade promotion bureaus that stock a variety of booklets and pamphlets describing audit and tax laws and import licensing regulations. You should be able to get the following questions answered from either a country's embassy or its trade promotion office.

1. What are the financial reporting requirements, and when do financial reports have to be filed?
2. Should these reports be verified by an in-country registered audit firm, or can that be done by your U.S. auditors?
3. Will audited consolidated financial statements from your parent company suffice or must the in-country entity be audited separately?
4. Has a Tax Information Exchange Agreement with the United States been executed?
5. What are the tax rates?
6. What income is included or excluded for corporate and individual tax purposes?
7. Is a tax levied on imports or direct sales?
8. Are there any tax incentives applied to foreign direct investments?
9. Are intracompany transactions with your U.S. company taxed?
10. Is there a withholding tax on earnings or royalties to be repatriated?

It's obvious that social, economic, and political conditions are changing rapidly all over the world. Legal systems that have worked for centuries are suddenly outmoded or, if not outmoded, certainly at variance with the judicial systems of a majority of Western nations. This is especially true of the Arab states where the Islamic Sharia is the governing law. Legal systems in those countries that are in a state of flux make market-entry planning especially difficult. Laws governing contracts, taxes, the protection of intellectual property rights, business permits and licenses, pensions, workers' security, and a host of other items continue to change. And one country's laws are significantly different from other countries. Moreover, the court systems in many countries are virtually inoperative. Cases take an inordinate amount of time to come to trial. Remedies are seldom granted to foreign companies. And even when you win a case, collecting an award can be very difficult.

In practical terms, the only way to learn about the current status and potential changes going on in business laws is to check with an attorney who is licensed to do business in that country. Fortunately, nearly all large U.S. law firms have correspondents around the world. Although the extent of your legal research will vary by country, the following are the broad questions to address:

1. Which correspondent firms does your attorney recommend?
2. What are the laws governing business permits, import licensing, and work visas?
3. What ethical problems, if any, might arise in dealing with host country correspondent firms?
4. What are the incorporation or business structure laws?
5. Are there any restrictions on or requirements for setting up joint ventures or partnerships with local firms?
6. What unique features of the host country's litigation laws pertain to American firms doing business there?
7. What liability do U.S. exporters have for actions taken by in-country representatives that may be in violation of the Foreign Corrupt Practices Act or other U.S. laws?
8. Which legal counsel, in the United States or in the host country, will review sales or purchase contracts, countertrade deals, or other contracts?
9. Are laws that protect intellectual property rights enforced?
10. Who will handle arbitration cases if they arise?
11. Do you have Washington contacts who can cut through red tape when we apply for export or import licenses, federal assistance, or financial aid?

COMMUNICATIONS BOTTLENECKS

I can't think of anything more frustrating for U.S. managers than trying to communicate with customers, sales representatives, distributors, or their own facilities only to find that telephones lines are down, electricity is out, and mail delivery takes four weeks. Although conditions are improving in many emerging nations, they still have a long way to go to meet modern day demands. The majority of businesses continue to live with grossly inferior communication infrastructures and are forced to get along with systems that are antiquated, unreliable, and very costly to use. Fortunately, cell phones are available in most countries

On more than one occasion, local mail handlers have opened mail, confiscated the contents, and then intentionally lost the envelope or package.

and e-mail is a feasible way to communicate in writing, provided both sender and recipient have electricity.

International mail service between some countries has improved a lot in recent years. In other countries, it remains almost nonexistent. Except for Brazil, internal mail service within emerging economies is dismal. On more than one occasion, local mail handlers have opened mail, confiscated the contents, and then intentionally lost the envelope or package. If you must send a package or a sheaf of documents, use an international courier. However, even with reputable couriers like DHL and FedEx problems arise.

INSIGHT... A couple years ago, I sent a bundle of documents to Georgetown, Guyana. The package arrived in about seven days. But it had obviously been opened and resealed, which, of course, DHL denied. Fortunately, the package contained only documents that were useless to anyone other than my client so no damage was done.

When gathering information about potential communications bottlenecks, it's a good idea to put what you are told to the test. More often than not, the official line about telephone service, couriers, and electronic mail is vastly different from actual practice. Nevertheless, as a start, the following are some questions to ask:

1. Does the country's telephone service operate on direct dialing for international calls?
2. If not, are local operators (hopefully English-speaking) used for placing international calls?
3. Can overseas calls be placed and received on private lines or does a central telephone office have to be used?
4. How much do international calls to and from the United States cost?
5. Can U.S. credit cards be used to pay for international calls placed from the host country?

6. Is e-mail used extensively or only sporadically?
7. How practical are cell phones for local calls and international calls?
8. Is fax service reliable? Does it cost extra?
9. Is voice over internet protocol (VOIP) a viable alternative?
10. How reliable is the electric power system?
11. Is it practical to use computers? How does the local weather affect their performance? Are backup generators readily available?
12. Are computer repair facilities and parts available?
13. How reliable is the local postal service, and what does it cost to send mail between the United States and the host country?
14. What is the mail delivery time to and from the United States?
15. Do major courier services deliver nearby your sales representative's or distributor's office? How long does a DHL or FedEx delivery take?

INSURANCE

In the United States, we assume that we can get insurance coverage for virtually anything merely by calling an insurance broker. This is certainly not the case in most countries of the world. Many types of coverage that we are accustomed to are either unavailable or grossly inadequate in less developed countries. Although your company's group health insurance program may include overseas coverage, many do not. Popular Blue Cross/Blue Shield policies or HMO plans, for example, generally exclude hospital or physician charges incurred while out of the United States. If your insurance carrier excludes international care and will not write a separate rider, specialized international healthcare bureaus are a good alternative. Be sure to select one that writes policies that include emergency transport back to the States (both Travel Assistance International and International SOS Assistance do so). This is essential in the event of serious illness or accident.

 Travel Assistance International, P.O. Box 668, Millersville, MD 21108; 800-821-2828; www.travelassistance.com and International SOS Assistance Inc., 3600 Horizon Blvd., Suite 300, Philadelphia, PA 19053; 215-942-8000; www.internationalsos.com

Some types of limited insurance coverage may be available within a host country. However, until very recently, most insurance companies were state owned, so don't expect the breadth of coverage, claim service, or low premiums offered by U.S. carriers. Some countries in Latin America and Eastern Europe have taken steps to privatize employee benefit programs, group health and life insurance, and nonhealth insurance companies. Compared to the United States, however, these carriers are very small. On the plus side, foreign firms are occasionally permitted to form joint ventures with local insurance companies.

Although privatized insurance companies and joint ventures with U.S. carriers offer limited opportunities for buying insurance locally, you will be ahead in the long run by arranging coverage through a U.S. carrier. This way you'll avoid any possibility of not getting adequate insurance at a reasonable cost.

In addition to health insurance, review your coverage for losses caused by work related accidents, damage to or disappearance of ocean shipments, destruction of property, product liability, vehicular accidents (especially with rental cars), and government expropriation of your property. Right off the bat, you can eliminate workers' compensation. Except in rare circumstances, the type of coverage we are accustomed to in the States is not available for offshore employees and must be purchased within the host country itself—if it's even available. Several marine insurance companies cover damage or loss of goods during ocean shipping. If you have trouble locating one, check with your state insurance commission. Property insurers are a different story. AIG (www.aig.insurance-website.com) is the largest carrier in this business. Lloyd's of London (www.lloyds.com)

Many types of coverage that we are accustomed to are either unavailable or grossly inadequate in less developed countries.

also insures offshore property. If you plan to have an in-country facility, coverage from the federal government's Overseas Private Investment Corporation (www.opic.gov) is hard to beat. And don't forget the UN's Multilateral Investment Guarantee Agency (MIGA) (www.miga.org). MIGA provides guarantees that serve as insurance policies to cover risks of currency transfer, expropriation, war and civil disturbance, and breach of contract by host country governments. This is a must if you expect to have in-country facilities or do business with a government agency.

Most insurance companies in emerging nations have never heard of product liability coverage. To offset this shortfall, a few U.S. carriers begrudgingly cover claims from U.S. companies' overseas customers. Also, since many markets are beginning to open to foreign investment, your U.S. carrier may already sell policies for local coverage through a subsidiary or joint venture with a host country carrier. Can't hurt to ask.

Your company fleet policy may or may not cover overseas rented or leased automobiles, although several U.S. insurers do. Since automobile rental insurance is usually several times more expensive when purchased in-country, make sure you are covered before leaving home.

That's about all you can do from the States. The rest of your survey will have to be conducted within the host country. It should focus on political and economic conditions, general business conditions, transportation options, security issues, personnel matters, and exchange controls. If you plan to have an in-country presence, you'll need information about labor conditions, local transportation, and expatriate living conditions. If such a presence involves manufacturing, information about the availability of materials or components, the extent of government subsidies, and the current status of infrastructure development are essential. If your market strategies are limited to exporting, the survey can be restricted to a review of competition, distribution options, advertising media, and other market conditions. Obviously, the amount of information and the time involved in gathering it depends on how much you can get from U.S. sources and your planned involvement within the country. Research procedures described in the rest of this chapter cover the waterfront and assume full involvement with an in-country presence.

Until you learn the ropes of global trade, it's prudent to make sure that markets will not only be accessible over a reasonable period of time but will also grow.

POLITICAL AND ECONOMIC ENVIRONMENT

To be effective, global market strategies must be long-term. It doesn't make sense to invest money and time in a country that is politically unstable or has a shaky economic future, even when the markets in that country demand products such as yours. Until you learn the ropes of global trade, it's prudent to make sure that markets will not only be accessible over a reasonable period of time but will also grow. Although certainty is a rare commodity on the global scene, by putting together as many specific facts and sound opinions as possible about a country's future potential, you should be able to reduce the risk of unrealistic growth projections.

Aside from international trade periodicals and U.S. government agencies focused on trade and foreign direct investment, some of which provide excellent coverage, the most reliable and current information about political and economic conditions will come from the host country offices of the American Chamber of Commerce, multinational banks, multinational accounting and consulting firms, and in-country subsidiaries or divisions of other American companies. The following questions should be asked of representatives from each organization:

1. Does more than one political party vie for office?
2. What are the views of each toward continuing economic reforms?
3. When is the next election? What is the prognosis?
4. Is the current government favorably or unfavorably disposed toward Americans and especially toward American imports?
5. What is the country's current relationship with the U.S. government?
6. What other American companies are doing business in the country?
7. What is the official attitude toward foreign direct investment, especially from U.S. companies? What is the unofficial attitude?
8. What does the country's main economic base consist of? Imports? Exports? Locally produced goods and services?
9. Are statistics available to show economic growth or decline (e.g., gross domestic product, interest rates, inflation rates, annual capital expenditures, imports, exports, wage rates, unemployment rates)? If so, what are they, and how reliable are they?
10. What are the country's demographic trends (e.g., age spread, income distribution, geographic dispersion, and so on)?
11. Are major businesses owned or controlled by the government?
12. If so, is there a privatization program under way, and which businesses are being sold?
13. How strong are local business cartels?
14. What specific trade barriers hinder foreign imports or foreign investment? Licensing? Exchange controls? Protected industries?

15. Do government regulations restrict the distribution of imported products?

MARKET SPECIFIC BUSINESS CONDITIONS

If you are planning to do your own marketing, as opposed to working through a trading company, the first step is to build a local sales organization. But first, you need to answer following questions.

1. What government regulations restrict the scope of in-country sales personnel?
2. What regulations govern contractual relationships with sales representatives?
3. Can sales representatives also distribute their own or competitors' products? Can distributors also sell retail? Do the same import licensing regulations apply to sales representatives, distribution centers, and end users?
4. Does the government encourage countertrade arrangements? What incentives or restrictions apply?
5. Do trading companies handle imported goods? Is this the dominant form of foreign sales representation?

Although much of this information can be obtained from government sources, the enforcement of official regulations should be confirmed with local merchants, producers, and sales representatives. The opinions of managers of in-country subsidiaries of American companies are usually reliable. If anyone knows the ins and outs of local business these people do and most are more than willing to show a compatriot the ropes. Also, if practical, try to get the opinions of sales representatives, distributors, and end users who import products. Their answers won't always be straightforward or necessarily reliable, but if you plan to use in-country representatives, you might as well find out now what regulatory obstacles you'll run into.

Cartels that control entire industries through a tight web of cross holdings are prevalent in some countries—but thankfully not many. Colombia probably has more business cartels than any other Latin American country.

Russian oligarchies control gas, oil, electricity, and several other industries. Taiwan, China, and Saudi Arabia are a few other countries with prominent cartels. Constraints imposed by these cartels can be devastating. Government officials won't admit to such informal barriers, but they do exist, nonetheless. If it looks as though cartels have control of your markets, it may be best to look into doing business in another country.

The same type of good ol' boy network that pervades the U.S. defense, petroleum, and pharmaceutical industries is very evident in developing countries, stretching across a wide range of industries. Personal relationships among sales representatives, bankers, bureaucrats, lawyers, and accountants create a steady crosscurrent of preferential treatment and favors. Try to identify such power brokers early in the game so that appropriate groundwork can be laid to smooth the way through customs, bank relations, government regulations, and grievance settlements. This can usually be accomplished surreptitiously with no one the wiser. First, ask government officials and sales representatives for referrals to bankers, lawyers, and accountants (under the guise of needing to engage these professionals for other matters). If Citibank, JPMorgan Chase, BankBoston, Bank of America, or other American banks have branch offices in the country or if a multinational accounting firm has a presence there these organizations should be the ones recommended to you. Any other referrals should be suspect. Then turn the table and ask the bankers, lawyers, and accountants for referrals to bureaucrats and sales representatives. Although it is more difficult to sort out relationships going this direction, recommendations from U.S.-affiliated organizations will be as straightforward as possible under the circumstances.

> If it looks as though cartels have control of your markets, it may be best to look into doing business in another country.

Competition

Business cartels also have a direct bearing on local competition and hence on pricing. Very seldom can imports compete on price with locally produced goods of similar quality, technology, or style. Additionally, cartels have even been known to block the sale of imported goods that have higher technology, better quality, or flashier styles.

Transnational companies with local manufacturing plants might also pose a serious threat to your ability to compete. Your market research should be extensive enough to uncover the names of competitors, along with their estimated market shares, growth prospects, and product development plans. Although this type of information is probably the most difficult of all to come by, the local AmCham office is a good place to start. Also, U.S. Commercial Service personnel at American embassies maintain extensive files on local companies. Interviews with potential competitors will quickly reveal the extent of their product lines as well as pricing structures.

If it looks like you'll have to compete with firmly entrenched transnationals it might pay you to join forces with one of them in some form of strategic alliance, either a joint venture or some other business structure. Two importers working together may be able to capture a larger market share than either could do separately.

Advertising and Sales Promotion

You can count on the fact that your advertising and sales promotion strategies that work well in the United States will not be effective in other parts of the world. Demographics, cultural norms, infrastructure deficiencies, and a variety of other conditions make it necessary to design promotional schemes that recognize subtle preferences unique to each market. To find out what forms of advertising work best for your products, you may want to test a few approaches. Or you may be lucky and find that research alone gives you the answers.

Pure observation can be invaluable. For instance, an aircraft parts manufacturer initiated an export program to Singapore and planned to use the same television spots that had proven effective in American markets. I was asked to produce comparative analyses of the effectiveness of Singaporean television, radio, newspaper, and direct-mail advertising. Unfortunately, the statistical data was very meager. During my visits to the city-state, I observed that radio and newspapers reached a wide segment of the population. Having verified these observations with the American manager of a local company, I relayed the findings to my client. The company dropped any thoughts of television commercials and hired a local agency to produce radio spots and a series of newspaper ads.

GOVERNMENT SUBSIDIES

Many governments offer direct subsidies of one type or another as incentives to attract foreign investment and trade. The form of subsidy varies but most can be grouped as follows:

- Reimbursements for labor training costs.
- Exemption from income and other taxes, often for periods of 10 years or more.
- Low interest, long-term financing.
- Exemption from import customs duties.
- Rent free housing for foreign managers.

Although some subsidies are part of publicly announced economic reforms that can be researched from the States, less obvious ones must be uncovered during an in-country investigation. Usually a visit to the country's ministry of finance will reveal the government's entire incentive package.

Some incentives are not granted to foreigners across the board and must be negotiated on a case-by-case basis. My experience has been that negotiating anything with government bureaucrats is at best a nightmare. You'll do better if you let a local attorney with government connections make the arrangements. You may be able to get your incentives without ever sitting down at a negotiating table.

American Chamber of Commerce offices, U.S. embassies or consulates, or in-country American companies won't be much help in obtaining special government handouts or exemptions. The exception, of course, is if the government views your product as critical to the country's well-being. In that case, be assured that officials will play up to embassy officers and U.S. executives in hopes of retaining Washington's goodwill. Don't expect direct help from U.S. embassies, however. These folks can point you in the right direction, but they can't overtly help you with business matters. That's against diplomatic rules. They will, however, brief you on the current status of government-to-government relationships and give you the names and titles of key bureaucrats.

> My experience has been that negotiating anything with government bureaucrats is at best a nightmare.

TRANSPORT, LICENSES, SECURITY, AND LABOR

Alternatives for inland shipping, import licenses, security measures, sources of raw materials, and the availability and cost of labor and management personnel need to be researched in-country if you plan to have a local production or distribution facility there. Are materials, supplies, and production equipment available locally, or will they have to be imported from the United States or other countries? If importing is necessary, are import licenses or permits required, and how do you get them?

Information about licenses or other formal import barriers needs to be ferreted out from government agencies. As for unofficial barriers, trading companies are the best sources of information. In-country American-owned companies are also reliable sources of information, especially if they have imported similar materials or equipment of their own. Managers of both willingly point out what must be done informally. In other words, how much do you pay and to whom to get your materials and equipment moved from the docks to your plant or distribution center. Furthermore, if materials, components, or equipment are to be sourced in-country but from a location far removed from your facility, these managers will fill you in on alternative modes of transport and the cost of getting the equipment or materials to your plant.

The safekeeping of company property is a problem in any country, just as it is in the United States. I suggest you make arrangements for enclosing any company facility with a 10-foot high metal fence topped with barbed wire. You should hire a 24-hour guard service while you're in the country doing the survey. By the time equipment, vehicles, and other company property begin to arrive, it may be too late. Better to be safe than sorry.

To get the scoop on labor regulations, stop in at the ministry of labor or any other government department that administers workers' rights and benefits laws. Get a copy of pertinent labor laws, and at the same time, find out which jobs are covered under collective bargaining agreements. Unions are very strong in some countries, and if this is true in your country of choice, you better find out right up front. Search out the local union hall and ask about both skilled and unskilled workers. Check out the rules governing hourly wage rates, vacation and holiday schedules, special benefit packages, and other labor related information. Try to get a feel for the availability of the particular skills needed in your facility. It may be necessary to recruit workers through labor brokers or to negotiate labor contracts through a local law firm in which case the names and addresses of both should be obtained.

Poke around the docks for a few days. Try to get a handle on some of the problems you might run into at the port of entry. Customs personnel will tell you about off-loading procedures as well as duties to be paid. Unofficially, however, bribes will be necessary. Local trading companies are the best source of information on that. Ask about the usual amount of such payments and to whom and when they should be paid. If materials or equipment must be transported overland, check with a contract hauler to find out about tariff rates, the availability of trucking lines, and on-loading and off-loading requirements.

> Poke around the docks for a few days. Try to get a handle on some of the problems you might run into at the port of entry.

INFRASTRUCTURES AND FREE TRADE ZONES

You need good intelligence on the quality of roads and rail lines, perhaps seaports and airports, and the availability and reliability of telephone service, electricity, and water supplies. Take the matter of roads. Typical questions should be:

1. Do toll roads connect your new facility with markets, suppliers, and ports of entry? If so, what are the tolls?
2. Are roadways paved?
3. How well are roadways, bridges, and tunnels maintained?
4. Can company leased trucks pass over bridges and through tunnels safely?
5. What are the dangers of highway bandits?

Any foreign company that trucks over these same roads is the best source of information. Ask about the status of roads currently under construction and whether they will impact the delivery of materials and equipment or, conversely, affect outgoing shipments. If you plan to export from the country, verify the accessibility and cost of freight forwarders, containerization, and on-loading facilities.

To get a fix on the availability and reliability of utilities, check with AmCham officials and local business managers. A short survey of businesses in the immediate area of your planned facility will quickly reveal any potential utility problems. The chamber office will provide a historical perspective on recent conditions that have affected a broader area.

Many countries have free trade zones (called foreign trade zones in the United States). These zones are restricted areas set aside by the government for duty-free storage of imported goods to be transshipped out of the country or, in some cases, converted to finished products by assembly or other operations. Try to get answers to the following questions about these zones:

1. Where are free trade zones located?
2. What facilities are available within the zones? What are the rental costs?
3. What support activities—labor recruiting, bookkeeping, transport, utilities, and so on—are available in the zones and what do they cost?
4. What types of goods can be moved through the zones?
5. What type of work (if any) can be performed on the goods held in the zones?
6. What restrictions are there on the destination of shipments out of the zones (e.g., sales to domestic markets, exports to specific countries, worldwide exports, and so on)?

If any of your people plan to carry samples into a country, you need to know which ones are duty-free and which are taxed. Import duties as well as extensive customs procedures can be avoided by obtaining an ATA (Admission Temporaire) Carnet. The ATA Carnet is a standardized international customs document used to obtain duty-free temporary admission of certain goods into countries that are signatories to the ATA Convention. Under the ATA Convention, commercial and professional travelers may take commercial samples, tools of the trade, advertising material as well as cinematographic, audiovisual, medical, scientific, or other professional equipment into member countries temporarily, without paying customs duties or taxes or posting a bond at the border of each country visited. Unfortunately, not all countries accept ATA carnets. Check out the Corporation for

International Business (www.atacarnet.com) for countries that do accept carnets.

 Corporation for International Business, Harris Bank Blvd., 325 North Hough St., 2nd Floor, Barrington, IL 60010

PERSONNEL MATTERS

If your marketing people are not fluent in the local language be sure to interview two or three interpreters recommended by an American branch bank or the local office of AmCham. Then contract with the one that shows the best perception of negotiating techniques and speaks the most fluent English.

Ensuring the safety of personnel, either traveling to the host country or relocating there, is obviously an important consideration but one too often overlooked. Three steps should be taken as soon as possible after arriving in any country:

1. American Embassy. Let the embassy know exactly where you will be staying, for how long, and whom to contact in the United States should an emergency occur. Don't expect any business help from embassy officials. And don't expect them to resolve your disputes with local government bureaucrats. However, in a genuine emergency, such as a coup d'etat or natural disaster, the American embassy may be the only place to get help, and embassy officers are anxious to give it.

2. American Chamber of Commerce. The local office can be extremely helpful in less serious emergencies. Officials always know who the power players are in the police department and government agencies. When push comes to shove, they will always try to help an American in distress. Tell your people to give the chamber office the same personal data given to the embassy.

3. Local Police Department. Let the police know who you are, why you are in their country, where you are staying, and whom to contact in the event of an emergency. Be sure to include both local contacts and those in the United States.

The best sources of emergency help may well be other expatriates, mainly other American, Canadian, or British expatriates. In addition to the American embassy, AmCham, and the local police, get to know the names and telephone numbers of expatriates in key business and banking positions. I have never known an American, Canadian, or British expat to shy away from helping a compatriot in need.

I have never known an American, Canadian, or British expat to shy away from helping a compatriot in need.

During all my travels around the globe, I have learned one trick that has benefited me more than any other. I always carry on my person two typed letters, one in English and one in the local language and dialect, containing my name, U.S. address and telephone number, local address and telephone number, passport number, where I'm staying, special medication I take and what I am allergic to, my blood type, and the names and addresses of at least three local people to contact in an emergency. To prevent theft, I always carry the letter in a pouch fastened to my body inside my shirt.

If your plans call for personnel to be traveling extensively or living in a country, gather as much information as possible about the cost and availability of accommodations, the cost and availability of local transportation (both public transport and private automobiles), educational facilities, and the names and telephone numbers of as many American- or English-speaking expatriates as possible.

EXCHANGE CONTROLS

What if you couldn't repatriate earned income, couldn't transfer working capital funds into the country, or didn't have access to these funds once they were deposited in a local bank? Wouldn't that be a disaster? Better take the time now to find out about laws relating to currency exchange and repatriation of profits and capital and then make arrangements for the secure movement of your company's money both in and out of the country. At the same time, open an account at a U.S. branch bank, arrange for the conversion of U.S. dollars into local currency, and get assurances that you will have access to this currency for paying bills.

When applying for permits to move or convert funds, be sure to arrange for business licenses, labor hiring clearances, tax identification numbers, and any other permits necessary to conduct business in the country.

SUMMARY

We have covered a lot in this chapter. Following the check lists provided in each section will enable you to do a complete market research survey. But don't assume that these are the only steps to be taken. Special situations require special research. Because we have covered so much territory, it might be helpful to summarize the whole process with the following lists of items to check out or obtain and steps to be taken:

1. Government restrictions that prevent the use of U.S. employees as in-country sales personnel.
2. Regulations controlling contractual relationships with local sales representatives.
3. Regulations governing sales representatives and distributors.
4. Local government's position on countertrade arrangements.
5. Names and addresses of local trading companies that import U.S. products.
6. Relative strength of business cartels.
7. Reference checks on important government bureaucrats and local sales representatives from banks, lawyers, public accountants, and independent U.S.-based investigation firms.
8. Names and market shares of local and multinational competitors.
9. Description of directly competing products and names and addresses of manufacturers and distributors.
10. Advantages or disadvantages of forming alliances with competing U.S. exporters.
11. Advertising and sales promotion options.
12. Relevant government incentives or subsidies, those that apply across the board as well as those that must be negotiated.
13. Availability and cost of skilled and unskilled labor.

14. Information about formal and informal barriers to the import of materials and production equipment.
15. Local sources of materials and supplies.
16. Current condition of port facilities and inland transport alternatives.
17. Reliability of electricity, water supplies, and telephone service.
18. Location, availability, and restrictions related to free trade zones.
19. Availability of security guards and property fencing.
20. Legal requirements for currency conversion and repatriation of earnings and capital.

In addition, the following steps need to be taken:

1. Open bank accounts with U.S. branch banks.
2. Make applications for business license, labor hiring clearances, tax identification number, and any other required permits.
3. Interview two or three interpreters and contract with the best one.
4. Test out potential personnel safety hazards.
5. Create safety/security checklist for company personnel.
6. Apply for carnets.

chapter sixteen
Assessing Country Risk

THE MEXICAN PESO DEVALUATION IN DECEMBER 1994, THE FINANCIAL MELTDOWNS in Southeast Asia and Russia during 1996–1998, and the currency upheaval in Brazil and Turkey in 1999–2001 took the wind out of the sails of many people who believed that emerging markets were ripe for the taking. All they thought they had to do was bring their products to market or build a manufacturing plant and returns would far exceed those possible in Europe, Japan, or the United States. Although devaluations in the global financial system taught a valuable lesson—the risks of doing business in emerging markets are far greater than previously thought—the rewards from burgeoning demand and strengthening economies have, in fact, continued to bring a flock of new U.S. entrants to global trade, especially smaller American companies. Still, the rash of global financial crises did generate a more sobering, realistic view of offshore business opportunities.

Although nearly all emerging nation governments have made real progress with their macroeconomic reforms, not one has adequately addressed the counter problems such reforms have brought to the social sphere. In fact, as we have seen, poverty levels and income inequalities are becoming more pronounced every year. These bureaucracies need to come to grips with political institutions ill equipped to deal with democracy.

The rash of global financial crises did generate a more sobering, realistic view of offshore business opportunities.

We would like to see all governments work toward the creation of genuine democratic political regimes so that elections are fair, free of fraud, and citizens feel secure in electing candidates of their choice. We would also like to see foreign exchange policies consistent with new international financial realities and the macroeconomic reforms of less developed countries. The biggest challenge of all is that we would like to see institutions that are capable of solidifying the economic reforms implanted during the last 20 years and allow social reform to progress unfettered. Boards of public health and education, antitrust agencies, healthcare distributors, an impartial judiciary, and tax enforcement bureaus, among many other political and social institutions, must be strengthened soon to prevent social ills from causing a massive backsliding of economic and political reforms.

It should be obvious that the external market risks faced by any U.S. company, whether exporting, sourcing, or operating an offshore facility, can be daunting. Foreign governments are more involved in everyday life. The military is visibly active. Infrastructures are depleted. Ports are crowded, and overland transport is abominable. Citizens are reticent to accept foreigners. In fact, it's fair to say that the entire mode of doing business in emerging markets is averse to traditional American marketing, production, and personnel policies. You will have to feel your way through the maze of market and cultural anomalies that at times seem bent on turning you back.

A surfeit of market risks must be recognized and dealt with. You must plan for the long haul. There is no quick fix.

While some risks are glaringly obvious, others are more subtle. Although the predominance and the importance of each risk varies from country to country, those that seem to present the biggest challenges can be loosely grouped as political, financial, social, and business. Let's take a look at each category and then put together a workable model that will help you decide how and where to begin your global quest.

POLITICAL RISKS

Regardless of the country you choose to do business in, you will find, to varying degrees, three political risks that must be dealt with:

1. The risk of unstable political institutions.
2. The risk of government interference.
3. The risk of bureaucratic corruption.

We are all aware of the inherent instability of governments in virtually all less developed nations. They may be elected and appear on the surface to be stable and permanent, but we must not for one moment ignore the volatility of the developing world. Democracy as we know it in the United States does not exist in Brazil, Russia, India, China, or any other country (although Brazil's federal system comes closest). Except for a handful of less developed nations, including the Arab states, most countries now have elected administrations. Maybe not elected the way we would like to see but elected nonetheless. In many cases, elections have taken place in a monopolistic single party system where one party has the continued support of the military establishment, national unions, and powerful trading families. In those countries that permit an opposition party to field a candidate, every election brings questions such as:

➡ Will this be a clean election?
➡ Will fraud be limited so that the winner does in fact have the support of the majority of citizens?

➡ Or will ballot boxes be stuffed or voters terrorized into casting their ballots for the power boss?

➡ Or will the front-runner be assassinated?

These are serious considerations when choosing which country and which markets to enter.

Political instability can disrupt the best developed plans. Consider these classic cases. A short time after Venezuela's President Hugo Chavez took office, he enacted new laws that revoked civil liberties and encouraged police intrusion in businesses and personal lives. This resulted in unwarranted arrests and confinement for hundreds of people. Businesses closed. Foreign investment dried up. Many foreign companies withdrew completely from Venezuela. Another classic case of how a duly elected president can throw a monkey wrench into the best developed plans occurred when Bolivia's President Evo Morales Aima nationalized the nation's natural gas companies.

You can't plan for these types of contingencies. However, you can attach a probability of occurrence to them and then factor that into your country risk assessment.

Risks of Government Interference

In Latin America, Eastern Europe, Asia, and the Middle East government interference in business matters is an accepted condition of life, although it's more pronounced in some countries than in others. In modern day Venezuela, Bolivia, Saudi Arabia, the U.A.E., China, Russia, and a host of other countries, to get anything accomplished you must go through one or more government bureaucracies. Governments dictate the hiring, firing, and pay scales of workers; the allocation of telephones and electricity; the granting of business permits and licenses; building codes; and a host of other matters. In some countries, the military also interferes in what are typically private business matters. At times, such interference can all but stop business activities; in other cases, it is more benign. But in every country, you must recognize, plan for, and deal with such interference in your everyday business affairs.

Risks of Corruption

What may not be so obvious is the widespread bureaucratic acceptance of payoffs, kickbacks, and bribes in the normal course of business. If you want to get anything done, no matter how menial the task, someone, somewhere must be paid off. Anyone who has done business in Russia, China, Malaysia, Indonesia, or any of the Arab states is well aware of the enormous power vested in government officials and, in some cases, military officers who must approve virtually everything a foreigner wants to do. Such overwhelming power tends to corrupt even the most dedicated civil servant. Not only is corruption very expensive, it is time consuming. To stop and pay everyone in the chain of command, usually with U.S. dollars, takes an inordinate amount of time.

Obviously, not all bureaucrats and military personnel demand payoffs. I have met some government officials who wouldn't dream of looking for or accepting bribes. I've even met a few military officers who have been very helpful without demanding kickbacks or payoffs. But enough do take bribes to make it seem like they all are corrupt.

FINANCIAL RISKS

In addition to political risks, financial upheaval is a risk that manifests itself from time to time in every emerging nation. The 2002 debt crisis in Argentina is a premier example. Faced with a default on its international debt obligations, Argentine Interim President Eduardo Duhalde had to do something. So, he decided to dump the nation's currency board and throw out the peso's 10-year-old, one-to-one peg to the dollar. This created a financial nightmare of massive currency devaluation and climbing inflation.

We are also all aware of the risks entailed when a country's currency fluctuates wildly against the dollar and when exchange controls prohibit repatriation of earnings or capital. One only has to look at Venezuela as a prime example of what can happen to prices and foreign direct investment when the national currency is unstable or when the government arbitrarily invokes exchange controls.

It would have been impossible to predict these outcomes. But we can assign probabilities of occurrence to them.

SOCIAL RISKS

Social risks may give you even more headaches than political or financial risks. We have already discussed the horrendous gender gap prevalent in many emerging nations. The following are a few more social risks that seem to be fairly universal:

- ➡ Rigid class structures.
- ➡ Great disparities in income.
- ➡ Wide variations in literacy.
- ➡ Street crime from citizens packed into urban areas.
- ➡ Distrust (fear) of foreigners.

While the modern world has done away with strict class structures, emerging nations have not. Class demarcation along income, racial, gender, and religious lines is very evident in all aspects of business. To overcome these barriers and structure your business to appeal to different social classes, you will need the help of a well-connected local partner.

While the modern world has done away with strict class structures, emerging nations have not.

Except for the very small percentage of developing world citizens who can be considered the elite class—about 2 to 3 percent of the total population of any country—the vast majority live below the poverty level, and in several countries, such as India and Pakistan, they live in abject poverty.

In more than a few places, education, medical facilities, housing, and sanitary conditions remind one of the regressive areas of sub-Saharan Africa. Unemployment continues at unacceptable levels. A large percentage of people have no land. Education beyond primary grades is mainly reserved for the urban elite. A vast underclass struggles for survival. And an informal economy provides the main source of income to millions of people.

Street crime has become a serious problem in many metropolitan areas. Indifference on the part of governments and the police merely exacerbates the problem. Furthermore, according to reports from several international watchdog agencies, court systems are so corrupt that they barely function. It's only natural that people who have lived a lifetime in this environment are now a bit leery of foreigners tempting them with jobs, steady income, and imported products. More than one person believes that behind the olive branch lurks another round of foreign domination.

BUSINESS RISKS

In addition to political, financial, and social risks, you will encounter a whole range of business risks. Again, the degree of risk varies from country to country but the following are a few that seem to be apply across the board:

➡ Infrastructure deficiencies.
➡ Inflation.
➡ Antiquated banking systems.
➡ Court systems that barely function.
➡ Cartel control of industries.
➡ Thriving underground economies.
➡ Preferential trade pacts.

The two risks that stand out as the most costly to foreigners are infrastructure deficiencies and inflation. No emerging nations have infrastructures that even come close to matching U.S. standards. In countries that have suffered years of civil strife, military dictatorship, or government neglect, one will find torn up roads, collapsed bridges, bombed out buildings, ruined schools and hospitals, contaminated water supplies, wrecked electric power generation and distribution facilities, and haphazard telephone service.

Unfortunately, every country except for a few Arab states is short of funds, so infrastructure improvements won't happen overnight. With economic development taking precedence over infrastructure rebuilding, most multilateral and bilateral aid has gone to create jobs through enhanced export production and subsidized investment in income producing projects.

Several countries still suffer from high inflation, although except for sub-Saharan Africa, the horrors of runaway inflation seem to have been squelched. As we all know when inflation is high, wages cannot keep up with local prices and customer buying power falls. Of course, this also diminishes demand for imported products. Moreover, high inflation makes selling on open accounts virtually impossible. Although you might be able to increase prices to keep up with inflation, it invariably becomes a very costly administrative nightmare. Regardless of your pricing policy, in a high inflation economy either you'll end up incurring much higher administrative costs, or you'll end up with lower product margins.

Recognizing risks is step one. But until you actually put your knowledge to work, you won't be any farther along in choosing the right countries and markets to tackle. Step two is to do a country risk assessment.

A COUNTRY RISK ASSESSMENT

Which country offers the least risk and greatest profit potential? Which market-entry strategy will yield the highest return on investment? These are key questions that must be answered prior to proceeding with your marketing plan. But even before analyzing country risk and market-entry options, you need to carefully define your objectives. Are you limited to exporting, with an FDI never entering the picture, or would you consider an in-country manufacturing plant, distribution center, retail store, or a sales and customer service operation?

Regardless of your pricing policy, in a high inflation economy either you'll end up incurring much higher administrative costs, or you'll end up with lower product margins.

With the leeway to consider several market-entry options, you can weigh one strategy against another. For instance, you might prefer to serve Polish markets solely by exporting directly from your U.S. plant or warehouse, but perhaps Poland's Byzantine customs procedures, high tariffs, and outlandish taxes make your imported products noncompetitive with goods produced in the EU. In this case, you might reach markets more effectively from an in-country factory or warehouse. Such a facility could handle products for local consumption as well as for export to other European countries. But that may not work either. Regulatory and legal bottlenecks may make such a direct investment inappropriate. You may have personal reasons for not even considering a foreign facility. And the pendulum swings back to exporting or perhaps a combination of exporting and FDI.

If your business is professional, financial services, communications, or other type of service industry, you could sell your services either from your U.S.-based office or from an in-country presence. By opting for the latter, you could provide services to customers or clients in other regional countries from this office.

If you are in a manufacturing business, how about producing parts or components or sourcing raw materials from a Malaysian location for use in your U.S. factory or to stock your U.S. warehouse. The savings in labor costs could then be passed along through lower prices to make your product even more competitive in U.S. markets. U.S. companies with Mexican and Central American maquila factories have been doing this for years.

In addition to defining your company's objectives, you need to evaluate the inherent risks of doing business in a given country. The best way to identify country risks is to conduct a country survey. With a firm understanding of your various market-entry options and the country risks that you have, you can perform a country risk assessment and devise strategies that will yield the highest return at the lowest risk.

DEFINING EXTERNAL COUNTRY RISKS

As we have discussed, external country risks are those political, financial, economic, and social conditions that you have no control over. You cannot exert any influence over them, and you cannot change the underlying factors that create these risks. They are external to your span of authority. They are present in every country. Yet, in the long run, these external risks will determine the success or failure of your strategic marketing decisions as much as or more than your management policies.

Political instability, financial upheaval, corruption, inflation, functional illiteracy, and several other conditions will unquestionably affect how successful you are in profitably marketing your products or services. A careful analysis of these risks will help you choose the market-entry strategy that best meets your objectives.

Under most circumstances, the greater the risk you're willing to take, the greater your profit.

MARKET-ENTRY OPTIONS AND RISKS

Global trade has never been straightforward. New risks seem to crop up every day to muddy the waters. These risks must be balanced against the available market-entry options. Under most circumstances, the greater the risk you're willing to take, the greater your profit. It is the old risk/reward formula. Nevertheless, entering a high risk market could result in significant losses. To compensate, you may have to alter one or more market strategies beyond those you originally conceived.

One way to determine the relative merits of alternative market strategies is to quantify the probable impact of external risks on these strategies through a country risk assessment. Before proceeding, I should clarify three assumptions that underlie such an analysis. They are:

1. Any risk assessment is valid only when one country is compared with another country (or countries) within a homogeneous region. For our purposes, we will look at countries in only one region: Eastern Europe. However, the same principles apply to markets in other regions as well.
2. The analysis of strategic benefits must be considered over a span of years. I prefer to use five years, although this may be too long a span for some companies.
3. By definition, all economic analyses are judgmental. In other words, the person preparing the analysis imparts his or her biased judgment to the statistical facts.

To begin, we must define two criteria: (1) the types of external risks that, to differing degrees, are present in all emerging markets that you are interested in and (2) the principal market-entry options available to your business. Looking at risks first, those that have the most influence on strategic market-entry decisions seem to be caused by:

➡ Political instability.
➡ Government interference.
➡ Corruption.
➡ Street crime.
➡ Inequality of income distribution that leads to social upheaval.
➡ Inferior education systems that result in functional illiteracy.
➡ Infrastructure deficiencies.
➡ High inflation rates.
➡ Exchange controls as part of inefficient banking systems.

When analyzing the impact of these external risks, it's necessary to look at how they affect each market-entry option in Eastern Europe, including Russia. Most U.S. companies should consider three market-entry scenarios:

1. Exporting products or services from the United States to an Eastern European country.
2. Establishing an Eastern European presence to produce goods or services for local consumption.
3. Exporting products or services from an in-country presence to other Eastern European countries or Russia.

Offshore sourcing of parts, components, or subassemblies at maquila plants would be a fourth strategy but probably not a viable choice for Eastern Europe. Obviously, all four options may be used alone or in tandem to develop any number of long- or short-term market-entry strategies. The next step is to quantify the impact external risks have on your choice of exporting, direct investment, and in-country export strategies.

Economists, statisticians, and bureaucrats have all developed models that purport to quantify external risks and their relevance to business strategies. Some models can be helpful while others are merely a play on numbers. However, they all have three common characteristics:

1. They rely on broad-based and often outdated data.
2. The mathematics employed in each can produce radically different answers.
3. They are difficult for business people to use.

Extensive research and experience have led me to believe that evaluating the magnitude and impact of rapidly changing risks and opportunities can best be done by applying informed judgments to relatively unsophisticated models without the use of complex mathematical compilations, although I'm sure professional economists and statisticians would disagree.

To illustrate the type of conceptual thinking involved in country risk assessments, I'll use a case study of one of my consulting clients, a midsize manufacturing and distribution company in the electronics industry named U.S. Fabrisource and Avionics Corp. (USFAC). USFAC is currently doing business in several regions of the world, including Latin America, Eastern Europe, and Russia. When the company was in the early stages of its global trade ventures, I was hired to help develop a meaningful index to be applied to the evaluation of external risks and market-entry options for South America. Since then I have used this model many times, and it always seems to work well. The president of USFAC was happy with the results of our South American study and, a few years, later commissioned me to apply the same model to assess options in Eastern Europe and Russia. The following discussion explains how the model worked.

A CASE STUDY: U.S. FABRISOURCE AND AVIONICS INC.

Looking for new markets that had the potential to expand European growth in both consumer and industrial product lines, the president of USFAC determined that Poland, the Czech Republic, Hungary, Bulgaria, and perhaps Russia looked promising, provided an intelligent assessment could be made of the potential medium-term risks involved. Calling his troops together, he agreed that the most viable market-entry options were: (1) exporting from the U.S. and (2) establishing a production or distribution facility within one or more European countries. In addition, the president wanted to investigate the possibility of sourcing certain components from one or more countries.

A team of marketing, production, and finance people was formed to implement a country survey for Eastern Europe and Russia. After completing its research, the team agreed that the previously described nine external risks did, in fact, apply to all countries. For each country, the team then assigned factors of zero to 10 to each of the risks and to the four market-entry options. The following shows the scoring system that was used.

SCORING RISKS AND MARKET-ENTRY OPTIONS

Risk	Market-Entry Options
10 = no risk	10 = sure bet
9 = extremely low risk	9 = extremely high benefits
8 = very low risk	8 = very high benefits

7 = low risk	7 = high benefits
6 = below average risk	6 = above average benefits
5 = average risk	5 = average benefits
4 = above average risk	4 = below average benefits
3 = moderately high risk	3 = moderately low benefits
2 = very high risk	2 = very low benefits
1 = extremely high risk	1 = virtually no benefits
0 = stay out of here	0 = no benefits

The next step was to determine how serious each of the nine risks was relative to USFAC's market objectives. For simplicity, the research team used a scale of one to five, with five being the most serious risk and one being the least serious. The team judged that political instability and social upheaval would be the most disruptive to USFAC's strategic plans and warranted a seriousness factor of five. An inefficient banking system was judged to be of virtually no risk to the company and was assigned a factor of one.

Obviously, the seriousness of political instability, corruption, functional illiteracy, or any external risk varies for every company. In other words, you must determine the seriousness of each risk relative to your business.

With a quantified evaluation of each risk in hand and a factor assigned to represent the relative seriousness of each risk, the USFAC team then calculated a weighted average of risks for each country. This was done by multiplying each risk factor (zero to 10) by the appropriate seriousness factor (one to five). The results were then totaled and the sum divided by nine (the number of external risks considered in the analysis).

This process was repeated for the four strategic market-entry options. Each market-entry option was assigned a benefit factor of zero to 10 and was then weighted on a one to five scale with five being the option that the team believed would result in the greatest benefit to USFAC and one assigned being the option deemed to be the least beneficial. The team then calculated a weighted average for each option. The results were totaled and the sum was divided by four (the number of options considered) to arrive at a single market-entry option factor. The final step was to add the weighted average of risks to the weighted average of strategic market-entry options to arrive at a risk assessment factor for each country. The results that this model produced are as follows:

RISK ASSESSMENT ANALYSIS

Potential Risks	Russia	Czech Republic	Poland	Hungary	Bulgaria
Political instability (5)*	7	6	8	4	3
Government interference (3)*	6	3	8	3	2
Corruption (4)*	5	2	5	3	3
Street crime (2)*	6	2	5	2	3
Income distribution/social upheaval (5)*	5	3	5	6	2
Functional illiteracy (2)*	4	3	8	6	8
Infrastructure deficiencies (3)*	7	5	4	4	6
High inflation rates (3)*	8	5	7	2	2
Inefficient banking systems (1)*	8	7	9	8	5
Weighted Average Potential Risks	19.0	12.1	19.7	12.6	10.4
Strategic Market-Entry Options					
Exporting to (5)†	9	7	7	6	8
Local satellite plants (2)†	2	3	1	5	4
Produce for local markets (4)†	8	8	8	3	7
Exporting from (2)†	9	8	9	8	9
Weighted Average Market-Entry Options	24.8	22.0	21.8	17.0	23.5
RISK ASSESSMENT FACTOR	43.8	34.4	41.4	29.6	33.9

Note: * = Seriousness of risk—5 equals greatest harm

Note: † = Benefits of market-entry decision—5 equals greatest benefit

Here is a summary of the results of this model building exercise.

RISK ASSESSMENT SUMMARY

	Risk Assessment Factor	Weighted Average Potential Risks	Weighted Average Market-Entry Options
Russia	43.8	19.0	24.8
Poland	41.4	19.7	21.8
Czech Republic	34.4	12.1	22.3
Bulgaria	33.9	10.4	23.5
Hungary	29.6	12.6	17.0

As illustrated, specific risks as well as potential benefits from different market-entry strategies varied widely among countries. In Russia, for example, with a risk assessment factor of 43.8, the nine external risks would impact USFAC's profitability and return on investment of the four market-entry options less than in any other Eastern European country. But because external country risks and the benefits from alternative market-entry strategies do not necessarily go hand in hand, the USFAC team recognized that it was necessary to look at both sides of the fence—risks and benefits.

In the case of Russia, the weighted average potential risk factor of 19.0 showed that risks were greater than in Poland (which had a factor of 19.7). However, the weighted average market-entry options factor of 24.8 was also greater than Poland's 21.8.

The results of the Czech Republic's risk assessment presented another interesting case. The Czech Republic's combined risk factor of 34.4 placed it as the third least risk country in the region. Yet its weighted average of risks alone, 12.1, placed it as the fifth least risk country (four other countries earned lower weighted average risk ratings). As an offset, the Czech Republic's weighted average of market-entry options of 22.3 placed it third after Russia and Bulgaria.

This demonstrates the importance of looking at the potential benefits that may be derived from alternative market-entry strategies as well as the probable impact external risks may have on these strategies. Looking at risks alone won't do the job. It also shows that risk assessment for a single country is meaningless. Scores for all countries under consideration must be compared.

The biggest advantage in the model we built for USFAC is its simplicity. Anyone can use it, and you don't have to be a mathematician or a statistician to benefit from it. I have used this model countless times for my own businesses and for clients. It may not be very scientific, but it does force you to evaluate many conditions you might otherwise miss.

By using the results of your market research to assess the desirability of each market-entry option and by applying your expert judgment to determine the severity of the nine external risks, you should be able to develop market-entry strategies for countries that will yield the greatest return at the least risk. But it's important to remember that any risk assessment model will yield useful results only in direct proportion to the accuracy of the data used and the experienced judgment of the preparer.

Many country risk assessment models are available. There is nothing magical about which one to choose. Some can be very helpful in quantifying seemingly unquantifiable market conditions while others are a waste of time. As an alternative, you could develop your own model. If you like to work with standard deviations and probability theory, or if you like to plot logarithm graphs, then by all means use statistical models that employ these tools. As long as the results of the calculation make sense relative to what you have learned from your market research, the analysis should be helpful in making strategic marketing decisions.

Spend the time looking at as many models as you can. Create your own model. Talk to other people in your industry and ask about the difficulties they have encountered in going global as well as the benefits they have derived from their choice of country and market-entry strategies. And by all means, spend sufficient time and resources preparing your market research so that you know exactly what obstacles you will likely encounter.

The main idea in any country risk assessment is to consider as many hazards and opportunities as time and resources permit. A reasonably reliable end result is the most important element of any analysis. The tools used to get there are not all that important.

chapter seventeen
Building Relationships with Strategic Alliances

AS WE HAVE SEEN, A LOCAL PRESENCE IS A PREREQUISITE FOR DOING BUSINESS in any emerging nation—in some countries because such a presence is mandatory, in others because it makes doing business so much easier and more profitable. Most companies find that a local sales representative, distributor, or both are all they need. In other cases, a full-blown joint venture might be the best route. Regardless of the form a strategic alliance takes, it should be formalized with a written contract and blessed by your American attorney and in-country consul.

A strategic alliance seems to work best when you have an exclusive agreement with your local partner, although this may not always be possible or practical. The sales representative or distributor may handle lines from other companies as well as yours, and that's OK as long as the lines don't compete. Whether or not you have an exclusive relationship or your representative/distributor handles multiple lines, try to initiate some form of partnership arrangement—preferably a formal joint venture. When I use the term partnership, I am not using the legal definition. In fact, most foreign joint ventures use the corporate or similar business form.

Strategic alliances of various types can be formed with sales representatives, distributors, and licensees, or for research projects, market research efforts, advertising campaigns, and countertrade arrangements. Virtually all transnationals, including General Electric, IBM, JP MorganChase, and Ernst & Young, use strategic alliances to manage cultural diversity and open bureaucratic doors. Midsize, privately owned companies like Washington Computer Corporation of America and Journal Electric Inc. use strategic alliances as a market-entry strategy.

INSIGHT... Two contrasting cases illustrate how crucial strategic alliances are for gaining rapid entry into very difficult markets. The first case involves a privately held company, Orso Corp., that distributes disposable healthcare products—bandages, needles, gloves, and so on. The company had been successfully exporting to Western Europe and South Korea for several years when Orso's marketing manager saw the potential for opening new markets in Brazil, specifically in Natal and Recife. As Orso's consultant, I strongly recommended an alliance partnership with a Brazilian distributor as the surest way to enter these markets, but Orso's CEO couldn't grasp the logic of this and elected to set up Orso's own distribution center in Natal.

Thirteen months later, stalled and frustrated by convoluted import regulations, by business license applications that went nowhere because of territorial disputes between local bureaucrats, and by costly thefts at the port of entry,

Orso gave up. A full year's efforts and $5 million went down the drain because Orso had stubbornly insisted on going it alone, without the benefits of a strategic alliance.

The second case involves a subsidiary of a well-known computer manufacturer. I was asked to assist the company in introducing a new line of peripheral equipment in Turkey. We negotiated a joint venture arrangement with a prominent local distributor who managed all licensing and customs clearances. Using his political connections, our Turkish partner convinced authorities to relax several onerous import regulations. His contacts with Ankara retail outlets provided a ready market for the peripherals. Of course there are always exceptions, but as these two cases dramatically demonstrate, some form of strategic alliance is the way to go for the smoothest road to market.

Strategic alliances take many forms and may vary from short-term agreements to long-term ventures. Transitional alliances, for instance, may be short-lived, lasting just long enough time to transfer technology. Countertrade alliances may be structured for a specific transaction, ending at its culmination. Franchising alliances may require a longer period, enabling your foreign partner to absorb necessary management know-how. Joint ventures are usually the longest-term form of alliance for selling, distributing, or manufacturing your products overseas.

Among the many advantages of strategic alliances, probably the most strategically important are that they:

➡ Provide direct links to key suppliers and local bureaucrats.
➡ Exert expert pressure to resolve customs logjams.
➡ Provide access to trade finance through host country government agencies.
➡ Create more efficient management of countertrade transactions.

Each strategic alliance should be uniquely designed to meet your company's needs on the one hand and your partner's needs as well as the requirements of markets, suppliers, and government regulations on the other hand. Joint ventures, licensing arrangements, and franchise agreements are by far the most popular forms of alliance, and of the three, joint ventures tend to be the easiest to monitor and usually bring the highest returns.

JOINT VENTURE BENEFITS

By definition, a joint venture involves the formation of a new operating entity (typically a corporation) that is independent of the joint venture partners. The equity contributed by the partners may take the form of money, facilities, technology, inventory, management know-how, or marketing expertise.

Although many problems can and generally do arise with joint ventures, a carefully structured contractual arrangement that spells out the responsibilities of and contributions from each party will minimize the severity of future disputes. Despite the fear of losing valuable assets by sharing closely guarded patents and proprietary know-how with a partner, companies of all sizes have found joint ventures an acceptable way to market their products and finance their businesses in foreign countries.

Joint Ventures as a Marketing Strategy

From a marketing perspective, the greatest benefit of using a joint venture comes from joining forces with a partner who sells complementary products through an established sales and distribution network. Such a partner may be either a foreign company already doing business in-country or a host country national. For example, assume that your company makes shortwave radios and you want to open new consumer markets in China. Marine Electronics Corp. has been selling its line of navigational equipment in China for several years. Your company and Marine Electronics form a Chinese joint venture specifically to sell and distribute certain types of navigational equipment and shortwave radios. Your company contributes working capital, and Marine Electronics contributes its sales and distribution network.

Another marketing reason for forming joint ventures is to break protective trade barriers. Although recent economic reforms have lowered import barriers in many emerging markets, high tariffs and quotas still protect more than a few national industries. A joint venture with a local partner who has access to import licenses may be the only feasible way to enter these markets.

Moreover, despite all the hoopla about state controlled economies converting to market economies, many governments continue to interfere in pricing policies and distribution channels. This makes it virtually impossible to penetrate these markets without an inside track to powerful bureaucrats. Your partner should know whom to contact, when to negotiate, and how to satisfy government officials who might otherwise block the import or distribution of your products. In other words, your partner should be in a position to grease the skids to obtain preferential treatment. This is a necessary part of doing business and mandatory in the Arab states.

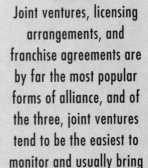

Joint ventures, licensing arrangements, and franchise agreements are by far the most popular forms of alliance, and of the three, joint ventures tend to be the easiest to monitor and usually bring the highest returns.

Joint ventures are also a convenient way to enter closed markets. Every country has certain industries protected from competition by government regulations. Telecommunications, power utilities, airlines, automobile manufacturers, mining, cement, and oil and gas field industries are a few prominent examples. These protected industries are usually dominated by one or two public or private sector companies. To sell in these markets, you must join forces with resident partners who already have government approvals and an established track record for dealing with these monopolies.

Joint Ventures as a Financing Mechanism

In addition to being an integral part of your marketing strategies, joint ventures can be a handy way to finance in-country production or distribution facilities or to finance reexports to other countries. Since many countries prohibit foreign companies from raising capital through local banks or capital markets and will not grant them access to government export/import trade credit, the only way to finance trade or expansion is through a joint venture with a local partner that has the legal right to do so.

Joint venture partners may also be in the best position to arrange financing through U.S. government and multilateral aid programs, development banks, and multinational foreign banks. Although exceptions certainly arise, each of these capital providers tends to favor arrangements in which the U.S. partner brings jobs and management know-how to emerging local companies. It is not unusual for a U.S. company to participate in a foreign venture without incurring any debt on its balance sheet or using any internal funds.

Studies by the Department of Commerce and several export trade organizations point to three prominent ways in which U.S. companies benefit from financing foreign trade and direct investments through joint ventures:

1. Host country export credit assistance. Several countries in Eastern Europe, Asia, the Middle East, and Latin America have export/import trade credit facilities that are easier to use and have much broader coverage than those available from Ex-Im Bank. However, most require that local companies participate in the transaction. Joint ventures that are by definition, local companies, open that door.

2. Sourcing host country capital markets. Stock markets in Moscow, São Paulo, Beijing, Mumbai, and Singapore can be excellent sources of large amounts of equity or debt capital for the purchase of either a local plant and equipment or a going business. However, since listings on these exchanges are generally restricted to national companies, a host country corporation formed with a local partner is the only way to qualify.

3. Tapping multilateral and bilateral aid programs. Multilateral and bilateral aid programs are another handy source of long-term capital. These programs always require equity participation by host country companies, however. To ignore such lucrative avenues because of ownership constraints makes little sense especially when a joint venture could open the doors.

You're not alone if you shudder at the thought of setting up a foreign partnership when all you really want to do is export. No one would dispute that exporting alone is a lot simpler and less costly than a joint venture. Nevertheless, you might have to include an alliance of one form or another in your strategic marketing plans.

Joint ventures are clearly not for everyone. In fact, to make a joint venture worthwhile, your company should meet a combination of four criteria:

1. It must be of sufficient size to warrant an overseas presence.

2. It should be well established in its U.S. markets. Foreign markets are not the place to experiment with new products or with products that don't sell in the United States.

3. It is facing or expects to face serious distribution obstacles in offshore markets—distribution practices, marketing customs, trade barriers, or local cartels that inhibit the sale and distribution of your products.

4. It encounters intense price competition that makes it necessary to write-off the costs of shipping, packing, customs, and other exporting expenses rather than increase selling prices.

If your company meets these criteria, a joint venture might be the best answer for establishing a viable marketing presence for your exports.

SETTING UP STRATEGIC ALLIANCES

All too often, strategic alliances are formed with insufficient preparation and without a clear market strategy in mind, creating relationship problems right from the beginning. To structure a successful alliance you need to:

➡ Set out clear objectives for the alliance.
➡ Qualify prospective partners.
➡ Negotiate a workable alliance agreement.
➡ Choose a name for the alliance.
➡ Set up controls.
➡ Structure policies for alliance managers.

Let's take a brief look at each of the steps.

Alliance Objectives

Without a clear strategy, it's easy to get caught up in the euphoric concept of a new venture, and it can lead to the wrong alliance structure or the wrong partner. For example, look at what happened when the Soviet Union broke up or when China opened its doors to the world. Many American firms were in such a hurry to establish strategic alliances that they gave little or no thought to their ultimate market strategy. They poured millions of dollars into unworkable and inevitably losing ventures. The same mistakes were made in Mexico soon after NAFTA was implemented. Enthralled by the prospects of Mexico's huge markets and cheap labor, many American companies charged ahead with Mexican joint ventures without a clear strategy either for running the business or for getting out of it at the appropriate time.

If a strategic alliance cannot be formed based on clearly defined corporate objectives that support long-term strategic marketing goals, it should not be entered into in the first place. To ignore this principle is to waste time, money, and effort.

Qualifying Prospective Partners

Companies who are already participating in foreign strategic alliances would certainly agree that if you choose the right partner, you're halfway home, but if you choose the wrong one, failure is right around the corner. The high worldwide demand for U.S. goods and technology has given foreign entrepreneurs a new lease on life, and you'll find sales representatives, agents, distributors, and manufacturers by the hundreds, not to mention an army of hustlers, scrambling to lure you into a partnership. The problem isn't locating a partner; it's choosing one that fits your corporate culture and management style and has the tools to meet your objectives.

If a strategic alliance cannot be formed based on clearly defined corporate objectives that support long-term strategic marketing goals, it should not be entered into in the first place.

A qualified partner with name recognition and a good market reputation is an invaluable asset. Many market-entry hazards can be avoided or at least mitigated by a partner who not only knows how to deal with influential bureaucrats but who also understands the nuances of the culture. (This is especially crucial in China and the Arab states.)

Negotiating the Terms of the Alliance

All successful alliances, especially joint ventures, require a champion, a booster, and a key player. You need someone who has the authority to make things happen. Perhaps your CEO, CFO, a vice president, or yourself (if you own the company). That person should head your team for negotiating an alliance agreement and be a member of the alliance's management committee or board of directors.

Having negotiated many strategic alliance agreements, I have found that to ensure a win-win arrangement, it's best to leave your lawyers at home. Bring them in only after the agreement has been reduced to writing. Even then, it is only to make sure that the contract complies with American and host country laws. Don't let them meddle in the negotiation itself or in other business matters, or you're likely to be maneuvered into making the wrong decisions.

Of course, both you and your foreign partner must benefit from a strategic alliance. If each party does not believe that the advantages of the partnership outweigh the costs, the alliance will inevitably fail. In other words, it must be a win-win arrangement.

Selecting a Name

An alliance's name can have a profound effect on its success in a given market. The obvious choice is to use the name of one of the partners. Perhaps customers in Taipei have never heard of your company but are very familiar with your partner's name. Then give the alliance that name. Conversely, customers in Warsaw may place a high priority on American products and welcome your company's name on the alliance banner. Perhaps neither your company nor your partner's company are well-known in St. Petersburg. In that case, a completely new name could be the best answer. Regardless of your choice, make sure to fit the alliance's name to the peculiar circumstances in the marketplace. This seems like a minor point, but a name can end up being the most important asset of your alliance.

Setting Up Controls

Most of us tend to over control. Auditors, government agencies, and stifling organization hierarchies preach that tight control over virtually every aspect of a business is the only way to prevent employee errors and theft, to comply with regulations, and to furnish top management with the flood of information it seems to want.

Try tight controls in your offshore alliance and I guarantee it will fall apart. No foreign partner wants close supervision by the Americans. They prefer to creatively react to circumstances as they develop. Or they may be more comfortable parroting government edicts, as in Russia, or government ideology, as in China. This may cause you severe headaches, but over the long-term, assuming you have chosen the right partner, you'll find that your alliance works as well as can be expected in the local environment. Don't try to control your partner's every move. And don't expect or demand written reports from them. Very few businesses in emerging nations use written reports. To insist on them will only alienate your partner.

Don't try to control your partner's every move.

Setting Policies for Alliance Managers

Hiring entrepreneurial spirited managers for your alliance should be a top priority. Regardless of the terms of the alliance agreement, ever changing condition in the host country will force frequent changes in operating policies. Such changes can only be managed by on-the-spot decisions. Let your alliance manager operate as an entrepreneur with full authority to take action as needed, even if that means changing alliance policies for pricing, delivery schedules, customer service, credit and collections, or even trade finance. Of course, it goes without saying that before you entrust anyone to manage your business affairs, whether an employee or a strategic alliance manager, that person must be thoroughly trained in your corporate culture and market objectives.

STRUCTURING A JOINT VENTURE AGREEMENT

Strategic alliances are a lot like marriages. They are much easier to get into than to get out of. That's especially true of joint ventures. Just like marriages, once a joint venture has been culminated, you need to constantly work to improve relationships with your partner. The agreement must be carefully drafted to meet the needs of both partners.

You and your partner may share equally or unequally in the ownership of the new company or in the responsibility for carrying on its business. You may also share the profits and losses of the venture proportionately or disproportionately to your ownership holdings. Some joint ventures are not intended to produce independent profits or losses but merely to generate long-term gains for each of the partners, as in arrangements to share technology and market intelligence. In most cases, however, a joint venture is a separate profit oriented operating entity.

Since no two joint venture agreements are alike, any attempt at universal contract language or format would be futile. However, the following standards seem to apply in most cases:

➡ **Multilingual.** The contract must be written in both English and the language of the host country. Even if personnel from your company and your partner's company are conversant in each other's language, contract terminology tends to have different meanings in different languages. Both of you must agree on the interpretation of all contract clauses under the laws and customs of each of your countries.

➡ **Objective of joint venture.** The objective of the joint venture should be clearly stated in the agreement, whether it is to market specific products, to build a manufacturing plant, to manage the operations of a facility, to export, to transfer technology and know-how, or to provide financing for a project.

➡ **Expiration date.** All joint venture contracts must have a definitive expiration date, regardless of how far into the future that may extend. In addition, the contract must spell out specifically how the venture's assets and liabilities, including inventory, receivables, plant and equipment, trade liabilities, and unpaid loans or other indebtedness will be distributed on dissolution.

➡ **Specific activities.** The joint venture's activities may require that specific functions be performed by either you or your alliance partner, such as managing the operation, arranging financing, marketing, engineering, or liaison with government officials. Regardless of the number of duties, each should be thoroughly described. The agreement should also include specific responsibilities for settling claims, lawsuits, any other legal or contingent matter that may arise during the operation of the joint venture, and for the paying of all taxes, license fees, permit fees, and so on.

➡ **Sharing profits and losses.** The contract must contain definitive language that spells out how the profits and losses of the joint venture will be allocated to you and your alliance partner. It must also describe how, when, and to whom cash will be distributed, and how compensation to each of you will be determined.

➡ **Board of directors.** A board of directors or other policy making body must be defined. Veto rights, withdrawal rights, new or additional equity contributions from partners, eventual transfer of ownership interests at the liquidation date, and other policy matters must also be defined.

➡ Escape clause. In the event that you or your alliance partner wish to withdraw from the venture, contractual provisions must spell out your right to do so, under what circumstances withdrawal will be permitted, what forfeiture or compensatory allowances will be paid, and any other items germane to the agreement.

Although joint venture contracts have many provisions similar to those in standard partnership agreements, they take on an added level of complexity. Now the parties must agree on such arcane issues as the relationship between the newly formed joint venture entity and its participating owners, initial and ongoing capital contributions, control of the venture, conflict resolution procedures, and termination provisions. The latter two issues, conflict resolution and termination provisions, seem to cause the most headaches.

Conflict Resolution

Disagreements are bound to arise in any joint venture. The contractual agreement must clearly spell out how conflicts that cannot be negotiated quietly and quickly will be resolved. Mutual approval of major decisions certainly helps, but additional provisions may also be required.

Ventures conceived between two companies with equal ownership often provide for a separate committee comprising senior members from both companies to act as a medium for dispute settlement. The committee's sole purpose is to meet periodically to resolve those major conflicts between the partners that the board of directors cannot handle.

Arbitration is another possibility. Every joint venture agreement should specify the conditions that could lead to arbitration, how an arbitrator will be appointed, and the finality of an arbitrator's decision. When agreement cannot be reached through normal channels, the contract may stipulate the buyout of one partner by the other.

Termination

Which brings us to termination procedures, probably one of the most misunderstood features of any alliance agreement. Clauses must spell out the joint venture's life span, specifying when and under what circumstances it will terminate. Specific provisions must identify how the venture's business will be wound down; how assets, including cash balances, will be distributed; and what liability each partner will assume for future claims that may arise once the venture is disbanded.

So much for the contractual aspects of joint ventures. Now let's take a brief look at locating and qualifying strategic alliances partners.

LOCATING PARTNERS

Large, well-known companies have a relatively easy time locating suitable joint venture partners for practically any purpose. Less well-known companies trip all over themselves trying to join up. Competitors, suppliers, customers, it doesn't make a difference. They all want to be in bed with a Microsoft, an IBM, or a Johnson & Johnson. Smaller companies, especially those relatively new to global trade, aren't as fortunate.

The problem isn't a dearth of partners. The problem is the sheer multiplicity of organizations eager to help you find one. An army of intermediaries, government bureaus, international publications, trade groups, and multinational agencies collect and disseminate leads and direct contacts to potential partners. In fact, the variety of sources is so staggering that it's easy to become mired in the process without achieving your end goal.

Chapter 4 described many governmental and private sector organizations that stand ready to help you find an alliance partner. Give agencies from the Department of Commerce and the Department of State as well as the local American Chamber of Commerce office a chance, and I guarantee you will have plenty of potential partners to choose from.

The care taken in selecting a partner and drafting a joint venture agreement often determines whether the arrangement will be beneficial or detrimental to one or both parties. Since the partners will be from different countries, accustomed to significantly different negotiating techniques, contract language, and interpretation of contract phrases, the most beneficial agreements are normally negotiated and drafted by intermediaries for both sides. Such intermediaries may be international management consultants, investment bankers, attorneys, government bureaucrats, or a combination thereof.

USING INTERMEDIARIES

With your first FDI, you will find it very difficult to get anything accomplished without the assistance of an intermediary. Intermediaries can also help set up your export program. When setting up any type of strategic alliance, intermediaries are a necessity.

You may also need in-country help. Host country trading firms that specialize in consulting to foreign companies can be a big help. Government bureaucrats in commercial related departments (e.g., the central bank or ministries of finance and trade) might also be helpful in some countries. Obviously, these emissaries do not advertise their talents and conduct business surreptitiously and informally. Still, you may find their services essential for arranging and setting up joint ventures and other partnership alliances. This is especially true in Arab states. In fact, it is impossible to get anything done in these countries without the direct assistance of a bureaucrat from one ministry or another.

When setting up any type of strategic alliance, intermediaries are a necessity.

Foreign affiliates of American law firms also take on intermediary assignments related to joint ventures. If you need to cut through bureaucratic red tape to get clearance for setting up a joint venture, in-country attorneys generally have more connections than anyone else. All international law firms maintain directories of correspondent firms capable of handling such engagements. Baker & McKenzie (www.bakernet.com) is one of the largest and probably the best-known international law firm. On occasion, I have had good responses from several of this firm's worldwide offices.

Another possibility is the local branch of an American or European bank. Bank managers generally know who is who in the local business community, and if qualified intermediaries are around, these bank managers know how and where to contact them. In smaller cities or resort areas, bankers rank right up there with political bureaucrats as sources of intelligence.

You'll get plenty of pressure from government bureaucrats and aid agencies to team up with certain consultants. If one of those being pressed on you seems competent, fine. If not, find some excuse, such as language difficulties, divergent work standards, or some other reason to dump those you cannot work with. It may be difficult to resist such pressure, but remember that the intermediary you choose will, in essence, be acting as your agent probably in several vital matters. Therefore, he or she must be trustworthy and able to communicate effectively with your home office.

Obviously there can be no guarantee that your strategic alliance will work as expected. Nevertheless, if you follow the suggestions outlined in this chapter, you will stand a much better chance of succeeding. As mentioned earlier, strategic alliances are an essential aspect of doing business in any emerging nation. The more care you take in choosing a partner and structuring the agreement the better chance you have of reaching your market objectives.

chapter eighteen
Selling Channels in Foreign Markets

WHETHER SELLING IN U.S. MARKETS OR OVERSEAS, YOU MUST SOLICIT potential customers; structure competitive pricing; reflect societal values and customs in your product's workmanship quality, utility, and style; warrant your product's performance; and, depending on the product, offer customer training, parts replacement, or other customer service features. We all know that. But selling in foreign markets requires something more. First, as we saw in Chapter 17, you definitely need a local partner as an in-country sales representative or distributor. Second, you have to allow extra time for making the sale and collecting your money. And third, with language barriers and cultural hurdles, every step along the way is significantly more complex than selling in the United States.

Several channels are available, and they all effectively recognize the special issues involved in offshore selling. Three are considered indirect and three are direct.

1. Indirect selling channels
    a. Sell to U.S.-based agents commissioned by foreign governments and foreign companies
    b. Sell to foreign export trading companies that represent one or more foreign customers
    c. Sell to U.S. export management companies and U.S. export trading companies who then sell to foreign buyers on their own account
2. Direct selling channels
    a. Sell through your own captive export trading company
    b. Sell through foreign sales representatives or distributors
    c. Sell directly to foreign customers either with your own sales personnel or through strategic alliance partners

The capabilities of your export sales department, your company's financial resources, and your level of interest in international trade determine whether an indirect or a direct marketing channel make the most sense. The easiest and least expensive way is to sell to U.S.-based agents commissioned by foreign governments and companies.

AGENTS COMMISSIONED BY FOREIGN GOVERNMENTS AND COMPANIES

A growing number of agents commissioned by foreign governments and companies roam the United States looking for products that cannot be purchased in their clients' countries. In many cases, these agents represent governments that need goods and services for infrastructure projects, military arsenals, or for state owned manufacturing, retailing, or service businesses (primarily financial services). They also represent the private sector, buying consumer products for retail chains or materials and components for manufacturers. It's fairly easy to make contact with these agents through various foreign embassies in Washington, New York, and other cities and through export trade promotion bureaus, U.S. government agencies, or trade shows.

There is nothing mysterious about selling to foreign commissioned agents. Everything is the same as selling to U.S. customers in Seattle, Denver, Kansas City, or Detroit. In fact, accountants record these sales as normal domestic sales and not as export sales.

Commissioned agents are not the best way to build the reputation of your company or the brand names of your products, however. An export management company (EMC), which is midway between a foreign commissioned agent and your own international sales department, might make more sense. An EMC is the least complicated selling channel that also establishes some product recognition in a foreign market—albeit not very much.

EXPORT MANAGEMENT COMPANIES

Before finalizing your export strategies, ask yourself the following questions:

➡ Do I have the financial resources to staff an export department with qualified sales personnel?

➡ Do I know how and where to find foreign customers?

➡ Am I confident that I can quickly master the intricacies of dealing with customs officials as well as in-country transport companies, sales representatives, and distributors?

➡ Do I have the time to devote to learning the various nuances of export markets?

If your answer is no to even one of these questions then you should seriously consider hiring an export management company. More than 5,000 small and midsize American companies—and a few very large ones, too—already use these organizations.

EMCs are a convenient outlet for American made goods. In some cases, EMCs act like manufacturers' representatives serving as the selling arm or export sales department for several manufacturers of noncompeting products, soliciting orders and transacting business in the name of the various producers they represent. In other cases, EMCs serve as your very own export sales department working exclusively for your company. These sales experts may be paid retainers, commissions, or a combination of retainers and commissions. A third option is for an EMC to purchase goods directly from manufacturers and then resell them overseas using its own account. Some combine all the three approaches. A few of the bigger EMCs with substantial resources will even help finance export orders. Most EMCs are quite small, however, and do not engage in trade finance.

EMCs maintain their own networks of offshore sales representatives and distributors. This puts them in a solid position to develop market strategies for U.S. clients. They can arrange for shipping and customs documentation, the purchasing of foreign risk and marine insurance coverage, and in some cases, supplier or buyer credit. As a seller, you don't incur any credit risks, shipping costs, overseas selling expenses, or customer service costs. In fact, you won't even know the identity of your customers.

An EMC is a clean way to increase sales without adding risk. However, the price for such a luxury is steep.

If your company is unwilling or unable to support its own export sales department, using an EMC is a clean way to increase sales without adding risk. However, the price for such a luxury is steep. Since EMCs on retainer earn their profits when they resell the goods offshore, they must buy the goods from you at prices significantly lower than market prices, which are generally your cost plus a small markup.

EMCs may also operate as commissioned sales representatives. In this case, your company retains title to the goods until the customer accepts shipment. This is less expensive than paying a retainer, however, you bear all the financing costs, credit risks, and carrying charges, plus storage costs of inventory stocked at the EMC's distribution warehouses.

Despite these drawbacks, EMCs are an effective way for smaller companies to test the waters of export markets without incurring the costs of full-blown international sales departments. They are very popular and have been around for a long time. You can get a list of EMCs from the Federation of International Trade Associations (www.fita.org.), export trading companies are another indirect selling channel.

EXPORT TRADING COMPANIES

In 1982, the U.S. Congress passed the Export Trading Company Act. This legislation permitted the formation of export trading companies (ETCs) by groups of competitors without fear of antitrust action. The avowed purpose of this legislation was to increase the competitiveness of U.S. companies by allowing them to market products jointly as the Japanese, British, and Dutch had done for more than a century. The Export Trading Company Act also permitted bank holding companies to form ETCs. The theory was that by allowing banks to engage in commercial, nonbanking transactions, they would be more receptive to requests for trade finance, thereby encouraging more American companies to export. This theory never proved to workout. As you have probably already learned, 9 out of 10 commercial banks still shy away from anything having to do with international trade.

After passage of the act, individuals, companies, trade associations, states, and cities jumped in. Enamored by the success of giant Japanese trading companies, Americans were eager to partake in the vast profits offered by global trade. Unfortunately, few actually took the time to understand the intricacies of international trade, and ETCs failed as fast as they were formed.

ETCs usually take title to products and then export them for the ETCs own account. They function independently, sourcing U.S. products from a variety of

INSIGHT . . . My favorite anecdote about ETCs involves a used car salesman from Keokuk, Iowa who married a woman whose family came from Paraguay. Tempted by the possibility of tapping his in-laws for local sales contacts, he quit his job, incorporated himself as an ETC, packed his bag for a four day stay, and took off for Asunción expecting to land several orders for whatever anyone wanted to buy. After landing, he was asked by his in-laws what product lines he represented. His response typified the naïveté of new traders, "Any product you want. I'm going to get the order first and then locate a supplier back in the States." Today, he is back in Iowa selling used cars.

manufacturers to meet the needs of known overseas clients. Typically, an ETC performs a sourcing or wholesale function between buyer and seller and does not assume any responsibility to either party in the transaction.

A few ETCs refuse to carry inventory or perform after-sales service. These companies operate strictly as commissioned agents, charging the seller or the buyer a percentage of the export value. Most export trading companies, however, do just the opposite. They buy everything from manufactured goods to raw materials (at 10 to 15 percent below the wholesale price) from a variety of U.S. manufacturers and then resell them for their own account. Your trade association is the best source for locating an ETC that meets your needs.

Brand loyalty is very hard to establish through intermediaries.

Whether you opt for foreign commissioned agents, EMCs, or ETCs, indirect selling channels impose some very definite disadvantages that you would not encounter if using your own international sales department. Some of them are as follows:

➡ Your personnel will not learn the complexities of exporting for future expansion to other offshore markets.

➡ Some foreign buyers will not deal with a third party intermediary, such as a EMC or ETC.

➡ With EMCs or ETCs, you have no control over defining your customers, setting selling prices, designing promotions, or handling after-sales service.

➡ EMCs and ETCs will always concentrate on those products that bring them the most profit shunning new product offerings or products with limited potential.

➡ The majority of EMCs and many ETCs are small businesses with limited financial resources available to stock your products or offer trade finance.

Furthermore, although U.S.-based commissioned agents, EMCs, and ETCs all offer convenient, low-cost ways to increase sales without becoming involved in complex international transactions, indirect selling channels will never be part of a viable long-term strategy. Intermediaries are just that, intermediaries. Brand loyalty is very hard to establish through intermediaries. Relying on intermediaries will neither gain you market prominence, nor establish your company's reputation as a quality supplier. In the end, a long-term stake in foreign markets cannot be a proxy to a third party.

As you have certainly discerned from the foregoing discussion, the distinction between ETCs and EMCs is often blurred, and it's hard to tell one from the other. However, as a general rule, ETCs handle products from many manufacturers and sell to a single customer or a select group of customers. EMCs, on the other hand, handle products from a single manufacturer and sell on the open market.

CAPTIVE EXPORT TRADING COMPANIES

Setting up your own captive export trading company (CETC) may be a better way to go. With an CETC, you avoid the loss in margin that occurs when selling to independent ETCs or through EMCs. Moreover, by marketing products for other exporters, your trading company in, say, Budapest or Jakarta will bring in extra profits. One of my favorite CETC cases involved a long-time client, Washington Computer Corporation of America, otherwise known as WCCA. Although I have related this anecdote many times, it is such a classic that it bears repeating.

INSIGHT... WCCA manufactured PC computers and peripheral hardware. The CEO was interested in both Venezuelan and Colombian markets but felt his company could only tackle one country at a time. He ordered his staff to proceed with surveys and risk assessments for both countries. The results indicated that a significant market existed in Colombia for WCCA's PC line. The company proceeded to form a joint venture with a Colombian distributor and hired two Spanish-speaking sales managers for its export sales department.

Before turning the Colombian partner loose, however, WCCA's CEO and his staff developed a strategic marketing simulation model to determine the impact of various forms of Colombian competition, demographic trends, import regulations, and other customs peculiarities; the role of certain influential government officials; and a distribution option for Bogotá and Cali.

By asking "what if" questions and varying their assumptions, the group evaluated the influence of each factor on the company's export program. They concluded that Colombian markets could be penetrated much faster and broader with a CETC, so WCCA formed one with its main office in Bogotá and a branch office in Barranquilla. The result? In the first two years, WCCA exceeded its Colombian sales forecast by 300 percent. It also picked up a whole new business using its CETC to market computer peripherals for other U.S. firms.

A typical CETC will take title to exportable goods and handle all export operations independent of its parent company. The CETC may handle one product line or multiple lines. It may export to one country or trade worldwide. Furthermore, CETCs can be formed with partners from banks, other manufacturers, state and city agencies, trade groups, or service organizations. These passive partners can provide working capital while your company handles all management and administrative duties. With the CETC assuming all trading risks, your parent company can concentrate fully on other operating matters.

If you decide to form a CETC with other companies, banks, or government agencies, don't forget to apply immediately for a Certificate of Review. This certificate is a legal document issued by the Department of Commerce with the concurrence of the Department of Justice that provides antitrust protection for the export activities specified in the document. In other words, this certificate makes it perfectly legal to collude with other companies in the formation and operation of a CETC.

If you are interested in exploring the possibilities of forming a CETC, the U.S. Office of Export Trading Company Affairs lays out the requirements and advantages in the booklet *The Export Trading Company Guidebook*. This office also sponsors seminars and regional conferences on various aspects of the Export Trading Company Act.

Export Trading Company Affairs, Room 7021, U.S. Department of Commerce, International Trade Administration, Washington, DC 20230; www.trade.gov/td/oetca/index.html

FOREIGN TRADING COMPANIES

Exporters from Great Britain, the Netherlands, Japan, and several other trading nations learned a long time ago that trading companies could market and distribute products on a global scale more efficiently than any single producer. More recently, exporting companies from nontraditional, newer trading nations such as Argentina, Brazil, and South Korea have learned the same lesson. Today, it's safe to say that trading companies have become the principal form of marketing medium worldwide. Major trading companies now operate in all large, metropolitan markets.

Foreign trading companies are as different from U.S. export trading companies as night and day. The only similarity is the designation "trading company." Many Japanese, Dutch, British, and German trading companies are huge conglomerates with marketing, financial, and distribution arms that truly permit a global reach. The Japanese trading companies Mitsui, Komatsu, Mitsubishi, and Sumitomo have been active for years throughout the world as have British trading companies. German and Portuguese trading companies compete fiercely in Brazil. A few American corporations have formed joint venture trading companies with foreign partners. Some trading companies handle specific product lines for smaller companies. The easiest way to make contact with foreign trading companies active in your markets is through that country's trade development bureau.

DIRECT SELLING CHANNELS

Sooner or later, you'll have to set up your own international marketing organization, either with sales managers who monitor foreign distributors out of your home office or through a network of sales personnel stationed in key submarkets throughout the region. Dumping exporting activities on your U.S. marketing organization might be a big mistake. Nine out of 10 times it will not work. The selling, distribution, and administrative activities related to exporting are so much more complex and time-consuming than comparable functions for domestic sales that a separation of duties is the only efficient way to operate.

Structuring an International Marketing Organization

Your international marketing group should have offices apart from your U.S. sales department, hopefully in a separate building or at least on a different floor. I realize that sounds simplistic, but I've seen international and domestic sales groups combined either to save space or to satisfy idiosyncrasies and it never works satisfactorily. If your company exports two or more distinctly different product lines or plans to enter more than one country, it might be advantageous to organize a separate international marketing group for each product line or country right off the bat.

I know of several U.S. companies that have exported successfully for a long time and believe strongly that their success is a result of a well-organized sales force and the specific methods used to sell and distribute their products. Yes, they all agree that their products are superior to their competition, but it's their marketing people who get the sales.

Foreign Agents and Sales Representatives

After setting up an international marketing organization, the next step is to determine how to distribute your products. Agency and representative laws vary by country but are always different from ours. For instance, in Venezuela market conditions and business protocol are seldom as advertised. Corrupt customs officials, arrogant bureaucrats, unfathomable trade laws, and cagey

INSIGHT... One broadly reported example involves difficulties with sight draft payments. Venezuelan buyers either delayed or refused to claim merchandise from the receiving port. Customs officials impounded the products, and the U.S. shipper was charged large fines and the goods were sold at auction. To complete the circle, the agents to whom the goods were originally shipped purchased them at severely discounted auction prices. Since Venezuelan law does not require an importing company to pay its bank before obtaining the original documents necessary to get the merchandise transferred out of customs, officials may release the goods to anyone who presents a copy of the bill of lading and posts a bond for duties.

hustlers pretending to be import agents can all too easily frustrate the unwary American exporter.

Wrongful transfer of goods at the port of entry occurs regularly throughout the world. Abuses of local laws have been reported at seaports and airports in Indonesia, the United Arab Emirates, Russia, Ecuador, and Guyana. It definitely pays to check references for all sales representatives and distributors before you agree to any type of contractual arrangement in any country.

One seldom disclosed hazard has to do with agents. By definition, an agent has the authority to act in the place of a principal. Agents may commit your firm contractually. They may execute contracts of various types, handle banking matters, change pricing as they see fit, represent your company to local bureaucrats, and a variety of other matters that you would do yourself if you were in-country. Be aware, however, that savvy exporters seldom use agents unless required by the host country's government. Entrusting such authority to a local company without immediate supervision from your own source is far too dangerous.

Savvy exporters seldom use agents unless required by the host country's government.

Foreign sales representatives do practically the same work as manufacturer representatives in the United States. They sell— and that's about it. Don't expect any additional help from them. Representatives call on customers, present your brochure or product information, and handle many different noncompeting products lines. They earn commissions on sales. However, they do not take title to your goods and do not have any authority to sign contracts or otherwise act on your behalf except to offer your products for sale. Some representatives want to represent your firm only on an exclusive basis for a given territory. This is a good strategy. Theoretically at least, an exclusive representative will give your company its undivided attention.

When you interview potential representatives, several questions need to be answered. The most important one is: What are the sales potential for my products? Since you will already have a fairly good grasp on the answer, the response from the representative organization, positive or negative, will reveal whether they know your industry and products or whether taking on your lines would be a new experience for them.

In addition to a basic knowledge of your industry, the representative should furnish references (bank references and trade references), a credit report, the current status and background of its officers, and how your product line will be introduced. If you have any doubt about the answers to these questions but still think you want to go with this firm, it pays to spend the extra dollars to hire an independent intermediary to dig deeper into the rep's background. Several U.S. firms do this type of work but I like Kroll Associates the best.

 Kroll Associates 900 Third Ave., 7th Floor, New York, NY 10022; www.kroll.com

Here are some additional questions to ask:

- Can at least one principal communicate effectively in English?
- What minimum sales volume would the representative need to make handling your line worthwhile?
- What types of customers does the rep contact now?
- What sales territory does it cover? The entire country? Specific provinces? Cities only?
- Does it have any branch offices in territories you are especially interested in?
- What type of promotion programs will the representative recommend? Radio? TV? Newspapers? Billboards? Cinema? Will you be expected to finance these promotions?
- How many sales people does the representative have to handle your products?
- What is the average sales volume expected per sales person?
- How does the representative compensate its sales personnel? Commission? Salary? Combination? Bonus program?
- Does the representative handle lines from other U.S. Companies? If so, how many different lines? Would there be a conflict of interest with your line? (Get references from these companies.)

When you finally locate the representative you want, draft a Sales Representative Contract. It pays to get your agreement in writing for the psychological effect, if nothing else. The structure of the contract should be virtually identical to the strategic alliance contract described in Chapter 17. Don't be surprised if you can't enforce it, however. Many deals in emerging markets are consummated verbally, knowing that no judge will take the time to enforce a written contract unless, of course, he is paid a handsome fee.

When Is a Sales Representative Your Representative, and When Is It Something Else?

Murky distinctions between forms of representation, including the separation between sales representatives and customers, have caused confusion for more than one U.S. exporter. For example, a local company can act as a manufacturer's representative, import/distributor, dealer, wholesaler, and retailer—all at the same time. The same company that acts as a sales representative and takes orders on commission can also maintain inventory for distribution to other companies and operate a retail store. Many retailers who import directly from exporters also buy through sales agents, jobbers, and dealers.

Several countries around the world do not require import licenses. They also don't publish a list of importers, which means that anyone can import anything. This, in turn, makes it very difficult to find out who is actually doing the buying. Fortunately, some emerging countries lack general merchandise importers and rarely do agents or distributors take on competing lines, making it a bit easier—but not much—to identify who are buyers,.

Loose definitions of sales representatives, distributors, agents, and customers are not restricted to any specific country. Each has its own peculiar commercial laws and no two are alike. Before beginning an export program, be sure to clarify these agency and representation laws.

Other Confusing Laws

In addition to agency and representation laws, other provisions in a country's commercial code affect the way agreements with representatives or distributors are written. Most countries require that to be valid, contracts must be written in that country's language and use metric measurements. They also require that all monetary values be in the local currency. Contracts must be signed by an attorney and notarized. Although a few countries have not yet enacted a complete set of contract laws for representatives or distributors, even those that have such laws seldom enforce them. This means that when a contract is canceled, indemnification clauses are difficult to invoke. Moreover, if possible, keep all personnel off your payroll, or you may get stuck with profit sharing, bonuses, pension payments, and separation allowances. Labor laws in most countries are far more stringent than in the United States.

Laws that regulate sales to government agencies or state owned businesses are another matter entirely. With little or no uniformity, compliance requirements must be researched case by case.

Don't forget to obtain all licenses and permits necessary to conduct business in that country and register your company with the appropriate government bureaus. You have to also do this to get on the right bidder's lists.

DISTRIBUTORS

Distributors are different from representatives. They actually purchase your products and store them in their own warehouses or distribution centers along with other noncompetitive but complementary product lines. Because they hold title to the products, they have the right to establish pricing structures and determine distribution services. It is not unusual for distributors to provide after-sales service, offer product repair facilities, and stock spare parts inventories.

As with agency and representation laws, regulations affecting both the definition and actions of distributors vary country by country.

Distributors provide valuable services that cannot be offered directly or can only be offered directly at great expense to U.S. exporters. For example, as residents of the host country, distributors know the characteristics of local markets. They understand customs regulations, pricing strategies, distribution peculiarities, and customer expectations. Competent distributors can also handle customer complaints and questions about technical product applications. Furthermore, since foreign distributors are not bound by the restrictions of the Foreign Corrupt Practices Act and other legislation that hampers U.S. companies, they are more competitive than U.S. firms selling directly.

Some companies set up training programs for their foreign distributors to teach them the technical aspects of a product. Others stock parts and materials at the distributor's warehouse for repair and maintenance work. Regardless of the specific relationship, putting contractual terms in writing will avoid future misunderstandings about what you want your distributor to do and how the compensation package will be structured.

MONITORING SALES REPRESENTATIVES AND DISTRIBUTORS

If you have trouble locating acceptable sales representatives or distributors, try the Agent/Distributor Service (www.buyusa.gov) of the U.S. Department of Commerce. This agency maintains a comprehensive database of the names, addresses, and specialties of foreign representatives and distributors. Agent/Distributor Service reports contain information on up to six qualified representatives who have expressed an interest in handling the types of products sold by your company and are already working in your markets. The reports can be obtained for a small fee in about 60 days.

INSIGHT... A small business client, A-Voval Inc., sold computer accessories and supplies in Southeast Asia through local distributors. It maintained sales offices in Singapore, Taipei, and Kuala Lumpur. The CEO was confident in his distributors and representatives, but knew that when the cat's away, the mice will play. One-on-one supervision was a must. He insisted that the regional marketing managers from the three offices travel regularly to all representative and distributor locations. This gave the managers the chance to monitor their activities and simultaneously provide technical, customer service, and, when necessary, financing assistance. As the A-Voval marketing vice president preached to his sales staff, "You can't supervise sales representatives or distributors by e-mail or phone. You have to meet face-to-face at least once a month." His philosophy was that if you're not willing to spend the resources on adequate field supervision, you might as well forget about selling internationally.

SALARIED SALES PERSONNEL

Some companies choose to have their own international sales force in addition to local sales representatives, bypassing both trading companies and distributors. If you decide to go this route, don't force your employees to operate out of your U.S. office. It can be a huge mistake. To be effective, sales personnel must spend an inordinate amount of time traveling to meet customers and sales representatives, inevitably diminishing their marketing effectiveness as well as their efficiency in taking care of paperwork at home. When you add in the extra time and cost of traveling from the States, you have practically paid for a local presence. Moreover, when customers are thousands of miles away, it's virtually impossible for sales people to provide quick answers to questions about pricing, contract terms, or technical product performance. And for the clincher, having international sales personnel operating out of your U.S. office makes your company look like it's pinching pennies, especially when competitors' sales people are stationed in-country.

Despite the cost of maintaining overseas offices, it usually pays to have at least one or two sales people based in-country. Not only does a local presence improve customer relations, it enables your employees to make face-to-face sales calls, test market alternative bidding options, and immediately negotiate sales contracts. Each sale is different and has its own delivery requirements, technical criteria, guarantees, financing schemes, and/or contract terms. Chances are good that only your own sales people will be qualified to deal with these matters.

INSIGHT... A small company with an ornery owner, Tell-It-Now Corp., is a good example of a U.S. contractor that marched to a different drum. During the early stages of its venture into Latin American markets, Tell-It-Now delegated contract negotiations and monitoring responsibilities to me, instead of using in-house personnel. Initially, I was asked to investigate the possibility of bidding on an upcoming hospital development job in western Mexico. I did my job and, with time to spare, helped my client's personnel prepare the bid documents. So far, so good. But when Tell-It-All won the bid, instead of sending company executives to Mexico City to negotiate and execute a sales contract, the company delegated those responsibilities to me. I tried to dissuade the owner, but he was adamant claiming that he didn't want his personnel to waste time on such a simple matter. I agreed to do the negotiation against my better judgment, and in retrospect, I should have said no. Within four months, the obstinate owner acknowledged that his company could not comply with the contract terms and stopped work, blaming me for executing an unmanageable sales contract.

Even if a trading company or other sales representative solicits customer inquiries, your own sales personnel should be responsible for building and maintaining market share. Although consultants and other intermediaries can pave the way, it's up to your people to close sales contracts and negotiate terms and conditions.

PRICING

It goes without saying that pricing strategies must reflect your company's market objectives. Are you looking for a way to get rid of excess inventory, make a quick killing, or enter and leave a market in short order? Then perhaps high prices supported by aggressive advertising campaigns are the answer. Are you looking for long-term growth in market share? If so, competition and market demand will dampen pricing flexibility. If your objective is to dump products that are obsolete in your home markets, then fire-sale prices or large discounts might be in order.

However, you may have less control over pricing than you would like. The factors that typically determine prices in the United States—market demand, competition, and cost to produce and sell—are, to a very large extent, overshadowed by external market forces beyond your control in foreign markets. Market demands in emerging nations are driven by income levels, literacy rates, infrastructures, and local customs. In most countries, active underground economies and business cartels strongly influence the form and magnitude of competition. Government regulations put a lid on pricing in protected industries, and to make matters worse, these regulations change rapidly as powerful social and financial forces buffet fragile political institutions.

In fact, about the only element of pricing that companies do have a modicum of control over is product cost. Even there, however, trade pacts, bureaucratic meddling, security factors, and union influence bear strongly on the cost of producing products and then selling and distributing them in-country. Moreover, since prices are mostly negotiated order by order, price sheets are worthless. Still, if you are going to have any control over product pricing, it will involve some markup over your total costs.

In most countries, active underground economies and business cartels strongly influence the form and magnitude of competition.

Putting external market forces aside for a moment, the costs you incur in foreign markets will be different from those incurred in U.S. markets. Although exported products may be produced in the same U.S. facilities and have the same labor content as their domestic counterparts, getting these products to market involves extra costs that can be significant.

If you have an in-country manufacturing plant, you may find labor costs much lower than in the United States. The cost of materials and components, whether sourced locally or imported, will certainly differ from the cost of domestic purchases—lower if purchased locally, probably higher if imported. Selling, distribution, and administrative costs may be higher or lower than in your U.S. facility, but they definitely will be different.

This is not the place to discuss pricing theories or worry about accounting protocols that dictate how you build product costs. But it is important to recognize the costs that are seldom seen in domestic markets beginning with the several types of incremental costs that relate directly to the exporting process. Although every cost listed on Worksheet A (see the end of this chapter) is not incurred for all export sales, most do apply. You will likely find that prices charged in your U.S. markets will have to be increased by a fair amount to cover these incremental costs. In and of itself, this might make your exports noncompetitive. Perhaps then you should consider a host country facility to service local markets.

Developing a cost estimate for goods to be produced offshore and perhaps including the sourcing of materials or subassemblies from third countries is a complex procedure especially if estimated costs are compared with domestic costs. All costs of transporting value-added materials, components, or subassemblies from one location to another must be included. And don't forget the expenses of getting products to market. Although these incremental costs are obviously different for each country, Worksheet B (see the end of this chapter) serves as a guide for building cost estimates for project bids or for comparisons with other sales strategies.

Price sheets are seldom used in foreign markets. Since prices for the same products sold to different customers will vary significantly, even without volume discounts, the basic pricing principle is that everything is negotiable. Whether bidding on a construction project or selling capital equipment, computer chips, or ladies' gloves, expect to negotiate mutually agreeable prices for each order. The cost estimates calculated on Worksheet A and B should only be used as starting points and not for determining final prices. Furthermore, negotiated prices must take into account any extra costs that may arise from the previously described external market forces.

THE SALES (PURCHASE) CONTRACT

Nearly all foreign sales or purchase transactions require a formal contract between buyer and seller. Since contracts serve as the basis for resolving conflicts, they must be negotiated with the utmost care. Both buyer and seller must have a clear understanding of all contract terms and conditions and both parties must agree that they can and will perform within the confines of the contract. The odds are very high that you will have to write the contract under the laws of the host country. In that case, hire the best in-country attorney you can find regardless of cost.

Sales contracts may take a variety of forms and may be either verbal or written. When written, they may be in the form of a letter, a telex, a cable, or a formally drawn contract. Regardless of the medium, such documents represent binding contracts to buy and sell. The minimum provisions should include:

➡ A description of the goods or services, price, weight, quantity, and a reference to any special customer defined specifications.

➡ Shipping and delivery instructions and all documentation, such as export or import licenses and permits required under the laws of both countries.

➡ Payment terms, conditions, and payment currency including the assignment of responsibility for paying customs duties, taxes, and other special fees.

➡ The designation of responsibility for providing goods in transit insurance coverage and for paying the premium for such insurance.

Although inclusion of the following items will make the contract more difficult and time consuming to negotiate, I guarantee they will save you untold hours in resolving future disputes over long distances.

➡ Method of packaging and marking.

➡ Inspections and tests by the buyer before goods are accepted.

➡ Seller warranties.

➡ Provisions for bid and performance bonds or guarantees.

➡ Special financing provisions.

➡ Mechanisms for patent and trademark protection.

➡ Remedies allowed either party in the event of default.

➡ Designated mediation service and location for arbitration.

➡ Jurisdiction under which disputes will be resolved.

Obviously, every transaction is different. The points listed above are examples of the type of items to be included. Specific clauses must be negotiated among the buyer, seller, and legal counsel. In the United States, sales and purchase transactions occur daily without any reference to a contract and disputes are usually readily settled. But in international trade, language disparities and unforeseen external forces confuse the issue. Taking the time to negotiate a formal contract may prevent a profitable shipment or project from turning into a disaster.

PROTECTING INTELLECTUAL PROPERTY

The piracy of intellectual property—copyrights, patents, trademarks, and so on—continues to be a major deterrent to free or fair trade. Biotechnology and computer software companies, music and film producers and distributors, publishers, and others know that the effective protection of intellectual property rights is crucial to the prosperity and even survival of their businesses. However, as you know, U.S. patent, trademark, and copyright laws do not apply overseas.

Regardless of the efforts by the U.S. government under Special 301 section of the Omnibus Trade and Competitiveness Act of 1988 that requires the U.S. Trade Representative to annually list countries on the priority watch list that are known or suspected of intellectual property piracy, political considerations—as in the case of China—often overshadow rigid enforcement.

Pragmatically, there are only two ways to reduce piracy infringement:

1. Register your patent, trademark, or copyright in the host country. If infringement laws do exist, at least you have a possibility for recourse. Of course, this means retaining local counsel.

2. File your patent under the Patent Cooperation Treaty to which 40 countries are signatories. This can be difficult and expensive, however. The fees are substantial and all claims and documents must be translated into other languages. Nevertheless, if piracy is a real problem and your property is crucial to the survival of your company then it may be worth the cost and effort.

 You can reference the treaty on the website of the World Intellectual Property Organization (www.wipo.int)

Unfortunately, many countries that have laws protecting intellectual property rights do not enforce them. If piracy is suspected, two choices are available: retain local counsel and bring suit in the appropriate foreign court or try to pressure the pirates to stop. The best way to accomplish the latter is to get both local government officials and the U.S. government on your side. This sounds like a reasonable expectation, but too often, it is not. Without political pressure, it seems doubtful that intellectual property theft will diminish much.

The International Chamber of Commerce (www.iccwho.org) commissioned an initiative called Business Action to Stop Counterfeiting and Piracy with the objective of surveying business executives about the degree to which countries protect or fail to protect intellectual property. The results are interesting to say the least. Of the 53 counties perceived by respondents to have the least favorable intellectual property environment, China and Russia were singled out as far and away the least favorable. A second survey, this time by European Union executives, revealed that China accounted for two-thirds of all counterfeit goods seized in the EU, with Russia, Ukraine, Chile, and Turkey close behind.

Returning to the ICC study, China, Russia, India, Brazil, Indonesia, Vietnam, Taiwan, Pakistan, Turkey, and Ukraine were favored with the top 10 spots as the worst countries for counterfeiting and piracy. The second 10 spots included, among others, Romania, Thailand, Mexico, and Poland.

It is indeed unfortunate that the four BRIC countries that have the largest consumer bases and the highest growth rates among emerging nations seem to be unable or unwilling to stop or even reduce intellectual property piracy. Apparently, many U.S. companies of all sizes have chosen to ignore this sad state of affairs and continue to export to these countries. Moreover, FDI from U.S. companies is a major factor stimulating their economic growth. One has to wonder how these transnationals live with the extensive intellectual property piracy so prevalent in these markets.

Information about protecting intellectual property can be obtained from any of the following U.S. government offices: Patent and Trademark Office (www.pto.gov), Office of the Trade Representative, U.S. and Commercial Service, Department of State's Bureau of Economic and Business Affairs.

WORKSHEET A
ESTIMATING INCREMENTAL EXPORT COSTS FROM A U.S. LOCATION

Customer
   1. Name _____
   2. Address _____
   3. Cable/telex address _____
   4. Telephone _____

Product

5. Product description _____
6. Quantity _____
7. Gross and net weight of order_____
8. Dimensions _____
9. Cubic measure_____

Product Cost

10. Manufacturing cost per unit _____
11. Number of units _____
12. Total manufacturing cost of order _____
13. Allocated selling, general, and administrative costs of order _____
14. Allocated interest expense _____
15. Other allocated costs _____
16. Total cost of order before export _____

Export Costs
Selling and Administrative

17. New product packaging_____
18. Promotional and sales literature_____
19. Foreign trade exhibitions _____
20. International travel expenses _____
21. Credit search _____
22. Risk insurance_____
23. Financing costs_____
24. Commissions and retainers_____
25. Export license_____
26. Certificate of origin licenses_____

Shipping

27. Export packaging _____
28. Freight forwarding charges _____
29. Export documentation fees _____

30. Cargo insurance _____
31. Labeling and packing _____
32. Inland freight _____
33. Loading and unloading charges _____
34. Customs duties _____
35. Total export costs _____
36. Total cost of order _____
37. Markup percent _____
38. Estimated selling price_____

WORKSHEET B
ESTIMATING INCREMENTAL EXPORT COSTS FROM A NONU.S. LOCATION

Customer

1. Name _____
2. Address_____
3. Cable/telex address _____
4. Telephone _____

Product

5. Product description _____
6. Quantity _____
7. Gross and net weight of order_____
8. Dimensions _____
9. Cubic measure _____

Product Cost

10. Manufacturing cost per unit _____
11. Number of units _____
12. Total manufacturing cost of order _____
13. Allocated selling, general, and administrative costs of order _____
14. Allocated interest expense _____
15. Other allocated costs _____
16. Total cost of order before export _____

Export Costs

Selling and Administrative

17. Promotional and sales literature_____

18. Foreign trade exhibitions _____

19. International travel expenses _____

20. Credit search _____

21. Risk insurance_____

22. Buyer credit costs_____

23. Commissions and retainers_____

24. Export license_____

25. Certificate of origin licenses_____

26. Warranty and after-sales service _____

27. Value-added tax (VAT)_____

28. Favors, gifts, and other promotions_____

29. Field service training_____

30. Customer training _____

31. Legal and audit _____

32. Special in-country taxes _____

Shipping

33. Export packaging _____

34. Freight forwarding charges _____

35. Export documentation fees _____

36. Cargo insurance _____

37. Labeling and packing _____

38. Inland freight _____

39. Loading and unloading charges _____

40. Customs duties _____

41. Total export costs _____

42. Total cost of order _____

43. Markup percent _____

44. Estimated selling price_____

chapter nineteen
E-Commerce and Advertising

W E ALL KNOW HOW IMPORTANT ADVANCED TECHNOLOGY IS IN OUR
lives. Cell phones, high definition TV, computer games, ipods, the
internet, and a host of other high-tech
gadgets play crucial roles in our everyday existence.
The same holds true in emerging nations. Advanced
technology has even infiltrated backward countries
like Yemen, Myanmar, Belarus, and sub-Saharan
African nations. Technology has truly become a
global phenomenon. The World Bank recently published a report called Global Economic Prospects, which

attempts to quantify the advance of technology in emerging nations. Its results are staggering—yet disappointing. Yes, on one the hand advanced technology has reached the far corners of the globe. On the other hand, vast swaths of people who live in less developed regions are not reaping the full benefit of high-tech products. The report describes 67 high-tech products currently available in emerging markets—only six reached enough people to claim at least half of a national market. It seems that these countries have done a good job of arranging for access to new technology but a much worse job of putting it to widespread use. As a result, high-tech products are concentrated in urban areas.

For example, the sales of most high-tech products in China are confined to the four industrialized areas of the coast. In Russia, Internet usage in Moscow and St. Petersburg is mushrooming, but it is dead in the water throughout the rest of the country. The same holds true in India where cell phones are a common sight in Mumbai, Kolcata, Delhi, and Chennai but hardly observable in rural areas. Few villages in Latin America have any advanced technology, and the entire region has less installed bandwidth and fewer broadband subscribers than East Asia. Overall, it seems that the citizens of less developed countries are doomed to miss the magical moments of the internet—at least for now.

> Countries have done a good job of arranging for access to new technology but a much worse job of putting it to widespread use.

Nevertheless, every time new statistics on internet access are released the number of users seem to double. Throughout the world, websites enable consumers and businesses to choose from a wealth of products and services that put shopping malls and catalogs to shame.

Only five years ago, consumers and businesses in emerging nations had meager choices and sometimes no choices at all. Payment systems were weak, mainly because of inefficient banking systems. Credit card purchases were given short shrift. Debit cards had just begun to gain popularity in a limited number of countries. B2B e-commerce was about the only type of transaction found on the net. Consumers didn't trust it. And websites didn't know how to reach them. Advertising was in its infancy. A few companies tried this relatively new media, but most either ignored it or tried it once and gave up. Elementary networking groups of websites sprung up, enticing small business owners to join. Pop-up advertising was the rage, even as consumers said no. Easing the return of goods seemed to be an unsolvable issue. Customer service was at best ragged.

Then search engines gained sophistication and began to solicit newer, broader, and fancier ads. Google was born, and a whole new generation of businesses and consumers began to realize the power of the net. Advertising agencies followed suit. No longer married to staid one-dimensional ads, they began to experiment with movement and sound. Payment systems were refined. Internet security was embellished with a variety of schemes to prevent fraud. Encryption put the fear of credit card theft to bed. The returns problem was solved with preprinted, prepaid shipping labels. Customer service improved with 24-hour phone lines and interactive e-mail. Today, several countries have found that B2B and B2C are viable commerce tools.

In a few countries, debit cards are the preferred payment method of e-commerce. But for most websites that accept plastic, credit cards rule the roost. The Carnegie Endowment for International Peace (www.carnegieendowment.org) reported that at last count the four BRIC countries had a total of 157.5 million credit cards. Brazil reported about half of these cards (2.5 people per card), China about 25 percent (33 people per card), Russia about 15 percent (six people per card), and India about 10 percent (65 people per card). Contrast this to the United States with 1.5 billion credit cards in use or five cards for every man, woman, and child, and you can see how far the BRIC countries have to go before B2C becomes a viable media choice

Mechanically, the internet still involves risks. In early 2008, two undersea cables north of Alexandria that carried 90 percent of the data traffic through the Suez canal and provided links between Europe, the Gulf states, and South Asia were damaged. Egypt lost 70 percent of its connectivity. Potential customers from Bangladesh to Algeria to southern Europe lost the use of the internet. The next month another cable was damaged, this time in the Persian Gulf off of Dubai. Then another cable went down between Qatar and the U.A.E. Earthquakes, accidents, sabotage? No one knows for sure. However, you don't need to be prescient to imagine a terrorist attack that would disrupt the world's commerce, especially with thousands of companies and consumers relying on e-commerce for their livelihoods or as their sole source of products and financial transactions. An answer to this dilemma has yet to be found. Regardless of such dangers, however, e-commerce will continue to be used and will likely expand in the years to come.

Although customers in rich countries love e-commerce, neither consumers nor businesses in emerging nations are sold on this new media. The internet is great for doing research, but buying merchandise? No thanks. So far, it hasn't caught on the way the gurus predicted. In fact, most consumers and businesses have not taken kindly to e-commerce or e-advertising. Of the 40 countries in this book, internet users account for only 414 million or just over 10 percent of a total population of 4.1 billion. By comparison, internet users in rich countries total 604 million, about 23 percent of a population of 2.5 billion. Ten percent in emerging nations compared with 23 percent in rich nations shows that e-commerce in less developed nations has a long way to go to before becoming a major selling channel. Combining emerging nations and rich countries, internet users total about 1 billion people or just over 15 percent of the 6.6 billion worldwide population.

Although a 10 percent penetration isn't anything to brag about, if predictions of population growth compiled by the UN's Population Fund are believed, even a 10 percent market share will result in substantial growth in pure numbers of users over the next 40 years. Figure 19-1 presents a brief summary of the UN fund's predictions of population growth for a few key countries.

The UN fund also predicts that the populations of older rich countries—Great Britain, France, Germany, and Italy—will decline by 2050, as will that of Eastern European nations.

Although looking at growth predictions for a few countries is interesting, it doesn't help you make a decision about whether to use e-commerce or e-advertising in a specific country. For that, we have to look at each region and the countries within that region. What we find may surprise you. Within a given region, some countries experience substantial internet access while other have virtually none. Let's begin this journey with Eastern Europe, which has a higher percentage of internet users than any other region of emerging nations.

EASTERN EUROPE

About 68 million Eastern Europeans use the internet. That's more than 22 percent of a total population of 306 million, about the same percentage of

	Population 2000	Population 2050	Percent
Country	(000)	(000)	Growth
World	6,056,715	9,322,252	54
Saudi Arabia	20,346	59,683	200
Pakistan	141,256	344,170	144
India	1,008,937	1,572,055	56
Mexico	98,872	146,651	48
Argentina	37,032	54,522	47
Indonesia	212,092	311,335	47
Brazil	170,406	247,244	45
United States	283,230	397,063	40
Canada	30,757	40,407	31
China	1,275,133	1,462,058	15
Japan	127,096	109,220	–14
Russia	145,491	104,258	–28

FIGURE 19-1
Population Growth

Source: United Nations Population Fund

users as in the rich countries. Figure 19-2 shows a breakdown of internet users by country.

The Czech Republic leads the way with half of its citizens having internet access. Slovakia and the three Baltic countries are right behind, although the small populations of these four countries combined, about 5.3 million, does not make much of a market for e-commerce.

Although 50 percent is a very high percentage of users, Czechs as a rule play games and do research rather than shop online. This is changing, however. During 2006, e-commerce grew by more than 13 percent, hitting $464 million in B2C sales and $353 million in B2B sales. The Czech Republic has traditionally been a cash economy, similar to most other emerging nations. But now credit cards are on the rise and the Ceska Sporitelna Bank provides e-commerce retailers with secure transactions.

FIGURE 19-2
Internet Users and Percent of Population (Eastern Europe)

Country	Percent of Population	Number of Users
Czech Republic	50.0	5.1 million
Slovakia	45.9	2.5 million
Latvia	44.3	1.0 million
Estonia	42.7	690,000
Lithuania	33.6	1.2 million
Hungary	31.3	3.1 million
Poland	27.5	10.6 million
Turkey	22.5	16.0 million
Romania	22.0	4.9 million
Russia	16.8	23.7 million

Source: Internet World Stats; CIA Fact Book, 2007

Russia's low internet access is somewhat surprising. Of course, this is a huge country and usage is quite high in Moscow and St. Petersburg, about 30 percent. However, large populations live in rural areas, many hundreds of miles apart with sparse access to electricity or telephones. When you add the number of rural dwellers to urban populations, the usage percentage drops way down to 16.8 percent. Nevertheless, Russia's 23.7 million internet subscribers account for more than one-third of all Eastern European users.

E-commerce in Russia runs nearly $6 billion per year. B2B sales top out at 30 percent of this amount or about $1.8 billion. However, Russian e-commerce and B2B commerce are constrained by a lack of efficient online payment mechanisms. Although the use of debit and credit cards is increasing rapidly, many online merchants still refuse to accept them as payment. But this is not the biggest hurdle. The main constraint comes from consumers who refuse to use their plastic online for fear of theft. Instead, the preferred method of payment is cash payment on delivery. Still, the number of Russian web merchants has steadily increased to about 4,000 at last count, with home appliances and electronics as the biggest sellers. Online cosmetics sales are also growing very fast.

E-advertising is not popular in Russia. This isn't too surprising considering the low penetration of internet usage. In Moscow and St. Petersburg, internet ads are becoming more popular but certainly not as much as in rich countries. The most effective Russian advertising relies on print media, TV and radio, billboards, and trade shows. The country has a large number of magazines and newspapers that reach out to nearly all rural areas as well as cities. And trade journals are used extensively to advertise commercial products. Trade shows are also very popular. Aside from the traditional Russian preference of displaying products face-to-face with potential customers, trade shows provide everyone with an excuse to take time off from their dull everyday lives.

In fact, trade shows tend to be popular throughout Eastern Europe, probably because of tradition. After all, exhibiting at trade shows dates back to the Middle Ages. In addition to trade shows, the most effective advertising media in all countries combines the traditional ones—radio, TV, magazines, newspaper, and billboards. Telemarketing does not work, mainly because of the low percentage of households with landline telephones. E-advertising has yet catch on to any large extent in Eastern Europe, although ads do appear on many websites.

In Turkey, more than one-fifth of the population has access to the internet. However, except for banking, e-commerce has not caught on. Nearly 70 percent of all e-commerce relates to banking and financial services, although nonbanking companies are trying hard to get consumers interested. B2B is hardly ever used. E-advertising actively promotes airline ticketing, hotel accommodations, food delivery, clothing, and the old internet standbys—books, CDs, and DVDs.

LATIN AMERICA

Somewhat surprisingly, online commerce is growing faster in Latin America than anywhere else in the world. In 2007, estimates place total e-commerce at well over $120 billion in the region. B2B e-commerce amounts to about 95 percent of that total. Equally surprising is that retail sales account for such a tiny percentage. Several reasons explain why.

First, Latin Americans do not trust the internet. Second, the region's antiquated banking system constrains the use of credit cards as a payment medium. Third, most of the population prefers to shop in malls where they can see and feel the merchandise. Fourth, only a very small percentage of the region's population can afford a computer with internet access. And fifth, there aren't very many ISPs, hardly any broadband service companies, and only recently, the beginnings of a cable market. Surprisingly, a few smaller countries, such as Guyana, now have cable internet service that works almost as well as it does in the United States. Figure 19-3 shows a breakdown of internet usage by country.

Brazil, Mexico, and Argentina account for 80 percent of Latin America's 68 million internet users. Brazil is clearly the most advanced e-commerce user in the region. Almost 26 million internet users are online regularly, often using broadband. According to a study by Fundação Getulio Vargas, e-commerce in Brazil has more than doubled within the last two years. B2B sales account for about 20 percent of all commercial sales, and B2C accounts for about 7.5 percent of all consumer sales. In 2006, Brazilians spent more than $6.5 billion shopping online. The hottest selling products were books, magazines, newspapers, CDs, DVDs, and electronics. The average purchase totaled $140 with most buyers between the ages of 35 and 49. And the most popular website is MercadoLivre, Brazil's equivalent of eBay. Not only does this country have the largest business and consumer markets in South America, Brazil is also the most important advertising market.

FIGURE 19-3 Internet Users and Percent of Population (Latin America)		
Country	Percent of Population	Number of Users
Argentina	24.8	10.0 million
Chile	24.2	1.0 million
Costa Rica	24.2	1.0 million
Mexico	17.1	18.6 million
Peru	16.0	4.6 million
Trinidad and Tobago	15.2	160,000
Brazil	13.6	25.9 million
Colombia	10.6	4.7 million
Dominican Republic	10.0	938,300
El Salvador	9.2	637,100
Guatemala	5.9	756,000
Source: Internet World Stats; CIA Fact Book, 2007		

Brazilian online shoppers are much less concerned about credit card theft or other types of online fraud than shoppers in any other country. Perhaps the reason has to do with the uniquely Brazilian culture trait that one's social position is a direct result of the friends one has. This translates into a lot more trust in others than is the case anywhere else. As the Brazilians say, "Mais vale ter amigos na praça que dinheiro em caixa." (It is worth more to have friends in the marketplace than cash.)

Argentina and Mexico round out the trio of Latin American countries with the most internet usage. And prospects for growth are excellent. By 2011, Argentina is expected to have 13.1 million internet users representing 31.3 percent of its population. Mexico is projected to have 39.5 million users or 34.7 percent of its population. Brazil's forecast is 43.7 million internet users or 22.1 percent of its population.

B2B e-commerce gives companies the same advantages as in the United States—lower costs, smaller inventories, faster billing, and quicker payments. Also, sourcing new bidders is a lot easier and faster on the internet than trying to do so in country. B2C retailing might be viable, but only for a very small market of the elite class.

The development of e-advertising relates directly to the success of B2B and B2C commerce. As e-commerce sales increase, e-advertising becomes more effective. That's obvious. However, while this holds true in countries like Brazil, Argentina, Mexico, Chile, Colombia, and, to a lesser extent, a few Central American nations, the net will not be a major advertising medium for some time to come, especially not in Brazil. This country has a well-developed postal service, making direct marketing an excellent way to reach 35 million middle-class Brazilian consumers who get only about 10 percent of the amount of junk mail that Americans do. Commercial advertising in catalogs and at trade shows also works well in most Latin nations. Advertisers readily admit that old-fashioned TV, radio, and billboards work better than the internet. Even in Brazil, Mexico, and Argentina, these older advertising mediums are used extensively.

SOUTH AND SOUTHEAST ASIA

The emerging nations of Asia have far and away more internet users than any other less developed region. The 11 Asian countries in our study report

257.5 million users. Compare this to Eastern Europe and Latin America with 68 million users each or the Middle East with a paltry 19 million internet users. Figure 19-4 shows the breakdown by country.

Clearly, Asians love the internet. Hong Kong reports 70.2 percent of the population with internet access. Taiwan has 57.6, Singapore 52.2, and Malaysia 44.8. This compares with 68 percent internet access in the United States and 65 percent in Canada. Because of their huge populations, the largest number of internet users come from China and India.

Despite the huge number of Chinese who access the internet, e-commerce has not caught on. Big swaths of the population continue to ignore it. The main reason for this is that China is a cash-based society with very limited use of plastic. The small amount of e-commerce that is transacted must be paid for on delivery. Moreover, getting your net purchases delivered can be difficult since delivery systems are at best sketchy and unreliable. And strange as it seems, Chinese don't seem to be aware of the need for internet security software.

FIGURE 19-4 Internet Users and Percent of Population (Asia)		
Country	Percent of Population	Number of Users
Hong Kong	70.2	4.9 million
Taiwan	57.6	13.2 million
Singapore	52.2	2.4 million
Malaysia	44.8	11.1 million
China**	16.0	210.0 million
Thailand	12.9	8.4 million
Philippines	8.6	7.8 million
Indonesia	6.8	16.0 million
Pakistan	6.4	10.5 million
India	5.3	60.0 million
Sri Lanka	1.3	280,000
** Official Chinese government statistics released December 2007		
Source: Internet World Stats; CIA FactBook, 2007		

Notwithstanding these negatives, internet usage in 2007 was up 50 percent from the previous year. China had three times ore internet users than India. And 70 percent of Chinese internet users are under 30 years of age. Before the end of 2008, Morgan Stanley estimates that China will have more internet subscribers than the United States.

Even though a large number of people have access to the internet, a multitude of barriers severely constrain e-commerce. Until they can be knocked down, the internet is not a good medium for business transactions. It's great for research, games, blogs, and other applications—but not for commerce.

The Chinese government's tight control over the internet creates another, more insidious barrier. Blogs and certain websites, such as Wikipedia, that the Beijing government finds offensive have been blocked. And Google is filtered to keep out any material that the government deems offensive. This censorship smacks of the same callous approach as Arab countries and will certainly retard China's advance in the high-tech age of globalization.

Advertising in China is strictly regulated, just like the internet. Print, TV, radio, billboards, and internet advertisements must, and I quote from the Advertising Law of the People's Republic of China, "be good for the physical and mental health of the people" as well as "conform to social, public, and professional ethics and safeguard the dignity and interests of the state." That pretty well sums up what you can and cannot do in your ads. So what is the internet used for in China? You guessed it, to distribute pirated music, TV shows, films, and of course, games.

The internet isn't quite as popular in India as it is in China. However, 60 million people, mostly middle-class and located in the four major cities, clearly make this a viable marketing channel. The Internet and Mobile Association of India estimates that 35 million people shop regularly online. This is expected to increase to 100 million in a few years. B2C e-commerce amounted to $1.2 billion in 2007 with more than 440,000 transactions per month. Airline tickets, hotel accommodations, banking, and stock trading are very popular. Additionally, books, videos, jewelry, watches, electronics, and apparel sell well. Although B2B e-commerce is not as popular, industry experts expect this to increase substantially in the next few years.

Practically every known advertising medium in India is used, including the internet, movie theaters, billboards, TV, radio, and all types of print. The advertising industry is thriving, turning out $3.4 billion a year in revenues.

Newspapers are an especially lucrative media with many daily, weekly, monthly, and business publications.

As one would expect from a country as far advanced as Singapore, the internet is a viable media for e-commerce and e-advertising. If your product sells well on the net in the United States, chances are good it will sell well on the net in Singapore. Ad format is also similar to that of rich countries. Print, TV, radio, and the internet all seem to bring good results from both consumers and businesses.

Conversely, although the Malaysian internet is widely used, e-commerce has yet to find its niche. Only in the last few years have Malaysians begun to trust the internet. First came banking and then airline ticketing. Gradually, consumers and businesses are beginning to see the advantages of e-commerce. However, internet security remains a major concern.

Malaysia has several English-language newspapers and magazines. These are all good advertising media. Eight TV channels are also very popular, broadcasting in English, Mandarin, and Tamil. Extravagant product launches for consumer goods, similar to those used in rich countries, are the norm.

ARAB STATES AND ISRAEL

At the 2008 annual meeting of interior ministers from all Arab countries, the central issue was a discussion of the methods they would use to limit the freedom of the publishing, recording, and media distribution industries. In the past, each country had its own methods of dealing with such nefarious issues. Reporters, recording artists, and distributing agents that were deemed guilty of, and I quote a Syrian release, "disseminating false information" were either thrown in jail or killed.

However, since nonArab media permits countries to be scrutinized by the court of world opinion, such tactics won't fly any more. Instead, more subtle methods were called for, and new laws were passed. This frees Arab governments from criticism. It places the entire responsibility for enforcing the laws on the police—making them the bad guys—and lets the royal family and the bureaucrats off the hook. Instead of being jailed, reporters, artists, and distributors are now assessed exorbitant fines. Those who can't pay up are then thrown in jail. Such draconian censorship bites into the very fabric of commercial endeavors and is sufficient reason for many U.S. companies to defer from doing business in any Arab state. It also makes one hesitate to design any type of website or advertisement that might in any way infringe on or question the sagacity of Arab morality. Obviously, neither e-commerce nor e-advertising play major roles in Arab countries.

Israel leads the Middle East with 57 percent of its population having internet access. However, this amounts to only 3.7 million users, hardly enough to make e-advertising or even e-commerce websites economical. The few Israeli e-commerce transactions that do occur are mostly for the sale of electrical appliances and computer products, which account for 60 percent of net sales. Books, food, tickets for entertainment venues, and airline tickets are also sold online. Figure 19-5 shows the internet usage statistics by Middle East country.

Some e-commerce flows through Saudi Arabia but only a scant $150 million. High-speed DSL connections are available and several ISPs and internet cafés operate in Riyadh and Jeddah.

All Arab states are cash economies. Credit and debit cards are scarcely used. This means that the only way e-commerce can function is with COD deliveries or prepaid cash cards (similar to prepaid telephone cards) and these aren't popular. All told, don't be concerned about using the internet for business in any Middle East nation. It isn't worth the cost or the aggravation.

FIGURE 19-5 Internet Users and Percent of Population (Middle East)		
Country	Percent of Population	Number of Users
Israel	57.6	3.7 million
United Arab Emirates	31.5	1.4 million
Kuwait	27.9	700,000
Qatar	24.1	219,000
Morocco	13.6	4.6 million
Saudi Arabia	9.1	2.5 million
Oman	7.6	245,000
Egypt	6.2	5.0 million
Algeria	5.7	1.9 million
Source: Internet World Stats; CIA FactBook, 2007		

TV and radio are both excellent advertising media in Israel. In the Arab states, however, although many people have TV and radio, government restrictions on what can be broadcast limits the creativity of advertisements. Companies keep trying with satellite TV and internet blogs, but hyper-regulation and catch-all laws that intentionally misinterpret ads as well as hard news make truth in advertising a foreign concept.

That concludes our look at e-commerce and advertising. A few emerging nations have grasped the importance of the internet and enjoy rapidly advancing coverage and programming, approximating the usage in rich countries. Conversely, most emerging nations still operate in the Dark Ages, refusing to consider the net as a viable business tool or entertainment media. Then we have those governments, like China and the Arab states, who are afraid to allow their citizens to know the truth. They seem to think that banning programs and websites will somehow safeguard their minions from the immoral Western media. Perhaps some day this will change—but not in the foreseeable future.

chapter twenty
Moving Your Goods to Market

ALTHOUGH THE PRINCIPLES INVOLVED IN TRANSPORTING GOODS TO OVERSEAS customers are the same as those for shipping within in the U.S., the mechanics are entirely different, and the complexities much greater. Packing and labeling, shipping licenses and declarations, collection documents, and cargo insurance must be uniquely managed. Moreover, every country has special regulations for the inland transport of goods. Although the shipping and transportation practices described in this chapter generally apply worldwide, it's important to recognize that modifications will be necessary to comply with a given country's regulations and practices.

The following discussion assumes that you already have experience in the preparation of invoices, bills of lading, packing lists, and so on for domestic shipments. If you are unfamiliar with these documents, you can get sample forms from any freight forwarder.

FREIGHT FORWARDERS

Although experienced export shipping personnel can certainly handle the preparation and submission of export documentation, nearly all companies find that freight forwarders perform these tasks more efficiently and cost effectively. Freight forwarders act as shipping and transport agents of exporting companies. They serve as primary coordinators among exporting companies, shippers, bankers, customs officials, and a variety of other parties.

Freight forwarders prepare all the documentation necessary for shipping goods, insuring cargo, and collecting from a customer. They also provide information for bid packages. All licensed international freight forwarders are familiar with international letters of credit (L/Cs). When the L/C is prepared, a copy of it—and any special shipping instructions—goes directly to the forwarder, who then advises you on any special packing, labeling, and export/import licensing that may be required. Ocean forwarders are licensed by the Nonvessel Operating Common Carriers organization, and the International Air Transportation Association licenses air forwarders. Most freight forwarders handle both ocean and airfreight.

Although a complete compilation of services performed by freight forwarders is beyond the scope of this book, the following are their primary services:

- Research tariff rates and determine the most economical method of transport.
- Offer advice about current conditions in the buyer's country relative to dockage and airport facilities.
- Arrange for licenses, permits, certificates, consular invoices, legalizations, and other regulatory documents to satisfy U.S. laws as well as the laws of the country of destination.

- Make appropriate contacts for arranging inland transport to the port of embarkation in the U.S. and to the customer's location in the destination country.
- Consolidate shipments, including containerization, and then transport the goods to the appropriate carrier.
- Arrange for special crating, packing, loading, and unloading equipment.
- Receive a clean bill of lading or waybill consistent with L/C or shipping instructions.
- Prepare export declaration, customs clearance documentation, bank documents for L/C drawdowns, and claims against airlines or ocean carriers.
- Arrange for cargo insurance.
- Track the shipment to its destination.
- Provide communications and courier service during the entire transportation period.

As you can surmise, these services are not only valuable but also absolutely necessary if you don't have a full complement of experienced export shipping and transportation personnel.

In certain situations, you may want to retain control over customer collections. In that case, the forwarder sends all the documents to your office for verification before presentation to a bank. However, you will then be expected to track your own shipments on vessels leaving and arriving in various ports around the world. This is not difficult and can easily be done by following the announcements of arrivals and departures in the *Pacific Shipper* (www.pacificshipper.com), the *Journal of Commerce* (www.joc.com), and for the East coast, the *Shipping Digest* (www.shippingdigest.com.) The best way to locate a qualified freight forwarder is to ask other companies in your area or industry who have been exporting for a while. The following criteria will help you choose the right freight forwarder. A freight forwarder should:

- Be large enough to have clout with major shipping lines but small enough to give personal service. Forwarders that handle major corporations are often too busy to care about small accounts.

- ➡ Have a location near the U.S. port that you plan to ship from.
- ➡ Be willing and able to prepare all license applications, declarations, collection documentation, and customs forms.
- ➡ Maintain listings of import restrictions from foreign countries worldwide.
- ➡ Come highly recommended from the international department of your bank.
- ➡ Offer consolidation services.
- ➡ Be willing to hold meetings in your office rather than at the freight forwarder's office.
- ➡ Furnish references from other customers and permit them be to checked.
- ➡ Provide bank references and permit them to be checked.

GETTING PRODUCTS READY FOR SHIPMENT

Although freight forwarders perform a variety of services for their customers, you must do some things yourself. When getting your shipment ready for the freight forwarder, you need to use packing that will protect the cargo against moisture, breakage, or pilferage while minimizing the cargo weight; choose among unitizing, palletizing, and containerization; and create an appropriate exterior identification for the cargo.

While proper packing ensures the first step, the size of the product and the quantity of parcels dictates the second step. If your product involves hazardous material, this must be indicated on the external labeling.

Packing

A variety of packing materials and holding forms are available to protect goods against moisture and breakage. Their suitability in any given situation depends on the nature of the product. Fiberboard boxes continue to be the most popular type of exterior container for hard goods. They are relatively inexpensive, strong, and light weight. Proper support by tension straps, water-resistant glue and tape, and staples should prevent breakage in cartons with a test strength of at least 275 pounds per square inch. Impregnated, multiwall fiberboard boxes are usually impervious to moisture —except when submerged for extended periods. Moreover, fiberboard is one of the lightest weight materials around.

A wooden nailed box around fiberboard cartons provides added security and strength. The wooden box won't keep out moisture, but it will protect against breakage. However, weight is an important factor in overseas shipping, and wooden boxes are heavy.

Wirebound boxes and crates, cleated plywood boxes, drums, and kegs (steel, fiber, or wood) are good packing containers for heavy loads or granular, liquid, or gelatinous products. However, these containers add significantly to the shipping weight. Multiwall shipping sacks and bales are used primarily for agricultural, powdered, or granular products, especially dry chemicals. However, both bales and sacks are subject to moisture damage, pilferage, and breakage by lift hooks, so they should be containerized.

> **Although freight forwarders perform a variety of services for their customers, you must do some things yourself.**

Fragile or brittle goods must be cushioned against shock and vibration. The type of material chosen depends on the size, weight, surface finish, and built-in shock resistance of the goods. Any freight forwarder can advise you on the best holding form and material for a specific shipment.

Unitizing, Palletizing, Containerization

Whenever possible, try to use unitizing, palletizing, or containerization to facilitate the movement of goods and to protect the cargo during stowage. In shipping parlance, unitizing means the assembly of one or more items into a tightly compacted load, secured together with cleating or skids for ease of handling. Palletizing refers to the assembly of one or more containers securely fastened on a pallet base. Most overseas shipments of hard goods are either unitized or palletized. Both systems offer several advantages, such as:

- ➡ Manual handling damage is eliminated. Forklifts, cranes, and other mechanical devices must be used to move the load.
- ➡ Since the load is handled as a unit, individual packages are further protected from handling damage.
- ➡ Theft is reduced.
- ➡ Loading and unloading from the vessel is faster.
- ➡ Physical inventory counts are facilitated.
- ➡ Waterproof coverings are more easily attached.

To further protect against moisture, breakage, and pilferage use shipboard containerization. Shipboard containers are large, metal, freestanding enclosures that contain several unit loads or pallets. They can be stacked, saving space aboard ship. They are easily loaded and unloaded by cranes. They may reside dockside for long periods waiting for a ship or inland transport without damage to the enclosed goods.

Nearly all ocean freight vessels accumulate loads for containerization. Ideally, you'll fill one or more containers with your own merchandise. But this isn't necessary. Partial loads can be combined to save space and secure the loads with the approval of the vessels' captain. When goods from two or more shippers are consolidated in a container, they share loading and unloading costs. Freight forwarders normally arrange for shared containers.

Exterior Identification—Labeling

Your buyer will specify the type of labeling to be affixed to the exterior of the cartons, crates, or other shipping containers. These markings may be in pictorial form, stenciled, or marked with any other indelible ink process. Labels should be at least two inches high and appear on the top of the package and on at least one side. Sacks should be marked on both sides, and drums should be marked on both the top and side. The reasons for accurate labeling are probably obvious, but it can't hurt to review the major ones. Markings and labels must identify the following:

- ➡ Shipper, consignee, reference number, and contract or purchase order number.
- ➡ Country of origin.
- ➡ Weight in both pounds and kilograms.
- ➡ The number of packages, if there are more than one in the shipment.
- ➡ Handling instructions such as markings for fragile, this side up, store in heated place, and so on.
- ➡ Final destination and the port of entry (e.g., Guatemala City via Livingston).
- ➡ Whether the package contains hazardous material.

All labels and markings should be in both English and the language of the destination country. It's extremely important to label shipments according to the laws of the host country. Freight forwarders keep track of these constantly changing laws for every port in the world.

SHIPPING LICENSES AND DECLARATION

In international trade, shipping documents serve a far broader purpose than merely authorizing the shipment and providing a record of the transaction. All kinds of harmful conditions can occur when you don't pay close enough attention to the preparation of shipping documents. Without proper documentation, payment may not be received on time—or at all. The shipment may not clear customs at the destination port, which results in charges, fines, and penalties. The goods may be returned to the exporter, incurring additional freight charges and customs fees. In some ports, goods without proper documentation will be seized by custom officials and either kept by them or auctioned off.

> With a few exceptions, the United States has the most restrictive and rigid barriers to export trade of any nation.

There are three broad types of shipping documents: general export licenses, validated licenses, and export declarations. Some licensing activities are controlled by the Bureau of Export Administration (BXA) in close association with the Department of Defense and the Department of State. Licensing for the export of arms and related technologies en route to a restricted nation is controlled by a 40 nation agreement inaugurated in 1996 called the Wassenaar Arrangement on Export Controls for Conventional Arms and Dual-Use Goods and Technologies (www.wassenaar.org).

The primary purpose of licensing exports is to enforce export trade barriers. With a few exceptions, the United States has the most restrictive and rigid barriers to export trade of any nation. Intense lobbying by special interest groups ensures that many of these onerous restraints will remain in effect for an interminable time, at least until relations improve with Cuba, North Korea, Iran, Myanmar, and so on.

General License

One of the first steps in preparing shipping documents is to get a blanket permit from the BXA that allows the export of different types of goods to be shipped to a variety of countries. Any freight forwarder can file the application for you. Be sure to do it before finalizing a sales contract, so you can be certain that the goods to be shipped are not defined as strategic commodities. It's also necessary to determine that the buyer's country is not included as a sensitive destination. Approximately two weeks are needed for the application to wind its way through the approval cycle. Information about its status can be obtained from the Office of Export Licensing.

Validated License

A validated license authorizes the sale of particular goods to specific countries. It must be obtained for the export of goods as defined from time to time by Washington as strategic. It also permits exports to a country on the government's restrictive list. This license requires a lengthy and costly application and review process with both the Department of Defense and the Department of State in the approval loop. The normal time for processing an application through the entire approval chain is 120 days, although partial approvals can be obtained in less time. However, continuing shifts in world politics and U.S. trade policies influence changes in both the strategic product list and restrictive country classifications, creating wide variations in the time estimates. When you get ready to submit an application, call the Export Licensing office for the current status.

Special Licenses

Special licenses apply to specific situations. One type of special license is a project license that covers the export of all goods requiring validated licenses for certain large-scale construction or development projects. Another type of special license is a one-year distribution license. This is granted for exports to consignees in countries that maintain good relations with the United States. A third type, a service supply license, is required to provide services on equipment exported from the United States or produced abroad with parts imported from the United States.

Foreign Export Licensing

Each country has its own export trade barriers with various definitions of strategic goods and restrictions. Few developed nations are as paranoid as the United States about what can and can't be done. Traditional trading nations such as the United Kingdom and Japan realize that the well-being of the country depends on an active export program. Exporting from these nations, or even from less developed nations, usually involves substantially less paper work than exporting from the United States. Regardless of where your export facility is located, some type of licensing will likely be required. Contact your local trade or commerce office for details.

Shipper's Export Declaration

A shipper's export declaration must be completed for all shipments valued in excess of $1,000 and for which a validated license is required. An export declaration identifies the license funder from which the products are being shipped. It verifies that the shipment complies with authorization regulations. And the declaration shows appropriate U.S. government product codes, quantities shipped, the value of the shipment, and destination. The Census Department requires this data for its monthly statistical reports.

COLLECTION DOCUMENTS

Collection documents must be submitted to the importer, the importer's bank, and most likely, your bank before payment can be made. These documents vary from country to country, importer to importer, and bank to bank. Although a specific transaction will probably never require all of the following documents, various classes of shipments to different destinations usually require one or more.

- ➡ Commercial invoice. As with domestic sales, a commercial invoice follows every export shipment. Some countries require special certification to be incorporated with the invoice, often in the language of the host country. The Department of Commerce keeps a list of each country's requirements.
- ➡ Consular invoice. In addition to a commercial invoice, most emerging nations require a consular invoice prepared on forms supplied by their respective consulates. These invoices must be prepared in the language of the host country. They are visaed by resident consul, who certifies the authenticity and correctness of the documents.

➥ Bill of lading. Of the two types of bills of lading, straight (nonnegotiable) and shipper's order (negotiable), the latter is used for sight draft or L/C shipments. According to the set of internationally recognized trading terms as specified in the Guide to Incoterms, 2000 edition (issued by the International Chamber of Commerce), a bill of lading acceptable for credit purposes must be marked clean on board. This means that the carrier has not taken any exception to the condition of the cargo or packing and that the goods have been loaded aboard the carrying vessel. A bill of lading is the most important document accompanying a foreign shipment. It serves as (1) a contract between the carrier and the shipper, (2) a verification of the receipt of goods, and (3) an identification of the right of title to the goods. A signed copy of a negotiable bill of lading is sufficient evidence of ownership to take possession of the goods.

➥ Packing list. A packing list is even more important for overseas than domestic shipments. Very often customs officials at both the port of embarkation and the port of debarkation use the packing list to verify the type and quantity of goods in the shipment. The list should include a complete description of the goods being shipped.

➥ Certificate of origin. Some countries require a separate certificate stating the origin of the goods. This certificate is normally countersigned by a chamber of commerce member and visaed by the country's resident consul at the port of embarkation.

➥ Inspection certificate. Many buyers request an affidavit, called an inspection certificate, from the shipper or an independent agent that certifies the quality, quantity, and conformity of the goods as specified in the original order.

➥ Dock receipts, warehouse receipts, and so on. When a shipper's responsibility is limited to moving the goods to a warehouse or dock at the port of embarkation, buyers often request receipts from the storage company that the goods have been received and await further disposition.

➥ Certificate of manufacture. The manufacturing cycle for certain goods can be quite long. If a buyer intends to make a down payment or an advance payment before the goods are shipped, the manufacturer prepares a certificate of manufacture, which serves as evidence that the goods have been produced in accordance with the order and have been set aside awaiting shipping orders. As soon as payment and shipping orders are received, the goods ship.

➥ Insurance certificate. In cases where sellers provide cargo insurance, an insurance certificate must be furnished, indicating the type and amount of coverage.

For a small charge, freight forwarders will prepare any or all of these documents as required by a customer's order. Even large exporters rely on forwarders to take care of this voluminous paperwork. Obviously, you should do the same. Although the form of these documents varies among countries, the content remains roughly consistent. Since international freight forwarders know the special requirements of the U.S. Customs Service as well as the regulations of foreign countries, it only makes good sense to let them handle all paperwork chores.

MARINE CARGO INSURANCE

Coordinating payments, following proper shipping procedures, and reducing the amount of risk in a transaction are all essential ingredients of successful exporting. Regardless of the country of origin, all three elements must be managed efficiently to remain competitive. Insuring marine cargo may seem of minor importance relative to getting paid and reducing political risk, but companies that slight this area, more often than not, live to regret their inaction. Any number of mishaps can occur during an ocean voyage, and it is only prudent business to safeguard against the damage or loss of goods by purchasing adequate insurance. Piracy on the high seas is one mishap that should have been snuffed out long ago. But that's not the way life works.

Insuring marine cargo may seem of minor importance relative to getting paid and reducing political risk, but companies that slight this area, more often than not, live to regret their inaction.

Although an increasing amount of merchandise is shipped overseas by air, the high cost, weight, and size restrictions imposed by air carriers makes ocean shipping the predominant mode of transport for most products. Ocean shipments are exposed to several unique hazards. Damage or loss of cargo from fire, stranding, moisture, collision, rolling of

INSIGHT... A client of mine shipped a container of high-end furniture to Singapore. The ship's route took it across the South China Sea. One very dark night pirates attacked, disabled the entire crew, broke open several containers, and for reasons that have never been explained, stole some furniture and damaged others. By morning, some of the crew disentangled their bonds and contacted the local authorities, much too late, of course. Fortunately, my client had adequate insurance so the only loss was the time involved to reship the container.

the ship, or theft is a real possibility—in addition to piracy. Because of the dangerous nature of ocean shipping, the Carriage of Goods by Sea Act of 1936 (www.access.gpo.gov/uscode) strictly limits the liability of carriers to $500 per package. The only problem is that there is no agreement among carriers, shippers, insurers, and the court about the definition of a package. Still, the act remains in force, albeit frequently litigated.

Practically all ocean shipments should be independently insured against damage or loss. In fact, banks, most joint venture partners, private financing organizations, and government agencies require marine cargo insurance. Depending on the terms in the sales contract, either the importer or the exporter can arrange for insurance.

Types of Policies

There are two types of marine cargo insurance: specific or special policies written for each individual shipment or open policies covering all shipments by the insured as long as the policy is in effect. The first is used by infrequent exporters, the latter by everyone else.

With an open policy, the shipper must inform the underwriter of each shipment made, including all the particulars. Premiums are billed each month depending on the number of shipments reported. An insurance certificate issued by the underwriter evidences effective coverage for a specific shipment.

It is difficult to get an open policy directly from an underwriter until you have established a record of continuous and fairly substantial shipments.

Therefore, you'll probably have to purchase your insurance through a broker. Brokers know which underwriters are currently available to handle your shipment size to your customer's destination. Furthermore, since underwriters, not exporters, are responsible for the payment of brokerage fees, it won't cost your company a penny extra to use one.

Cost

Premiums for marine cargo insurance vary all over the lot and are based on the type of coverage, shipping routes, types of conveyances, nature of goods being shipped, and duration of the voyage. The best type of coverage for smaller exporters is an all-risk policy that covers loss or damage to cargo for any reason. You should also insure against losses warehouse to warehouse which means that coverage begins when the goods leave your shipping dock and remains in effect until the goods arrive at your customer's receiving location. Policies cover both marine and inland transport.

Losses of shipments made by aircraft and connecting conveyances can also be included in all-risk policies. Generally, premiums for airfreight coverage are substantially less than charges for ocean shipments because the risks of loss are lower and the time duration is shorter.

Limitations

All-risk policies generally exclude war risks but do cover losses resulting from strikes, riots, and civil commotion. The exception, of course, is for those countries or parts of the world where the likelihood of such losses is high. Premiums can then become exorbitant.

Additional limitations to cargo insurance generally include the following:

→ Losses due to the inherent nature of the goods being shipped for example, losses incurred because the goods deteriorated on the journey (perishable goods), because of improper packaging, or because of normal wear and tear.
→ Loss of market due to delays en route.
→ Shipments that are illegal. By definition, a shipment is only legal when it complies with the laws of the export country and any international agreements in effect at time of shipment.

INSIGHT... Cost, inconvenience, and complexities notwithstanding, you'd be foolish to ignore marine and door-to-door cargo insurance. This lesson was painfully learned by a client who shipped products to Guatemala for the first time. This small international contractor was installing a replacement turbine for a power station in the hills of Guatemala. Ignoring my advice to purchase an all-risk policy to cover door-to-door transport, he decided to insure only the ocean part of the voyage. The equipment reached the dock at Puerto Barrio safely. It was then offloaded onto several trucks for the long overland run to northwestern Guatemala. When the trucks finally arrived at the job site two weeks later, the contractor discovered that substantial damage had occurred to several turbine parts. A claim was first filed with the ocean carrier. The carrier turned it down flat claiming that the damage occurred during inland transport. Efforts to obtain reimbursement from the Guatemalan trucking company were frustrated when the trucking company claimed that the damage occurred onboard the ship. In the end, no amounts were recovered, and my client stood the cost of replacing the damaged equipment to the tune of $262,000.

There are many reputable marine insurance companies to choose from. CIGNA, for example, offers as complete a package as most companies. There are many others, however. Your freight forwarder can make helpful recommendations, an insurance broker can find an insurer, or you can select one yourself. Regardless of who does the selection, the following will help you qualify an underwriter. The underwriter should:

➥ Have an office in close proximity to your shipping location.
➥ Be willing to meet in your office.
➥ Offer a comprehensive package of marine, air, and overland cargo insurance, including an all-risk policy.
➥ Encourage the all-risk option.
➥ Not push for third party joint beneficiary.

- Offer competitive rate comparisons.
- Provide a claim procedure you can understand.
- Have representatives and adjusters stationed throughout the world.
- Provide financial statements and bank references.
- Encourage reference checking with other customers.

INTERMODAL SHIPPING

Today, intermodal shipping is as common as snow in New England. It hasn't always been that popular but having a single carrier responsible for door-to-door delivery, whether by ocean, air, truck, rail, or a combination of carriers, makes it much easier for a shipper to file claims and collect on those claims.

Large international carriers such as American President Companies and CSX actively market intermodal shipping to American exporters and importers. From a shipper's perspective, door-to-door transport solves a huge problem in determining where the loss occurred. An intermodal carrier assumes full responsibility regardless of which carrier does the actual transporting.

Unfortunately, not all American shipper's have bought into the intermodal way because of the structured transportation departments within large shipping organizations and the lack of cooperation among American ocean, rail, air, and truck carriers. Nevertheless, the favorable economics of integrated transportation, including less shipping time, single insurance coverage, and simplified rate tariff charges makes the concept viable.

Several trade organizations continue to actively sell the idea. These advocates have also encouraged carriers to restructure their organizations to handle intermodal shipping. The Intermodal Marketing Association, the National Railroad Intermodal Association, and the Intermodal Transportation Association all work diligently to find the right answers as dynamic transport conditions continue to change. All three organizations have merged into the Intermodal Marketing Association (www.intermodal.org).

Intermodal transport companies are well known overseas. Any U.S. company that exports from a foreign country, especially from an Asian facility, should either seriously consider sourcing an intermodal steamship line to carry their products or work through a broker/packager who can do the same.

AIRFREIGHT

Although ocean shipping remains the predominant form of transport for large cargo, it has some definite drawbacks. The high cost of cargo insurance and the risk of damaged goods in transit are two of the most difficult to cope with. The length of time it takes to move merchandise across the high seas could lead to disgruntled customers or market changes by the time the merchandise arrives. Multiple handlings during loading and unloading and lengthy dock storage increase the likelihood of damage or pilferage. Moreover, if you can't fill an entire shipboard container, you may have to share one with another shipper. That can lead to mixed merchandise, delaying receipt at the buyer's destination.

To overcome these hazards, try airfreight. Mergers and combinations of worldwide delivery services further enhances airfreight as a viable alternative. FedEx, UPS, DHL, and other couriers offer worldwide intermodal shipping. With their vast worldwide stable of inland transport contacts, each offers door-to-door service to most areas of the world. Some analysts believe that air cargo companies offering intermodal service could heat up the entire industry and jeopardize the role of freight forwarders. Maybe, but not likely. DHL, UPS, and FedEx have been in business for a long time, as have freight forwarders. Over the years, they have all learned to live together.

Even with the rapid, reliable service offered by many carriers, airfreight is still the most expensive way to ship products. Shipping containers must be small enough to fit on a Boeing 747 or an Airbus A-380. The goods must be relatively insensitive to low pressure and wide variations in temperature. The value of the products must be high enough to justify the significantly greater transport costs. The lack of capacity and competitors who can match the quick delivery schedules has made airfreight a seller's market and this tends to keep rates high. Nevertheless, for certain types of goods, airfreight can't be beaten.

Most reliable freight forwarders handle airfreight as well as ocean shipments. When choosing an air carrier, the same reliability criteria applied to ocean shippers should be used, and the same shipping and collection documentation is required.

chapter twenty-one
Trade Finance and Ensuring You Get Paid

WHETHER YOUR PLANS CALL FOR EXPORTING, OPENING AN OFFSHORE manufacturing plant or distribution center, or engaging in a joint venture, you will need financing. Countertrade is probably the most profitable way to finance a foreign direct investment and is explained in detail in Chapter 22. In this chapter, we'll strictly deal with the financing of exports, otherwise known as trade finance.

When selling to U.S. customers, you don't normally need to worry about helping them finance the purchase of your products. That's their business—not yours. But global trade adds a new dimension. As an exporter, you are expected to help customers get the financing to pay for your goods. And that's why trade finance is the key to profitable exporting.

More often than not, arrangements for trade finance that satisfy your customer's needs determine whether or not you even get the order. As a marketing tool, trade finance provides competitive advantage just as readily as price discounts, after-sale customer service, or free deliveries. Fortunately, many federal and state agencies, private organizations, and international banks stand ready with a variety of financing options. And customized trade finance strategies are crucial regardless of the country your customer resides in.

INSIGHT... A personal experience with a Malaysian customer demonstrates the importance of trade finance. A few years ago, I owned a manufacturing company that designed and produced a wide range of metal parts for the automotive after-market and for off-road construction equipment manufacturers. My marketing vice president romanced several contractors who were bidding on a massive industrial project outside of Kuala Lumpur. One company that he was especially interested in seemed to be in the driver's seat to win a major bid. This contractor also had strong political connections in the Malaysian government. I cautioned my vice president that we must be prepared to offer long-term financing for an order that would have shipments extending over four or five years. He disagreed and insisted that the contractor pay cash in advance for one-half of the order and open a straight letter of credit for the other half. The customer rebelled, and we lost the order.

You need to make trade finance an integral part of your marketing plan. It is just as important as product design, pricing, and customer service. Both public and private sector customers expect American exporters to help arrange financing for them to pay for the goods, mainly because these countries have very weak financial systems. In-country banks may be unable or unwilling to grant import credit. Export-import banks are either nonexistent or too small to finance larger import orders. Without homegrown bank support, customers must look to foreign exporters for trade finance. Moreover, your competitors stand ready to offer financial terms of various tenures, so you must do so as well.

In addition to financing, you'll need to take measures to ensure that your customer pays for the goods. Getting reliable credit references on a foreign customer can be very difficult—if not impossible. Even with a good credit reference, you customer may not be willing to pay. So what do you do? How can you be certain that you will get paid? Probably the easiest and least expensive way to do this is with credit insurance. You can get it to cover losses from customers who refuse to pay, political expropriation, breach of contract, and many other causes. While it is certainly possible to export without insurance, it doesn't seem prudent when coverage against practically any contingency is readily available at a reasonable cost.

In this chapter, we will explore a variety of trade finance strategies together with ways to guarantee the timely collection of customer accounts. Some methods are available only through U.S. government sponsored programs, some derive from state and city agencies, and others can be arranged through private means. To help organize the vast array of options, these finance strategies can be divided into four categories, according to the payment schedule negotiated in the sales contract:

1. Short-term strategies when payment terms are less than 180 days.
2. Intermediate-term strategies when payment terms run from six months to five years.
3. Long-term strategies when payment periods are greater than five years.
4. Countertrade strategies when customers cannot or will not pay in hard currency. (See Chapter 22.)

SHORT-TERM STRATEGIES

The most common forms of short-term trade finance, documentary letters of credit and bankers' acceptances, place the collection burden on banks. Occasionally, open account terms may be used, but this is the exception rather than the rule. Unless your customer has an excellent credit rating, is willing to securitize the transaction with accessible collateral, or you know the principals very well—and trust them—stay away from open account sales.

Documentary Letters of Credit

A documentary letter of credit (L/C) can be used to reduce the risk of non-payment or delay of payment. It is called documentary because the terms of the letter specify payment against the presentation of certain sales and shipping documents. Nearly all L/Cs used in international trade are documentary. Payment terms may involve *sight drafts* or *time drafts* or other demands for payment. Time drafts are also referred to as *usance drafts*.

L/Cs do not, in and of themselves, guarantee payment and should not be substituted for common sense credit judgment. The instructions embodied in the L/C determine the payment security. Therefore, specific instructions must be written into the L/C that payment will be made in compliance with the sales contract.

Letters of credit come in many forms and carry a wide range of provisions. They can be revocable or irrevocable, confirmed or advised, straight or negotiated, payable at sight or over an extended period of time, transferable, assignable, or restricted. They can be written to cover partial shipments, full shipments, or transshipments. An L/C can cover one shipment or it may be revolving, covering several subsequent shipments.

Regardless of other provisions, L/Cs should be irrevocable and confirmed by an American bank. (When I say an American bank, I include the U.S. operating branches of foreign-owned banks.) Irrevocable means that the issuer cannot change the terms of the L/C, and confirmed means that an American bank is obligated to make payment upon presentation of proper documentation. Proper documentation means bills of lading or other transport documents proving that the goods have been delivered as specified in the order. However, L/Cs must be properly prepared and executed to be valid. A bank will not honor an L/C unless all supporting documentation called for in the letter accompanies a payment request. The following is an example of what happens when payment is made against an irrevocable L/C confirmed by a U.S. bank:

1. After the exporter (USA Sales Inc.) and its customer (Moscow Markets, Ltd.) agree on the terms of a sale, Moscow Markets arranges for its bank, Chase, to open a letter of credit.

2. Chase prepares an irrevocable L/C in favor of USA Sales, including all negotiated instructions covering the shipment.

3. Chase sends the L/C to a USA Sales U.S. bank, Citibank, requesting confirmation.

4. Citibank prepares a letter of confirmation and sends it to USA Sales along with the L/C.

5. USA Sales carefully reviews all conditions in the L/C to be certain that the conditions agree with the negotiated terms. USA Sales' freight forwarder is then contacted to ensure that the shipping date can be met. (If USA Sales cannot comply with one or more of the conditions, Moscow Markets is immediately contacted to arrange new language for the L/C.)

6. USA Sales arranges with its freight forwarder to deliver the goods to the appropriate port or air terminal.

7. When the goods are loaded, the forwarder completes the necessary documents, including the bill of lading.

8. USA Sales or its freight forwarder presents the documentation to Citibank.

9. Citibank reviews the documents and, if they are in order, sends them to Chase for review and transmittal to Moscow Markets.

10. Moscow Market or its agent then uses the documents to claim the goods when they arrive in Russia.

11. On the date specified in the L/C, Citibank honors the draft that accompanies the letter of credit. As an alternative, Citibank discounts the draft for payment at an earlier date.

No matter how carefully we prepare L/Cs, errors that prevent payment seem to creep up. The following are the most common errors:

➡ Omission of clauses stating irrevocable or confirmed by a designated American bank.

➡ Misspelled name and/or address of exporter or customer.

➡ Credit insufficient to cover full cost of shipment, including forwarding fees, consular fees, insurance, inspection charges, and so on.

➡ Incomplete or inaccurate description of merchandise, prices, and terms of payment.

➥ Failure to allow for variations in shipping quantity due to shrinkage, damaged goods, and so on.

➥ Omission of the words about or approximately (which allows for a 10 percent variance) preceding the amount of credit.

➥ Marks and numbers on the invoice that differ from those on other documents.

➥ Wording in customer's draft different from that in the L/C.

➥ Inappropriate or incomplete markings on bill of lading that do not conform to L/C instructions.

➥ Bill of lading shipping date later than allowed in L/C.

➥ Failure of all drafts and other documents to carry a date prior to the expiration date of the L/C.

➥ Instructions in L/C different from those specified in the invoice.

Variations on Documentary Letters of Credit

There are many variations of a straightforward documentary letter of credit, far too many to be included here. However, the following are the most common options:

➥ Back-to-back L/Cs are used when vendors or subcontractors demand payment from the exporter before collections are received from the customer.

➥ Off-balance sheet credit extension is a variation on the back-to-back L/C theme. By extending off-balance sheet credit, a bank uses the exporter's general credit line, not the buyer's L/C as collateral, which permits the bank to issue new L/Cs directly to the exporter's vendors.

➥ Assigned proceeds can be used when an exporter desires to use a buyer's credit to raise working capital. This is achieved by assigning the proceeds from the buyer's L/C to companies that supply the exporter with parts and materials.

➥ Transferred L/Cs are used when exporters require that certain materials or products be shipped directly from their supplier to the foreign customer rather than relayed to the exporter's for inclusion in the complete order. Terms of payment, shipping instructions, insurance provisions, product markings, drawdown documentation, and all other terms and conditions stipulated in the L/C remain intact.

➡ Standby L/Cs are used as guarantees of performance or payment in lieu of bank guarantees. They are essentially unsecured lines of credit to customers.

When your customer does not have sufficient credit or capital to warrant the issuance of a confirmed, irrevocable L/C as immediate payment, other financing instruments can be used. A documentary banker's acceptance is one possibility.

Documentary Bankers' Acceptances

A documentary bankers' acceptance (BA) is an instrument that guarantees payment to an exporter directly from a customer's bank. This eliminates any risk of nonpayment thereby eliminating any credit risk for the exporter. The following is how a typical BA works:

➡ Colombo Electronics wants to buy a shipment of TVs, radios, and computers from U.S. Electronics but can't afford to pay in advance. Also, Colombo Electronics has not yet established its credit with U.S. Electronics.
➡ Colombo Electronics asks its Sri Lankan bank to issue a draft to U.S. Electronics for the full amount of the shipment based on Colombo Electronics credit record with that bank. The draft's payment date is set at two weeks after the shipment arrives in Colombo, Sri Lanka.
➡ Since the Sri Lankan bank knows that its customer is good for the amount of the draft, the bank "accepts" the draft on behalf of Colombo Electronics. The bank stamps the draft with its acceptance stamp and sends it to U.S. Electronics.
➡ U.S. Electronics takes the accepted draft to its U.S. bank and receives payment for the shipment. The U.S. bank then collects the amount from the Sri Lankan bank. In two weeks, Colombo Electronics settles the draft with its Sri Lankan bank.

Both sides win with bankers' acceptances. As an exporter, you get your cash immediately, while your customer conserves cash for the holding period.

One glitch may arise to invalidate the BA, leaving your bank and therefore your company holding worthless paper. This happens when your customer and the bank collude to defraud. Either the foreign bank doesn't exist, it is in financial default, or it doesn't have sufficient capital to match the draft. This is not a fiction. Each of these circumstances has actually happened. Therefore it is crucial to determine that your customer's bank is in fact good for the BA before you agree to ship products. Your U.S. bank should be able to verify this, or you could contact the International Chamber of Commerce for confirmation.

 International Chamber of Commerce, 38 cours Albert 1er, 75008 Paris, France; www.iccwbo.org

OVERSEAS BRANCHES OF U.S. BANKS

In addition to documentary drafts, L/Cs, and bankers' acceptances, you may be able to arrange customer financing directly from a U.S. bank. This can be a viable strategy when your bank has branch offices or a line of credit with a bank in your customer's country. In this case, the bank's U.S. office and its foreign branch office work in tandem to grant import L/Cs for host country companies. Such credit lines are usually secured by guarantees or insurance from Ex-Im Bank (www.exim.gov) or from other commercial and political risk insurers. Your customer may also be able to arrange financing with its own bank if it has offices in the United States.

GETTING PAID

After arranging financing for customers, it's only prudent to ensure that you get paid. Since, in practical terms, you have virtually no legal recourse in the United States if your foreign customer breaches a sales contract, other collection methods must be in place.

Before making the first shipment be sure to verify your customer's credit rating. Fortunately, several organizations, both federal and private, offer credit reports on foreign customers. Be aware, however, that credit reports on foreign companies tend to be outdated and inaccurate.

This is where the U.S. Commercial Service (USCS) can be very helpful. The USCS is the promotion arm of the International Trade Administration. One of its missions is to help U.S. small and midsize exporters. In addition to other assistance, the USCS will provide you "with an opinion as the to viability and reliability of the overseas company or individual you have selected as well as an opinion on the relative strength of that company's industry sector in your target market."

It does this by issuing International Company Profile (ICP) background reports. These reports include:

- A detailed credit standing on prospective customers, potential sales representatives, or prospective partners.
- A listing of a company's key officers and senior management.
- Banking and other financial information about the company.
- Market information, including a company's public record sales and profit history.

Dun & Bradstreet (www.dnb.com) and a few smaller credit bureaus provide reports on larger companies, but they are not necessarily reliable or current. Commercial banks are a better source of credit reports. All major banks maintain their own credit departments and chances are good that your bank can get credit information on virtually any customer who has purchased goods within the last few years from an American company. You can also get a credit report online from an English company, International Company Profiles. They are a good resource for information about customers in Eastern Europe and Russia.

> Be aware that credit reports on foreign companies tend to be outdated and inaccurate.

International Company Profiles, 6-14 Underwood Street, London N1 7JQ; www.icpcredit.com

Ex-Im Bank's Credit Insurance

In addition to checking credit reports, it makes sense to purchase credit insurance. Insurance against both political and commercial risk is available from private carriers or from Ex-Im Bank. Ex-Im Bank issues five types of policies that cover a wide range of risks, including expropriation, customer's failure to pay, and currency fluctuations. The following is a breakdown of the policies:

- New-to-export policies for short-term credit sales of companies just getting started in exporting.

➡ Umbrella policies that are available only to export agents such as EMCs and ETCs who administer single policies on behalf of multiple exporters.

➡ Multibuyer policies for companies who export to several buyers in the same country.

➡ Short- and medium-term single buyer policies that cover several exporting companies shipping to a single buyer, such as a government agency or a state-owned electric company.

➡ Operating lease policies that cover lease payments and the value of leased products.

Private Insurance Companies

Of the few private insurance companies that sell export policies, AIG World-Source (www.aig.com), a subsidiary of American International Group, is probably the most active. It insures against expropriation, money transfer loss, and contract repudiation by foreign governments. It also sells performance bonds required in bidding arrangements.

FCIA Management Company (www.fcia.com), a wholly owned subsidiary of Great American Insurance Company, is another comprehensive insurer of all types of potential export losses. At one time, FCIA was a subsidiary of Ex-Im Bank, but in the early 1990s, it was spun off to the private sector. Between FCIA and AIG WorldSource, you should be able to get all the export coverage you'll ever need.

INTERMEDIATE-TERM STRATEGIES

When a sales order calls for payments that extend over periods of 180 days to 10 years, intermediate-term financing is necessary. Although both the Private Export Funding Corporation (PEFCO) and Ex-Im Bank provide inter-mediate-term financing, their strong suit is funding long-term orders. Inter-mediate-term orders can be financed more effectively with forfaiting, factoring, leasing, or alternative transaction financing.

Forfaiting

Would you like to negotiate a sales contract with payment terms well beyond one year, and perhaps as much as 10 years, without the risk or attendant problems of collecting against a dated letter of credit; get paid 100 percent of the selling price when the shipment is made; and have your customer pay all the financing costs? If this sounds appealing, you may want to look into forfaiting, a relatively new technique in the United States that has been used by European exporters for years.

The middleman in a forfaiting transaction is a forfaiter, which is a specialized type of bank or lending institution that deals in the nonrecourse financing of export sales. Several nonbank organizations offer forfaiting services, as do a half dozen or so U.S. money center banks and virtually all European and Canadian banks. None of these institutions, however, forfait short-term orders. The forfaiting process is best suited for customers that need medium-term credit from three to eight years but cannot obtain buyer credit from other sources.

Forfaiting is also popular when direct buyer credit is too complex to arrange; export credit insurance is not available; competitors offer forfaiting; or buyers insist on fixed-rate financing to close the order. Export orders can be as large as $50 million or as small as $50,000. The forfaiting procedure is relatively simple. The following is an example of how it works:

1. A customer seeking intermediate-term credit negotiates with an exporter a series of notes, drafts, bills, or other instruments. These documents will be used to pay off balances due the exporter over the term of the transaction.
2. The exporter then contacts a forfaiter, and the forfaiter and the customer negotiate with a bank, usually the customer's bank, to guarantee the customer's note, draft, or bill. The simplicity of this transaction has great appeal to both bankers and customers because no contracts are involved that could require litigation in the event of default.
3. Finally, when the exporter presents the forfaiter a complete set of documentation, the forfaiter releases the funds.

Forfaiting has four broad advantages:

1. It provides medium- to long-term financing when short-term credit doesn't work.
2. It covers the entire sale, not just 85 percent of the contract value, which is the maximum covered by Ex-Im Bank.
3. It costs less than borrowing from a commercial bank.

4. In its simplest form, forfaiting is very much like traditional accounts receivable factoring, except that forfaiting requires a bank guarantee from the customer.

Forfaiting isn't for everyone. But if it fits your needs, it is one of the fastest and cheapest ways to finance a medium-term export order. Forfaiting transactions are mostly handled by European financial institutions. However, a few have sprung up in the United States. Trade and Export Finance Online

Forfaiting isn't for everyone. But if it fits your needs, it is one of the fastest and cheapest ways to finance a medium-term export order.

(www.tefo.org) can help you find a forfaiter, provided you are located in California. Its website also carries a very good description of the pluses and minuses of forfaiting. Standard Bank of South Africa (www.standardbank.co.za) has a forfait department and a New York branch office. The London Forfaiting Company (www.forfaiting.com) has been active in forfaiting for many years. It was recently taken over by the First International Merchant Bank of Malta, which has expanded its U.S. forfaiting activities. British American Forfaiting Company is one of the more active U.S. forfaiting houses. This company will forfait transactions over $100,000, and you can get a quote by completing a form on the company's website. If all else fails, you can get names and contact information of forfaiters from the International Forfaiting Association.

British American Forfaiting Company, 1 The Pines Court, St. Louis, MO 63141; www.british-americanforfaiting.com and International Forfaiting Association, P.O. Box 432, CH-8024 Zurich, Switzerland; www.forfaiters.org

Export Factoring

Most people are familiar with factoring domestic receivables and the stigma of financial difficulties that attach themselves to it. Export factoring brings far greater benefits without the stigma. Export factoring does, however, involve selling receivables at a discount, usually 70 to 90 percent of the invoice value. But once this is done, your company is off the hook for any collection default. In other words, the factor assumes commercial risk and political risk. Export factors also provide a variety of other services including credit investigations, bookkeeping functions, monthly reports issued to the exporter, and a choice of payment cycles.

If export factoring seems like a viable option, your best bet is to contact one of the following international factoring organizations through their web-sites to get the names and addresses of reputable export factors in your area:

➥ Factors Chain International (www.factors-chain.com) is a global network of leading factoring companies, whose common aim is to facilitate inter-national trade through factoring and related financial services. This network claims to represent 206 factors in 59 countries. These factors presumably handle more than 50 percent of the world's cross-border export factoring.

➥ International Factors (www.ifgroup.com) is an international factoring association with around 78 members in 50 countries.

➥ First Commercial Credit (www.firstcommercialcredit.com) is a large factor house that also does other types of trade finance.

Leasing

Leasing is another viable way to finance the sale of capital goods. Although primarily used for intermediate-term orders, leasing applies equally well to orders with payment terms that extend beyond 10 years. International leasing is not straightforward, however. It involves a wide range of legal and tax peculiarities, such as customs and contractual requirements, collateral rights, foreign tax laws, creditor/debtor rights, government expropriation risks, and other matters unique to each country.

Cross-border leasing works well for transactions between large exporters and large customers, usually government-owned businesses, but is too complex for smaller companies. If you're interested in exploring leasing as a means of financing the export of capital goods, check out both U.S. and European multinational banks. Most of them have international leasing divi-sions or subsidiaries. Also, here are three companies that can help you structure international leases independent of banks.

➥ eLease International Inc. (www.eleaseinternational.com)
➥ LeaseForce International (www.leaseforce.com)
➥ mosaic International (www.mosaicleasing.com)

Alternative Transaction Financing

The reluctance of commercial banks to look beyond a company's balance sheet to determine its creditworthiness has opened the door to a variety of nonbank organizations that specialize in trade finance. These organizations finance individual export transactions rather than entire companies. In other words, their level of interest is determined by the viability of a specific export order, not by a company's profitability or debt to equity ratio.

Some of these transaction finance organizations are outgrowths of state foreign trade programs while others are privately owned by manufacturing, shipping, distribution, or trading companies. Still others are subsidiaries of major international commercial and investment banks.

Transaction finance is ideally suited to companies that are entering new markets, partnering with new foreign suppliers or customers, investing in new inventory for seasonal reasons, or to restocking a single customer. Transaction finance also applies to companies who need to finance large, single export orders while leaving current borrowing facilities intact. It works well in tandem with export factoring, especially when factor houses cannot handle staggered payments.

Most private sector transaction finance organizations specialize in a particular form of trade credit or in specific industries. They offer a variety of finance services, including factoring, forfaiting, foreign exchange management, loans, and equity contributions (primarily for companies interested in establishing maquila plants). Check out Creative Capital Associates based outside Washington, DC (www.ccassociates.com) or InterNetLC.com (www.internetlc.com) based in California. Alternately, get the names of transaction finance organizations in your area from your state export trade promotion bureau or a money center bank.

SMALL BUSINESS ADMINISTRATION

Export financing assistance from the SBA Office of International Trade (www.sba.gov) encompasses three programs: (1) SBA Export Express, (2) the Export Working Capital Program, and (3) the International Trade Loan Program.

Bank loans through the SBA Export Express guarantee program can be used for several purposes:

- Financing export development activities such as participating in a foreign trade show or translation of product literature.
- Revolving lines of credit for export purposes.
- Standby LCs used as bid or performance bonds on foreign contracts.
- Transaction specific financing associated with the completion of actual export orders.
- Acquiring, constructing, renovating, improving, or expanding facilities and equipment to be used in the United States for the production of goods or services for export.

For qualified exporters, the SBA will guarantee 85 percent of bank loans of up to $150,000 and 75 percent of loans between $150,000 and $250,000. But you have to negotiate loan terms with your bank, within the restrictions imposed by the SBA, of course. Banks may charge up to 6.5 percent over prime rate for loans of $50,000 or less and 4.5 percent over prime for loans over $50,000. These are pretty steep rates, and you can probably do a lot better by shopping banks. The good news is that maturities generally run 5 to 10 years for working capital loans and 10 to 15 years for equipment loans. That's hard to get from a bank without a third party guarantee.

Export Working Capital Loan Program

The SBA's Export Working Capital Loan (EWCL) program is a handy way to finance export sales when you have already reached your borrowing limit with your bank. Under this program, the SBA guarantees up to 90 percent of the loan amount up to $1 million for exports comprised of either a single transaction or multiple transactions on a revolving basis. When an EWCL is combined with an SBA International Trade Loan, the guarantee can be up to $1.25 million. EWCL financing can be used for:

- Purchase of finished goods or other inventory for export.
- Preexport costs of labor and materials used in the manufacture of goods to be exported.

➥ Cost of U.S. labor and overhead for service company exports.

➥ Standby letters of credit used for bid or performance bonds.

➥ Foreign accounts receivable for exports sold on open account.

The SBA charges a guaranty fee of one-quarter of one percent on the guaranteed portion of the loan for maturities of 12 months or less. It insists on the following loan collateral:

➥ A first lien on all items financed by the EWCL, including export inventory and foreign receivables.

➥ The assignment of proceeds from L/Cs, documentary collections, and foreign accounts receivables.

➥ Personal guarantees of key principals or owners of 20 percent or more of the exporting company.

International Trade Loan Program

SBA guarantees under the International Trade Loan (ITL) program can be as high as $1.25 million in combined working capital loans and facilities and equipment loans. Either the working capital portion or the fixed asset portion can be up to $1 million, but the two cannot exceed $1.25 million. Maturities of up to 10 years apply to working capital loans and maturities up to 25 years apply to fixed asset loans.

Proceeds under the ITL can be used for the purchase or renovation of buildings and equipment located in the United States and used to produce export goods. The working capital portion can be transaction specific or permanent. Coverage is 85 percent on loans up to $150,000 and 75 percent on loans between $150,000 and $1.25 million.

LONG-TERM STRATEGIES

There are three federal government related sources of long-term trade finance: The Private Export Funding Corporation, Ex-Im Bank, and Department of Agriculture programs. In addition, several states and cities have started export finance and development agencies that operate in conjunction with Ex-Im Bank's City-State Partners Program.

Private Export Funding Corporation

The Private Export Funding Corporation (PEFCO) (www.pefco.com) is owned by several U.S. banks and large corporations and is closely associated with Ex-Im Bank. PEFCO's mission is to bridge the gap between Ex-Im Bank's long-term financing and short-term bank instruments. Loans are given directly to foreign buyers of U.S. exports or to intermediary financial institutions (e.g., local development banks) for on-lending to foreign buyers. Although financing packages with unique interest rate and repayment terms can be structured on a case-by-case basis, nearly all require Ex-Im Bank guarantees.

PEFCO is considered a supplemental lender. As such, it enters a transaction only when financing is not available from traditional sources. Its principal contribution to the world of exporting has been that it can make long-term loans with fixed interest rates during periods of tight credit. PEFCO loans range from $1 million to well over $100 million. Applications are be made through your commercial bank.

Ex-Im Bank

Although the trade finance options discussed so far may be all you need to close an order, in the end, you might have to consider Ex-Im Bank. Ex-Im Bank goes beyond what banks can do and offers both medium- and long-term trade finance. Officially, any U.S. exporter of any size, in any industry can utilize Ex-Im Bank services. In practice, however, Ex-Im Bank is more responsive to larger manufacturing companies. I have known a few smaller exporters who have used Ex-Im Bank, but usually this government agency requires far too much excess collateral from small businesses.

The main programs offered by Ex-Im Bank follow:

- ➡ Pre-Export Financing. These are guarantees to commercial banks or other lenders specifically for working capital loans used to produce export orders.
- ➡ Credit Insurance. Export credit insurance guards against nonpayment by a foreign customer.
- ➡ Buyer Financing. Ex-Im Bank will extend loan guarantees covering 100 percent of the loan principal and interest for qualified buyers. It will also

make direct loans to buyers. The loans cover 75 percent of the contract price after a 15 percent cash down payment by the buyer.

➡ Structured and Project Financing. Ex-Im Bank offers direct loans and loan guarantees to international buyers specifically for the construction and operation of infrastructure and other projects with terms extending to 14 years.

➡ Transportation Equipment Financing. Specifically geared to financing exports of airplanes, locomotives, rolling stock, ships, and trucks. Includes special requirements such as asset-based leases. Terms extend to 14 years.

Although Ex-Im Bank offers direct loans and loan guarantees throughout the world it is currently very active in Brazil.

U.S. Department of Agriculture

Through its Foreign Agricultural Service (FAS) (www.fas.usda.gov), the Department of Agriculture administers several specialized assistance programs for the export of agricultural products. Programs vary, depending on the specific product being sold. To find out about financing assistance that matches your requirements, visit the FAS website.

City-State Partners Program

Ex-Im Bank's City-State Partners Program was designed to help new-to-export companies cut through federal red tape by using city, county, and other local export finance and development agencies. These agencies provide export loans and guarantees to businesses located within their jurisdictions.

In addition, many city and state agencies that cooperate in this program offer export seminars and technical support. According to Ex-Im Bank promotions, "this makes exporting more accessible and creates less confusion and wasted time for local banks." Although each city and state promotes slightly different programs, they all have the same objective—to involve more companies and lenders in export trade.

EXPORT ASSISTANCE CENTERS

For many years, small business exporters had to search out different federal government offices for each type of export assistance—Ex-Im Bank, the SBA, U.S. Department of *Commerce, and so on. That is no longer the case. Now the government has responded to the needs of smaller companies by putting all its resources in one location, an Export Assistance Center. These one-stop shops are located in Atlanta, Baltimore, Boston, Charlotte, Chicago, Cleveland, Dallas, Denver, Detroit, Miami, Minneapolis, Newport Beach, New York City, Philadelphia, Portland, Oregon, Sacramento, Seattle, and St. Louis. (See Appendix A for contact data.) At these centers you can learn about the government programs aimed at helping U.S. companies export. The services are free.

I would like to be more positive about these centers than I am. Some of them are extremely helpful and warrant your support. Unfortunately, as is true with all government bureaucracies, while some Export Assistance Centers are excellent, others are not so helpful. The good news is that personnel at these centers tend to turnover rather quickly, so if you have not received a warm welcome in the one nearest your facility, try again in a few months. You may be surprised.

chapter twenty-two
Countertrade as a Last Resort

COUNTERTRADE IS ONE OF THOSE ESOTERIC SOUNDING TERMS THAT DESCRIBES a very basic concept: the exchange of goods, services, and perhaps currency, for other goods or services. The most common form of countertrade, barter, has been used to transact business between two parties since caveman days. In the modern world, more convoluted countertrade techniques have evolved, but they all have one common element—paying for merchandise or services mostly with goods or services of equal value.

In some cases, currency payments form part of the transaction. In other cases, currency payments may be made by third or fourth parties, far removed from the original transaction. In all cases, however, countertrade transactions create their own financing, independent of a company's balance sheet or outstanding debt obligations. In this sense, countertrade is one of the original transaction financing mediums.

The opening of foreign markets with very low hard currency reserves has fostered a rebirth of countertrade, once the sole domain of military hardware suppliers. Today, it is almost impossible to develop emerging market strategies without including countertrade as a viable marketing and financing tool.

For the most part, countertrade is a relatively new concept in the United States. U.S. regulatory bodies are generally opposed to the technique, refusing to officially sanction it, although in a free market economy they can do little to stop it. The Securities and Exchange Commission, the Internal Revenue Service, and the Justice Department have yet to figure out how to write rules to control this strange beast. And the American Institute of Certified Public Accountants seems befuddled by the nonconformity of countertrade with generally accepted accounting principles. Fortunately, enough powers in Washington recognize that for American firms to compete in world markets, countertrade is a necessity. Desultory regulations that some would like to impose have so far been avoided. Undoubtedly, as American industry begins to accept countertrade as a beneficial tool, public and private regulatory organizations will devise methods for coping with it. During the current transition period, however, further confusion and misunderstandings can be expected.

Nevertheless, to effectively compete in emerging markets, you must learn to use countertrade techniques as an alternative to straightforward marketing channels and financing instruments. With that in mind, this chapter looks at various countertrade techniques and the pros and cons of getting involved in these highly complex, potentially expensive but very effective transactions.

FORMS OF COUNTERTRADE

I'm sure you'd agree that you would prefer hard currency as payment for any export sale. However, to compete, it is sometimes necessary to negotiate countertrade arrangements specifically suited to a given customer. Moreover, if a joint venture seems appropriate, the odds are high that some form of countertrade arrangement will take place, if for no other reason than your partner has used it before and likes it.

What, then, is countertrade? Countertrade is a contractual arrangement that links exports from one country and imports to another country with the limited use—or no use—of currency. Although many people have tried to define countertrade more succinctly, it defies pigeonholing. *Barter, offsets, compensation, coproduction, counterpurchase, compensating trade, switch trade, evidence accounts,* and *buybacks* are all terms used to describe various forms of the same concept—giving up something of value, usually exported products, in exchange for something else of value, usually cash, plus other products or services.

For many years, countertrade was the exclusive domain of military hardware suppliers. Lockheed, Boeing, Grumman, General Dynamics, and so on used countertrade to sell airplanes, guns, and ships to foreign buyers. Selling into currency poor countries in Africa encouraged global pharmaceutical companies to use countertrade in place of currency. Today, the top five countertraders in the world are Lockheed Martin, Boeing Ventures, British Aerospace, the European ABB Structured Finance division of ABB, and Siemens KFU. For many

Although many people have tried to define countertrade succinctly, it defies pigeonholing.

years economists attributed 40 to 50 percent of all global trade to some form of countertrade. In 2003, *FDI Magazine* quoted the United Kingdom's minister for international trade, Baroness Symons, as claiming that this ratio was closer to 10 to 15 percent of world trade. Interviews that I have had with several marketing and financial executives of American, Latin American, and European companies indicate that countertrade accounts for more than half of all global trade and significantly more than Latin America. Which ratio is correct? Apparently, that's anyone's guess. However, it seems clear that in many parts of the world, the use of countertrade as a primary marketing tool rather than a financing technique is becoming more popular every year.

As José Luis Yulo, president of the International Association of Trading Organizations of Developing Countries, stated at a countertrade conference, "No one denies that it [countertrade] is not as efficient a system as the free, multilateral system. No one denies that it is complex, risky, and sometimes costly. No one denies that it is not everyone's cup of tea. However, most people agree that it is a rational and practical approach to difficult international economic circumstances, such as lack of foreign exchange, protectionism, and structural limitations facing many developing countries in the global economy."

Countertrade contracts vary with each deal and from customer to customer—the form and content limited only by the imagination of the parties involved. Some contracts involve only the exporter and customer. Others involve third or even fourth parties. They may entail payment entirely in goods or services, or payment partly in goods and services and partly in cash. The cash portion may be denominated in the currency of the buyer or the exporter. Moreover, a contract may require additional services to be performed either by the exporter or buyer beyond the mere delivery of goods. The many variations of countertrade can be viewed under several broad headings.

Barter

Barter is the oldest form of countertrade and involves exchanging one type of goods or services for another. The amount exchanged from each party is determined by negotiation, and no invoicing or exchange of money takes place. Obviously, both parties must either be able to use the goods or sell them at a profit.

Compensation

Compensation is merely a variation on the barter theme. In this case, the exporter is paid a combination of goods and currency, with the currency denominated either in U.S. dollars or in the buyer's home currency. In the latter case, of course, the exporter must either convert the soft currency to a hard currency or use it in the buyer's country. As with straightforward barter, the exporter must either use the exchanged goods internally or sell them, usually through a countertrade broker.

Parallel Trade

Parallel trade involves two separate contracts, one for the export sale and one for the purchase of goods from the buyer. Two contracts are mandatory if you buy export insurance or finance sales through a bank because both insurance underwriters and financing institutions want to be able to enforce each side of the transaction separately.

Counterpurchase

Counterpurchase is one of the terms used to describe a parallel trade arrangement involving actual cash transfers. Under such an arrangement, the exporter and customer each pay the other for the goods received with drafts, letters of credit, or wire transfers. These payments may be in one currency, or they may be denominated in the home currency of each party. Many Latin American countries encourage counterpurchase arrangements as a way to balance imports and exports as well as stabilize their currencies and control inflationary pressures.

Offsets

Offset transactions, a more complex form of parallel trade involves a third or even a fourth party to the transaction. Exchanged goods then come from a supplier other than the exporter's customer and often from a different country altogether. Most offset transactions involve a corporate seller and a sovereign purchaser. Products are typically large, highvalue items, such as aircraft, military hardware, or infrastructure equipment like turbines, boilers, smelting furnaces, and so on. Large volume purchases of pharmaceuticals from Big Pharma companies have also been made through offsets, mainly by African governments. The deal typically involves a package of transactions carried out over a defined period of time and theoretically compensates the importing country for loss of jobs, currency, and the development of similar technologies within the buyer's country.

Offset transactions can be very convoluted. Here is how one might be structured:

➡ Assume you want to sell mining equipment to the Peruvian government, which doesn't have enough hard currency to pay for it.

➡ Your company agrees to finance the building of a state owned fertilizer plant in Peru in exchange for a 40 percent equity interest.

➡ Fertilizer is then exported to Argentina for Argentine pesos, which are used by the Peruvian government to pay you for the mining equipment.

➡ Your company uses the Argentine pesos to pay operating expenses in your Buenos Aires plant. This plant produces components for your mining equipment, which is assembled in the United States.

Everyone wins in this kind of deal. The Peruvian government creates jobs, foreign exchange, and a viable industry. Most of the funding for the building of the fertilizer plant comes from the U.S. Agency for International Development. As the fertilizer business grows, you should reap profits from your 40 percent equity ownership. And, of course, you succeed in closing the original export order.

Buybacks

Buyback arrangements are quite common for the sale of technology, licenses, production lines, or even complete factories and are frequently used to import subassemblies, components, or parts back to the United States for assembly into finished products. Buyback products can also be sold on the open market. When you export parts or components to a foreign customer, you usually receive payment (in full or in part) in the form of products manufactured in the new facility or using the new license or technology.

Buyback arrangements are especially popular for *turnkey infrastructure projects*. Here is an example of how a turnkey infrastructure transaction might be structured as a buyback:

➡ The customer first pays you for the project with government backed long-term credit.
➡ As the exporter, you then agree either to buy back products or services from the completed facility or serve as a distributor for products exported from the host country to your U.S. warehouse.
➡ The host country buyer uses these hard currency payments to liquidate the original long-term credit.

In a variation on this scheme, no cash changes hands and no credit arrangements are necessary. The countertrade contract merely states that the output from the newly constructed facility will be applied to the original price of the exports. However, with this type of arrangement you should insist on a bank guarantee to be certain that the output from the new facility will be produced and shipped on schedule.

Coproduction

Coproduction is a specialized form of buyback countertrade used principally for the transfer of technology or management expertise. The following example describes a typical coproduction arrangement:

- Assume that you want to sell desktop printers in Thailand.
- A Thai company wants to purchase the printers but also wants the technology to produce them at home in the future.
- Your two companies form a joint venture to build a suburban Bangkok plant to manufacture the printers.
- Your company takes an equity interest in the Thai project and may also furnish management support to run the facility. In either case, the facility is usually co-constructed between you the exporter and your customer.

Since both parties remain responsible for the operation of the facility, manufacturing the printers is known as coproduction. The benefits of such as arrangement are that:

- With equity interests, both parties profit from printer sales.
- The Thai customer gains new technology.
- Most importantly, you have made an export sale.

To avoid any misunderstanding, I'd like to clarify one point. The terms used in countertrade—*compensation, counterpurchase, coproduction,* and so on—are not essential to the structuring of a countertrade deal. You can call the deal whatever you want, as long as it benefits both your company and your customer.

Making countertrade deals is never easy. Many long-term benefits and risks need to be considered. Because of financial, contractual, and administrative complexities, countertrade should only be used when more conventional arrangements for closing an order are not practical.

Although certainly not inclusive, the following guidelines provide a good starting point for minimizing countertrade risks:

1. Establish a risk threshold that is measurable in terms of money expended, time required, and administrative difficulty. Beyond this threshold, the transaction will become uneconomical and should be terminated.
2. Identify a countertrade broker capable of selling the exchanged goods.
3. Insist on adequate shipping and collection insurance as well as bankguarantees of customer performance.
4. Get a clear interpretation of the terms of the countertrade contract from a competent professional.
5. Structure the deal as simply as possible to reduce the risk of an unmanageable contract.

Finally, I must reiterate that every countertrade deal stands alone, with features unique to that transaction. No set formula can be applied. No regulations muddy the waters. And, with a few minor exceptions, neither foreign governments nor Washington will interfere with the details of the transaction as long as the economic and political policies of both countries are not violated.

BUSINESS CLIMATE FOR SUCCESSFUL DEALS

Be aware that when using countertrade, you need to be constantly alert to the changing economic and political environments in your host country and region. External market factors over which you have little control will most likely determine how you structure the transaction—or whether you use countertrade at all. Five conditions seem to have the greatest impact on your success:

1. The types of products involved in the deal.
2. The degree to which your customer wants or needs the goods or services.
3. The amount of support the host country government gives the transaction.
4. The ownership of your customer—whether it is a public or private sector company.
5. The cost of the deal.

But before you worry about these matters, a logical first step is to clearly define your corporate objectives for entering a countertrade deal. In other words, what do you expect to achieve from the transaction?

Your Corporate Objectives

Broadly speaking, companies have either one or two primary objectives for entering into a countertrade arrangement: (1) to finance a specific export transaction when more conventional means are not available or (2) as a means of establishing a direct investment on foreign soil.

You should only use countertrade when other means to close the deal are not available. Nearly every other form of financing promises higher cash throw-off, faster collections, and in most cases, greater profits. If the transaction can be financed through a federal assistance program, such as Ex-Im Bank, a state sponsored aid package, letters of credit, nonbank trade finance organizations, or joint venture funding, countertrade is a poor substitute.

You should only use countertrade when other means to close the deal are not available.

Moreover, countertrade transactions cover long time periods. Exchanged goods must be disposed of for at least the value traded and this could be difficult. The administration of countertrade contracts almost always require the addition of qualified staff personnel to manage the deal. Countertrade is costly, time-consuming, and allows plenty of room for errors in judgment and execution.

Most companies that use countertrade successfully engage a qualified third-party broker to provide assistance throughout the entire transaction. A competent broker will protect you not only by arranging a manageable contract but also by identifying exchange products that may be sold in other countries. On the downside, the use of brokers does mean an extra cost.

Although countertrade has evolved primarily as an exporting tool, the greatest benefits usually occur when the technique is used to establish an off-shore presence. Any of the buyback or parallel trade arrangements previously described work well. But using countertrade for this purpose requires a long-term strategic game plan. If viewed as a short-term tactic, countertrade becomes an end in itself rather than a means to an end. This invariably results in lower profits than with other, less complex tactics.

Bearing in mind the long-term nature of the transaction, you need to negotiate a way to get out of the deal at a later date. This should be done at the same time you execute the original countertrade contract. One way to get out is through a barter arrangement to swap ownership in one facility for a stake in a different one at a later date. Of course, there are many other ways to end the relationship, too.

Types of Products Involved in the Deal

Although buyback arrangements typically lend themselves to construction or construction related projects, companies selling products can also benefit. The secret lies in structuring the right contract. One of the same problems that exists with international licensing agreements—the potential loss of intellectual property rights—occurs with buyback or coproduction agreements. Once the technology, management skill, or process is put in place with joint ownership, products are no longer proprietary.

As a general rule, large, high-cost products, such as boilers, furnaces, aircraft, or major infrastructure equipment are the easiest type of products for which to structure a countertrade deal. Countertrade can also be used for low-cost products, but in this event either one of two conditions should be present. Either payment terms must extend well beyond five years or your customer cannot pay for the goods in hard currency.

Level of Demand for Your Products

Another element to consider when deciding whether to pursue a countertrade transaction is the level of demand for your products in your customer's home country. How great is the market demand for your products, and what role do government trade barriers or incentives play?

Even though your customer may be a private company, it may be subject to onerous government regulations. For instance, the government may make it difficult to get import licenses and approvals or it may prohibit foreign currency conversion. Consequently, the ease of making a countertrade deal and the potential benefits of the transaction depend to a large extent not only on market demand but also on how much the host country government needs or wants the products or project. If market demand is strong, the host country government will probably smooth the way through any protective trade barriers. This will allow both parties the freedom to negotiate price, terms, delivery schedules, and a host of other matters.

Public Sector or Private Sector Customer

The desirability of entering into a countertrade transaction will be influenced by whether your customer comes from the public sector or private sector. Contracts with sovereign customers tend to be far more complex. There is much less negotiating room for structuring beneficial terms. And political favors usually count as much or more than equitable price and terms. These conditions tend to dissuade smaller companies from public sector countertrade deals.

Trying to arrange a countertrade with a large transnational company can be equally maddening. Unless your products or technologies happen to be in great demand and face weak competition, the likelihood of negotiating a favorable transaction with one of these giants is almost as difficult to achieve as with sovereigns.

For your first countertrade deal, it's a good idea, if practical, to concentrate on customers of a size similar to that of your company. Once your organization gains some experience, adds competent countertrade staff, and identifies third-party brokers, it becomes easier to venture further afield into more complex transactions.

Cost Considerations

Cost is another consideration. Countertrade is significantly more costly than traditional trade finance. When you try to sell the exchanged goods, you will likely find that the disposal cost can easily reach 10 percent or more of the value of the goods. Using a third-party broker (a countertrade house or trading company) can double the cost. Furthermore, third-party brokers seldom handle deals of less than $1 million.

Time is another cost, although hard to measure. Any countertrade transaction slows the selling process. With potentially lengthy negotiations and complex side arrangements, countertrade transactions easily take four to six months to close. And if they don't close, the time spent is wasted.

Accounting and Tax Issues

The American accounting fraternity is still trying to figure out how to account for countertrade transactions. A variety of questions remain unanswered, such as:

➡ At what point in time do you record a sale?

➡ At what value is the sale recorded?

➡ When and at what value are exchanged goods recorded?

➡ How should unsold exchanged goods be shown on your balance sheet?

➡ How should you record transactions that extend over several years?

➡ Are credit transactions recorded in U.S. dollars, the currency of your customer's country, or the currency of a third-party to the transaction?

➡ How do you record exchanged goods used internally?

While the accounting profession struggles with financial statement niceties, taxing authorities wrestle with issues involving the timing and the amount of countertrade taxable income and deductible expenses:

➡ What constitutes taxable income?

➡ When is taxable income recognized?

➡ What expenses can be offset against revenues?

➡ What income or expenses arise from exchanged goods that are used internally? Or sold in a third country?

➡ When is an asset an asset? And when and how much is it depreciable?

Although certainly not openly acknowledged, one of the reasons the United States government, and specifically the Internal Revenue Service, frowns on countertrade transactions is that no one can figure out how to tax them effectively and equitably.

INTERNATIONAL CONSULTANTS

Most companies, large and small, find international consultants useful in one phase or another of countertrade transactions. Acting as independent intermediaries, consultants will work with your marketing, contract administration, and financial executives to break logjams, not only with the customer, but also with host country bureaucrats. Smoothing the way through the maze of strange cultural and trade barriers, international consultants more than pay their way, especially for companies unfamiliar with countertrade. In many first time countertrade deals, consultants provide the only reasonable safeguard against being outsmarted by far more savvy customers. No, as I said earlier, I cannot take on any new clients. I can, however, suggest a website that will lead you to international consultants, www.barternews.com. This site also has some excellent countertrade articles.

International consultants perform five services in a typical countertrade transaction. They help a client:

1. Structure and negotiate a countertrade transaction.
2. Recruit and train internal staff to source countertrade customers and then administer contracts.
3. Locate appropriate third parties to dispose of traded goods in the United States, the host country, or a third country.
4. Monitor the performance of countertrade partners.
5. Develop strategies to utilize the countertrade exchange for expansion into other product lines or businesses.

Although these intermediaries certainly add a measure of cost to the transaction, 9 times out of 10 it will be minor compared with the total profitability of the transaction. Also, in most situations, international consultants provide the only feasible, cost effective way to handle constantly changing countertrade techniques.

PROS AND CONS OF COUNTERTRADE

The basic countertrade philosophy is to create a transaction that benefits both trading parties beyond the single transaction itself and this can be accomplished with a minimum amount of currency exchange. Israel needs U.S. technology. U.S. companies need markets in South Africa. The South African government needs Israeli management know-how. If private companies, government agencies, or a combination of both can negotiate the right countertrade agreements, each company and country benefits.

In a general sense, countertrade is beneficial under four conditions:

1. When it is the only option. Other means of financing are unavailable for one reason or another. Supplier or buyer credit may be impossible to arrange. Performance or payment guarantees may be too costly. The

project might call for longer term financing than Ex-Im Bank allows. The political situation in your customer's country might preclude local government financing assistance. Or your customer's government might not permit currency repatriation.

2. When competitors offer countertrade. Japanese and European trading companies have used countertrade for centuries. Their techniques for arranging deals and disposing of exchanged goods are well honed. If one of these experienced global traders really wants an order, a smaller American company will not stand a chance with traditional financing. With countertrade you can at least stay in the race.

3. When countertrade makes a direct investment easier or less expensive. Countertrade provides a way to make a foreign direct investment without starting from scratch or going through the difficult process of buying a business. If structured properly, a coproduction arrangement can put you directly into new foreign markets. This might be in addition to exporting or, in some cases, take the place of further exporting. In either case, gaining access to local distribution channels through a foreign direct investment is an obvious advantage.

4. When nontrade benefits can be derived from the arrangement. Long-range management and technical benefits of joint venture partnerships can easily be achieved through buyback arrangements, particularly coproduction transactions. A foreign partner brings local management techniques and protocol to the partnership that may take you years to develop on your own. In some cases, your partner might bring technical or application techniques unique to the local cultural environment.

Countertrade also involves risks, such as:

1. Disposal of goods can be costly or time-consuming. Countertrade contracts involving the exchange of goods that cannot be consumed within your own company require their sale or trade on the open market. Even with an in-house trading specialist and assistance from an international consultant, the disposal of goods is time-consuming and costly. Using a third-party broker doubles or even triples the cost of disposing of the

goods. Added profits on their resale might compensate somewhat, but the net effect is often a loss.

2. Internal expertise is required. To achieve long-term success in counter-trade transactions you must establish internal expertise. This means setting up a department dedicated to arranging and managing counter-trade deals. This can be a costly addition and unless you get involved in several countertrade deals, the cost of this department is extra overhead.

3. Time period to close the deal is quite long. Countertrade deals require a long time to negotiate and close. Many months and dollars can be spent trying to arrange a transaction only to have the deal fall through in the end.

4. Final result may be uncertain. The final result of a countertrade trans-action is usually very uncertain. In most cases, the recognition of profits won't occur for several years. Political and economic conditions change rapidly, and it's entirely possible that when the deal finally culminates, the results may be different from those originally intended.

COUNTERTRADE SURVIVAL TACTICS

In addition, certain features peculiar to countertrade can cause unforeseen difficulties: (1) the complexity of the countertrade process itself, (2) host country objectives, (3) host country legal and trade regulations, and (4) finance and insurance options.

Complexities of Countertrade Contract

To succeed in countertrade, a clear grasp of the process is crucial. First, demands from customers—such as penalties for nonperformance, ratios of export volume to current consumption, impossible delivery schedules, and untenable deadlines—are nearly always unreasonable. These matters can usually be negotiated, however, assuming both parties want to enter the transaction.

Most countertrade transactions beyond straight barter require three sep-arate agreements. One contract stipulates the terms and conditions of the originating export transaction (primary agreement). A second agreement covers the terms and conditions of the exchanged goods shipped from the host country in counterpurchase, offset, or buyback arrangements. (It should be noted that two particularly critical clauses should be included in this second contract: (1) the right to cancel the contract if the primary agreement is canceled and (2) the broadest possible range of goods to be included without regard to geographic or other restrictions on resale.) The third agreement, often referred to as a protocol agreement, specifies the terms and relationship between buyer and seller.

Host Country Conditions

Every country has its own national objectives that influence trade. Political, commercial, economic, and social ambitions of the ruling bureaucracy together with the bureaucratic hierarchy that oversees trade policies will, in the end, determine the success of failure of any countertrade transaction.

If a countertrade transaction falls outside the scope of the government's agenda, the deal will fail.

Before entering a countertrade contract, it is crucial to thoroughly understand the current government's policies and attitudes. A government's objective might be to stabilize prices, reduce inflation, create hard currency, pay off debt obligations, develop infrastructures, bring in foreign technology, or to effect an overall improvement in the general economy. If a countertrade transaction falls outside the scope of the government's agenda, the deal will fail.

Legal Requirements and Trade Regulations

Along with a firm grasp of the host country's political objectives, be sure to research the country's company laws and trade barriers before executing a contract. Every country has its own set of import and export regulations. Some are restrictive, some are incentive laden. These regulations have been initiated either to protect or to stimulate certain aspects of the country's economy. Countertrade agreements that do not comply face certain failure.

Finance and Insurance Options

A popular misconception is that countertrade transactions do not involve cash, credit, or insurance considerations. But many countertrade contracts call for partial payment in currency. Whereas a great many choices exist for short- and long-term export financing, arranging such funding through normal bank channels won't work for countertrade transactions. Banks and most government export agencies rely on a verifiable, binding trade contract for granting credit. In a countertrade transaction, however, collecting against a contract is conditional on the performance by both parties. On the other hand, development banks and other funding sources within the host country should at least grant performance guarantees.

U.S. government export insurance agencies also avoid countertrade contracts. As an alternative, since insurance against political risk and nonperformance is such an important element in any international transaction, policies from private carriers should be purchased.

Probably the best way to visualize the components of a countertrade transaction is to look at how an actual deal was structured between a U.S. manufacturer and an Argentine customer.

CASE STUDY: GUARDALL INTERNAL MONITORING INC.

Guardall Internal Monitoring Inc. (GIM) manufactured electronic surveillance devices, all of which carried U.S. patents. One product line included a range of infrared cameras for use in banks, securities houses, hospitals, confidential government and private sector meeting rooms, or any facility where a recording of events is required. Another product line included micro listening devices to be attached to telephone transceivers (much like an old-fashioned "bug"). A third line consisted of a variety of micro tracking devices installed in vehicles, airplanes, boats, and other mobile apparatus.

GIM had annual sales of just over $100 million. Although it had been very profitable for a number of years, its U.S. market share began to slip away to Japanese and South Korean imports.

The GIM marketing department received an inquiry from a small but financially sound Argentine company, Corada, S.A., expressing an interest in purchasing GIM technology or as an alternative, several products from each of the three lines. After reviewing the inquiry, the GIM controller pointed out that protection against the piracy of intellectual property rights was virtually nonexistent in Argentina and warned against taking the order. However, the marketing manager pressed forward, reiterating that the inquiry could result in an order of more than $20 million (approximately 40 percent of GIM's total export sales). He presented the following facts to GIM's president:

1. The market for electronic surveillance equipment throughout the MERCOSUR countries was growing at 30 percent per year.
2. GIM had been trying for several years to penetrate South American markets without success.
3. GIM's local bank, FirstSecond National, had provided trade finance support for GIM exports to Europe but indicated that it would not be interested in South America.
4. GIM currently imports about 70 percent of its microchip parts from suppliers in Taiwan and Malaysia at an annual cost of $30 million.

In addition, GIM's chief financial officer provided the following information:

1. The company's cash reserves had recently decreased and currently stood at approximately $7 million.
2. Any new investment in offshore facilities would have to complement GIM's Italian plant, which made industrial electronic safety devices, either by throwing off hard currency or by producing components that could be used in the Italian plant.
3. The financial community had already been alerted that GIM's earnings the would be down 25 percent in the upcoming year, mainly because of soft U.S. markets.
4. The Inter-American Investment Corporation (www.iic.int), affiliated with the Inter-American Development Bank and the Overseas Private Investment Corporation (www.opic.gov), were currently financing direct investments in Argentina up to 75 percent of the project cost.
5. The potential Argentine customer, Corada, S.A., had been importing from Western Europe for several years. Therefore, it obviously had access to some hard currency reserves, but GIM personnel did not know how much.

Corada S.A. was a Buenos Aires industrial electronics manufacturer with annual sales equivalent to $20 million. Its major competitors, a subsidiary of

Toshiba and the recently privatized ARTO S.A., had initiated aggressive advertising campaigns that threatened to push Corada out of key markets.

Both Toshiba and ARTO were developing new electronic surveillance products to be introduced within 18 months. If Corada might beat them to market, it should be able to capture a commanding share. In addition to Argentine markets, demand in Brazil was escalating even faster, and with MERCOSUR, prices on exports to those markets would be competitive with Brazilian firms. Corada also planned to enter Colombian markets within two years, thereby qualifying for preferential trade with the United States, provided the U.S.–Colombia Free Trade Agreement went through.

The Corada board of directors voted to expand the company's product lines to compete against Toshiba and ARTO; however, a tiny R&D budget prohibited in-house product development. The purchasing department was, therefore, directed to acquire the technology from abroad.

Corada was profitable and enjoyed a positive cash flow. It appeared, however, that it would take about $20 million to acquire appropriate technology, far beyond the company's means. Furthermore, in recent months the Argentine peso had seriously sagged against the dollar. So much so that the government enacted a series of temporary exchange controls.

Hearing about state-of-the-art equipment developed by GIM Corada's executive vice president initiated an inquiry for the purchase of that company's surveillance technology or its products. However, Corada had limited access to hard currency and could not afford to pay more than $5 million. Any price above that figure would have to be financed by GIM. A joint venture to produce the products in Argentina seemed to be a logical option, but the cost of a facility and equipment was estimated to be $40 million, a figure Corada couldn't possibly meet. And the Argentine Ex-Im Bank was currently granting import guarantees.

When GIM sales personnel and Corada procurement personnel met to negotiate the deal, they had to answer the following questions:

1. What type of sales contract should be negotiated? Should it be for technology, products, or both?
2. How could the order be financed?
3. Should a joint venture countertrade arrangement be considered?
4. If yes, then how much equity should be contributed by each party?

5. Who should run the joint venture?
6. How could a joint venture finance imports of parts and subassemblies inventory?
7. How much, if any, Argentine produced components should be reserved for use in GIM's Italian plant? How should they be priced?
8. If the two companies agree to a joint venture, how will it be financed?
9. How, when, and under what circumstances would the joint venture be terminated?

After three months of negotiations, the two companies agreed on the following arrangement:

1. GIM would sell Corada certain products in its infrared camera line for a total sales value of $15 million. The sales contract called for delivery of unassembled components—not complete products. In this way, GIM hoped to mitigate the piracy of its complete product technology.
2. GIM and Corada formed an equal joint venture in Buenos Aires to assemble camera components imported from GIM-U.S. In addition, the facility would take direct shipment of $5 million worth of chips from the Taiwan supplier to be used in producing assemblies from the ground up. GIM management assumed it would take at least two years for Corada technicians to copy the assembly and testing technology.
3. A modest volume of assemblies would be exported to GIM's Italian plant.
4. Financing was as follows:
   a. Corada would contribute part of its current facility and equipment.
   b. Additional equipment would be financed with long-term debt through Corada's Argentine bank.
   c. GIM would contribute its technology and $5 million working capital.
   d. The Argentine branch of JPMorganChase (GIM's U.S. bank) agreed to provide a line of credit to purchase GIM assemblies, backed by guarantees from the Argentine Ex-Im Bank.

e. The Argentine Ex-Im Bank agreed to extend buyer credit to the joint venture to purchase the Taiwanese chips and buyer credit to GIM's Italian plant to purchase the assemblies.

f. A countertrade deal was negotiated whereby GIM would take 75 percent of the profits of the joint venture for five years and would have the exclusive rights to distribute joint venture products throughout MERCOSUR for eight years in exchange for its initial inventory of assemblies.

5. A GIM team would be responsible for the management of the joint venture.

6. The partnership would terminate in 10 years or after it had produced and sold the equivalent of $200 million of products, whichever came first. On termination, Corada would retain ownership of all equipment and inventory and would pay GIM $15 million over a two-year period.

Everybody was a winner in this deal. Moreover, five years later, GIM structured a second countertrade deal with a U.A.E. customer. This one was also a big winner for everyone.

There can be little doubt that countertrade is here to stay and will continue to play a major role in global trade for many years to come. Although most companies are still learning how to use the technique, many who have tried it remain convinced that in one form or another, countertrade makes both export sales and establishing a foreign presence possible when other financing methods are cost prohibitive or unavailable. And in some cases, countertrade is the only feasible way to gain access to foreign markets.

In conclusion, remember that every countertrade deal is unique and can be constructed in any way that satisfies both parties to the deal. For more information on how countertrade might fit into your marketing plans, contact the U.S. trade association.

Global Offset and Countertrade Association, 818 Connecticut Ave., NW, 12th Floor, Washington, DC 20006; www.globaloffset.org

chapter twenty-three
Foreign Sourcing (Importing) Made Easy

IMPORTING MATERIALS AND PRODUCTS HAS BEEN A WAY OF LIFE IN AMERICAN business for many years. Lower material and labor costs make importing from less developed countries a vital strategy for large, midsize, and small U.S. companies. Globalization has forced virtually all U.S. consumer and industrial products to carry some foreign material or labor. Automobiles, building materials, clothing, shoes, foodstuffs, athletic equipment, home appliances, farm implements, airplanes, machine tools, electronics, and military hardware are partially made in foreign lands. Materials, components, and subassemblies moving from one country to another through the various stages of manufacture provide companies with an ever expanding panorama of combinations from which to gain competitive advantage.

As we all know, to compete in today's markets, you must source the lowest-cost, highest-quality products, materials, and services, regardless of where suppliers happen to be located. However, cross-border sourcing has become increasingly complex, with protectionist trade policies rampant throughout the world. Although a thorough discussion of the pros and cons of sourcing from anywhere in the world would be desirable, it is beyond the scope of this book. Therefore, we will limit the following discussion to importing to the United States. If you do need to import products to other countries for use in your foreign branches, you'll want to check out applicable regulations in those nations.

If foreign sourcing is part of your competitive strategy, you must be cognizant of a variety of commercial, government, and legal matters regardless of how you plan to use the goods. However, except for financing, the topics discussed in this chapter are unique to importing and are not relevant for companies engaged solely in exporting. As an aside, letters of credit, bankers' acceptances, and other trade finance instruments used for importing goods and materials are identical to those used in exporting.

Once your shipment is on its way from a foreign supplier, you need to monitor its progress across the sea, in the air, or over land. Any number of catastrophes can occur in transit. Without monitoring the shipment, you'll never know it's missing until it doesn't show up on your receiving dock.

MONITORING THE MOVEMENT OF GOODS

Someone in your receiving organization must be responsible for monitoring the movement of goods from the point of embarkation in the country of origin to delivery on your receiving dock. More often than not, if you don't assign this responsibility to a specific individual, purchasing and receiving personnel inexperienced in global trade will expect goods to flow naturally from the foreign shipper to their door on schedule, just like U.S. purchases. But this doesn't happen. The importing process is so complex that to rely on shippers, carriers, or other outsiders to complete the transaction invariably leads to lost or damaged goods or, at best, late deliveries. The responsibility for monitoring and controlling the movement of imported goods must rest solely with your personnel and hopefully the responsibility of a single individual.

The following recap of the movement of imports shows that ocean or air-freight companies, brokers, terminal operators, U.S. customs officials, and domestic freight carriers all get involved:

➡ Ocean or airfreight company. Notifies consignee two days before arrival of goods at the port of entry. Provides freight release to terminal operator.
➡ Customs broker. Responsible for obtaining customs releases and necessary clearances at port of entry. Checks bills of lading and delivery orders for completeness. Forwards originals of these documents to motor carrier for pick up.
➡ U.S. Customs officers. Verifies compliance with customs regulations and collects duties.
➡ Terminal operator. Arranges with domestic carrier for pick up. Makes arrangements for payment, if any, of demurrage. Verifies accuracy of deliver order. Loads merchandise onto domestic carrier.
➡ Domestic freight carrier. Receives merchandise at port of entry. Verifies clearance documents and delivery order. Delivers shipment to importer's receiving dock.

With so many people involved something is bound to go wrong. Therefore, once notified by the shipping company of the shipment's arrival date try to station one of your people at the port of entry. This person not only coordinates the activities of each party but is available to open bottlenecks as they occur. Your representative should also be prepared to arrange payment of customs duties, demurrage, and any other required clearance fees.

INSIGHT... The president of a $21 million chemical processing plant readily admitted to me that he missed the boat the first time around—literally. Taking on a new line of industrial filter compounds, the purchasing agent for Closette Mack Inc. successfully located a Kuala Lumpur source for one of the compounds needed in the mixture. Arranging to purchase a full container of the compound, the company waited patiently for its delivery. Sixty days passed and nothing arrived. The Closett Mack president became concerned and asked the company's controller to trace the shipment. Three weeks later it was discovered that the steamship company forgot to unload the container in Philadelphia. Since no one from Closett Mack was at the port to coordinate receipt of the shipment, the container remained on board for the next port of call, Buenos Aires. And there it sat.

Maintaining close surveillance of ocean shipments may seem inconsequential, but in the long run, it's safer to spend the money and take the time to be sure. Don't rely solely on customs brokers, foreign suppliers, or carriers. Do it yourself.

U.S. CUSTOMS

Once cargo reaches an American port of entry, U.S. customs officials take over. All goods arriving at U.S. ports with a value of more than $1,000 must go through a formal entry process. This process consists of four steps:

1. The filing of appropriate entry documents.
2. Inspection and classification of the goods.
3. Preliminary declaration of value.
4. Final determination and payment of customs duty.

In most cases, customs processing takes about five working days. Once the amount of duty has been established, either you or your broker (or your on premise personnel) will receive instructions on how to make the payment and obtain release of the goods. If merchandise is not moved out within five working days after that, customs officials transfer the goods to a warehouse and you'll get charged for storage. If the goods remain in custody for 12 months, the government has the right to auction them for storage fees.

Entry Documents

Of the 22 different types of customs entries, the following six are the most common:

1. The Consumption Entry is the most common type. It is used for goods brought directly into the importers stock and intended for domestic resale.
2. An Immediate Transportation Entry allows merchandise to be forwarded directly from the port of entry to an inland destination for customs clearance.
3. A Warehouse Entry is used to store goods in a customs bonded warehouse for up to five years.
4. When goods are ultimately withdrawn from a bonded warehouse a Warehouse Withdrawal for Consumption Entry applies.
5. An Immediate Exportation Entry is used when goods are to be transshipped to a foreign country.
6. A Baggage Declaration and Entry form is filed by U.S. citizens returning from a trip abroad.

Before goods are allowed out of the U.S. Customs area certain documents must be made available to customs agents, specifically (1) a commercial invoice from the exporter, (2) a bill of lading from the exporter or freight forwarder, and (3) one of the previously mentioned entry forms completed by the importer or its broker.

Each of these entry forms must contain a description of the shipment, its value, and the amount of customs duty to be paid. Goods may be removed from the customs area by paying this customs duty immediately or by posting a bond guaranteeing payment at a later date. The bond may be in the form of a *single transaction bond* that applies to entry through one port or a *continuous bond* that covers all U.S. ports of entry. Either brokers or importers can arrange for such a surety bond.

Types of Duty

Whether an item is dutiable or free from duty inevitably impacts your decision to import or not. Import duties are classified by the following three types:

1. Specific duties assessed against a unit of the goods, such as 5 percent per pound.
2. Ad valorum duties assessed as a flat percent for the total value of the import transaction, such as 10 percent of the total imputed value of the goods.
3. A compound duty combining specific duties and ad valorum duties, such as $5 per pound of a commodity plus a percentage of the value of the transaction. Certain types of agricultural commodities are assessed in this manner.

All duties levied by the U.S. Customs Service are included in a voluminous document called the Tariff Schedules of the United States. It resembles freight tariff schedules for rail and trucking lines. An official ruling from the head office of the port of entry determines the type and rates of duties applicable to specific goods that for one reason or another are excluded from tariff schedules.

In addition to levying commodity duties, the U.S. Customs Service enforces statutory duties. These apply to the import of any goods, either directly or indirectly, from countries the federal government deems unfriendly. Obviously, this list keeps changing as foreign policy shifts. For purposes of valuation, currency exchange rates from the exporting country are determined by the daily buying rate for foreign currency established by the Federal Reserve Bank of New York.

Duty-Free Items

The U.S. Customs Service defines certain types of imported items as duty-free. A bond must be posted with the service to guarantee that they will either be exported or destroyed. Although slight variations occur periodically, the following list includes those items that are currently duty-free. In addition, foreigners may import personal items (cars, films, boats, and so on) for use while temporarily in the United States.

1. Materials or goods imported specifically to be repaired, modified, or processed in the U.S. with the intent of shipping the final product off-shore. The product may also be totally destroyed while in bond rather

than exported. The end product cannot contain perfume, alcohol, or wheat. A complete accounting of the articles must be made and any scrap or waste turned over to a U.S. Customs Service officer.

2. Women's clothing to be used strictly for modeling in a U.S. garment maker's establishment.

3. Samples used solely to attract sales.

4. Motion picture advertising films.

5. Items intended solely for review, testing, or experimentation, such as drawings, plans, or photos.

6. Containers for handling or transporting items.

7. Items used solely in the preparation of illustrations for catalogs, pamphlets, or advertising.

8. Professional equipment, trade tools, repair components for these tools and equipment and articles of special design for temporary use in the manufacture or design of items for export.

9. Props, scenery, and apparel for temporary use in theatrical performances.

The items on this list change regularly so be sure to check with the U.S. Customs Service for products that are currently duty-free goods.

DRAWBACKS

The term *drawback* refers to refunds of customs duties previously paid on imported goods. Normally, drawbacks on imported goods are not allowed if the goods are subsequently exported after being released from the customs area. However, as with other government regulations, there are always exceptions, such as the following:

➡ A total of 99 percent of duties paid are refundable if the goods are used in the manufacture or production of final products in the U.S. and these final products are exported.

➡ If an importer rejects the goods as not meeting order specifications they may be returned to the U.S. Customs Service for supervised shipment back to the exporter. A 99 percent drawback is allowed.

➡ The same 99 percent drawback is allowed if the imported goods are returned to the exporter within three years in the same condition as they were received.

➡ Goods found to be banned from import by U.S. government decree. They must be returned to the exporter or destroyed by customs officials. All duties paid are included in a drawback.

➡ Total refunds are also granted if goods are exported from a customs bonded warehouse or if the goods are withdrawn from the warehouse for repair, supplies, or maintenance of vessels and aircraft (under certain conditions).

The application for drawbacks is complicated. Most companies that import and then export hire customs brokers who specialize in drawback management. Companies that qualify for drawbacks are "importers who export their products or exporters of articles manufactured with imports." If you meet either of these two tests, contact a drawback broker to get your refund.

A drawback broker or specialist handles the entire drawback process including the preparation of all paperwork and the processing of all claims. A competent drawback broker can also design in-house procedures to help identify drawback items. I'm certain that you will find that drawback specialists more than pay for themselves in cost savings and actual cash recoveries.

U.S. IMPORT RESTRICTIONS AND QUOTAS

As we have seen, every country enforces protectionist policies on imported goods. The United States imposes four such restrictions.

1. Goods that the government deems detrimental to the well-being of its citizens as a whole or to special interest groups of citizens.
2. Quantities or quotas of specific goods.
3. Anti-dumping regulations to protect certain U.S. industries from foreign competition.
4. Preference regulations that apply to favored nations.

Goods Detrimental to U.S. Citizens

Special interest groups have convinced Washington to designate certain products as harmful to U.S. citizens. Consequently, trade barriers either prohibit or severely restrict the importing of these goods. The most severe restrictions call for the seizure of the goods by the U.S. Customs Service. Less severe barriers include limiting entry of the goods to certain ports; restricting the routing, storage, or use of the goods; or requiring special labeling or processing before goods can be released to the market.

These restrictions apply to all imported goods, whether or not they pass through a foreign trade zone. The list of items falling under these restrictions is voluminous and constantly changing. Although U.S. Customs Service offices retain complete up-to-date listings, the following are the better known items considered to be detrimental to U.S. citizens:

➡ Alcoholic beverages.
➡ Arms, explosives, ammunition, and implements of war.
➡ Automobiles and accessories.
➡ Coins, stamps, currencies, and other monetary instruments.
➡ Eggs and egg products.
➡ Fruits, vegetables, plants, and insects.
➡ Milk and cream.
➡ Electronic products.
➡ Food, drugs, and cosmetics.
➡ Animals.
➡ Wild animals and endangered species.
➡ Wool, fur, textile, and fabric products.
➡ Livestock and meat.
➡ Pesticides and toxic substances.
➡ Viruses and serums.
➡ Rags and brushes.
➡ Narcotics.
➡ All products from communist countries.

It seems ludicrous that items such as rags, brushes, coins, stamps, automobiles, and milk can harm U.S. citizens, but that's what the law says. Clearly, such items are restricted solely to protect U.S. companies from foreign competition and not to protect U.S. citizens from harm.

Quotas of Specific Goods

Most import quotas are administered by the District Director of Customs. Other government agencies handle special products. For example, quotas for dairy products are established by the Import Branch, Foreign Agricultural Service, U.S. Department of Agriculture. Quotas for imported fuel and oil products are set by the Director of Oil Imports at the Federal Energy Administration. Watches and watch movement quotas are controlled by the Special Import Programs Division of the Department of Commerce.

Because all quotas are for specific periods of time, it is impossible to predict with any certainty in advance of shipment whether or not a given import transaction will be restricted by quotas when the goods arrive at a U.S. port of entry.

There are two types of import quotas: (1) tariff rate quotas and (2) absolute quotas. U.S. protectionist policies use tariff rate quotas to control the pricing of imported products sold in the United States. If market prices are higher than the government wants, it sets tariff rate quotas that allow the importing of specific products at very favorable duty rates to force prices down. One example of this is the tariff rate quotas that are imposed to keep the price of agricultural products down when, for example, bad weather causes free market prices to temporarily rise. A few of the current products subject to tariff rate quotas include milk, fish, tuna, and potatoes. Quotas also apply to whisk brooms and large motorcycles. Hard to believe but true.

Absolute quotas have nothing to do with favorable duty rate adjustments. They are established solely to control the quantity of specific goods that may be imported during any given period of time. Examples of imports restricted by absolute quotas include: peanuts, ice cream, steel bars and rods, cotton, sugar, and condensed milk. These are obvious attempts to protect noncompetitive U.S. companies. Because all quotas are for specific periods of time, it is impossible to predict with any certainty in advance of shipment whether or not a given import transaction will be restricted by quotas when the goods arrive at a U.S. port of entry. If your shipment hits when quotas have already been filled, an over quota customs duty will apply. The government hopes this will make your prices of these imports noncompetitive with U.S.-produced goods.

Anti-Dumping Regulations

Anti-dumping laws are another tool used by the federal government to support high cost American producers. These laws restrict the importing of goods that, according to the federal government, create a competitive disadvantage for U.S. producers. The determination is made solely on a comparison of the imported price of the goods with prices of similar domestic goods. The efficiencies of foreign suppliers are not considered.

The anti-dumping test is very straightforward. If the selling price of an import is less than that of similar goods produced in the United States, then imported goods are deemed to be dumped on U.S. markets. For goods that cannot be so tested because they are not sufficiently similar to U.S.-produced goods, the rules call for a *constructed value test*. Constructed value is the foreign manufacturer's total of materials and labor costs, factory and administrative overhead, packing and shipping expenses, and a reasonable profit, all estimated by U.S. bureaucrats. If a product falls within the anti-dumping provisions, additional customs duties will be assessed. Theoretically, these additional duties will increase the price of imported items to make them competitive with U.S.-produced goods.

Preferential Trade Partners

There are two classes of preferential trade partners: (1) designated less developed nations and (2) countries who have executed free trade agreements with the United States. Currently, more than 140 less developed nations qualify for preferential treatment, but the list changes frequently. Items deemed to be preferential fall within the General System of Preferences (GSP). Over 2,700 products in the Tariff Schedules of the United States are so classified.

Trade Policy Staff Committee, Office of the Special Representative for Trade Negotiations, 1800 G St., Washington, DC, 20506; www.ustr.gov/Who_We_Are/Executive_Branch_Agencies

FOREIGN TRADE ZONES

Nearly every trading country in the world has one or more free trade zones that enable companies to import goods and then export them duty-free. In the United States, such zones are called *foreign trade zones*. U.S. foreign trade zones, or FTZs, provide a convenient way to import products; repack, modify or otherwise finish them; and then ship them offshore to the ultimate customer, exempt from all customs duties and other import restrictions.

A foreign trade zone is defined by regulations as an "isolated, enclosed, policed area, operating as a public utility." Although FTZs are located within the boundaries of the United States, they are treated as if they were outside U.S. Customs Service territory. Currently, 141 FTZs operate in the United States.

FTZs may be used for a variety of purposes including storage, distribution, assembly, light manufacturing, modifications of products, or transshipping. Goods in an FTZ may also be sold, exhibited, broken up, repacked, repackaged, graded, cleaned, and mixed with other foreign or domestic merchandise. One of the most interesting applications of FTZs for a company that produces goods overseas is to use a foreign trade zone as an intermediate stop for adding value to the product prior to shipping to the ultimate offshore customer.

For example, assume you have a plant in Budapest that assembles washing machines. You want to ship the machines to a customer in Recife, Brazil. The most direct route would be to ship from Hungary to Brazil. However, ocean freight might be substantially less if you shipped only the components and perhaps some subassemblies, partway, say to a Jacksonville or Miami FTZ. Once there, they could be assembled, tested, and packed, and the final product could then be shipped to Recife. Ordinarily, U.S. duties would apply, as would insurance, taxes, and the completion of myriad forms. With a FTZ, however, no import duties apply. There is no tax liability, no additional insurance coverage required, and much less paperwork. In other words, an FTZ is treated as a foreign port, affording substantial savings to U.S. importers. Using an FTZ would also permit you to use American workers to complete and test final products.

One unusual and, at times, very helpful feature of FTZs is that importers may exhibit their wares to potential customers. Companies may maintain their own showrooms in the zone and display merchandise for an indefinite period of time. Since merchandise may also be stored and processed in the zone, you could stock products in a display room and then sell wholesale quantities directly from the zone without incurring any duty.

Get your list of FTZs by state from
www.ita.doc.gov/FTZPAGE/letters/ftzlist.html

IMPORTING WITH COUNTERTRADE

Countertrade has become a convenient and often necessary way to finance exports to, or investments in, soft currency countries. Countertrade arrangements also conserve cash for U.S. importers. For example, you could combine exports to a given country in exchange for imports from that country. The experience of a small, toy manufacturing client is a good example of how this works.

INSIGHT ... UltraSafe Inc. produced dolls, stuffed animals, and other soft products for handicapped preschool children. Several product lines required hand sewing. Other lines used a stuffing material treated with nonflammable chemicals. As sales tapered off and competition from foreign producers intensified, it became apparent that UltraSafe must find ways to cut costs to survive in their niche markets. At the same time, the company saw new markets for its products in Argentina. UltraSafe developed a strategy to take advantage of lower wage rates by setting up sewing shops in Guatemala. It purchased stuffing material from Malaysia. The final safety testing had to be performed in the United States by certified inspectors so that the products could then be sold domestically as well as in Argentina and throughout most of Latin America. Countertrade deals were structured as follows:

1. A major producer/distributor in Buenos Aires agreed to a three-year contract to purchase and distribute three lines of dolls and animals. In exchange, UltraSafe agreed to purchase processed beef from Buenos Aires.

2. The Argentine beef was shipped directly to a producer in Kuala Lumper. In exchange, UltraSafe imported Malaysian stuffing direct to its foreign trade zone plant in Los Angeles.

3. UltraSafe formed a joint venture with a Guatemalan company to perform the in-process sewing operations. These subassemblies were then imported to the Los Angeles plant.

4. The stuffing was added in Los Angeles and final sewing completed. The products were then safety tested. Some lines were shipped to the distributor in Buenos Aires, and the balance was sold in U.S. markets.

This countertrade arrangement enabled UltraSafe to resume its commanding position in its niche markets. Its president attributed the company's recovery entirely to the extra profitability provided by the countertrade deals.

A NEW TWIST

The Dominican Republic has long been a favorite location for maquila factories. Low labor costs, a pro-American political culture, close proximity, and beneficial subsidies from the Caribbean Basin Trade Partnership Act of 2000 and now the new DR-CAFTA have made the DR a principal exporter to the United States. In addition, the inclusion of the DR in the European equivalent of the Caribbean Basin Trade Partnership Act of 2000 gives Dominican producers duty-free access to the entire European Union. This provides U.S. manufacturers that have facilities in the DR a double-barreled advantage (1) shipping duty-free to the United States and (2) shipping duty-free to the EU.

In addition to an abundance of skilled and semiskilled labor and low wages, industrial free zones in the DR offer substantial tax, tariff, and regulatory incentives, including freedom from foreign currency holding and exchange restrictions and unrestricted repatriation of profits. Furthermore, the Dominican's pro-business climate encourages significant growth opportunities for U.S. businesses.

THE CUSTOMS AUDIT

If you import anything, you must keep and make available certain records for examination by the U.S. Customs Service. No one is exempt. All companies, regardless of size, classification of products, or the value or frequency of imports are subject to customs audits. And, as with IRS audits, discrepancies will likely be found.

In the past, the U.S. Customs Service has limited its investigations to large corporations that import fairly significant quantities. But times change. The age of the computer has hit. In fact, the U.S. Customs Service has now automated all import documentation and increased its audits of smaller importers.

National Entry Processing, also know as DABA, Paired Ports, and Triangular Processing, comprise a totally electronic environment for automated importers, including paperless entry and summary, electronic invoices, electronic payment of duties, preclassification of merchandise, and binding rulings attached to a company's specific style or part number. This information appears on an electronic invoice, which is then used to obtain an electronic release and entry summary to calculate the duty charges. Finally, the U.S. Customs Service automatically debits an importer's bank account. In other words, just about everything is out of your hands.

The Customs Service is quick to point out that electronic processing gives importers a more rapid access to their goods. And that is true. What the service does not reveal, however, is the price importers must pay for this more timely access. The biggest cost of any government audit, exclusive of discrepancy findings, is the substantial amount of nonproductive time spent by company personnel in arranging records for audit and answering auditor's questions. In addition, record keeping, which in the past could be somewhat haphazard, now must be formalized—and all this has a cost.

Record keeping for import transactions must be maintained in a manner that allows "rapid access to transactions in an orderly and systematic fashion" according to the Customs Service. Managers of importing companies must have more than a passing knowledge of the transaction. Customs regulation 19 CFR Part 162 is quite specific about which records must be made available for examination as well as about records that must be maintained by third-parties, such as customs brokers, and how they will be accessed by customs auditors apart from a broker's internal records. Invoicing requirements are also clearly delineated in 19 CFR Part 141.

 You can get current information on this regulation and all others from the Customs Service website at www.cbp.gov

Importers are responsible for all aspects of invoices relating to import transactions. To be certain that an invoice properly reflects all required information, your manager needs to be intimately involved in the detailed preparation of the purchase order and insist that exporting suppliers copy this data in total. (This appears to be a rather silly requirement because importers have absolutely no control over the actions of suppliers; however, that is what customs regulations require.) Information about terms, inclusions or exclusions from the price, shipping instructions, dangerous markings, insurance, and so forth, must be spelled out in detail.

In addition to verifying hard data, customs auditors determine whether importers have taken "reasonable and prudent actions" in the transactions (very nebulous terminology used by the Customs Service). This seems to mean that you must have qualified personnel as import managers. Of course. What else is new? Successful entrepreneurs make certain that all their managers are qualified.

You can prove you have competent management by hiring an international consultant to conduct an in-house audit of your international transactions prior to any customs audit. Corrective measures resulting from such an audit go a long way toward satisfying customs auditors that reasonable and prudent management actions have been taken. However, this costs money and, to me, seems like overkill.

The importance of maintaining good internal controls, adequate accounting records, and qualified management personnel cannot be overemphasized. It's too late to try to put things together once you are notified that an audit is imminent. Regardless of audit requirements, however, companies that enjoy success in either exporting or importing know that good record keeping and sound management practices are essential to remaining competitive.

QUALITY CONTROL

Global competitiveness requires quality products. That should be obvious to everyone. Throughout the United States billions of dollars are spent every year on quality assurance programs, testing procedures, and in-line inspection. Quality assurance auditors are stationed at major suppliers to ensure that purchased materials, parts, and components meet their specifications.

Unfortunately, the same degree of quality control cannot be exercised over imported materials, parts, and components. To determine if suppliers in Jakarta, Santiago, Port of Spain, or Tel Aviv maintain the same rigid quality standards as their American counterparts is a daunting task well beyond the means of smaller companies. Yet, to remain competitive, some effort at quality control must be made. The best way to avoid lengthy negotiations and perhaps litigation of quality defects in imported goods is to follow these few simple guidelines.

1. Know your foreign supplier. Check references from other American customers of the supplier. Verify the supplier's litigation record.

2. Understand the quality control standards in place in your supplier's plant. Visit the location. Talk to quality assurance managers. Obtain a copy of the testing and inspection procedure manual, if possible.

3. Make sure your supplier understands how important high quality standards are to you. The more dogmatic and obsessive you are about quality, the better. If possible, use a second or third verification source occasionally to impress on a supplier your insistence on quality products. Competition often does what mere words or contracts will not do.

4. Be sure your product specifications include quality testing and inspection procedures and that your supplier understands the specifications thoroughly.

5. For large orders of critical parts, spend the money to station your own quality inspector at the supplier's location at least intermittently. Aerospace and military hardware manufacturers do this all the time. Very often it's the only way to be sure of what you are getting.

6. When quality problems arise, communicate with the supplier immediately. Get on a plane and meet. Find out what caused the glitch. Be sure it is corrected before more products are shipped.

7. Make certain the purchase order or contract spells out litigation and arbitration procedures, including what laws apply in the event of dispute.

8. Use letters of credit for payment. Include receiving inspection procedures in the documentation that must be satisfied prior to payment.

9. Maintain close personal contact with your supplier. Meet at the supplier's location and invite local managers to visit your plant. Stay in constant contact by telephone, e-mail, and fax.

Although these guidelines won't ensure the quality of imported products, they are a good start. Once shipments reach your U.S. plant it may be too late to take action to correct materials or products that won't work, wear out, or otherwise do not meet your specifications. And recovering compensation from a foreign supplier is very difficult—if not impossible.

appendix

EXPORT ASSISTANCE CENTERS

ATLANTA
(GA, AL, KY, TN, MS)
International Trade Programs
Sunbelt U.S. Export Assistance Center
75 Fifth St., NW, Ste 1055
Atlanta, GA 30308
404-897-6089

BALTIMORE
(MD, Northern VA, DC)
International Trade Programs
U.S. Export Assistance Center
300 West Pratt St., Ste 300
Baltimore, MD 21201
410-962-4582

BOSTON
(ME, VT, NH, MA, CT, RI)
International Trade Programs
U.S. Export Assistance Center
World Trade Center, Ste 307
Boston, MA 02210
617-424-5953

CHARLOTTE
(VA, NC, SC)
International Trade Programs
U.S. Export Assistance Center
521 East Morehead St., Ste 435

Charlotte, NC 28202
704-333-4886

CHICAGO
(WI, IL, IN)
International Trade Programs
U.S. Export Assistance Center
200 Adams St., Ste 2450
Chicago, IL 60606
312-353-8065

CLEVELAND
(OH, Western NY, Western PA, WV)
International Trade Programs
U.S. Export Assistance Center
600 Superior Ave., Ste 700
Cleveland, OH 44114
216-522-4731

DALLAS
(OK, TX, LA, AR)
International Trade Programs
North Texas U.S. Export Assistance Center
1450 Hughes Rd., Ste 220
Grapevine, TX 76501
817-310-3749

DENVER
(WY, UT, CO, NM)
International Trade Programs
U.S. Export Assistance Center

1625 Broadway Ave., Ste 680
Denver, CO 80202
303-844-6623 ext. 18

DETROIT
(MI)
International Trade Programs
U.S. Export Assistance Center
211 West Fort St., Ste 1104
Detroit, MI 48226
313-226-3670

NEWPORT BEACH
(Southern CA, NV, AZ, HI)
International Trade Programs
U.S. Export Assistance Center
3300 Irvine Ave., Ste 305
Newport Beach, CA 92660
949-660-1688 ext. 115

MIAMI
(FL)
International Trade Programs
U.S. Export Assistance Center
5835 Blue Lagoon Dr., Ste 203
Miami, FL 33132
305-526-7425 ext. 21

MINNEAPOLIS
(MN, ND)
International Trade Programs
U.S. Export Assistance Center
U.S. Small Business Administration
100 North Sixth St., 210-C, Butler Square
Minneapolis, MN 55403
612-348-1642

PHILADELPHIA
(Eastern PA, DE, NJ)
International Trade Programs
U.S. Export Assistance Center
The Curtis Center
601 Walnut St., Ste 580 West
Philadelphia, PA 19106
215-597-6110

PORTLAND
(Southern WA, OR, Southern ID, Montana)
International Trade Programs
U.S. Export Assistance Center
One World Trade Center
121 SW Salmon St., Ste 242
Portland, OR 97204
503-326-5498

SEATTLE
(Northern WA, AK, Northern ID)
International Trade Programs
U.S. Export Assistance Center
2601 4th Ave., Ste 320
Seattle, WA 98121
206-553-0051 ext. 228

ST. LOUIS
(SD, NE, IA, KS, MO)
International Trade Programs
U.S. Export Assistance Center
8235 Forsyth Blvd., Ste 520
St. Louis, MO 63105
314-425-3304

SMALL BUSINESS ADMINISTRATION REGIONAL OFFICES

SBA REGION I OFFICE
(ME, NH, VT, MA, CT, RI)
10 Causeway St., Ste 812
Boston, MA 02222-1093
617-565-8415

SBA REGION II OFFICE
(NY, NJ, VI, PR)
26 Federal Plaza, Ste 3108
New York, NY 10278
212-264-1450

SBA REGION III OFFICE
(PA, MD, WV, VA)
Federal Building

900 Market St., 5th Floor
Philadelphia, PA 19107
215-580-2807

SBA REGION IV OFFICE
(TN, KY, NC, SC, MS, AL, GA, FL)
233 Peachtree St., NE, Ste 1800
Atlanta, GA 30303
404-331-4999

SBA REGION V OFFICE
(MN, WI, MI, OH, IL, IN)
500 West Madison St.
Citicorp Center, Ste 1240
Chicago, IL 60661-2511
312-353-0357

SBA REGION VI OFFICE
(NM, TX, OK, AR, LA)
4300 Amon Carter Blvd., Ste 108
Fort Worth, TX 76155
817-684-5581

SBA REGION VII OFFICE
(KS, NE, MO, IA)
23 W. 8th St., Ste 307
Kansas City, MO 64105-1500
816-374-6380

SBA REGION VIII OFFICE
(ND, SD, MT, WY, CO, UT)
721 19th St., Ste 400
Denver, CO 80202-2599
303-844-0500

SBA REGION IX OFFICE
(CA, NV, AZ)
330 North Brand Blvd., Ste 1270
Glendale, CA 91203-2304
818-552-3434

SBA REGION X OFFICE
(WA, ID, OR, AK)
2401 Fourth Ave., Ste 400
Seattle, WA 98121
206-553-5676

AMERICAN CHAMBER OF COMMERCE OFFICES

RUSSIA AND EASTERN EUROPE
www.amcham.ru

Bulgaria
www.amcham.bg

Czech Republic
www.amcham.cz

Estonia
www.acce.ee

Hungary
www.amcham.hu

Latvia
www.amacham.lv

Lithuania
www.acc.lt

Poland
www.amcham.com.pl

Slovakia
www.amcham.si

Romania
www.amcham.ro

Turkey
(Turkey-American Business Assocaition)
www.amcham.org

MIDDLE EAST/NORTH AFRICA
The following countries do not have an
American Chamber of Commerce office:
Algeria, Oman, and Qatar.

Egypt
www.amcham.org.eg

Israel
www.amcham.com.il

Kuwait
No website listed

Morocco
www.amcham.morocco.com

Saudi Arabia
(Dhahran, Jeddah, and Riyadh)
No website listed

United Arab Emirates
(Dubai and Northern Emirates)
www.abcdubai.com

United Arab Emirates
(Abu Dhabi)
No website listed

SOUTH AND SOUTHEAST ASIA

Asia-Pacific Council of American
Chambers of Commerce
www.apcac.org

China (Beijing)
www.amcham-china.org.cn

China (Guangdong)
www.amcham-guangdong.org

China (Shanghai)
www.amcham-shanghai.org

India
www.amchamindia.com

Hong Kong
www.amcham.org.hk

Indonesia
www.amcham.or.id

Malaysia
www.amcham.com.my

Pakistan
www.abcpk.org.pk

Philippines
www.amchamphilippines.com

Singapore
www.amcham.org.sg

Sri Lanka
www.amchamsl.lk

Taiwan (Taipei)
www.amcham.com.tw

Thailand
www.amchamthailand.com

LATIN AMERICA

Brazil (Rio de Janeiro)
www.amchamrio.com.br

Brazil (São Paulo)
www.amcham.com.br

Argentina
www.amchamar.com.ar

Chile
www.amchamchile.cl

Colombia
www.amchamcolombia.com.co

Costa Rica
www.amcham.co.cr

Dominican Republic
www.amcham.or.do

El Salvador
www.amchamsal.com

Guatemala
www.amchamguate.com

Mexico
www.amcham.com.mx

Peru
www.amcham.org.pe

Trinidad and Tobago
www.amchamtt.com

FOREIGN CHAMBERS OF COMMERCE
IN THE UNITED STATES REGIONAL
ORGANIZATIONS

U.S. Business Council SE Europe
1901 North Fort Myer Dr., Ste 303
Arlington, VA 22209
703-527-0280

U.S.-ASEAN Trade Council
425 Madison Ave.
New York, NY 10017
212-371-7420

Council of the Americas
680 Park Ave.
New York, NY 10021
212-628-3200

Latin Chamber of Commerce
1417 West Flagler St.
Miami, FL 33135
305-642-3870

National Council on U.S.-Arab Relations
1735 I St., NW, Ste 515
Washington, DC 20006
202-293-0801

LATIN AMERICA
Argentina-American
Chamber of Commerce
10 Rockefeller Plaza, 10th Floor
New York, NY 10020
212-698-2238

Brazilian-American
Chamber of Commerce in the U.S.
22 West 48th St., Rm 404
New York, NY 10036
212-575-9030

Colombian-American Association Inc.
150 Nassau St., Ste 2015
New York, NY 10018
212-233-7776

Guatemala-U.S. Trade Association
299 Alhambra Circle, #207
Coral Gables, FL 33134
305-443-0343

U.S.-Mexico Chamber of Commerce
1211 Connecticut Ave., NW
Washington, DC 20036
202-296-5198

Peruvian-American Association
50 West 34th St.
New York, NY 10036
212-964-3855

Trinidad and Tobago
Chamber of Commerce
c/o Trintoc Services Ltd.
400 Madison Ave., Rm 803
New York, NY 10016
212-759-3388

ASIA
U.S. Office of China
Chamber of International Commerce
4310 Connecticut Ave., NW
Washington, DC 20008
202-244-3244

India Chamber of Commerce
445 Park Ave.
New York, NY 10022
212-755-7181

Philippine-American
Chamber of Commerce
711 Third Ave., 17th Floor
New York, NY 10017
212-972-9326

MIDDLE EAST
U.S. Egypt Chamber of Commerce
330 East 39th St., #321
New York, NY 10016
212-867-2323

American-Israel Chamber of Commerce
350 Fifth Ave., Ste 1919
New York, NY 10118-1988
212-971-0310

Saudi Arabian Council of Chambers
of Commerce and Industry
c/o Hamed Jared
Washington Representative
Embassy of Saudi Arabia
601 New Hampshire Ave., NW
Washington, DC 20037
202-342-3800

index